Enhancing Sustainability in Global Supply Chains With Big Data Analytics

Mohammad Kamrul Hasan
https://orcid.org/0000-0003-3866-0090
Tongling University, China

Tahsina Khan
https://orcid.org/0000-0001-8032-3376
Bangladesh University of Professionals, Bangladesh

Arbia Hlali
https://orcid.org/0000-0002-1850-4579
Taibah University, Saudi Arabia

Md Mehedi Hasan Emon
https://orcid.org/0000-0002-6224-9552
American International University-Bangladesh, Bangladesh

IGI Global
Scientific Publishing
Publishing Tomorrow's Research Today

Published in the United States of America by
IGI Global Scientific Publishing
701 East Chocolate Avenue
Hershey, PA, 17033, USA
Tel: 717-533-8845 | Fax: 717-533-7115
Website: https://www.igi-global.com E-mail: cust@igi-global.com

Library of Congress Cataloging-in-Publication Data

Names: Hasan, Mohammad Kamrul editor | Khan, Tahsina, 1984- editor | Hlali, Arbia, 1983- editor | Emon, Md Mehedi Hasan, 1997- editor
Title: Enhancing sustainability in global supply chains with big data analytics / edited by: Mohammad Kamrul Hasan, Tahsina Khan, Arbia Hlali, Md Mehedi Hasan Emon.
Description: Hershey, PA : IGI Global Scientific Publishing, [2026] | Includes bibliographical references and index. | Summary: "This book aims to establish a structured framework for leveraging big data analytics (BDA) to achieve sustainability goals"-- Provided by publisher.
Identifiers: LCCN 2025042333 (print) | LCCN 2025042334 (ebook) | ISBN 9798337368962 hardback | ISBN 9798337368979 paperback | ISBN 9798337368986 ebook
Subjects: LCSH: Supply chain management | Sustainable development | Big data
Classification: LCC HD38.6 .E53 2026 (print) | LCC HD38.6 (ebook) | DDC 658.500285--dc23/eng/20260122
LC record available at https://lccn.loc.gov/2025042333
LC ebook record available at https://lccn.loc.gov/2025042334

British Cataloguing in Publication Data
A Cataloguing in Publication record for this book is available from the British Library.

We dedicate this book to the scholars, practitioners, and innovators who strive to build a more sustainable, ethical, and resilient global economy. In an era defined by rapid technological transformation and pressing environmental challenges, the pursuit of responsible and data-driven supply chain management is not merely an academic endeavor it is a global necessity.

We also dedicate this work to the next generation of researchers and students who will continue to explore the intersection of big data analytics, artificial intelligence, and sustainability. May their curiosity, critical thinking, and commitment to societal wellbeing shape supply chains that are transparent, inclusive, and environmentally responsible.

Above all, we dedicate this book to our families, whose patience, encouragement, and unwavering support sustain our academic journeys. Their understanding and belief in the value of scholarly contribution make endeavors such as this possible.

May this work contribute, even in a modest way, to advancing knowledge and fostering sustainable transformation across global supply networks.

Table of Contents

Detailed Table of Contents

management in urban and industrial contexts, are discussed, along with challenges such as data privacy, interoperability, and organizational preparedness. Additionally, the chapter illustrates how BDA aligns with circular economy principles, supporting product life extension, secondary market development, and material recirculation, while future directions point to blockchain traceability, ethical AI, and alignment with ESG and SDG frameworks.

This chapter explores how big data technologies are transforming circular supply chains, enabling firms to manage end-of-life products more efficiently while promoting sustainability. By integrating predictive analytics, IoT, AI, and digital twins, organizations can anticipate product returns, optimize reverse logistics, automate sorting, and make informed decisions on reuse, refurbishment, and recycling. The discussion highlights applications across electronics, automotive, and consumer goods industries, illustrating how data-driven strategies support circular economy practices, improve resource efficiency, and reduce environmental impact. Challenges such as interoperability, data quality, cost, privacy, and ethical considerations are also examined, alongside recommendations for governance, collaboration, and technology adoption. The chapter underscores the strategic potential of data-driven circularity in achieving long-term operational and environmental resilience.

Global supply chains are under increasing scrutiny to address environmental, social, and governance (ESG) challenges while maintaining competitiveness and resilience. Big data has emerged as a transformative tool that not only improves transparency but also enables the transition towards circular economy models. This chapter investigates how big data analytics can support the shift from linear practices to circular supply chains that prioritise resource efficiency, waste reduction, and product life-cycle optimisation. It examines the role of big data in enhancing supply chain visibility, enabling predictive decision-making, and fostering collaboration across stakeholders. Case examples will demonstrate how industries such as food, apparel, and manufacturing are using big data to achieve traceability, reduce carbon footprints, and enable closed-loop systems. The chapter will also critically discuss barriers, including governance, interoperability, and ethical concerns, while offering a practical framework for integrating big data into circular supply chain strategies.

The escalating complexity of global supply chains requires analytical capacity beyond that traditionally offered by big data systems. With such disturbances as pandemics, climate shocks and geopolitical tensions growing in scale and intensity, the simultaneous pursuit of sustainability and resilience has emerged as a key strategic challenge. In this chapter, the authors study how quantum-inspired big data analytics can be leveraged to facilitate sustainable and resilient global supply chain systems. Based on the synthesis of Resilience Theory, Complex Systems Theory and Sustainability Frameworks, the research propose a conceptual framework that demonstrates how quantum-inspired algorithms contribute to predictive modelling, decision optimisation and risk intelligence.

The study aimed to review and develop a policy framework for data-driven, sustainable supply chain governance and global collaboration in LDCs. The study was based on secondary data and an exploratory design based on general case studies of Bangladesh, Rwanda, Uganda, Nepal, Ghana, Cambodia, and Bhutan. The findings reveal that infrastructure deficits, institutional failure, technical power shortfalls, and political and administrative gaps hinder transformation despite hopeful changes. The study adopts a seven-step integrated policy approach to create digital infrastructure, data governance frameworks, analytics functionality, traceability frameworks, adaptive governance functions, multi-stakeholder cooperation, and inclusive socio-economic outcomes. The study provides a theoretical framework for sustainable supply chain

Foreword

In an era marked by intensifying environmental pressures, geopolitical disruptions, and rising expectations for ethical and transparent business practices, sustainability in global supply chains has shifted from a strategic option to an urgent necessity. Contemporary supply chains spanning continents and linking producers, intermediaries, and consumers have become increasingly complex, data-intensive, and exposed to risk. Climate change, resource scarcity, regulatory tightening around environmental, social, and governance (ESG) standards, and growing stakeholder scrutiny have collectively challenged organizations to rethink how supply chains are designed, managed, and evaluated. Against this backdrop, *Enhancing Sustainability in Global Supply Chains With Big Data Analytics* emerges as a timely and meaningful contribution to both scholarship and practice.

The convergence of sustainability objectives and big data analytics represents one of the most significant transformations in modern supply chain management. While sustainability has long been discussed in conceptual and strategic terms, its effective implementation has often been hindered by limited visibility, fragmented information, and reactive decision-making. Advances in big data analytics powered by artificial intelligence, Internet of Things (IoT), blockchain technologies, and digital platforms have fundamentally altered this dynamic. These tools now enable organizations to capture, integrate, and analyze vast volumes of real-time data, facilitating predictive insights into carbon emissions, supplier compliance, logistics efficiency, waste reduction, and ESG performance across global networks.

Having spent more than three decades engaged in teaching, research, and professional practice in supply chain management and sustainability, I have observed a gradual yet decisive shift from linear, cost-focused models toward more resilient, circular, and sustainability-oriented systems. My own scholarly work has consistently underscored that meaningful sustainability outcomes require not only sound theoretical frameworks but also robust analytical capabilities that translate data into actionable intelligence. This volume responds precisely to that need by demonstrating how big data analytics can move sustainability beyond compliance and reporting toward proactive, data-driven transformation.

Edited by an accomplished international team Dr. Mohammad Kamrul Hasan, Tahsina Khan, Dr. Arbia Hlali, and Md Mehedi Hasan Emon this book reflects strong editorial leadership and intellectual coherence. From an initial pool of nearly sixty-six accepted proposals, twenty chapters were selected through a rigorous peer-review process and subsequently organized into two complementary volumes. Ten chapters are included in this book, while the remaining ten chapters appear in a companion volume titled Sustainable Operations in the Age of AI and Big Data. This selectivity is evident in the quality of the contributions, which are theoretically grounded, methodologically rigorous, and closely aligned with contemporary industry challenges. The chapters address a wide spectrum of critical themes, including AI-driven carbon footprint tracking, predictive analytics for zero-waste operations, blockchain-enabled transparency, IoT-based sustainability monitoring, green manufacturing, reverse logistics, and the evolving role of Industry 5.0 in sustainable supply chains.

One of the book's notable strengths lies in its holistic and multidimensional perspective on sustainability. Rather than focusing solely on environmental performance, the chapters collectively engage with economic efficiency, social responsibility, ethical sourcing, supplier governance, and ESG compliance. This integrated approach reflects the reality that sustainability is not an isolated initiative but a systemic capability that must be embedded across organizational boundaries and decision-making processes.

The global orientation of this volume further enhances its relevance. Contributions from diverse geographical and institutional contexts offer insights applicable to both developed and emerging economies. Such diversity is particularly valuable at a time when global supply chains must balance international integration with local responsiveness, regulatory variation, and socio-environmental constraints.

For academics, this book offers fertile ground for advancing theory and guiding future research at the intersection of supply chain management, sustainability, and data analytics. For practitioners and industry leaders, it provides practical frameworks and evidence-based insights to support strategic and operational decisions in an increasingly data-driven and sustainability-conscious business environment. Policymakers and development organizations will also find valuable guidance for aligning data-enabled supply chain strategies with broader global agendas, including the United Nations Sustainable Development Goals.

I commend the editors and contributors for their scholarly rigor, collaborative spirit, and commitment to addressing one of the most pressing challenges of our time. It is my hope that this volume will not only inform and inspire its readers but also serve as a catalyst for continued innovation, research, and action toward building more sustainable and resilient global supply chains.

Abu Bakar Abdul Hamid
Kuala Lumpur University of Science and Technology, Malaysia

Preface

Global supply chains are at the center of today's sustainability challenge. Increasing environmental pressures, social responsibility expectations, regulatory demands, and recurring disruptions have exposed the limitations of traditional supply chain models. In this context, the integration of Big Data Analytics with enabling digital technologies such as the Internet of Things (IoT), Artificial Intelligence (AI), explainable AI (XAI), blockchain, and emerging quantum-inspired approaches offers unprecedented opportunities to transform global supply chains into systems that are more sustainable, resilient, transparent, and human-centered.

The book Enhancing Sustainability in Global Supply Chains with Big Data Analytics provides a comprehensive and interdisciplinary exploration of how data-driven technologies can support sustainability objectives across global supply networks. It brings together theoretical perspectives, analytical models, empirical studies, and governance frameworks to illustrate how Big Data enabled decision-making can improve environmental performance, promote ethical practices, optimize resource use, and strengthen supply chain resilience.

This edited volume addresses sustainability challenges across multiple sectors, including manufacturing, procurement, logistics, healthcare, and public administration, while also incorporating perspectives from both developed and developing economies. Special attention is given to emerging economies and least developed countries, where data-driven solutions can play a transformative role in addressing structural constraints and enhancing sustainable development outcomes. The book is intended for researchers, graduate students, practitioners, policymakers, and technology professionals seeking to understand and apply Big Data Analytics for sustainable supply chain management.

The book is organized to reflect a logical progression from foundational digital concepts to advanced analytical applications, governance challenges, and future-oriented perspectives on sustainable global supply chains. The chapters are sequenced to demonstrate how Big Data Analytics evolves from an enabling technology into a strategic driver of sustainability, resilience, and transparency across supply chain systems.

CHAPTER 1: BIG DATA ENABLED TRANSFORMATION OF GLOBAL SUPPLY CHAINS: INTEGRATING IOT, AI, XAI, AND GOVERNANCE FOR SUSTAINABLE AND RESILIENT OPERATIONS

This chapter examines how big data analytics is reshaping global supply chains by enabling a shift toward sustainability, resilience, and responsible decision-making. It explores the integrative roles of Internet of Things (IoT) generated data, artificial intelligence (AI), and explainable AI (XAI) in enhancing visibility, predictive capability, and managerial accountability across complex supply networks. The discussion highlights how data-driven insights support energy efficiency, emissions reduction, risk anticipation, and adaptive operational responses, while emphasizing the importance of governance frameworks in addressing cybersecurity, data privacy, and ethical concerns. By synthesizing technological, managerial, and policy perspectives, the chapter demonstrates that sustainable and resilient supply chain transformation depends not only on advanced analytics but also on transparency, trust, and robust data stewardship in an increasingly digitalized global environment.

CHAPTER 2: A BIG DATA–DRIVEN MCDM MODEL FOR SUSTAINABLE SUPPLIER SELECTION

In response to increasing environmental degradation and sustainability pressures, supply chain management (SCM) has expanded its focus to include sustainability alongside traditional performance goals. This study examines the use of Big Data Analytics (BDA) integrated with three Multi-Criteria Decision-Making (MCDM) methods—WASPAS, MAUT, and COPRAS—to support sustainable SCM decisions. Criterion weights are determined using the CRITIC method, enabling a more objective and data-driven evaluation framework. The study highlights how real-time data from Internet of Things (IoT), Enterprise Resource Planning (ERP) systems, and external sources enhance the accuracy and adaptability of sustainability assessments. A case study on supplier selection and logistics management demonstrates the effectiveness of the proposed approach. The results highlight a research gap in the comparative analysis of MCDM techniques in the context of improving decision quality, responding more quickly to change, and sustainability-focused supply chains.

CHAPTER 3: LEVERAGING BIG DATA ANALYTICS FOR SUSTAINABLE AND ETHICAL SUPPLY CHAINS

This chapter explores the transformative role of Big Data Analytics in advancing sustainable and ethical supply chains. It examines how data-driven decision-making enables companies to enhance transparency, reduce environmental footprints, and uphold labour and human rights across multi-tier supply networks. The chapter addresses challenges in data integration, ethical AI use, and balancing cost with sustainability objectives, supported by real-world case studies from fashion, food, and electronics sectors. It highlights technological innovations such as digital twins, AI, and blockchain that empower circular economy practices and supply chain resilience. Offering critical insights and future directions, this chapter serves as a comprehensive guide for academia and practitioners committed to responsible supply chain management.

CHAPTER 4: AI-DRIVEN BIG DATA AND BLOCKCHAIN CONVERGENCE FOR CARBON FOOTPRINT ACCOUNTABILITY IN GLOBAL SUPPLY CHAINS

The urgency of climate change has heightened the need for accurate carbon accountability in global supply chains. Conventional systems suffer from fragmented data, poor interoperability, and risks of greenwashing, reducing trust and compliance. This chapter explores the convergence of Artificial Intelligence (AI), big data, and blockchain as a transformative solution. AI and big data enable emission forecasting, anomaly detection, and process optimization, while blockchain ensures immutability, transparency, and tamper-proof reporting. Case studies from Walmart and Volvo illustrate practical applications. The chapter also examines socio-economic implications, regulatory aspects, and technological barriers, while highlighting opportunities such as AI-enabled smart contracts, blockchain-based neutrality certifications, and predictive sustainability with digital twins. Collectively, these innovations provide a pathway to low-carbon, ethical, and transparent supply chains aligned with global sustainability and ESG goals.

CHAPTER 5: BLOCKCHAIN AND BIG DATA INTEGRATION FOR TRANSPARENT AND TRACEABLE SUPPLY CHAINS: A LITERATURE SCOPING APPROACH

This chapter explores the integration of blockchain and big data technologies to enhance transparency and traceability in modern supply chains. Drawing on socio-technical systems theory, this chapter examines how decentralised ledgers and real-time analytics can collaboratively address challenges such as fraud, inefficiency, and lack of visibility across supply chain networks. Using the PRISMA methodology, a systematic review of peer-reviewed literature from 2015 to 2025 was conducted to identify trends, gaps, and empirical evidence supporting the integration of these technologies. Key findings reveal that blockchain ensures data immutability and provenance, whereas big data enables predictive analytics and operational optimisation. The synergy between the two technologies fosters trust among stakeholders and supports regulatory compliance. The chapter concludes with recommendations for policymakers, technologists, and supply chain managers, emphasising the need for interoperable platforms, data governance frameworks, and capacity-building initiatives.

CHAPTER 6: HARNESSING BIG DATA FOR REVERSE LOGISTICS AND WASTE MANAGEMENT: PATHWAYS TO SUSTAINABLE SUPPLY CHAINS

This chapter investigates the transformative potential of Big Data Analytics (BDA) in promoting sustainable practices within reverse logistics and waste management, highlighting its contribution to the development of circular supply chains. It delves into the basic concepts of reverse logistics, explores perspectives that guide sustainable operations, and examines the capabilities of BDA in predictive analytics, AI-supported decision-making, and real-time monitoring. Practical implementations, including product returns management, recycling process optimization, and integration of waste management in urban and industrial contexts, are discussed, along with challenges such as data privacy, interoperability, and organizational preparedness. Additionally, the chapter illustrates how BDA aligns with circular economy principles, supporting product life extension, secondary market development, and material recirculation, while future directions point to blockchain traceability, ethical AI, and alignment with ESG and SDG frameworks.

CHAPTER 7: BIG DATA-DRIVEN CIRCULARITY: ENHANCING SUSTAINABILITY THROUGH CLOSED-LOOP SUPPLY CHAIN MODELS

This chapter explores how big data technologies are transforming circular supply chains, enabling firms to manage end-of-life products more efficiently while promoting sustainability. By integrating predictive analytics, IoT, AI, and digital twins, organizations can anticipate product returns, optimize reverse logistics, automate sorting, and make informed decisions on reuse, refurbishment, and recycling. The discussion highlights applications across electronics, automotive, and consumer goods industries, illustrating how data-driven strategies support circular economy practices, improve resource efficiency, and reduce environmental impact. Challenges such as interoperability, data quality, cost, privacy, and ethical considerations are also examined, alongside recommendations for governance, collaboration, and technology adoption. The chapter underscores the strategic potential of data-driven circularity in achieving long-term operational and environmental resilience.

CHAPTER 8: FROM TRANSPARENCY TO CIRCULARITY: ENHANCING SUPPLY CHAIN SUSTAINABILITY THROUGH BIG DATA

Global supply chains are under increasing scrutiny to address environmental, social, and governance (ESG) challenges while maintaining competitiveness and resilience. Big data has emerged as a transformative tool that not only improves transparency but also enables the transition towards circular economy models. This chapter investigates how big data analytics can support the shift from linear practices to circular supply chains that prioritise resource efficiency, waste reduction, and product life-cycle optimisation. It examines the role of big data in enhancing supply chain visibility, enabling predictive decision-making, and fostering collaboration across stakeholders. Case examples will demonstrate how industries such as food, apparel, and manufacturing are using big data to achieve traceability, reduce carbon footprints, and enable closed-loop systems. The chapter will also critically discuss barriers, including governance, interoperability, and ethical concerns, while offering a practical framework for integrating big data into circular supply chain strategies.

CHAPTER 9: QUANTUM-INSPIRED BIG DATA ANALYTICS FOR SUSTAINABLE AND RESILIENT GLOBAL SUPPLY CHAINS

The escalating complexity of global supply chains requires analytical capacity beyond that traditionally offered by big data systems. With such disturbances as pandemics, climate shocks and geopolitical tensions growing in scale and intensity, the simultaneous pursuit of sustainability and resilience has emerged as a key strategic challenge. In this chapter, the authors study how quantum-inspired big data analytics can be leveraged to facilitate sustainable and resilient global supply chain systems. Based on the synthesis of Resilience Theory, Complex Systems Theory and Sustainability Frameworks, the research propose a conceptual framework that demonstrates how quantum-inspired algorithms contribute to predictive modelling, decision optimisation and risk intelligence.

CHAPTER 10: POLICY, GOVERNANCE, AND GLOBAL COLLABORATION FOR DATA-DRIVEN SUSTAINABLE SUPPLY CHAINS (A STUDY ON THE LEAST DEVELOPED COUNTRIES): DATA-DRIVEN SUSTAINABLE SUPPLY CHAINS IN LDCS

The study aimed to review and develop a policy framework for data-driven, sustainable supply chain governance and global collaboration in LDCs. The study was based on secondary data and an exploratory design based on general case studies of Bangladesh, Rwanda, Uganda, Nepal, Ghana, Cambodia, and Bhutan. The findings reveal that infrastructure deficits, institutional failure, technical power shortfalls, and political and administrative gaps hinder transformation despite hopeful changes. The study adopts a seven-step integrated policy approach to create digital infrastructure, data governance frameworks, analytics functionality, traceability frameworks, adaptive governance functions, multi-stakeholder cooperation, and inclusive socio-economic outcomes. The study provides a theoretical framework for sustainable supply chain digitization in a resource-scarce context and offers practical guidance for policymakers, practitioners, and international development organizations.

As editors of this volume, we are pleased to present Enhancing Sustainability in Global Supply Chains with Big Data Analytics, an edited collection that brings together international scholars and practitioners to examine how advanced data-driven technologies can support the transition toward more sustainable, resilient, and transparent global supply chains. This book is the result of a shared recognition that sustainability challenges in global supply networks can no longer be addressed through isolated technological or managerial solutions, but require integrated approaches that combine Big Data Analytics, digital innovation, governance, and policy perspectives.

Mohammad Kamrul Hasan
Tongling University, China

Tahsina Khan
Bangladesh University of Professionals (BUP), Bangladesh

Arbia Hlali
Taibah University, Saudi Arabia

Md Mehedi Hasan Emon
American International University-Bangladesh, Bangladesh

Acknowledgment

We express our sincere gratitude to all those who have contributed to the successful completion of this book, *Enhancing Sustainability in Global Supply Chains With Big Data Analytics*. This work represents a collective intellectual journey grounded in interdisciplinary collaboration, empirical inquiry, and a shared commitment to advancing sustainable development through technological innovation.

We are deeply thankful to the contributing authors whose scholarly rigor, analytical depth, and innovative perspectives have enriched the intellectual quality of this volume. Their expertise across supply chain management, sustainability, artificial intelligence, big data analytics, governance, and emerging technologies has made this book both comprehensive and forward-looking.

We also extend our appreciation to the peer reviewers and academic colleagues who provided valuable feedback and constructive insights during the development of this manuscript. Their critical evaluations significantly strengthened the conceptual clarity, methodological robustness, and practical relevance of the chapters.

Our heartfelt thanks go to our respective institutions for fostering a research-driven academic environment that encourages interdisciplinary exploration and scholarly excellence. The institutional support, access to research resources, and encouragement for innovation have been instrumental in shaping this work.

We further acknowledge the practitioners, policymakers, and industry experts whose real-world challenges and experiences continue to inspire research in sustainable and resilient supply chains. Their insights have ensured that this book bridges theory and practice effectively.

Finally, we extend our sincere gratitude to our families for their patience, encouragement, and unwavering support throughout this demanding yet rewarding academic endeavor. Their understanding and motivation have been invaluable in bringing this project to completion.

We hope this book contributes meaningfully to academic discourse and practical transformation toward more sustainable, transparent, and data-driven global supply chains.

Mohammad Kamrul Hasan
Tongling University, China

Tahsina Khan
Bangladesh University of Professionals (BUP), Bangladesh

Arbia Hlali
Taibah University, Saudi Arabia

Md Mehedi Hasan Emon
American International University-Bangladesh, Bangladesh

Chapter 1
Big Data-Enabled Transformation of Global Supply Chains:
Integrating IoT, AI, XAI, and Governance for Sustainable and Resilient Operations

Md Mehedi Hasan Emon
http://orcid.org/0000-0002-6224-9552
American International University-Bangladesh, Bangladesh

Tahsina Khan
http://orcid.org/0000-0001-8032-3376
Bangladesh University of Professionals, Bangladesh

Mukut Sikder
http://orcid.org/0000-0002-1415-2203
Institute of Blue and Green Development, Shandong University, Weihai, China

Mohammad Kamrul Hasan
http://orcid.org/0000-0003-3866-0090
Tongling University, China

Lei Xunping
http://orcid.org/0009-0000-2899-3428
Tongling University, China

Arbia Hlali
http://orcid.org/0000-0002-1850-4579
Taibah University, Saudi Arabia

ABSTRACT

This chapter examines how big data analytics is reshaping global supply chains by enabling a shift toward sustainability, resilience, and responsible decision-making. It explores the integrative roles of Internet of Things (IoT) generated data, artificial intelligence (AI), and explainable AI (XAI) in enhancing visibility, predictive capability, and managerial accountability across complex supply networks. The

DOI: 10.4018/979-8-3373-6896-2.ch001

discussion highlights how data-driven insights support energy efficiency, emissions reduction, risk anticipation, and adaptive operational responses, while emphasizing the importance of governance frameworks in addressing cybersecurity, data privacy, and ethical concerns. By synthesizing technological, managerial, and policy perspectives, the chapter demonstrates that sustainable and resilient supply chain transformation depends not only on advanced analytics but also on transparency, trust, and robust data stewardship in an increasingly digitalized global environment.

INTRODUCTION

The present context of global trade has experienced a shift in supply chain to become dynamic connected socio-technical ecosystem where sustainability and resilience have become the important methods. The combination of the Big Data Analytics (BDA), Internet of Things (IoT), Artificial Intelligence (AI), Explainable AI (XAI), and powerful governance systems, are reshaping the design, management, and transformation of supply chains. The growing rate of digitization has increased the volume, rate and range of data generated at various points of contact within the supply chain that facilitates real-time visibility and analytic insights previously unavailable. Sensors, corporate systems, logistics, and external entities produce data streams that are used to make both strategic and operational decisions through these digital ecosystems which simultaneously meet sustainability objectives and enhance dynamic capability to shocks. The blistering increase in the amount of data and blistering development of AI and machine learning (ML) approaches and design forced researchers and practitioners to redesign the supply chain models found on the data-centered paradigm. BDA and AI have not only become widely acceptable as a means of optimization of the operations but also as important models in developing smart supply chains that provide predictive and prescriptive decisions and efficiencies in resource deployment, and an improved environmental output. As the latest research states, supply chain resilience and the facilitation of sustainable practices across the majority of industries is possible because of the integration of the BDA and AI since these tools allow predictive risk mitigation and more adaptive responses to volatility (Kamble et al., 2023; Kumar et al., 2024; Talwar et al., 2021). The development is consistent with the global practices of sustainability and governance where there is need for transparency, accountability and ethical data and decision-making practices.

This rate notwithstanding, complex analytics adoption in global supply chains is a huge load especially in interpretation of complex model outputs, information security, and ethical integrity. To curb such concerns, the idea of XAI has come out as an important area of research that will render AI-generated information comprehensible to stakeholders hence hold the AI responsible in critical supply chain decisions. XAI frameworks are particularly relevant in the instillation of trust and obedience in governance systems whose black box models are not justified in an ethical and legal manner. The chapter will consider the potential of integrated digital technologies (and the IoT in particular) in supporting sustainable and resilient supply chain operations. It is also concerned with the empirical and literature-based knowledge that aims at charting a vast framework of the deliberate correspondence of data and analytics to sustainability, ethical governing and resilience objective measures.

BACKGROUND

The supply chain development using digital technology has been based on various areas of scholarly research that offer varying theoretical and practical perspectives. The key performance indicators that the scholars started to focus on are the resilience and sustainability of supply chain performance because the traditional definition of the efficacy, cost-saving and inventory optimization was disrupted by the global pandemic, geopolitical crises and climate-related disruptions, which made the scholars include them in the center of the supply chain research. Resilience may be considered as the ability of the supply networks to foresee, withstand and recuperate following disruption and sustainability can be considered as the long-term commitment to being a steward of the environment and social responsibility. The scholarly opinion is that quantitative technologies have a focal point in this change. Interconnected IoT devices, including sensors, actuators, and platforms, create huge quantities of information that can help to improve the situational awareness of manufacturing, logistics, and distribution processes. This connection between IoT and BDA has been found to be useful in providing sustainable supply chain models by allowing real-time monitoring of the energy use, emissions, and resource distribution (Bechtsis et al., 2022). The AI and ML algorithms are used to extract actionable insights on the complex information and predict, optimize, and identify anomalies to enhance the outcomes of operational resilience and performance (Zekhnini et al., 2021). Technology is the backdrop of what modern literature has dubbed as intelligent, adaptive and sustainable supply networks.

Despite high potential in the digital transformation of supply chains, there are obstacles to the implementation thereof, especially, on the data governance, cybersecurity, and ethical aspect. The system of governance that enhances data quality, compliance and oversight are significant in making sure that advanced analytics and AI products work within ethical and regulatory boundaries particularly as supply chains keep becoming automated and autonomous. In the case under consideration, XAI can be utilized to mitigate the trade-offs between AI analytics complexity and interpretability, making the stakeholders explore, validate and rely on model results. This chapter puts the realization of the advanced technologies in the globalization of supply chain research in a context that would facilitate the same and is in the relation to the prevailing sustainability and resilience demands, as well as the growing necessity to build explainable and controlled analytics platforms, which will enable ethical decision-making.

The central theme of this chapter is to give a detailed framework on how the integration of BDA, IoT, AI and XAI, and robust governance models will bring the world supply chains to the place of sustainability, resilience and ethical responsibility. It will also be the goal of the chapter to show how the utilization of IoT-data can make industrial operations sustainable, how AI and XAI can ensure transparency and resiliency in the decision-making process, and how policy and managerial behavior can be guided in the emerging economies and the Least Developed Countries (LDCs) by using governance strategies to address issues related to cybersecurity, data privacy, and ethics.

This chapter is also significant to academic and practical knowledge since it delves into the critical meeting point of digital transformation, sustainability, and resilience in global supply chains. First, it facilitates a more efficient integration of theory, establishing a group of fields of study in BDA, AI, IoT, XAI, and governance into a unified analytical framework and considers both environmental and operational goals. Secondly, it satisfies new demands in the literature about explainable and accountable AI applications in the supply chain setting that is virtually untapped despite the extensive implementation of AI (Gebhardt et al., 2022). The chapter is more significant to policy and industry because it provides actionable information to supply chain managers, technology designers and policymakers on how to address the issue of implementation like that of data governance, cybersecurity, ethical compliance as critical issues that are encountered in resource constrained and emerging economies. Sustainability and resilience, as essential performance requirements, are employed to support strategic decision-making and, as a result, help create data-driven, ethical, and adaptive supply networks focused on meeting the global environmental and social governance provisions, are highlighted in this chapter.

DATA-DRIVEN FOUNDATIONS OF SUSTAINABLE SUPPLY CHAINS

BDA as a Catalyst for Sustainable Supply Chains

BDA has emerged within the recent years as a key enabler of sustainable and resilient supply chains. The growing complexity of international supply chains and the high legal and social expectations on environmental and social responsibility have necessitated a shift towards data based, analytics-oriented models of decision making as compared to traditional approaches. Aggregation, integration, and analysis of large volumes of structured and unstructured data of different types, including enterprise resource planning (ERP) systems, IoT systems, social media, supplier networks, and market intelligence systems, make up BDA. The capability to process and understand large amounts of data can assist companies in uncovering operational actionable insights that could result in a higher rate of operational efficiency, reduced environmental footprint, and enhanced long-term sustainability goals (Bechtsis et al., 2022; Fernando et al., 2025).

Figure 1. Conceptual Framework of BDA-Enabled Sustainable Supply Chains

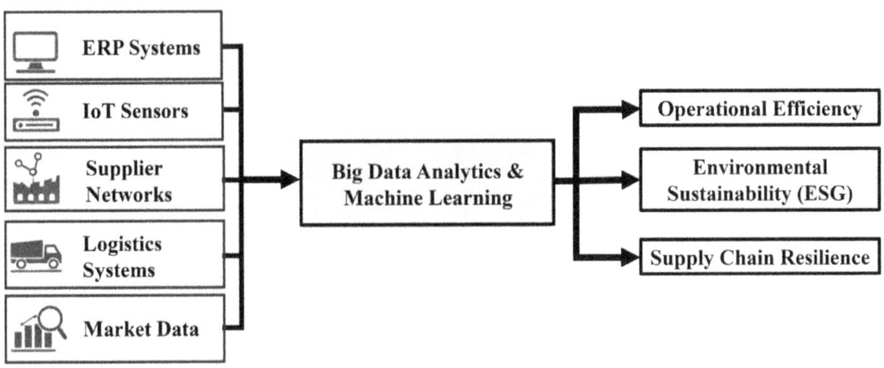

Source: Conceptualized and designed by the authors

The most significant positive aspect of the BDA on supply chains is the fact that it can optimize the resources and minimize the waste of the entire value chain. The Production schedule, inventory, transportation, and the consumption of energy will help the companies to know the inefficiency of the whole process and corrective action will be taken in real-time. Predictive analytics can see ahead in time to know when production or stock obsolescence might happen, enabling companies to adjust their buying and production plans. Similarly, the carbon emissions and fuel consumption during the operation can be reduced through the optimization of the routes using the BDA and maintain the level of service and cost-efficiency of the logistics (Maheshwari et al., 2021). These functions are complemented by the fact that the principle of ML algorithms that allow the supply chains to learn the tendencies of the past, discover non-linear tendencies, and adapt to the changing environment ad-hoc are introduced. BDA also leads to accomplishment of sustainability goals besides improving efficiency in the operations which are not strategic. ESG performance is being introduced to the company strategy, the supply chain activities have become a critical point of the strategy. Big data helps companies to measure, monitor and report sustainability data, such as carbon footprint, water usage, amount of waste and compliance of labor in multi-tiered supply chain. As an illustration, preventing actions and achieving sustainable sourcing decisions would be simpler with a more fined analytics understanding of suppliers that are more prone to environmental risks or that would experience some climate-related interference (Bechtsis et al., 2022). The cost-effectiveness of the supply chain available will be put into consideration and the ESG and operational analytics will not undermine the cost-effectiveness of the supply chain choices, and nothing will be compromised in the process of meeting the societal and regulatory requirements. The other BDA effect is that it enhances resiliency. The threats facing the international supply chains are classified under different categories including natural calamities, geopolitical conflicts, pandemics, and market shocks. BDA provides forecasting and prescriptive data that may assist firms to peep into the future disruption and come up with backup plans. Simulation of different scenarios and stress test of the supply chain designs would help the businesses to identify the areas of weakness and devise risk management strategies and simplify the distribution of resources. The ML models will be capable of detecting the appearance of a supply chain interrupt, such as a surge in demand, supplier failure, or logistical bottlenecks and taking suitable and prompt decisions to preserve continuity and make the overall economic and environmental costs as limited as possible (Stroumpoulis & Kopanaki, 2022).

Figure 2. Role of BDA in Enabling Sustainable and Resilient Supply Chain Outcomes

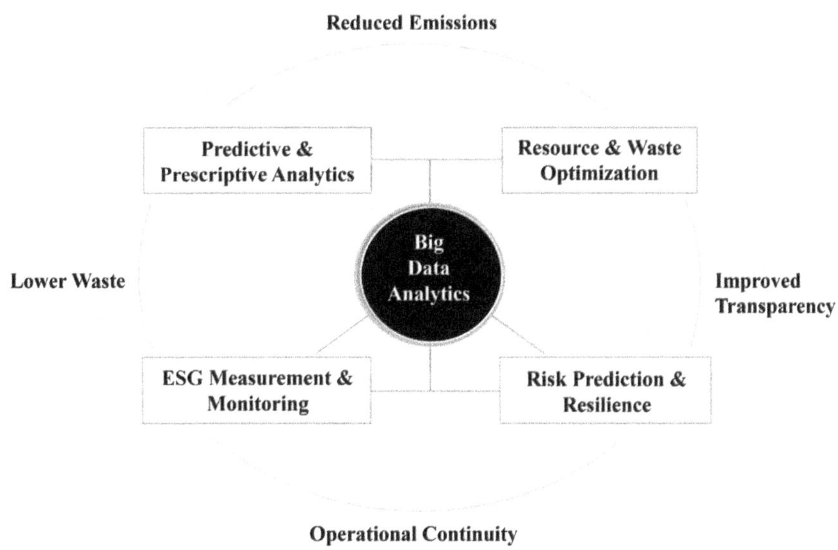

Source: Author's illustration based on literature synthesis

In addition, the integration of additional technologies is the IoT, blockchain, and AI, which enhances the capacity of BDA to sustainability and resilience. The IoT sensors keep providing the operation information that can be analyzed with the frameworks of BDA to present the information about the energy consumption patterns, machines' performance, and the impact directly influenced on the environment. Realizing with the assistance of blockchains, traceability allows managing the sustainable practices within the supply chain by facilitating the checking and transparency and accountability of the processes in accordance with the expectations of the stakeholders. The AI based optimization and the BDA allow dynamic inventory, intelligent routing, and predictive maintenance, thus, minimizing waste, optimizing efficiency, and improving the resilience of the entire supply chain (Núñez-Merino et al., 2020; Rossini et al., 2023). Irrespective of this disruptive nature, there are difficulties in applying BDA to supply chains. The issue of data quality, data governance, interoperability, and privacy is still a significant challenge with which the businesses would have to address to effectively utilize the benefits of analytics-based sustainability. The creation of end-to-end data governance models, the assurance that analytics are utilized in an ethical way, and the incorporation of various data sources are important needs in determining successful execution of the BDA in a global supply chain. Researchers have stressed that, to achieve sustainable supply chains, both technological skills and organizational willingness are needed, the alignment of strategies, and coordination of stakeholders to translate the results of data into the practical and long-term results (Akbari & Do, 2021).

IoT-Generated Data in Contemporary Operational Ecosystems

The fast development of IoT technology has entirely transformed the work process of industry and manufacturing so that data has become a driving force of change that is oriented towards sustainability. Smart sensors and embedded controllers, RFID tags, and connected machines are Internet-of-things devices that produce high rate, detailed, data on energy consumption, emissions, health equipment, material flows, and operational conditions on a continuous basis. The IoT infrastructure provides real-time visibility in the production processes and industrial assets unlike in traditional monitoring systems, which need periodic audits or consolidated reports to have visibility. It has turned into a critical competence since businesses are experiencing mounting pressure to minimize their environmental impact and meet regulatory requirements, not to mention to increase operational stability in an increasingly unpredictable global landscape (Turskis & Šniokienė, 2024). Regarding sustainability, IoT-related data offers the empirical basis of attaining specific monitoring and evidence-based decisions. Consumption of energy in industrial processes like manufacturing, processing, and heavy engineering has been inefficient always due to the inability to see through the consumption of energy by machines as well as inability to predict processes. The current IoT sensors on the factory machines also enable the business to trace consumption of electricity, fuel, water, and materials with great accuracy, which makes it easy to detect abnormalities in their application and the wastage of energy. Taking the information of this kind and analytical solutions to work, companies have an opportunity to optimize the production plans, balance the loads, and change the parameters of work to achieve the minimum waste and emissions without declining productivity (Malik, 2024). The data-driven projects provide the opportunity to implement the measurable rise in efficiency of energy consumption and to adjust the industrial process to the overall objectives of sustainability and decarbonization.

In addition to energy conservation, the data, which is offered by IoT, is required to verify the emissions, as well as to control the environmental compliance. Instantaneous feeds of sensors to track the quality of air, temperature, humidity, and pollutants allow businesses to stop being reactive in their compliance strategy to actively safeguarding the environment. Corrective actions can also be taken by firms in real time as opposed to attempting to correct the breach of regulation after it has taken place. This transformation is especially applicable to the sphere of business where there are severe environmental regulations governing every detail, and the inability to follow them will result in financial and reputational losses. Recent studies focus on the fact that tracking the environment with the help of the IoT and analytics will increase transparency and accountability and allow extending possibilities of environmental performance in the long term (Anjaria, 2025). Predictive maintenance and asset management is one of the excellent contributions of the data generated by IoT to sustainable operations in industries. The customary maintenance process, which is typically founded on the series of schedules or the responsiveness machine to the failures of the equipment, is costly and eco-unfriendly. The IoT sensors continuously accumulate the information on machine use, temperature, pressure, and vibrations to enable the models to give a prediction on equipment degradation and breakdown before it succumbs to a breakdown. Predictive maintenance also minimizes downtime and disruptions during the operation due to the extension of the equipment life or the waste of the materials used as well as energy, which is the result of the inefficient or defective equipment (Saeed et al., 2023).

Figure 3. IoT-Based Predictive Maintenance and Asset Sustainability

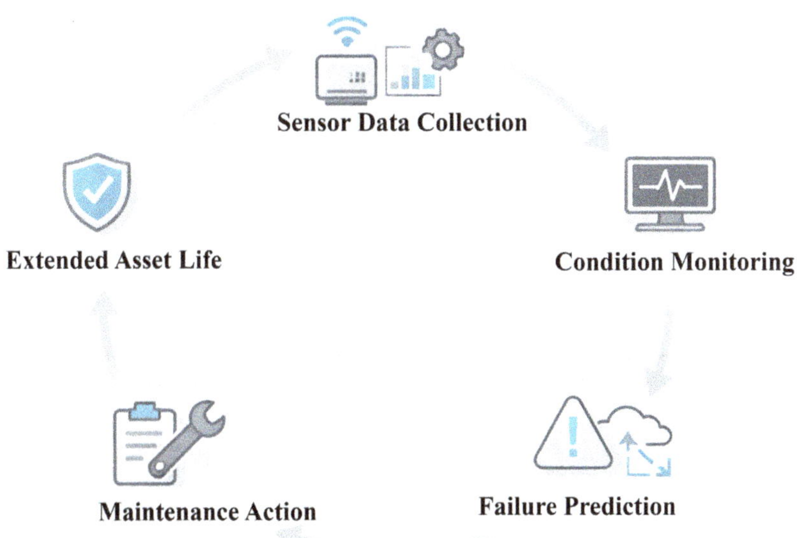

Source: Developed by the authors based on prior studies

Within the framework of sustainability, the conservation and minimization of the emissions is done directly through the increase of the asset's lifetime and the maintenance limitation that are not planned.

Integration of the data provided by the IoT with advanced AI and analytics will make it more involved in sustainable processes of industries. The IoTs have the potential to produce complex and high dimensional data that can be processed with ML algorithms to indicate non-linear correlations and concealed trends that are otherwise not detected in regular analysis. AI-based analytics may be able to find the most optimal operating points where the result is maximum productivity with a minimum of energy consumption or prescribe modification to the processes that will decrease the waste that is produced during peak demand times. The systems are smart and provide flexible and self-optimizing industrial operations, which are becoming the key to sustainable production and Industry 4.0 models (Lin & Wang, 2024).

Figure 4. Integration of IoT Data with AI for Adaptive and Resilient Industrial Operations

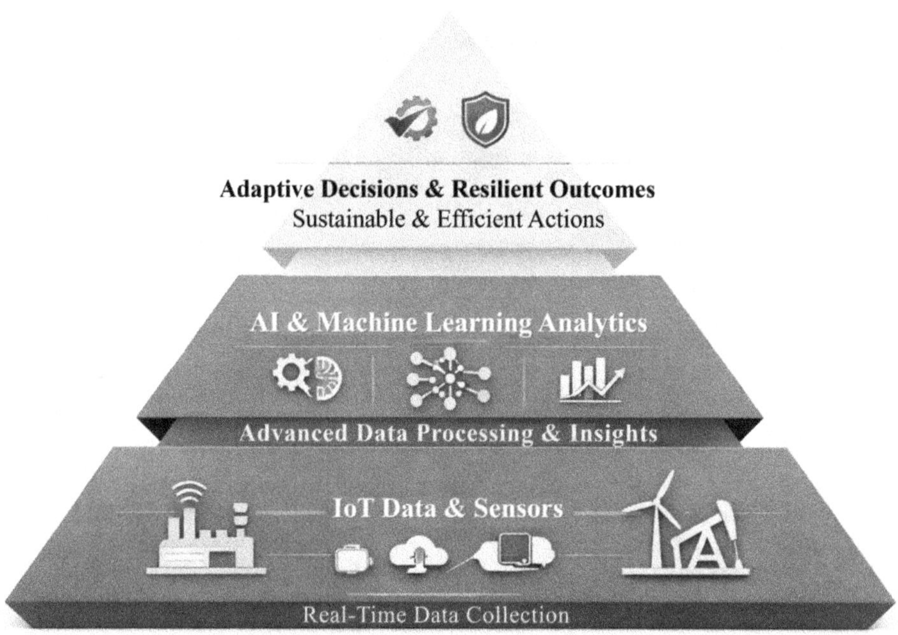

Source: Authors conceptual representation

It is noteworthy that the information given by the IoT will enhance resilience in industries which is directly proportional to sustainability. The actual time industrial system requirements are that, in case of a failure in the supplies, equipment failures or other environmental disruptions happen, the situation awareness is the state of knowledge that needs to be acted upon. The IoT offers round-the-clock awareness in the systems to enable the businesses to identify irregularities, resource allocation, and alteration of production activities due to the disruption. This dynamic capability minimizes the threat of catastrophic failure and minimizes the environmental and financial cost of unavailability. Advocates of the resilient industrial operation as more sustainable as such, are increasingly coming to be interested in arguing that they are not objects to unwarranted recovery interventions, and may not be able to cope with the ensuing emergency (Beheshti & Mansoor, 2025). The ease of access to the data generated by the IoT implies the necessity to utilize the generated data and is based on a variety of organizational and technological considerations. The lack of interoperability in the data, the potential to interface with the older systems, the risk of cybersecurity and governance models are one of the grave issues. The IoT data and its growth rates can either overpower businesses and make them less valuable unless they have effective data management and data governance systems. Moreover, privacy, surveillance and monitoring of the ethical issues in labor should be prudently factored in the pursuit of delivering the socially viable and plausible sustainability initiatives. It is also unanimous in the literature to postulate that it is not merely the technology that, which is present in the organization, but effective industrial change should involve a strategy, organizational preparedness and interaction among functions to transform the observations of the IoT to a meaningful change within the organization (Simionescu & Strielkowski, 2025).

The IoT produced information is a significant facilitator of green industrial processes, which offers real-time visibility, and allows to optimize energy and emissions, predict maintenance and operational lifespan. Combined with analytics and AI based systems supporting decision making, IoT data can assist the businesses to make significant improvements to the marginal efficiency improvements to complete sustainability improvements. The tactical exploitation of the information provided by the IoT will be on the tip of the success of the eco-friendly, durable, and forward-looking industrial procedures, as the industries will have to deal with the environmental problems, compliance requirements and uncertainty in their work.

INTELLIGENT MANUFACTURING AND RESILIENCE-ORIENTED ANALYTICS

Smart Manufacturing as a Strategic Enabler of Environmental Resource Efficiency

The concept of efficiency, sustainability and long-term competitiveness of industrial systems changed with the development of smart production. Intelligent manufacturing is more than the automation that has been in use and involves data-driven intelligence, advanced analytics, AI, robotics, and cyber-physical systems (CPS) to develop adaptive and self-optimizing manufacturing systems. Within such a design, the effectiveness of the environmental resource has been made part of the core values of operating industries as opposed to being considered an achievement. Being more interconnected and having more information, the manufacturing systems can perceive, analyze, and optimize energy, material consumption, and waste production in real-time and balance the operations performed by the manufacturing systems with their sustainability interests (Andronie et al., 2021; Krishnan, 2024).

Smart manufacturing is based on a unified layer of sensor networks, Industrial Internet of Things (IIoT) platform, and analytics-driven decision-support systems. With the help of such systems, it is also possible to constantly record the information on the machines and production lines, and in the processes within the plant. The smart factories rest on the feedback loops when compared to the conventional production models in which processes have been highly configured and periodic performance measurement undertaken. The actual time data about the machine work, power usage, material flows are calculated to identify the inefficiency and take proactive actions. The AI control systems can adjust the settings of the machines to either reduce the amount of energy used when the demand is low or to attain the desired balance between the input used to produce materials and scrap and rework. The characters also play a significant role in the effectiveness of the resources despite the lack of reduction in throughput and quality requirements (Kaniappan Chinnathai & Alkan, 2023).

Figure 5. Smart Manufacturing Architecture for Environmental Resource Efficiency

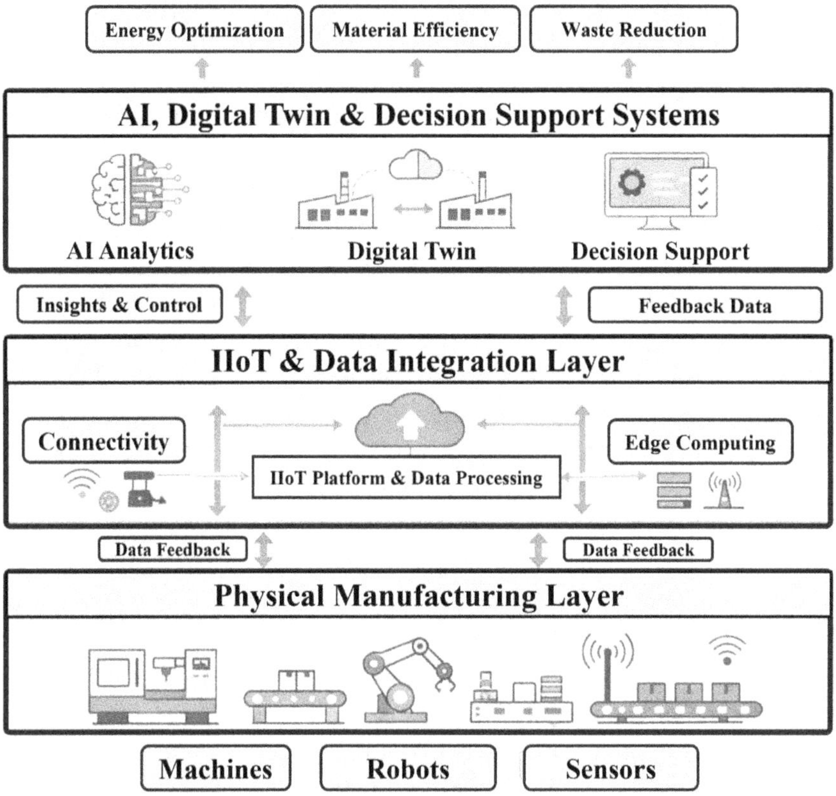

Source: Authors conceptual representation

Another technology that is bought along with intelligent manufacturing ecosystems is digital twin technology. A digital twin is a computer simulation of a physical object, process or manufacturing system that will continuously update itself using real time operation data. With the help of digital twins, the simulation of many operating scenarios can ensure that they can test changes in processes, energy-efficient, and waste-reduction programs without interfering with the actual processes. Speaking of the digital aspect, which is concerned with the environmental impact, the digital twins are more likely to make certain choices depending on the analysis of the effect of resources and emissions of various strategies associated with production. Through the help of digital twins, it has become possible to optimize the energy consumption and waste of materials by a considerable percentage i.e. in the energy-intensive economy of the automotive industry, electronics industry, and process industry (Sachan et al., 2025).

Smart manufacturing sustainability is enormous, due to the cyber-physical systems (CPS) that are distributed across computational intelligence and physical processes in a complex way. CPS is an autonomous process that is applied to make the machine and systems to interact and coordinate their actions, reactions to the changes that take place in the surrounding and working conditions. This freedom is especially effective in cases of complicated material flows and waste streams. CPS can divert or reassign material and dynamic supply of working with bottlenecks to accomplish even distribution of the workload on machines to prevent energy spiking and sort waste stream to be re-used and recycled. The CPS also assist the circular manufacturing models in the dimensions of the closed control mechanisms and allow the resources to be recovered to be utilized in the manufacturing processes of the products instead of being wasted (Chinnathai & Alkan, 2023). The industry needs intelligent production as per the aspects of the circular economy in the industrialization process. Circularity is skewed in the use of virgin materials, longer life of commodities and assets, and reclaiming value in waste. The streamlining of the processes with the support of AI and data-based analytics can potentially assist manufacturers in creating production systems that can potentially reduce wastage and provide an opportunity to reuse and re-manufacture. Another example is the fact that the defects in the production process can be identified in the actual process thus minimizing the scrap rates and wastages of materials. Equally, the by-products and waste streams are monitored through smart monitoring in order to generate the possibility of reusing them within or without the organization or even collaborate with the members of the supply chain of an industrial symbiosis system (Sachan et al., 2025).

Figure 6. Smart Manufacturing–Driven Circular Resource Optimization Model

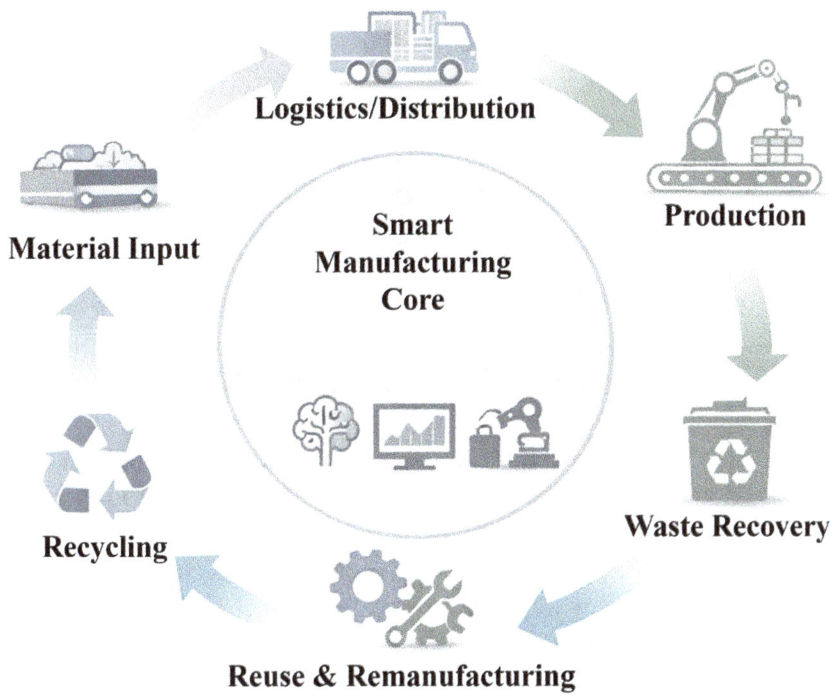

Source: Developed by the authors

Empirical information gathered by the installations of smart factories, is that the efficiency of the utilization of environmental resources can be offered with the competitive advantage and even complements it. The subsequent astuteness in production that the companies embrace tends to result in efficiency in the energy expenditure, decrease in spoilage, greater production, flexibility, and capacity to reply to the market demands. This power to react promptly to the shift in products to suit the shift in demand will offset heavy production and wastage of stocks that cause colossal waste to the environment. Moreover, smart manufacturing promotes transparency and traceability, due to which the company can prove that it is in accordance with the environmental law, as well as with the sustainability standards, and this aspect is particularly relevant to remain relevant in the international markets (Waltersmann et al., 2021). To be successful, smart manufacturing would demand that sustainability potential should be founded on different organizational and structural factors. They have been too high in their initial investment spending, the lack of skilled labor and the lack of integration with the already existing systems was a major concern especially to the small and medium enterprises. With the increasing popularity of data-driven automation, the issues of data management, responsible behavior, and cybersecurity emerge. The lack of an adequate system of governance may result in the emergence of new spheres of failures or more injustices of industrial ecosystems in the wake of technologies in which the efficiency of resources is facilitated. The introduction of the technologies, as the latest study demonstrated, should be matched with the organizational strategy, the working force development, and the sustainability governance as one of the means of ensuring that the smart manufacturing can achieve both the long-term environmental and economic benefit (Sachan et al., 2025).

The idea of smart manufacturing is an extreme approach to efficiency of the industrial processes regarding the use of environmental resources. Smart factories will become capable of optimizing their energy and material flows, waste disposal in real-time, and using digital twins, AI-based decisions, and cyber-physical systems and sensor-enhanced analytics. Such functions render it more sustainable and round-trip economic goals and as well as flexible and competitive in terms of its operations. Intelligent manufacturing will be a part of the general implementation of the ecologically sustainable, resilient, and visionary manufacturing process when the manufacturing systems will be technologically advanced with Industry 4.0 and other technological successes.

Simulation and Predictive Analytics for Enhancing Supply Chain Resilience

The remarkably large and acute form of interruption of chains of supply because of natural disasters, geopolitical unrest, and international pandemics have shown the result lessness of the traditional, reactive risk management strategy. In this case, resilient supply chains should be able to withstand shock in addition to forecasting, adjusting as well as recovering losses brought about by disruption at minimum operational and economic costs. Big data systems, ML, and AI that enable the creation of simulation and predictive analytics have become a critical tool that will enable business enterprises to transform their crisis management attempts into proactive resilience planning. The technologies allow decision-makers to simulate complex systems of supply chains and simulate possible scenarios and develop contingency plans to develop continuity, flexibility, and resilience in an uncertain environment (Aljohani, 2023; Smyth et al., 2024). One of the essential approaches of the comprehension of the dynamics of supply chains in different states of affairs is simulation modeling.

Figure 7. Simulation-Driven Supply Chain Risk Modeling Framework

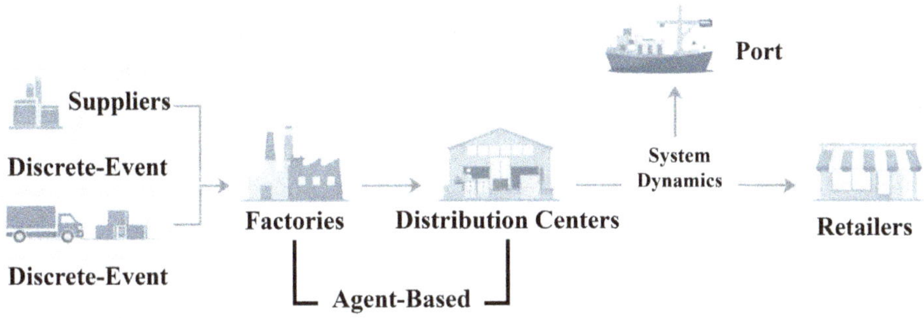

Source: Developed by the authors

Through the establishment of a virtual supply chain, organizations can explore the propagation of any disturbance situation, port closure, supplier breakdown or transport delays using the network nodes. The three most popular methodologies that may be applied to visualizing and quantifying the effects of disruptions to the inventory level, lead times, and service performance are discrete-event simulations, agent-based models and system dynamics. To simulate the processes of the material flows within a multi-tier supply chain, the simulation of the discrete-event simulation is applicable, and the planners can observe the congestion and bottlenecks at the time when demand is high or when there are few suppliers. Such knowledge is necessary to define weaknesses in the structures and establish the efficiency of solutions used to mitigate these weaknesses before they could be applied to the real world (Iftikhar et al., 2024). Predictive analytics is an enhancement of simulation; it takes the past and real-time data to predict a future event and identify potential risks. Sophisticated AI and ML systems can consider complicated data patterns and spot early indicators and calculate the potential and the probability of disruption events. The predictive models can enumerate suppliers that are very vulnerable due to geopolitical instability or forecast demand based on market indicators and seasonality. When predictive data is synthesized and combined with the simulation findings, the supply chain planners can be able to formulate more informed and robust risk mitigation strategies. This may be achieved by holding inventories at key locations, diversifying supply chain or avoiding straddling risky transport routes (Belhadi et al., 2024).

The most effective area of use of simulation and predictive analytics is inventory management. The classical inventory models tend to presuppose fixed equations of the safety stocks that fail to put into consideration the fluidity of disruptions. Conversely, the dynamically computed safety stock can be done by methods with analytics that consider probabilistic forecasts of demand variations and supply variations. As new data streams into the ML algorithms, they will continuously be able to enhance demand forecasts, enabling companies to make stock objectives adjustments within minutes. Not only does it increase the extent of services, but it also contributes to the minimization of the risk of surplus and limited supply of goods that are not only expensive to the economy, but the environment as well. The demand patterns that have strongly diverged in comparison to the historical ones could be followed within the frames of real-time analytics and the inventory could be adjusted to keep the balance and the resilience (Dubey et al., 2021).

Figure 8. Integrated Predictive Analytics and Scenario Planning for Resilient Supply Chains

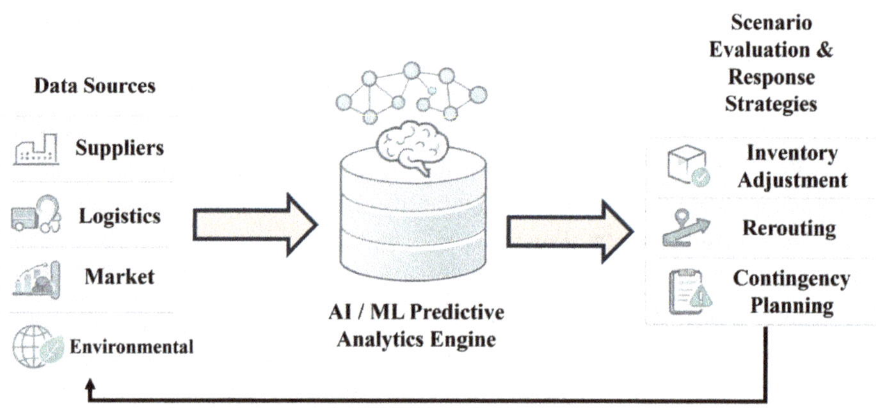

Source: Developed by the authors

Simulation and predictive analytics must be part of the operation in optimization of logistics and port operation which in most cases constitutes the operational core of global supply chain. Ports receive a lot of consignments, sort, and distribute cargo making them susceptible to these challenges such as labor unions, harsh weather conditions, or lack of communication. Simulation also enables port authorities and logistics companies to establish how disruption conditions under various conditions of disruption affect throughput, queue length, and turnaround times. Predictive models can be used to predict congestion times or equipment failures, and this enables the planning of resource allocation ahead of time and redirection of deliveries to keep the flow going. The latter analytical capabilities are especially necessary in the sphere of the emerging economies that have to struggle with the infrastructure limitations and externalities (Burgos & Ivanov, 2021). The additional threats to resilience planning include multi-tier supply chains that have complicated relationships of interdependence between suppliers, manufacturers, distributors, and retailers.

To make proper forecasting and simulation, cross-layer visibility is necessary. The more recent studies indicate the combination of supply chain visibility systems with predictive analytics to provide a detailed risk profile. The supplier data in the upstream can be used to refine the precision of prediction model and the simulation may reveal the implications of disruption at the lower levels on the end customer risks. Linked analytics systems enable coordinated response e.g. coordinated production adjustments, joint inventory, and coordinated contingency plans between the partners. This kind of coordination minimizes the impact of impacts and also builds resiliency in the form of a collective strategic goal within the supply network (Shekarian & Mellat Parast, 2021).

Although simulation and predictive analytics offer numerous opportunities, a lot of implementation issues continue to persist. Accessibility and quality of data have been a major limitation particularly in areas with low digital infrastructure or in isolated data systems that discourage easy information exchange. Besides this, advanced analytics are complex, and some skills in technology and organizational preparedness are required, which may be unavailable in small and medium-sized businesses. The ethical issues of how the algorithms work, and the accountability of the decisions taken must be strictly controlled, which means that predictive algorithms are not to introduce bias and adverse outcomes without a strategy. To solve such problems, one will need to invest in data governance systems, create cross-functional capacity, and collaboration platforms that encourage learning as a team and resiliency innovation (Bahrami & Shokouhyar, 2022). The two important methods of creating resilient supply chains that can anticipate, absorb, and recover shocks are predictive analytics and simulation. These technologies allow exploration of the situations, dynamic forecasting, and adaptive inventory and logistics to provide companies with analytical sight to make a step through uncertainty with strategic certainty. As global supply chains grow and become more complicated and volatile, continuity, operational resilience, risk mitigation and sustainable competitive advantage of global supply chains will entail the incorporation of simulation and predictive faculties through resilience planning.

ETHICAL, EXPLAINABLE, AND CIRCULAR SUPPLY CHAIN INTELLIGENCE

XAI as a Foundation for Sustainable and Ethical Supply Chain Decision-Making

The rapid integration of AI into the global supply chains has been accompanied by the prospects of boosting its performance, minimizing risks, and being more strategic than ever. This has resulted in a major paradox of how complex AI models may exist and then there is a need to make transparent and reliable decisions. The classical AI systems, particularly the ones that are based on deep learning or ensemble systems, are commonly black boxes, which give a high level of accuracy in the forecasting, but they cannot be interpreted. It is quite problematic as well within the context of the supply chains where the implication of the decisions that have such a colossal effect on the ethical, environmental, and social aspects is unclear (Hao & Demir, 2024). XAI has arrived to solve this and provide methodological competence by which the inner rationality of AI systems could be made clear to the human decision-makers and that the AI-related practices would be able to adhere to the principles of sustainability and morals. The primary goal of XAI is to find the balance between the complexity of computation and human comprehension. Rather, AI can be seen as an opaque oracle, and XAI models will be defined by the style of explanation, which is more often written in natural language, in the form of a heatmap or rules, and may give reasons why a model has made a given output. This kind of transparency is essential in supply chain operation management and governing ethics. When the AI models propose to source, carry inventory, or reduce carbon, the supply chain executives ought to be aware of the rationale of the choices to make sure that the offerings do not discriminate against the marginalized suppliers in an unintended manner, eradicate environmental risks, and operate contrary to the current ESG (Environmental, Social, and Governance) standards. It is especially important because accountability in algorithmic decision-making is becoming of greater interest among regulatory organizations and investors (Vaio et al., 2024).

The idea of XAI is not easily implementable when making a sustainability-based supply chain decision. The supplier evaluation and assessment process, as well as the procurement, entails the evaluation of large and complex sets of the cost structure, delivery performance, labor practices and environmental records using AI models to provide prioritized or ranked potential partners. Without such explainability, such rankings can conceal biases based on data quality issues, proxy variables or form an unsophisticated model with the consequence of unwittingly propagating inequalities or undermining ethical sourcing requirements. The XAI tools such as SHAP (SHapley Additive exPlainations) values and Lime (Local Interpretable Model-Agnostic Explanations) would be capable of providing information about the feature that can affect a model and give the procurement manager the opportunity to estimate the extent to which the environment performance or social compliance can influence the outcome. That way, the decisions made by XAI are not just efficient but also acceptable by the morals as stipulated by the company values and as per the international standards (Wu et al., 2024).

Figure 9. XAI–Driven Sustainable Supply Chain Decision Framework

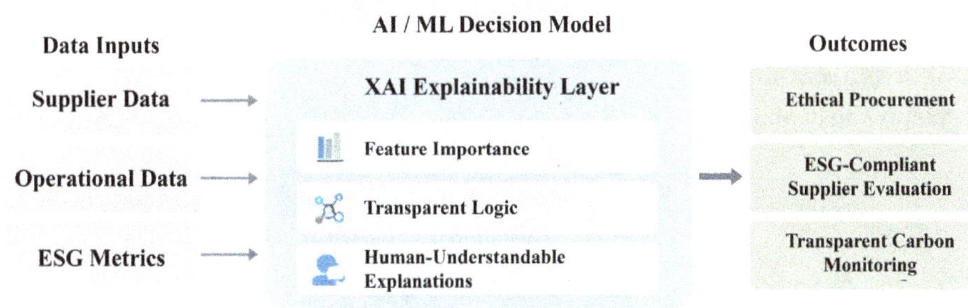

Source: Developed by the authors

Transparency is essential in managing and controlling carbon footprints in the processes of supply chains. Emission-related to production, logistics, and supply chain networks are evaluated using AI models on a grand scale. However, the factors of carbon performance including energy make up, transportation approach, and intensity of production are complex and interact with operational and contextual variables in non-linear ways. XAI tools can explain such connections showing which factors have the strongest effect on emissions projections and why some actions should be recommended. Such level of clarity is critical to sustainability officers and outside auditors where they could review the emissions reduction strategies, identify intervention leverage points, and explain the rationale of action plans to stakeholders, including regulators, customers, and investors (Hoffmann & Reich, 2023). Explainability is an important aspect beyond operational openness, which includes ethical accountability and trustworthiness. AI systems have strong impact on strategic decision-making that influences corporate outcomes, human wellbeing, nature and business forces. This interpretability may reduce the level of confidence between the internal decision-makers and the external stakeholders, as it may undermine the trust of the employees and deter the sense of legitimacy of the people in case the decision made impacts on the small suppliers, the local communities, or the vulnerable population. Conversely, XAI promotes responsibility, which is informed and enables decision-makers to justify AI-based recommendations, analyze unforeseen results, and put in place a governance structure that can support ethical standards. Sustainable supply chain management depends on reliable AI, as the concept of transparency is also associated with ethical control (Ha & Kim, 2024).

Figure 10. Role of XAI in Ethical Governance and Trust Building in Supply Chains

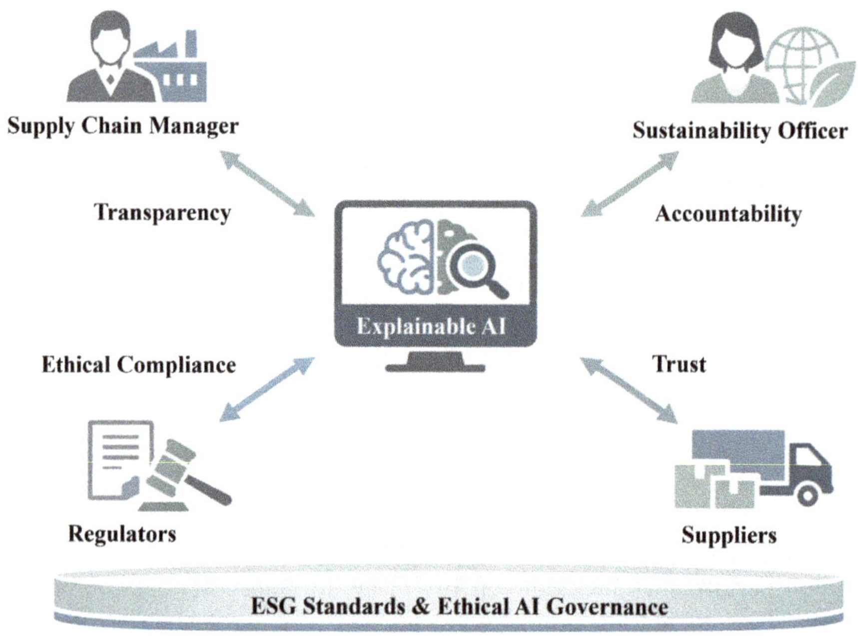

Source: Developed by the authors

The integration of XAI into the supply chain systems has practical challenges despite its potential. To begin with, predictive power of models, such as deep neural networks, which are most predictive, is traded off with simpler and explainable models that can induce less predictive power. The challenge of achieving this trade-off is to be careful with the choice of models and explanatory strategies that are to be used in specific decision-making situations. The veracity of explanations has an enduring influence on the integrity and fineness of input information. The inference of incorrect interpretations due to poor quality of data, null values, or biased samples may occur, and in this case, tight data governance principles ought to be implemented as well as XAI is to be adopted. Third, the organizational readiness that develops itself due to the presence of analytical literacy, technical infrastructure, and a culture of belief in ethical AI is very heterogeneous in organizations, which influences the effectiveness of XAI application, and the sustainability of the explainable products (Hao & Demir, 2024; Janssen et al., 2022). To overcome these obstacles, researchers and professionals propose to develop the XAI potential in parallel and the structures of governance that will enable the ethical issues to be considered in the patterns of supply chain decision-making. This would entail establishing specific explainability standards in model building practice, educating the decision-makers on the use of AI explanations, and incorporating the XAI products into the established audit and compliance practice. It also involves building of cross-functional groups of data scientists, sustainability specialists, operations managers and legal advisors to make sure that the explanations have a contextual value and value. As part of the business procedures, AI is becoming more of an open instrument of strategic decision making and less of a mysterious predictive instrument with the introduction of XAI into corporate practices. XAI is a breakthrough to sustainable and ethical supply chain decision making. XAI leads to the increased transparency and explainability of AI rationale and enables managers to justify, validate, and explain the judgment of the algorithms in the context of the ESG requirements, and ethics. Its use in the procurement, supplier evaluation, emission management, and risk management makes it more accurate on the analysis and responsible management within the organization, therefore, giving confidence to the stakeholders. As supply chains grow more complex and the role of AI alters, explainability frameworks will be necessary to develop technical advancement and ethical responsibility and sustainability.

Circular Economy, Reverse Logistics, and Waste Management Analytics

The environmental degradation pressures, the scarcity of resources, and the need to be controlled have resulted in the fact that the supply chains are not necessarily linear and rely on the take- make -Dispose model but should be more regenerative and restorative. Among the created models that have been adopted as one of the best methods is the circular economy which attempts to concentrate on resources efficiency, by reusing, recycling, remanufacturing and recovery. Circularity of supply chains is not only an environmental goal, but a reconstruction of the material flows, the life cycle of goods and product value creation processes. BDA, AI, and the higher-order information systems would also be needed to represent forward and reverse supply chain operations and make them visible, synchronized, and optimized, all of which would require the implementation of the very concept of the circular economy (A. Mishra et al., 2023; Rodrigues et al., 2025).

The presence of the reverse logistics operations in the normal operations planning is one of the features of the circular supply chains. Reverse logistics involves the activities, which concern product counteractions, fixing, refurbishing, reusing along with the safe disposition. The reverse flows are not certain compared to way forward logistic but rather are uncertain in terms of time, quantity, quality and place of origin. This ambiguity has rendered circular systems economical and not scalable in the past. Reverse logistics, however, has been handled a lot better by the analytics-based approaches to reverse logistics. Using the historic data of returns offered, sensor monitoring systems and client usage logs, the firms can know the volume of returns, evaluate the state of products and create an effective collection and redistribution process. Most of the operations in the reverse logistics planning are optimized with the help of the enriched predictive models: it minimizes the wastage of the products that lead to transit, it minimizes the cost of processing, and it maximizes the use of the valuable materials (Ni et al., 2023).

Figure 11. Analytics-Enabled Circular Supply Chain and Reverse Logistics Flow

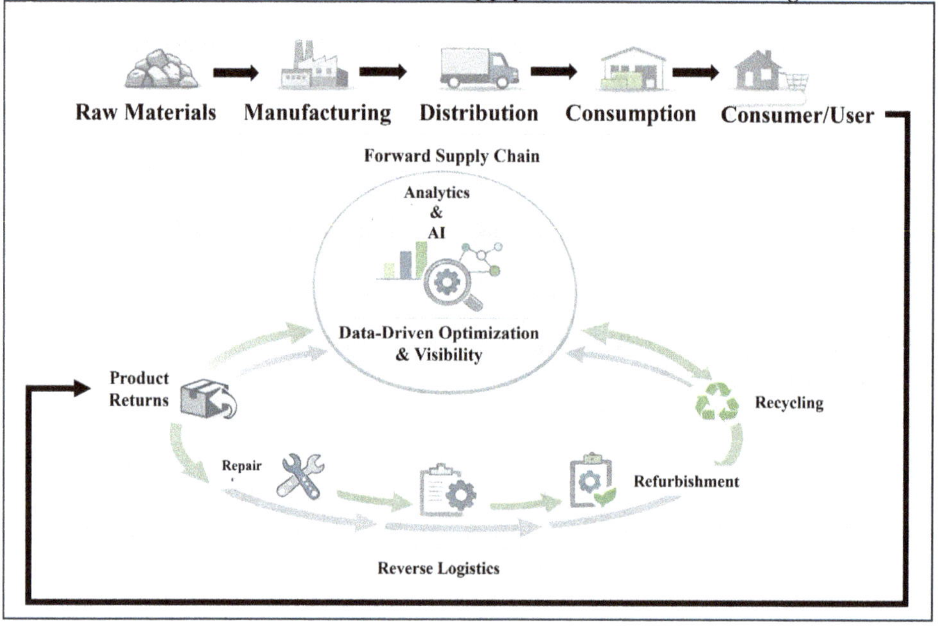

Source: Developed by the authors

The latter is what improves the enhanced utilization of circular supply chains as the former is applied to get the entire picture of the flow of material through the product lifecycles. Wastes constitute a natural by-product of production and consumption in the concept of traditional supply chains. Circular models, in their turn, view the trash as the resource that can be reused within the production systems. The analytics systems integrate the industrial process data, data on the inventory, waste and downstream consumption data to indicate the potential opportunities in reusing and recovering the materials. Analytics will be able to detect unreasonable scrap production at some point in the manufacturing process and modify the operations to minimize waste production at its source on the fly. The data on the post-consumer waste may help the companies to create specific waste recycling and take-back programs in order to regain the materials more effectively and reduce the quantity of adverse effects on the environment (Wilson et al., 2022). Problems such as AI in decision made contribute significantly to optimization of solutions employed in managing waste in the chain of supply circles. The ML algorithms will be able to learn to process complex and high-dimensional data, identify types of waste, and the recycling process will be successful and has suggested an appropriate treatment or recovery process. In the manufacturing and logistical industries, computer vision systems and AI, in turn, are increasingly employed to automatize the process of garbage sorting and quality inspection and reduce contamination and maximize the efficiency of the recycling process. These technologies facilitate the overall environmental results and at the same time add economic value through increasing a percentage of materials that can be reclaimed. Empirical data indicate that the cost cut and the revenues received with the assistance of the waste management powered by analytics help to make an argument regarding implementing the circular economy (Gaur et al., 2022; Mallick et al., 2024).

Figure 12. AI-Driven Waste Management and Material Recovery Decision Framework

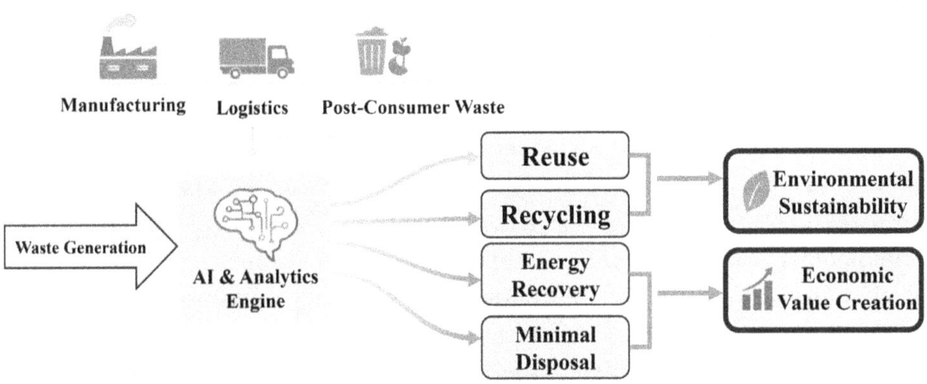

Source: Developed by the authors based on prior studies

Operational efficiency is not the only strategic implication of the analytics-based circularity but also the product lifecycle. The concepts of the circular economy mean that companies must take into consideration the sustainability aspects of each phase of the lifecycle of the product that consists of design, procurement, use, and end-of-life recovery. The lifecycle-oriented decision making that could be offered by the big data and AI will assist in the evaluation of alternative solutions of designs, the substitution of the materials, and the recovery plans. The effect of design changes on a product in terms of durability, repairability, and recyclability can be evaluated with the use of analytics, and this would assist the companies in adjusting the design considerations to the goals of the circular. In the segments of automotive, electronics, and fast-moving consumer products, the lifetime perspective is crucial, as the generation of waste and obsolescence is particularly challenging to sustainability (Wijewickrama et al., 2021). Supply chain coordination perspective This is since the implementation of a circular economy requires further cooperation between the manufacturers, the logistics companies, the recyclers, and the downstream partners. Collaboration is achievable by using analytics systems that create common data environments that enhance coordinated planning and performance evaluation. The analytics of material flow can be adjusted to congruent with the production schedules and recycling capacities, and the analytics of demand can be applied to make the decision regarding the offerings of the products that have been remanufactured. Collaborative, data-driven strategies also maximize system efficiency, and will decrease chances of rebound effects, whereby the individual efficiency gain changes may cause changes in aggregate resource utilization without any anticipation. The scholars are beginning to say that the circular supply chains could only be equipped with complete sustainability functionality with the support of coherent analytical systems that do not merely cross the organizational boundaries (Rajput & Singh, 2022).

The transformation into the circular supply chain based on analytics is associated with multiple challenges despite its potential. The absence of standards and scattered data, as well as reduced traceability of multi-tier networks, can slow down the efficacy of the projects associated with the implementation of the circular economy. The processes of reverse logistics and recycling represent economic processes that are reliant on the market conditions, legislative incentives, and technological advancements. These especially exist in the emerging economies in which informal waste industries; troublesome deficiency of infrastructural set-ups and governance deficiencies are present to impede the gathering of information and system incorporation. These limits need to be reduced, and this should be done through technical investment that enables legislative frameworks, capacity building, and cross-sector alliances and which align the incentive of the economy with the sustainability objectives (Mukherjee et al., 2024). The ideas of a circular economy, backed by big data and analytics that are driven by AI, will provide a way to find the ecologically friendly and economically powerful supply chains. Analytics alter the idea of the circularity between a theory and an actual practice by creating properly developed reverse logistics, optimizing waste management, and progressing the decision-making that is grounded in the lifecycle. Circular supply chains based on analytics demonstrate that there is a way to ensure environmental sustainability and be effective and profitable at the same time. When properly operated in a way that does not compromise the operational risk and develops new value streams, circular models can increase the productivity of the resources utilized by the firm and help it to perform well in the conditions of increasing environmental and societal demands.

GOVERNANCE, SECURITY, AND TRANSPARENCY IN DIGITAL SUPPLY CHAINS

Cybersecurity, Data Privacy, and Governance Challenges

The heightened dependency on BDA, AI, and a network of digital systems has essentially altered the way the modern-day supply chains are run. Although these technologies provide unparalleled visibility, efficiency and sustainability, they present a major challenge related to cybersecurity, data privacy and control in supply chains. As the process of supply chain is increasingly becoming more data-oriented and digitally linked, the problem of cyber-attack, data misuse, and ineffective systems of governance, appear as significant opportunities to destabilize the operational resilience and trust in stakeholders. That way, cybersecurity and data management have not only turned into technical issues but also strategic demands of sustainable and responsible supply chain management. The implementation of IoT devices, cloud-hosted models, and real-time information exchange between organizational boundaries are additions to cybersecurity threats in the data-based supply chains. The machines used in manufacturing, logistical equipment, warehouses etc. will always produce relatively large volumes of operational data that are transmitted throughout elaborate digital networks through sensors. Such inter-religious systems substantially augment the size of attack surface to cyber-attacks that comprise ransomware attacks, cyber breaches, and system interruptions. Empirical researchers have discovered that supply chains are more susceptible to hackers because of their interdependence where failure of one node in the network can extend to the entire network halting the operation and stealing sensitive data (Ogbuke et al., 2022; Wylde et al., 2022). In terms of sustainability, such disruptions may lead to stagnation of the production process, excessive production of waste, crisis logistics, and a lack of trust in the stakeholders, which undermine the long-term environmental and social goals.

Figure 13. Cybersecurity Risk Landscape in Data-Driven Supply Chains

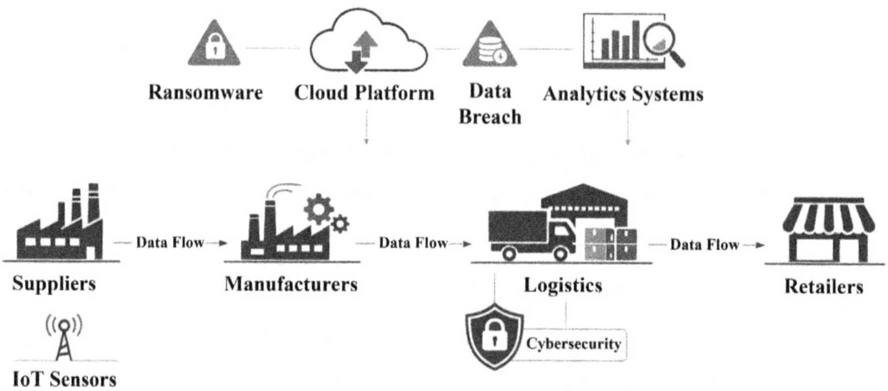

Source: Developed by the authors

It is possible to speak about such significant problems of analytics-based supply chain as the data privacy, because companies tend to become increasingly dependent on the highly specific information regarding suppliers, employees, and consumers. Advanced analytics usually demand access to confidential information, e.g. supplier cost capacity, manufacturing capacity, employee performance metrics and customer consumption dynamics. Faulty or illegal leakage of such kind of data may result in a legal repercussion, loss of publicity and loss of confidence of partners in supply chains. Corporate responsibility has been put under more pressure by government laws like the GDPR in the European Union, growing data protection legislations in Asia and Africa, regarding privacy policies. Recent studies also state that adhering to the requirements of data privacy is exceptionally complicated in global supply chains, in which data crossing its various jurisdictions must be able to meet numerous legal requirements and implementation practices (Aarland, 2025; Wylde et al., 2022). The issue of governance also exists due to the necessity to harmonize the data ownership, accessibility, accountability and ethical utilization of the supply chains networks at the multi-tier levels. The government structures that prevail in conventional supply chains are largely concerned with the contractual ties and observable streams. The data-driven supply chains, on the other hand, need elaborate governance mechanisms that specify the data gathering, sharing, storing, and the utilization in the decision-making process. This may also result in the presence of data silos, poor data quality, and misuse of the analytical results due to poor governance thereby minimizing the effectiveness of sustainability initiatives. Researchers begin to claim that sustainable supply chain analytics should be provided with efficient governance structures to match the technology capacity with the corporate values, regulatory needs as well as the stakeholders demands (Masip-Bruin et al., 2021).

The ethical aspect problem is also contributing to the complexity of cybersecurity and data management in supply chain analytics. Even though strong, AI-based decision-making systems can subconsciously support biases, encourage intrusive monitoring, or act in an unethical way by prioritizing efficiency over social responsibility. Predictive analytics that are used to review suppliers or optimize workforce would have to trust or penalize the smaller suppliers or discriminated labor groups unless ethics are incorporated into a system design. Firms should have visible, auditable, and consistent data-driven decisions according to the regulations of ESG on a governance approach. Not only reputational risks of the companies of subjects subject them to the risks of ethics but also their reduced potential of analytics as the instrument of sustainable development (Al-Farsi et al., 2021). Cybersecurity and data governance issues are beginning to see risk mitigation strategies taking a more focused approach towards the combination of technological, organizational and policy-based approaches. Technology suggests that encryption, secure authentication, blockchain based tracing and zero-trust architecture are highly sold to improve data safety in the supply chain of the network. It has been possible to provide data integrity, traceability, and tamper resistance when applied to a multi-party context; this has also caught the attention of blockchain in the implementation of the risk of data tampering and fraud (Boyson et al., 2022). Technological solutions cannot be adequate unless other organizational measures are included, i.e. training of the staff, incident response planning, as well as ongoing risk evaluation.

In the aspect of governance, organizations are more taking on the data stewardship strategy that assigns evident roles in the management of data, data quality certification, and ethical compliance. According to such models, it is necessary to ensure that the IT, operational, legal and sustainability departments have cross-functional relationships allowing that the analytics activities should align with the overall business goals. In the inter-organizational risks, collaborative governance systems such as the common data standards, collective cybersecurity activities, and contractual agreements on the use of data are required. It can be said that the supply chains have more capacities of leveraging analytics to deliver sustainability and reduce the vulnerability to cyber and privacy risks because of the well-established data governance policies (Rauniyar et al., 2023). There is a specific prevalence of cybersecurity issues and data management in less developed economies that may have an unevenly developed range of digital infrastructure, regulatory requirements, and organizational possibilities. Rapid digitalization tends to keep up with effective governance system building in such a case making it more susceptible to hacking and data use. Nevertheless, the developing economies promise the opportunities of leapfrogging with the help of implemented integrated systems of governance and security which incorporate sustainability and ethics at the early stages. Policy makers, industry associations and international bodies are very important to assist in capacity building, standardization and knowledge exchange to enhance data management in global supply chains.

Figure 14. Integrated Data Governance Framework for Sustainable Supply Chain Analytics

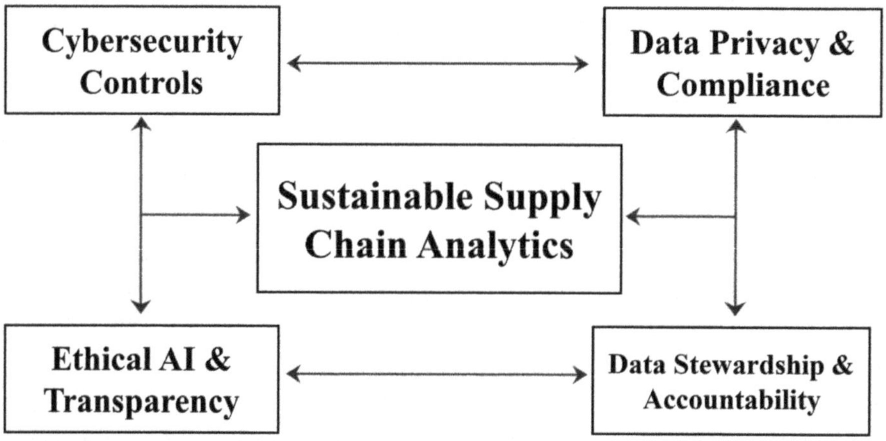

Source: Developed by the authors

The cyberspace, privacy of data, as well as the issues of governance represent a critical boundary of sustainable supply chain development. With the growing reliance of businesses and organizations on grand data and sophisticated analytics to improve their environmental and operational outcomes, data protection and data ethics have become vital drivers of subsequent stability. Well-planned cybersecurity measures, well-defined data management frameworks, and decision-making processes grounded in ethics do not only lower the risk but also strengthen the credibility of the company and trust in the stakeholders. Sustainable supply chain analytics does not only entail extracting value out of data but also has ethical management of data to promote economic viability, environmental integrity, and social legitimacy in an increasingly digitalized world.

Blockchain-Enabled Transparency and Carbon Accountability

The traditional systems of information on the location of their products and sustainability performance are not effective anymore, in the time when the environment has become more sensitive and more buyers require to know what is happening with their products and sustainability performance. It is in this light that blockchain technology has become of significant scholarly and real-life interests as a tool to give irrefutable and decentralized documentation that can transform the processes through which supply chains document and attest to environmental and ethical practices. Contrary to a system in the traditional database that could be manipulated, copied, and lack transparency, blockchain builds a distributed registry where all the records of the transactions are cryptographically regulated and that the chain of the parties involved of the system may be tracked. This natural transparency puts the companies in a better position to be more responsible in reporting sustainability indicators, including carbon emissions, fair sourcing, and environmental, social, and governance (ESG) standards (Alotaibi et al., 2024; Zhu et al., 2024). In essence, blockchain has value proposal that is grounded on three aspects that are interrelated, which include immutability, decentralization and transparency. Immutability also ensures that a transaction cannot be altered without approval of the networks such as a batch of raw materials getting into a supply chain. Decentralization means that no one in charge of the ledger exists and therefore there are less chances of manipulation of the data or selective reporting. Transparency provides all the parties concerned with a chance to see, evaluate, and ratify documented information virtually in real-time. As the traceability infrastructure can be the heart of the blockchain that might monitor product features, emissions data, and sustainability assurances along the supply chain to the end with the help of such ancillary technologies as IoT and AI.

Blockchain technology with IoT device improves its use in carbon responsibility and environmental monitoring. The IoT sensors on the production equipment, the transport fleet, the warehouse facilities provide data on the operational data, e.g. energy consumption, temperature, and rates of emissions, in unending data streams. The data of these sensors can be automatically written to blockchain and create a timely record according to which the actual performance is factored in rather than self-reported or audited information. This will reduce the possibilities of green-washing and make the carbon accounting practices more legitimate. To provide an example, the IoT-blockchain interfaces are used to monitor cold chain temperatures and energy consumed to support a cold chain to improve the quality of goods and precision of environmental reporting in the food and beverage sector (Khanfar et al., 2021; Parmentola et al., 2022).

Figure 15. Blockchain-Enabled End-to-End Transparency and Carbon Accountability Framework in Sustainable Supply Chains

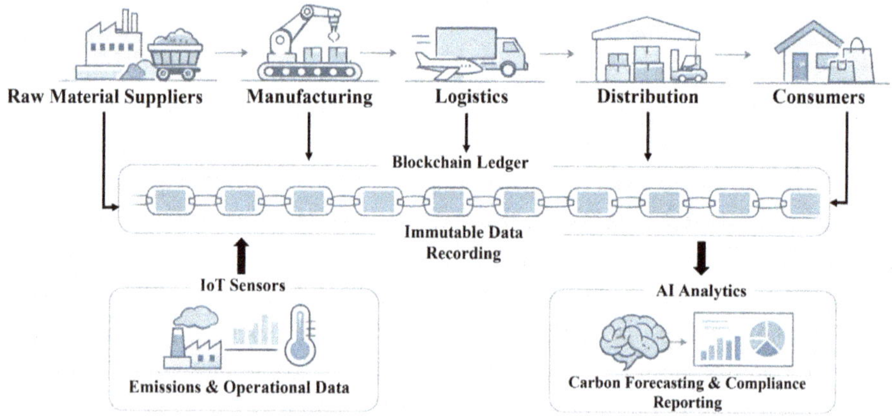

Source: Developed by the authors

The improvement of the tracking systems involving blockchains with the help of AI is achieved by managing the smart data processing and creation of insights. It is expected that the application of blockchain will guarantee the integrity, the impossibility of any kind of information changes that have been added in the records, and AI algorithms will be used to synthesize the previous and the current information and comprehend the tendencies in the emissions and determine the ineffective areas that should be improved. Within it, there are predictive models that can be used to make predictions of carbon emission in the future given the different operations and prediction models despite the presence of anomaly detection algorithms that can be employed to identify the difference or the anomalies in the reported data. Passive transparency, dynamism of accountability which is accomplished with blockchain and AI and enhances compliance and strategic sustainability plan. The application of blockchain industries which is empirical has been applied to facilitate sustainability traceability. The fashion industry has embraced the trendy brands that have integrated blockchain technology in tracking the origin of raw cotton in addition to ensuring that the products are produced in factories that are in tandem with the prevailing labor and environmental regulations. The entire manufacturing processes are registered in a decentralized list of these technologies, which allows the customers, auditors and regulators to confirm the claims on sustainability and ethical sourcing. One of the uses of blockchain, which relates the material provenance, usage history, and end-of-life practices, is the monitoring of lifecycles of valuable components, including batteries, in the automotive industry. Specifically, it can be applied to carbon accounting, which enables companies to trace the emissions to certain levels in the supply chain and take mitigation actions (Thanasi-Boçe & Hoxha, 2025). Regardless of the disruptiveness of the potential, the use of blockchain in the supply chain is associated with its own serious challenges, which cannot and should be regarded thoughtfully. It is faced with a problem of interoperability and scale of the technology with the preexisting legacy systems. The number of players in a supply chain, especially the small and medium size firms in the developing countries, lack digital infrastructure and technology to fully participate in blockchain networks. In the absence of such a huge amount of involvement, it minimizes the decentralized authority of blockchain, and a shortage of transparency is not destroyed. Second, blockchain applications should possess a good governance mechanism, which guarantees the integrity of the data, confidentiality, and adherence to new regulatory actions. The impossibility of undoing blockchain may also be presented to the list of risk factors in the situation where the wrong introduction of information or misleading information can be made during the initial stage which also implies the necessity of the strong control of the verification process by the stakeholders (Dasaklis et al., 2022).

The other aspect is privacy, which defines the supply chain blockchain and analytics implementation. Although the strength of openness is strong, the ease with which the whole information about the operations could be provided could add to the issues which relate to the disclosure of competitive intelligence, or the disclosure of proprietary information. The blockchain models are authorized to provide the trade-off between transparency and anonymity, such that the authorized users should be allowed to access them. In these types of models, a given firm has the freedom to practice selective disclosure of information if sustainability is involved but not sensitive financial information. According to some recent studies, the desperate need is to have governance structures which would establish the parameters of data access, permission plans and dispute management processes to have ethical and safe blockchain adoption (Basu et al., 2024). Institutional environment is also important in determining whether blockchain would be successful in the sustainability projects in a timely fashion. Regulatory incentives, industry conventions and collaborative governance frameworks can facilitate or hamper the adoption. The low carbon reporting policies or the incentive production policy that is supplemented with the low carbon requires traceable and verifiable information system and, therefore, creates the need of the blockchain experimental (Zhu et al., 2025). On the same note, companies within the industry that come up with standardized data protocols and interoperability requirements lessen fragmentation and will not complicate data sharing between businesses. Blockchain applications will otherwise be decentralized in local projects which are not large systemics unless the environment is friendly. The future of the proposed research and practice will be considered. To start with, further empirical research should be conducted to establish the role of blockchain in real carbon reduction achievements, beyond the hypothetical assertions of transparency. It can be extremely enriching that this blockchain is introduced with the introduction of new technologies like digital twins and edge computers, the traceability and accountability of which can be real-time. Lastly, blockchain systems constituting equitable and inclusive sustainability may be available in the social-economic impact particularly in the global value chains that considered the informal sectors and the small-scale suppliers. One of the potential solutions that may be adopted to make the modern supply chains more transparent and carbon responsible is also the blockchain technology. Intelligently integrated with IoT and AI, blockchain has the potential to offer non-corruption records, end-to-end visibility and real-time traceability, which can support plausible sustainability programs. This good governance commitment, institutional support and reasonable plans for interoperability and data quality must, however, be brought into existence. Having the solutions to these issues, the businesses will be capable of using blockchain as a technical solution and as a constituter of responsible and practical supply chain ecosystems.

POLICY, LDC PERSPECTIVES, AND MANAGERIAL IMPLICATIONS

It is also factual that there is growing trend of data-driven and sustainability-driven supply chain operations, increased in the developed economies, but the rate of its implementation in the emerging economies and in LDCs is skewed and very selective. Although the potential of analytics is high, the AI and digital platforms have the potential to improve efficiency, resilience, and the environmental performance of LDCs, the structural constraints of LDCs are likely to act as the hindrance to the successful operation of technology. The limitations include absence of digital infrastructure, fragmented policies, absence of source of funding, and overly high human resource shortages. Thus, the transformation to the supply chains of the sustainability of the LDCs that are based on analytics cannot be perceived as the simple imitation process of the models of the economies that are prosperous. It requires that policy interventions and management methods be put into perspective so that they can be able to align the technology aspirations with the existing institutional conditions, developmental agenda, and resource limitation (Akbari, 2024).

Policy Challenges and Strategic Priorities in LDC Contexts

The remaining option to the policy LDCs is to proceed with the accelerated digitalization process and provide equitable and sustainable development, which is complex. The relevance of the digital supply chains to commercial competitiveness, progress, and eco-social-fundamental validation are welcomed in most countries, especially the export-based economies whose internationalized structure is made up of light manufacturing-based, agricultural-based, and textile manufacturing industries. Nevertheless, the absence of sufficient digital infrastructure which can be reflected in non-accessibility of broadband, insufficient electricity supply and high prices of technological equipment is among the biggest obstacles to the spread of advanced analytics and data systems. These physical inadequacies make the dissemination of the technology more complicated and unequal relations between large corporations and small suppliers which have been integrated into global value assemblages (De Marchi & Alford, 2022).

The policy scattering is associated with the problem of adoption. The regulatory design of number of LDCs data governance, cybersecurity, environmental regulation and industrial policy is not based on the consideration of one another and results in an imbalanced or overlapping regulatory need. This kind of uncertainty renders it difficult to make investments that companies would prefer to make in analytics-based sustainability. The current studies have also suggested the necessity to implement the frameworks of joint policy, which would resolve the issues of the digital revolution, the control of the environment, and the development of industries simultaneously. The country-level measures or, in other words, the package of incentives to invest in digital capacity and the precise carbon reporting policies can be implemented to kick-start the businesses to roll out the analytics-based sustainability solutions to mitigate the compliance uncertainty (Epede & Wang, 2022). The policy interventions in the LDCs should also be capacity-based generation of conjunction and regulation. The digital investments in competencies, data literacy and institutional capacity will most likely lead to the collapse of even the most thought-out policies. International development agencies, multilateral institutions are becoming increasingly favorable to blended policy responses, which involves a certain component of regulatory re-alignment, public/private partnerships, and pilot projects that are donor funded. This is since the initiatives could help the LDCs to avoid the phases of gradual improvement by integrating the sustainability and analytics opportunity in the modernization of the supply chain at their initial phases (Santiago et al., 2024).

Managerial Implications for Analytics-Driven Supply Chains in Resource-Constrained Environments

The environment of decision making by managers in LDC is very different from the industrialized economies. The shortage of resources, the fluctuating demand, and the uncertainty of the infrastructure require pragmatic and progressive solutions to the analytics implementation. The managers in LDCs usually discover that modular scalable solutions have immediate gains of operation but can expand to make use of any emerging opportunities that might come out later rather than hooting into fully integrated and costly digital platforms. The potential directions to the construction of data-driven capacities of the supply chain with a limited budget are generally viewed as the use of cloud-based analytics, mobile-based data collection, and open-source platform (Pacheco et al., 2025). Managerial strategy must include the fact that informal and small-scale suppliers are the ones with large populations in LDC supply chains. They tend to be less digitally equipped, have low protocols, or written documents and, thus, restrict access and reliability of data. The managers are at the center of the engagement of the suppliers and capabilities development facilitation. Commonly used data-sharing agreements render reporting tools slimmer and educational programs can contribute more to transparency and data quality without imposing compliance expenses on them. It is also demonstrated that relational governance and the use of trust-based coordination is especially beneficial in the context of less developed country (LDC) where formal enforcement tools may not be adequate (Abdullah et al., 2025). The managers must ensure that analytics operations are correlated with local ESG priorities from the sustainability perspective. Social factors, such as the state of work, a secure salary, or the community effect in LDCs, are likely to be as good, or even better, than environmental measures only. Consequently, the analytics-based supply chain tools must be shaped in such a way that it will consider the multidimensional measures of sustainability as opposed to efficiency or carbon reduction. In this manner, the businesses will be capable of enhancing the degree of confidence among the local population and meet the expectations of global purchasers and governmental agencies (Polater, 2025; Saran & Kesswani, 2025).

Coordinated Roles of Governments, NGOs, and the Private Sector

The sustainable supply chains in the LDCs can only be successfully executed through the cooperation between the non-governmental organizations (NGOs), the non-governmental organizations and the governments. The prevailing role of government is to possess a favorable climate by investing in infrastructures, excellence and encouragement in green technology in regulation. The digital and green tech could either be digitally subsidized or tax-preferred or preferentially financed to lower the adoption cost particularly among the small and medium-sized enterprises that constitute most of most LCD economies. These ecosystems are some of the key middlemen who include the non-governmental organizations and development partners. These tend to favor pilot projects, technical assistance, and act as neutral intermediaries that dampens the passion of the foreign buyers, local vendors and that of the government entities. With the last years NGOs have resorted to digital solutions to boost traceability, labor monitoring and environmental reporting on the export driven supply chains. In addition to enhancing compliance, such types of programs generate learning results that disseminate analytics knowledge to broader industry circles (Zarei et al., 2023). It is the massive undertaking of the leaders of the private sector, particularly the multinational corporations that buy their products in the LDCs, to make certain that they establish inclusive and sustainable supply chains. Supporting the development of ability and minimizing the risk of being displaced Lead businesses may make analytics requirements included in the supplier development programs rather than mandatory requirement in the compliance requirements. The shared data sources, shared investment in the digital environment, and long-term sourcing engagements have already enhanced the sustainability results and the resiliency of the supply chains in a resource constrained environment (Mishra et al., 2025).

FUTURE RESEARCH DIRECTIONS

Despite the development of the sphere of large data analytics, AI, and digital technologies at an impressive speed in the sphere of the supply chain management, the existing body of knowledge remains inadequate and fragmented, particularly evaluated around sustainability and resilience. The surrounding literature has been largely based on technological capability or organizational performance objective, and sustainability, governance and social implications were pushed to the periphery. The future study in supply networks must move beyond the specific technology perceptions and cross-functional, holistic perceptions in which the supply network is considered more multi-dimensional, interdependent and data intensive. This part offers the areas of critical action that the study should consider in the future to potentially assist in the improvement of the theory, regulate its real-life use, and contribute to the creation of stable and robust supply chains, both in the developed and developing world. Multi-disciplinary integration is an important field. The sustainability of the supply chain problem is an issue with a multi-dimensional nature and involves the operations management, information systems, environmental science, economics and organizational behavior. The number of empirical studies has been many and restricted to specific regions; hence, the fact that empirical studies are more restrictive to explain. The research in the future should strive to generalize concepts of these areas to establish a collection of assimilating models that would signify a combination of digital technologies, environmental factors and socio-economic pressures. The combination of life cycle assessment tools with the application of the BDA and behavioral decision theory will be capable of providing more information about the transfer of digital interventions into measurable sustainability gains at the levels of supply chains (Talwar et al., 2021). Mixed-method research, with a good portion of analytics and qualitative case studies, methodologically can be of use in sealing the gap between the abstract and the practical.

The other second priority is associated with AI ethics and ethical analytics concerning supply chain decision-making. The ethical considerations have been addressed inappropriately though the use of AI-based solutions is primarily aimed at forecasting, assessing the suppliers, and managing the risks. The issues of algorithm prejudice, the absence of proper transparency, and the disproportion of spreading the benefits to the participants of the supply chain are not adequately researched. Perhaps, in the future, the question of whether the supply chain analytics systems can be implemented in the principles of fairness, accountability, transparency, and inclusiveness when applied with the help of AI ethics, should be answered. The research should be conducted on the governance practices that can be applied to ensure that the AI-assisted decisions are not contradictory to the goal of ESG and that they do not affect small suppliers or group stakeholders under threat. The alternative assumption of the proposed study could be the heightened interest in XAI; however, further empirical results are to be acquired to define how explainability affect managerial trust, the quality of decisions, and the sustainability outcomes in the real world (Kumar et al., 2024; Maheshwari et al., 2021). The standardization and development of the sustainability indicators and the data-based performance evaluation is one of the potential research opportunities. Although digital technology may be used to allow a more accurate control over the emissions, energy spending, and flow of resources, the optimal standards of a sustainability performance measurement in the scale of a supply chain have not been determined yet. The range of further research should be focused on the development of the integrated methods of measurements that would be centered on the environmental, societal and economical aspects and would be rational to be implemented by the management in practice. This entails research to get the insights on the application of real-time analytics to enable real-time sustainability assessment as opposed to retrogressive cumulative reporting. Particularly, longitudinal research on the effects of analytics-enabled measuring systems on strategic decision-making and long-term performance would be interesting (Bechtsis et al., 2022).

The other solution that is interesting is the human-AI collaboration in the supply chain management. The current state of literature tends to believe that the adoption of AI-based systems will replace human judgments; however, the latest data demonstrates that the most effective one is possible with a balance between human and AI interaction. The perception, faith, and response of the managers to the knowledge about analytics is to be investigated, and the study below is needed, especially in the conditions of uncertainty and confusion. The study on cognitive load, decision making and learning responsibility within an organization is one of the topics that should be researched on. One can determine the decision-support mechanisms that support and not disrupt sustainable and resilient supply chain operations by using the knowledge of the role of human skills and contextual knowledge and algorithmic recommendations (Ogbuke et al., 2022). The other frontier is the position of the triumphant digital twins and autonomous systems. The opportunities created by AI-enhanced digital twins in the form of real-time virtual networks of the supply chains are unprecedented in terms of the opportunities to analyze different scenarios, plan on ways of resilience and enhance sustainability. However, lack of empirical research that has been done on their uptake, scaling implication and governance is paucity. Future research will have to realize the incorporation of digital twins into predictive analytics, blockchain, and IoT to deliver end-to-end visibility and carbon responsibility. It is the autonomous technologies like self-organizing warehouses and AI-equipped transportation systems that lead to the questions of the need to spend energy, labor relations, and willingness to act by regulators and need to be scrutinized more closely (Zekhnini et al., 2021). Finally, the adoption of technology in LDCs and an emerging economy is a field that has received inadequate studies. The available empirical evidence on digital supply chains is anchored mostly in the developed countries, and this reduces the generalizability of the findings. The second phase of research should be concerned with context specific adoption patterns, institutional constraints, and institutional capacity building in resource starved environments. Such implications of the legislative framework, access to infrastructure, and how the culture influences the performance of the analytics-based sustainability programs can be understood with the help of comparative analyses, both on the national and regional levels. Alongside it, it is also possible that the candidature approach to research, involving local business, non-governmental and politicians may generate feasible ideas that can make the digital transformation inclusive and just (Akbari & Do, 2021; Chauhan et al., 2022).

CONCLUSION

This chapter has discussed the radical redesigning of global supply chains with the help of technologies provided by the big data regarding efficiency and responsiveness, sustainability and resilience as the elements of the operating model. The discussion has also revealed that the transformative nature of BDA is the sharpest when the support of other digital enablers, i.e. the IoT, AI, XAI and full governing system is magnified. All these are united together in a bid to create just one socio-technical system that makes informed, ethical and visionary decisions within the supply chain. One of the most significant concepts of this chapter could be stated as the fact that the value is determined by the capability of an organization to develop a flexible insight to transform a lot of heterogeneous data with high frequency into value that can bridge the organizational purposes and environmental and social responsibility. The data produced by the IoT is more accurate and timelier and is extremely essential to the cognition of energy consumption, emissions, material flow and efficiency of assets to the supply chains concerned that are intricate in nature. With this information, it is through AI-assisted analytics that predictable, adaptive, and self-optimizing supply chain activity can be realized to minimize wastage, smother risks and enhance continuity when facing uncertainty. Sustainability and resiliency are not contrary objectives but on the contrary the garnishing results of evidence-based collaborations and vision. The chapter has established that a combination of technological innovation and transparency and accountability should be there. Being a novel use of AI in supply chain preparation, sourcing and risk control, it casts valid concerns of higher salience, favoritism and moral accountability. To address these issues, XAI is among the solutions required to reduce the risks of such issues because the rationale behind them as an algorithm in the human decision-maker must be understandable. The XAI fosters trust and resulting ESG relevant decision-making and contributes to greater organizational legitimacy among regulators, partners and society by allowing managers to interpret, critique and justify AI-based recommendations.

Explainability is not a technological aspect as such, it is a governance model between analytics and ethical surveillance. One of the critical factors of sustainable digital change is governance, and its display in this chapter has been proved. Their inter-organizational structures of governance and privacy and safety issues in cyberspace are the presence or absence of systemic resilience or systemic risk in analytics-driven supply chains. Data custody quality, the explicit accountability and style models of leadership, and collaborative types of governance are very significant in ensuring that data shared and high order analytics promote as opposed to restricting long-term sustainability goals. This is enhanced by inclusion of technology like blockchain which triggers the layer of governance through multi-levels supply chains hence enhancing the traceability, carbon responsibility and reliability of the supply chain sustainability reporting. The ideas in this chapter demonstrate that even the future of the global supply chains is founded on the way technology, the government and human judgment are tactical in the coordination. It is not such a linear process of digital adoption, which can be enhanced by big data, but a long-term process of reorganizing capabilities and relations, and decision-making paradigms. The businesses which manage to succeed in this change, are the ones that regard digital technologies as the method of complete improvement that should seek to find a balance between efficiency and responsibility, innovation, and clearness, rivalry and the establishment of the society values process.

REFERENCES

Aarland, M. (2025). Cybersecurity in digital supply chains in the procurement process: Introducing the digital supply chain management framework. *Information and Computer Security*, *33*(1), 5–24. DOI: 10.1108/ICS-10-2023-0198

Abdullah, F., Naeem, H. M., & Aslam, H. (2025). Big data, bigger ideas: The role of big data analytics management capability in supply chain sustainability. *Industrial Management & Data Systems*, ●●●, 1–23. DOI: 10.1108/IMDS-09-2024-0913

Akbari, M. (2024). Revolutionizing supply chain and circular economy with edge computing: Systematic review, research themes and future directions. *Management Decision*, *62*(9), 2875–2899. DOI: 10.1108/MD-03-2023-0412

Akbari, M., & Do, T. N. A. (2021). A systematic review of machine learning in logistics and supply chain management: Current trends and future directions. *Benchmarking*, *28*(10), 2977–3005. DOI: 10.1108/BIJ-10-2020-0514

Al-Farsi, S., Rathore, M. M., & Bakiras, S. (2021). Security of Blockchain-Based Supply Chain Management Systems: Challenges and Opportunities. *Applied Sciences (Basel, Switzerland)*, *11*(12), 5585. DOI: 10.3390/app11125585

Aljohani, A. (2023). Predictive Analytics and Machine Learning for Real-Time Supply Chain Risk Mitigation and Agility. *Sustainability*, *15*(20), 15088. DOI: 10.3390/su152015088

Alotaibi, E. M., Khallaf, A., Abdallah, A. A.-N., Zoubi, T., & Alnesafi, A. (2024). Blockchain-Driven Carbon Accountability in Supply Chains. *Sustainability*, *16*(24), 10872. DOI: 10.3390/su162410872

Andronie, M., Lăzăroiu, G., tefănescu, R., U ă, C., & Dijmărescu, I. (2021). Sustainable, Smart, and Sensing Technologies for Cyber-Physical Manufacturing Systems: A Systematic Literature Review. *Sustainability*, *13*(10), 5495. DOI: 10.3390/su13105495

Anjaria, K. (2025). *Analytics for Harnessing IoT and Industry 4.0: Data Flows in S-ERP* (pp. 197–219). https://doi.org/DOI: 10.1007/978-981-96-7734-4_7

Bahrami, M., & Shokouhyar, S. (2022). The role of big data analytics capabilities in bolstering supply chain resilience and firm performance: A dynamic capability view. *Information Technology & People*, *35*(5), 1621–1651. DOI: 10.1108/ITP-01-2021-0048

Basu, P., Deb, P., & Singh, A. (2024). Blockchain and the carbon credit ecosystem: Sustainable management of the supply chain. *The Journal of Business Strategy, 45*(1), 33–40. DOI: 10.1108/JBS-09-2022-0157

Bechtsis, D., Tsolakis, N., Iakovou, E., & Vlachos, D. (2022). Data-driven secure, resilient and sustainable supply chains: Gaps, opportunities, and a new generalised data sharing and data monetisation framework. *International Journal of Production Research, 60*(14), 4397–4417. DOI: 10.1080/00207543.2021.1957506

Beheshti, A., & Mansoor, W. (2025). Exploring the convergence of Internet of things and big data technologies in the age of generative artificial intelligence. In *Empowering IoT with Big Data Analytics* (pp. 333–354). Elsevier., DOI: 10.1016/B978-0-443-21640-4.00004-1

Belhadi, A., Mani, V., Kamble, S. S., Khan, S. A. R., & Verma, S. (2024). Artificial intelligence-driven innovation for enhancing supply chain resilience and performance under the effect of supply chain dynamism: An empirical investigation. *Annals of Operations Research, 333*(2–3), 627–652. DOI: 10.1007/s10479-021-03956-x PMID: 33551534

Boyson, S., Corsi, T. M., & Paraskevas, J.-P. (2022). Defending digital supply chains: Evidence from a decade-long research program. *Technovation, 118*, 102380. DOI: 10.1016/j.technovation.2021.102380

Burgos, D., & Ivanov, D. (2021). Food retail supply chain resilience and the COVID-19 pandemic: A digital twin-based impact analysis and improvement directions. *Transportation Research Part E, Logistics and Transportation Review, 152*, 102412. DOI: 10.1016/j.tre.2021.102412 PMID: 34934397

Chauhan, S., Singh, R., Gehlot, A., Akram, S. V., Twala, B., & Priyadarshi, N. (2022). Digitalization of Supply Chain Management with Industry 4.0 Enabling Technologies: A Sustainable Perspective. *Processes (Basel, Switzerland), 11*(1), 96. DOI: 10.3390/pr11010096

Dasaklis, T. K., Voutsinas, T. G., Tsoulfas, G. T., & Casino, F. (2022). A Systematic Literature Review of Blockchain-Enabled Supply Chain Traceability Implementations. *Sustainability, 14*(4), 2439. DOI: 10.3390/su14042439

de Jesus Pacheco, D. A., Koundal, D., Gunasekaran, A., Attaran, M., Sgarbossa, F., & Narayanan, A. (Chalam), & Zailani, S. (2025). Challenges and opportunities for empirical research on data analytics in supply chain management. *Supply Chain Forum: An International Journal, 26*(4), 431–436. https://doi.org/DOI: 10.1080/16258312.2025.2581507

De Marchi, V., & Alford, M. (2022). State policies and upgrading in global value chains: A systematic literature review. *Journal of International Business Policy*, *5*(1), 88–111. DOI: 10.1057/s42214-021-00107-8

Di Vaio, A., Latif, B., Gunarathne, N., Gupta, M., & D'Adamo, I. (2024). Digitalization and artificial knowledge for accountability in SCM: A systematic literature review. *Journal of Enterprise Information Management*, *37*(2), 606–672. DOI: 10.1108/JEIM-08-2022-0275

Dubey, R., Gunasekaran, A., Childe, S. J., Fosso Wamba, S., Roubaud, D., & Foropon, C. (2021). Empirical investigation of data analytics capability and organizational flexibility as complements to supply chain resilience. *International Journal of Production Research*, *59*(1), 110–128. DOI: 10.1080/00207543.2019.1582820

Epede, M. B., & Wang, D. (2022). Global value chain linkages: An integrative review of the opportunities and challenges for SMEs in developing countries. *International Business Review*, *31*(5), 101993. DOI: 10.1016/j.ibusrev.2022.101993

Fernando, Y., Sroufe, R., Tseng, M.-L., & Shaharudin, M. S., Wahyuni-TD, I. S., & Jawo, M. (2025). The circular supply chains in smart cities: A catalyst for sustainable development. *Journal of Industrial and Production Engineering*, *42*(7), 730–754. DOI: 10.1080/21681015.2025.2497867

Gaur, A., Gurjar, S. K., & Chaudhary, S. (2022). Circular system of resource recovery and reverse logistics approach: key to zero waste and zero landfill. In *Advanced Organic Waste Management* (pp. 365–381). Elsevier., DOI: 10.1016/B978-0-323-85792-5.00008-3

Gebhardt, M., Kopyto, M., Birkel, H., & Hartmann, E. (2022). Industry 4.0 technologies as enablers of collaboration in circular supply chains: A systematic literature review. *International Journal of Production Research*, *60*(23), 6967–6995. DOI: 10.1080/00207543.2021.1999521

Ha, T., & Kim, S. (2024). Improving Trust in AI with Mitigating Confirmation Bias: Effects of Explanation Type and Debiasing Strategy for Decision-Making with Explainable AI. *International Journal of Human-Computer Interaction*, *40*(24), 8562–8573. DOI: 10.1080/10447318.2023.2285640

Hao, X., & Demir, E. (2024). Artificial intelligence in supply chain decision-making: An environmental, social, and governance triggering and technological inhibiting protocol. *Journal of Modelling in Management*, *19*(2), 605–629. DOI: 10.1108/JM2-01-2023-0009

Hoffmann, R., & Reich, C. (2023). A Systematic Literature Review on Artificial Intelligence and Explainable Artificial Intelligence for Visual Quality Assurance in Manufacturing. *Electronics (Basel)*, *12*(22), 4572. DOI: 10.3390/electronics12224572

Iftikhar, A., Ali, I., Arslan, A., & Tarba, S. (2024). Digital Innovation, Data Analytics, and Supply Chain Resiliency: A Bibliometric-based Systematic Literature Review. *Annals of Operations Research*, *333*(2–3), 825–848. DOI: 10.1007/s10479-022-04765-6 PMID: 35611176

Janssen, M., Hartog, M., Matheus, R., Yi Ding, A., & Kuk, G. (2022). Will Algorithms Blind People? The Effect of Explainable AI and Decision-Makers' Experience on AI-supported Decision-Making in Government. *Social Science Computer Review*, *40*(2), 478–493. DOI: 10.1177/0894439320980118

Kamble, S. S., Mor, R. S., & Belhadi, A. (2023). Big Data Analytics for Supply Chain Transformation: A Systematic Literature Review Using SCOR Framework. In *Digital Transformation and Industry 4.0 for Sustainable Supply Chain Performance* (pp. 1–50). https://doi.org/DOI: 10.1007/978-3-031-19711-6_1

Kaniappan Chinnathai, M., & Alkan, B. (2023). A digital life-cycle management framework for sustainable smart manufacturing in energy intensive industries. *Journal of Cleaner Production*, *419*, 138259. DOI: 10.1016/j.jclepro.2023.138259

Khanfar, A. A. A., Iranmanesh, M., Ghobakhloo, M., Senali, M. G., & Fathi, M. (2021). Applications of Blockchain Technology in Sustainable Manufacturing and Supply Chain Management: A Systematic Review. *Sustainability*, *13*(14), 7870. DOI: 10.3390/su13147870

Krishnan, R. (2024). Challenges and benefits for small and medium enterprises in the transformation to smart manufacturing: A systematic literature review and framework. *Journal of Manufacturing Technology Management*, *35*(4), 918–938. DOI: 10.1108/JMTM-07-2022-0255

Kumar, D., Singh, R. K., Mishra, R., & Vlachos, I. (2024). Big data analytics in supply chain decarbonisation: A systematic literature review and future research directions. *International Journal of Production Research*, *62*(4), 1489–1509. DOI: 10.1080/00207543.2023.2179346

Lin, H., & Wang, J. (2024). Enabling AI into business operations: Investigating the impact of IoTs, big data, and IT-enabled technologies on supply chain performance. *International Journal of Electronic Business*, *19*(2), 123–138. DOI: 10.1504/IJEB.2024.137703

Maheshwari, S., Gautam, P., & Jaggi, C. K. (2021). Role of Big Data Analytics in supply chain management: Current trends and future perspectives. *International Journal of Production Research, 59*(6), 1875–1900. DOI: 10.1080/00207543.2020.1793011

Malik, S. (2024). Data-Driven Decision-Making: Leveraging the IoT for Real-Time Sustainability in Organizational Behavior. *Sustainability, 16*(15), 6302. DOI: 10.3390/su16156302

Mallick, P. K., Salling, K. B., Pigosso, D. C. A., & McAloone, T. C. (2024). Towards a circular economy: Development of a support tool for designing reverse logistics systems. *Journal of Environmental Management, 351*, 119819. DOI: 10.1016/j.jenvman.2023.119819 PMID: 38104465

Masip-Bruin, X., Marín-Tordera, E., Ruiz, J., Jukan, A., Trakadas, P., Cernivec, A., Lioy, A., López, D., Santos, H., Gonos, A., Silva, A., Soriano, J., & Kalogiannis, G. (2021). Cybersecurity in ICT Supply Chains: Key Challenges and a Relevant Architecture. *Sensors (Basel), 21*(18), 6057. DOI: 10.3390/s21186057 PMID: 34577264

Mishra, A., Dutta, P., Jayasankar, S., Jain, P., & Mathiyazhagan, K. (2023). A review of reverse logistics and closed-loop supply chains in the perspective of circular economy. *Benchmarking, 30*(3), 975–1020. DOI: 10.1108/BIJ-11-2021-0669

Mishra, V., Ishdorj, A., Tabares Villarreal, E., & Norton, R. (2025). Collaboration in agricultural value chains: A scoping review of the evidence from developing countries. *Journal of Agribusiness in Developing and Emerging Economies, 15*(6), 1168–1192. DOI: 10.1108/JADEE-12-2023-0311

Mukherjee, S., Nagariya, R., Mathiyazhagan, K., Baral, M. M., Pavithra, M. R., & Appolloni, A. (2024). Artificial intelligence-based reverse logistics for improving circular economy performance: A developing country perspective. *International Journal of Logistics Management, 35*(6), 1779–1806. DOI: 10.1108/IJLM-03-2023-0102

Ni, Z., Chan, H. K., & Tan, Z. (2023). Systematic literature review of reverse logistics for e-waste: Overview, analysis, and future research agenda. *International Journal of Logistics Research and Applications, 26*(7), 843–871. DOI: 10.1080/13675567.2021.1993159

Núñez-Merino, M., Maqueira-Marín, J. M., Moyano-Fuentes, J., & Martínez-Jurado, P. J. (2020). Information and digital technologies of Industry 4.0 and Lean supply chain management: A systematic literature review. *International Journal of Production Research, 58*(16), 5034–5061. DOI: 10.1080/00207543.2020.1743896

Ogbuke, N. J., Yusuf, Y. Y., Dharma, K., & Mercangoz, B. A. (2022). Big data supply chain analytics: Ethical, privacy and security challenges posed to business, industries and society. *Production Planning and Control*, *33*(2–3), 123–137. DOI: 10.1080/09537287.2020.1810764

Parmentola, A., Petrillo, A., Tutore, I., & De Felice, F. (2022). Is blockchain able to enhance environmental sustainability? A systematic review and research agenda from the perspective of Sustainable Development Goals (SDGs). *Business Strategy and the Environment*, *31*(1), 194–217. DOI: 10.1002/bse.2882

Polater, A. (2025). Building resilient supply chains: Unveiling the interplay of reflexivity, supply chain innovation and improvisation capability. *Benchmarking*, *32*(9), 3524–3555. DOI: 10.1108/BIJ-10-2024-0930

Rajput, S., & Singh, S. P. (2022). Industry 4.0 model for integrated circular economy-reverse logistics network. *International Journal of Logistics Research and Applications*, *25*(4–5), 837–877. DOI: 10.1080/13675567.2021.1926950

Rauniyar, K., Wu, X., Gupta, S., Modgil, S., & Lopes de Sousa Jabbour, A. B. (2023). Risk management of supply chains in the digital transformation era: Contribution and challenges of blockchain technology. *Industrial Management & Data Systems*, *123*(1), 253–277. DOI: 10.1108/IMDS-04-2021-0235

Rodrigues, S. P., Gomes, L. de C., Peres, F. A. P., Correa, R. G. de F., & Baierle, I. C. (2025). A Framework for Leveraging Digital Technologies in Reverse Logistics Actions: A Systematic Literature Review. *Logistics (Basel)*, *9*(2), 54. DOI: 10.3390/logistics9020054

Rossini, M., Powell, D. J., & Kundu, K. (2023). Lean supply chain management and Industry 4.0: A systematic literature review. *International Journal of Lean Six Sigma*, *14*(2), 253–276. DOI: 10.1108/IJLSS-05-2021-0092

Sachan, S., Barve, A., Muduli, K., Kumar, A., Samadhiya, A., & Luthra, S. (2025). Can smart manufacturing benchmark the complex landscape of global success? *Benchmarking*. Advance online publication. DOI: 10.1108/BIJ-10-2024-0879

Saeed, N., Malik, H., Naeem, A., & Bashir, U. (2023). Incorporating big data and IoT in intelligent ecosystems: State-of-the-arts, challenges and opportunities, and future directions. *Multimedia Tools and Applications*, *83*(7), 20699–20741. DOI: 10.1007/s11042-023-16328-3

Santiago, F., Haraguchi, N., & Lavopa, A. (2024). Global Trends and World Order: Implications for New Industrial Policies in Developing Countries. *Journal of Industry, Competition and Trade*, *24*(1), 5. DOI: 10.1007/s10842-024-00419-4

Saran, N., & Kesswani, N. (2025). An analytics-driven framework for securing industrial IoT-Enabled Supply Chain Management Systems. *Supply Chain Analytics, 11*, 100128. DOI: 10.1016/j.sca.2025.100128

Shekarian, M., & Mellat Parast, M. (2021). An Integrative approach to supply chain disruption risk and resilience management: A literature review. *International Journal of Logistics Research and Applications, 24*(5), 427–455. DOI: 10.1080/13675567.2020.1763935

Simionescu, M., & Strielkowski, W. (2025). The Role of the Internet of Things in Enhancing Sustainable Urban Energy Systems: A Review of Lessons Learned from the COVID-19 Pandemic. *Journal of Urban Technology, 32*(1), 103–132. DOI: 10.1080/10630732.2024.2411932

Smyth, C., Dennehy, D., Fosso Wamba, S., Scott, M., & Harfouche, A. (2024). Artificial intelligence and prescriptive analytics for supply chain resilience: A systematic literature review and research agenda. *International Journal of Production Research, 62*(23), 8537–8561. DOI: 10.1080/00207543.2024.2341415

Stroumpoulis, A., & Kopanaki, E. (2022). Theoretical Perspectives on Sustainable Supply Chain Management and Digital Transformation: A Literature Review and a Conceptual Framework. *Sustainability, 14*(8), 4862. DOI: 10.3390/su14084862

Talwar, S., Kaur, P., Fosso Wamba, S., & Dhir, A. (2021). Big Data in operations and supply chain management: A systematic literature review and future research agenda. *International Journal of Production Research, 59*(11), 3509–3534. DOI: 10.1080/00207543.2020.1868599

Thanasi-Boçe, M., & Hoxha, J. (2025). Blockchain for Sustainable Development: A Systematic Review. *Sustainability, 17*(11), 4848. DOI: 10.3390/su17114848

Turskis, Z., & Šniokienė, V. (2024). IoT-Driven Transformation of Circular Economy Efficiency: An Overview. *Mathematical & Computational Applications, 29*(4), 49. DOI: 10.3390/mca29040049

Waltersmann, L., Kiemel, S., Stuhlsatz, J., Sauer, A., & Miehe, R. (2021). Artificial Intelligence Applications for Increasing Resource Efficiency in Manufacturing Companies—A Comprehensive Review. *Sustainability, 13*(12), 6689. DOI: 10.3390/su13126689

Wijewickrama, M. K. C. S., Chileshe, N., Rameezdeen, R., & Ochoa, J. J. (2021). Information sharing in reverse logistics supply chain of demolition waste: A systematic literature review. *Journal of Cleaner Production, 280*, 124359. DOI: 10.1016/j.jclepro.2020.124359

Wilson, M., Paschen, J., & Pitt, L. (2022). The circular economy meets artificial intelligence (AI): Understanding the opportunities of AI for reverse logistics. *Management of Environmental Quality, 33*(1), 9–25. DOI: 10.1108/MEQ-10-2020-0222

Wu, H., Liu, J., & Liang, B. (2024). AI-Driven Supply Chain Transformation in Industry 5.0: Enhancing Resilience and Sustainability. *Journal of the Knowledge Economy, 16*(1), 3826–3868. DOI: 10.1007/s13132-024-01999-6

Wylde, V., Rawindaran, N., Lawrence, J., Balasubramanian, R., Prakash, E., Jayal, A., Khan, I., Hewage, C., & Platts, J. (2022). Cybersecurity, Data Privacy and Blockchain: A Review. *SN Computer Science, 3*(2), 127. DOI: 10.1007/s42979-022-01020-4 PMID: 35036930

Zarei, H., Rasti-Barzoki, M., Altmann, J., & Egger, B. (2023). Cooperation, coordination, or collaboration? A structured review of buyers' partnerships to support sustainable sourcing in supply chains. *Environmental Science and Pollution Research International, 30*(31), 76491–76514. DOI: 10.1007/s11356-023-27541-w PMID: 37280495

Zekhnini, K., Cherrafi, A., Bouhaddou, I., Benghabrit, Y., & Garza-Reyes, J. A. (2021). Supply chain management 4.0: A literature review and research framework. *Benchmarking, 28*(2), 465–501.

Zhu, Q., Duan, Y., & Sarkis, J. (2024). Supply chain carbon transparency to consumers via blockchain: Does the truth hurt? *International Journal of Logistics Management, 35*(3), 833–864. DOI: 10.1108/IJLM-03-2023-0109

Zhu, Q., Duan, Y., & Sarkis, J. (2025). Blockchain Empowerment: Unveiling Managerial Choices in Carbon Finance Investment Across Supply Chains. *Journal of Business Logistics, 46*(1). Advance online publication. DOI: 10.1111/jbl.12405

KEY TERMS AND DEFINITIONS

Artificial Intelligence (AI): An artificial model of computer-based calculations that enable machines to gain knowledge, identify trends and generate predictions or recommendations that optimize the planning process, operations, and risk control within the supply chain.

Big Data Analytics (BDA): The process of the rational assessment, and analysis of extensive, varied, and rapidly created amounts of data created in the business of a supply chain to enable efficient, timely, and strategically smart decision making that is driven by efficiency, sustainability, and resiliency.

Circular Economy: This refers to economic and operation models in which the main emphasis is resource efficiency in terms of reuse, recycling, remanufacturing, and recovery of trash to reorganize the linear supply chains into regenerative and closed-loop systems.

Data Governance: A collection of policies, guidelines, accountability policies that regulate ownership, quality, security, ethical usage of data and accountability to secure quality and reliable analytics-based supply chain business processes.

Explainable Artificial Intelligence (XAI): A system of the development of the AI systems which guarantees transparency and interpretability and enables human decision-makers to trust and understand the logic of the results offered by algorithms and assess them.

Internet of Things (IoT): IoT is a network of physical objects, sensors, and systems that perpetually gather and transmit operational real-time data concerning the operations of energy consumption, emissions, logistics flow and equipment condition.

Supply Chain Resilience: This is the ability of a supply chain to predict, absorb, adapt and recover to the disruptions, and a continuity of the operations of a supply chain combined with mitigating financial, environmental, and social losses.

Sustainable Supply Chain: A model of design and management which makes a compromise between the economic intelligence of the supply chain and conservation of the environment and social responsibility of all supply chain processes which include sourcing, production, distribution and end-of life management.

Chapter 2

A Big Data-Driven MCDM Model for Sustainable Supplier Selection

Beyzanur Cayir Ervural
http://orcid.org/0000-0002-0861-052X
Necmettin Erbakan University, Turkey

ABSTRACT

In response to increasing environmental degradation and sustainability pressures, supply chain management (SCM) has expanded its focus to include sustainability alongside traditional performance goals. This study examines the use of Big Data Analytics (BDA) integrated with three Multi-Criteria Decision-Making (MCDM) methods—WASPAS, MAUT, and COPRAS—to support sustainable SCM decisions. Criterion weights are determined using the CRITIC method, enabling a more objective and data-driven evaluation framework. The study highlights how real-time data from Internet of Things (IoT), Enterprise Resource Planning (ERP) systems, and external sources enhance the accuracy and adaptability of sustainability assessments. A case study on supplier selection and logistics management demonstrates the effectiveness of the proposed approach. The results highlight a research gap in the comparative analysis of MCDM techniques in the context of improving decision quality, responding more quickly to change, and sustainability-focused supply chains.

INTRODUCTION

In response to increasing global concerns over environmental degradation, social inequality, and economic instability, sustainability has become a fundamental dimension of supply chain management (SCM) in recent years. (Morana, 2013; Seuring

DOI: 10.4018/979-8-3373-6896-2.ch002

& Müller, 2008; Stefan Schaltegger et al., 2014). Once considered a minor goal of a company's operation, sustainability has now risen to being one of the most important indicators of a company's performance due to not only the forceful regulations but also the expectations from stakeholders and the marketplace (Contini & Peruzzini, 2022; Epstein & Roy, 2001). Supply chain models, which have been traditionally focused on cost-effectiveness and operational speed, cannot effectively meet the many complexities associated with sustainable performance. Therefore, supply chain executives have had to increasingly evaluate their supply chain strategies using a multidimensional perspective that integrates economic feasibility, environmental sustainability and social responsibility (Elkington, 1998).

Additionally, advancements in Big Data Analytics (BDA) have provided companies with a rich source of information to monitor, manage, and analyze the large amounts of diverse data they possess in real time. Information is derived from many sources including, but not limited to, Internet of Things (IoT) devices, Enterprise Resource Planning (ERP) solutions, social media data and third-party environmental and regulatory datasets (Alyahya & Agag, 2025). When used in conjunction with actionable data, BDA enables an organization to have greater visibility, agility and accuracy when making decisions. For this reason, Multi-Criteria Decision-Making (MCDM) methods are necessary for complicated real life issues. MCDM provides a systematic and tough framework for rating alternatives based on several, often conflicting criteria. In the area of sustainable SCM, the use of MCDM techniques has been extended to a wide range of decisions such as supplier selection, facility location, transportation planning, and product design (Govindan et al., 2013). Nonetheless, most current implementations depend on static, expert-driven input data - such as responses from surveys or Delphi methods - that do not acknowledge the ever-changing, data-rich environments in which today's supply chains are functioning. The merger of BDA with MCDM models is a potential, though largely unrecognized, way of resolving this issue, thus granting not only real-time responsiveness but also organized decision support. There is an increasing amount of research published in the academic world that shows the interest in the combination of BDA and sustainability. For example, Dubey et al. (2020) argue that BDA capabilities can be a major driver for the company to achieve environmental and social performance if they are deeply integrated with supply chain strategies. However, most of these studies, especially in comparative contexts, end without detailing the operational linkage between specific decision-making frameworks such as BDA and MCDM. Besides, most of the researches have only one MCDM technique (e.g., Analytic Hierarchy Process (AHP), Technique for Order Preference by Similarity to Ideal Solution (TOPSIS), or VIšekriterijumska Optimizacija I Kompromisno Rešenje (VIKOR)), and only a few have investigated the relative strengths and weaknesses of different methods when combined with current big data inputs.

This study fills these gaps by suggesting a comparative integration of three successful MCDM methods - Weighted Aggregated Sum Product Assessment (WASPAS), Multi-Attribute Utility Theory (MAUT), and Complex Proportional Assessment (COPRAS) -in a BDAs-powered setting. Using the CRITIC method, criterion weights are first obtained and then introduced in the three MCDM methods to form a holistic and integrated decision-making model. Each of the approaches has different advantages in dealing with multi-faceted criteria: WASPAS merges additive and multiplicative utility models, MAUT lets the decision-maker specify his/her preferences directly, and COPRAS produces normalized rankings by separating beneficial from non-beneficial criteria (Ghorabaee et al., 2017; Zavadskas & Turskis, 2011).

In this study, we aim to compare these techniques side by side for effectiveness, clarity, and flexibility in sustainability-related decision-making on one and the same dataset derived from BDA sources. Another valuable contribution of this study is theoretical progress in big data operationalization within decision-making models, moving from conceptual frameworks to prescriptive tools. While there is a number of studies that have emphasized the potential of BDA in decision quality, such as Akter et al.(2016), most of them suffer from methodological weaknesses and are hard to implement. In this respect, current research exemplifies comprehensive, seamless workflow-from data gathering to MCDM modeling and output-that can be replicated or modified in different industries and settings. This chapter contributes to the sustainable supply chain management (SSCM) literature by showing the way real-time big data inputs can be operationalized within a comparative MCDM framework for supplier selection. The study integrates objectively derived CRITIC weights with three underexplored yet powerful MCDM methods—MAUT, COPRAS, and WASPAS. So, it moves beyond conceptual discussions and delivers a fully implementable, data-driven decision support model. The study, through a real-life case in the electronics manufacturing industry, depicts how economic, environmental, and social sustainability criteria can be met at the same time under dynamic data conditions. The comparative findings reveal the differences in the ranking logic and decision sensitivity of the methods, thus providing theoretical insight and practical guidance for the choice of MCDM techniques in sustainability-oriented supply chain.

The remainder of this chapter is organized as follows: Section 2 summarizes relevant literature on SSCM. Section 3 describes the decision-making instruments used to conduct this study, identified as COPRAS, MAUT, WASPAS, and the CRITIC method. Section 4 illustrates the application of the proposed model. Finally, Section 5 represents the conclusion and suggests possible directions for future research.

LITERATURE REVIEW

The evolution of SCM towards environmental sustainability has been largely influenced by digital technologies in general and BDA in particular. At the same time, MCDM methods have been widely used to make complex decisions involving multiple, often contradictory criteria. Scholars point out that although significant research has been conducted in both areas, the combination of BDA and MCDM for environmentally friendly supply chain management is yet to be sufficiently explored. BDA gives companies the ability to collect, process, and analyze huge volumes of both structured and unstructured data, thus paving the way for more informed and faster decision-making in SCM. The researchers argue that BDA can be used as a main source of supply chain sustainability by increasing supply chain visibility, hence enabling the instant tracking of environmental and social metrics and the use of predictive models for the detection of risks and the handling of disruptions

Beinabadi et al. (2024) discussed a SSCM framework in an automotive company using multi-stage models comprises forecasting approach, BWM and DEA methods to provide a successful production planning with adapting sustainable development goals. Yildizbasi and Arioz (2021) evaluated a big data analytics based on hybrid fuzzy AHP and TOPSIS methods to optimize a green supplier selection process. Momena et al.(2024) considered CRITIC based MULTIMOORA model for assessing performance of supply chain companies under diverse scenarios. Tajally et al. (2025) considered a sustainable supplier selection and order allocation problem with a multi-phase data driven decision making method such as fuzzy BWM, fuzzy normalized weighted sum and chance constrained fuzzy goal programming model to evaluate the most significant factors related to agility, resilience and sustainability context. Gholami et al. (2025) proposed a data driven model for sustainable and resilient supplier selection in manufacturing systems with using AI techniques and fuzzy based approach in Python program. Feng et al. (2025) presented a Pythagorean fuzzy decision making structure using big data approaches to see capabilities of various enterprises under manufacturing supply chains.

Akter (2016) and Hasan et al.(2024) argued that the use of big data results in better decisions in the supply chain, especially when the analytical model includes environmental and social aspects. Nevertheless, the most common drawback pointed out in the research is that most of them relies heavily on theoretical frameworks or results of surveys, without much fusion of the real-time or operational data coming from IoT and ERP systems (Haddud et al., 2017; Ivanov, 2020; Wijesinghe et al., 2024). Furthermore, although a great number of studies put forward the framework of sustainable decision-making with the use of BDA, only a handful of them incorporate prescriptive or comparative modeling instruments for assisting structured decision-making.

SSCM poses a challenge of having to weigh environmental, economic, and social factors, which are the criteria that complicate the decision-making processes. MCDM methods have been employed to a great extent in the SSCM decision-making process to help the decision-makers evaluate the different options and choose the ones that are most suitable for them under the most criteria that are usually conflicting. Among them, Analytic Hierarchy Process (AHP), VIšekriterijumska Optimizacija I Kompromisno Rešenje (VIKOR), Technique for Order Preference by Similarity to Ideal Solution (TOPSIS), ELimination Et Choix Traduisant la REalité (ELECTRE), Preference Ranking Organization METHod for Enrichment Evaluations (PROMETHEE), Step-wise Weight Assessment Ratio Analysis (SWARA), and Simple Additive Weighting (SAW) are some of the most frequently used techniques in SSCM.

AHP is a widely used technique because it breaks down the issues into a hierarchy and compares the elements in pairs. The method has been applied in various SSCM issues, particularly for the purpose of sustainable supplier selection, while being able to take into account economic, environmental, and social factors at the same time. For example, Govindan et al.(2013) used a combined AHP-TOPSIS model to assess suppliers in the electronics industry, pointing out that economic factors are still the most influential ones even if the sustainability factors are taken into account. TOPSIS evaluates the options on the basis of how far they are from the best and the worst solution, thus being the most suitable for sustainability assessment where the trade-offs among multiple criteria are involved. Chen (2000) demonstrated the effectiveness of TOPSIS in the optimization of internal supply chain operations and thereby pointed out supplier relationships and inventory planning as critical factors.

VIKOR is concerned with ranking alternatives by taking into account their closeness to the ideal solution and also stressing the compromise solutions. It has been utilized to select the best electric trucks, where the emission of pollutants, the management's approval, and the observance of the regulations were the most important factors (Opricovic & Tzeng, 2004). ELECTRE is a method that allows the ranking by comparing pairs and hence it has been employed in analyzing the green supply chain practices and understanding environmental performance as the leading factor (Zavadskas et al., 2014). Likewise, PROMETHEE has been used in the selection of sustainable logistics providers where it was instrumental in capturing the qualitative as well as the quantitative criteria reflecting the decision-makers' preferences (Agrawal, 2022; Jamshidi et al., 2019; Siagian & Gwynne, 2023). SWARA is a weighting approach that identifies the importance of the criteria in a stepwise manner and has been used for evaluating successful factors in green supply chain implementations (Ajalli, 2025; Akram et al., 2025; Šarić & Abramović, 2025). The Simple Additive Weighting (SAW) method, though being a very simple one, is still widely used for making initial judgments. In a comparative study of methods namely SAW, AHP, TOPSIS, VIKOR, and MABAC for the selection of pharmaceutical suppliers, it was found that the results obtained by SAW and AHP were quite similar thus pointing to their trustworthiness in certain SSCM scenarios (Putro et al., 2025).

On the other hand, other multi-criteria decision-making methods such as MAUT, COPRAS, and WASPAS are mentioned in very limited numbers in the sustainable supply chain management literature and are therefore not used sufficiently. All these issues present a challenge in terms of tool diversity for decision-makers dealing with complex sustainability issues. Furthermore, there is very little study on the integration of these methods with the sophisticated weighting methods like CRITIC. Also, numerous studies make use of expert opinions or historical data; however, the use of real-time, data-driven inputs via BDA is still at the early stage of development in the context of correspondence between SSCM and MCDM. As a result, a gap has emerged wherein dynamic and objective data-informed decision-making models can significantly improve sustainability outcomes. The present study fills the gap by integrating BDA inputs with less frequently utilized yet highly promising MCDM methods such as MAUT, COPRAS, and WASPAS. Besides, the CRITIC approach is employed in the study for the objective weighing of criteria by making use of the correlations between criteria and data variability to enhance the decision-making process. This study provides a comprehensive comparative analysis under real-world conditions and dynamic data, making a significant contribution to SSCM decision-making processes in terms of a new methodological development.

APPLIED MCDM METHODS

To gain a detailed, clear, and comparative understanding of environmentally friendly supply chain options, this research utilized four widely accepted multi-criteria decision-making (MCDM) methods: COPRAS, MAUT, WASPAS, and CRITIC. Each of the chosen methods is justified by the respective decision setting, data structure, and the weights of criteria. In this study, weighted decision matrices are created using the weights obtained from the CRITIC method, and then the other three MCDM methods are applied in sequence. Their methods and readiness for solving the sustainability issues in decision making are briefly described:

COmplex PRoportional ASsessment (COPRAS)

Initially introduced by Zavadskas et al. (1994), COPRAS is a decision-making method composed of several key steps:

- First, a decision matrix $K = \left[x_{ij}\right]_{m*n}$ *is* constructed, where x_{ij} represents the evaluation of the ith alternative against the jth criterion.
- The matrix is then normalized to ensure comparability across criteria using:

$$x_{ij}* = \frac{x_{ij}}{\sum_{i=1}^{m} x_{ij}} \tag{1}$$

(i=1,…,m j=1,…,n)

- Next, the normalized values are weighted by their respective criterion weights w_j, producing the weighted normalized decision matrix as follows.

$$\left[d_{ij}\right]_{m*n} = x_{ij}{}^{*} w_j \tag{2}$$

- Two indices are calculated: S_{+i} which sums weighted normalized values for beneficial criteria, and S_{-i} which does so for cost criteria. Higher S_{+i} and lower S_{-i} indicate better alternatives.

$$S_{+i} = \sum_{j=1}^{n} d_{+ij} \tag{3}$$

$$S_{-i} = \sum_{j=1}^{n} d_{-ij} \tag{4}$$

- The relative significance Q_i of each alternative is computed by combining these indices, where a higher Q_i denotes greater importance.

$$Q_i = S_{+i} + \frac{S_{-\min}\sum_{i=1}^{m} S_{-i}}{S_{-i}\sum_{i=1}^{m}(S_{-\min}/S_{-i})} = S_{+i} + \frac{\sum_{i=1}^{m} S_{-i}}{S_{-i}\sum_{i=1}^{m}(1/S_{-i})} \tag{5}$$

(i=1, 2, …,m)

- Finally, the quantitative utility U_i is derived by normalizing Q_i against the maximum Q_{max}, allowing alternatives to be ranked based on their utility percentages.

$$U_i = \left[\frac{Q_i}{Q_{max}}\right] * 100\% \tag{6}$$

U_i shows the overall utility value of alternative *i*.

Multi Attribute Utility Theory (MAUT)

MAUT is an example of a classical decision theory method which involves the use of utility functions to represent the preferences of a person over several attributes. Each factor is converted into a utility measure ranging between 0 and 1, expressing the decision-maker's internal assessment of the attribute's performance. The steps of MAUT are given as follows:

- o Define utility functions $U_j(x_{ij})$ for each criterion j and alternative i
- o If necessary, normalize the data and determine the utility values corresponding to each criterion.
- o Calculate the total utility for each

$$U_i = \sum_{j=1}^{n} w_j U_j(x_{ij}) \tag{7}$$

U_i offers the overall satisfaction.

Weighted Aggregated Sum Product Assessment (WASPAS)

WASPAS, which combines the Weighted Sum Model (WSM) and Weighted Product Model (WPM) to evaluate alternatives, was created by Zavadskas et al. (2012). The steps of the WASPAS method are shown as:

- The decision matrix $X = [X_{ij}]_{m*n}$ is established.
- Normalization is implemented based on the type of the criterion: if the criterion is a benefit one, the values are divided by the maximum value within the criterion, while if it is a cost criterion, the minimum value is divided by the actual value, thus making the results.

$$\bar{x}_{ij} = \frac{x_{ij}}{\max_i x_{ij}} \tag{8}$$

$$\bar{x}_{ij} = \frac{\min_i x_{ij}}{x_{ij}} \tag{9}$$

- Two separate scores are calculated:
  - o $Q_i^{(1)}, the weighted sum of normalized values (WSM).$

$$Q_i^{(1)} = \sum_{i=1}^{n} \bar{x}_{ij} w_i \tag{10}$$

- $Q_i^{(2)}$, *theweightedproductofnormalizedvalues(WPM).*

$$Q_i^{(2)} = \prod_{i=1}^{n} \left(\bar{x}_{ij}\right)^{w_i} \tag{11}$$

- The final score Q_i is computed as a weighted combination of $Q_i^{(1)}$and $Q_i^{(2)}$, controlled by parameter λ (ranging from 0 to 1).

$$Q_i = \lambda Q_i^{(1)} + (1 - \lambda)Q_i^{(2)} = \lambda \sum_{i=1}^{n} \bar{x}_{ij} w_i + (1 - \lambda)\prod_{i=1}^{n} \left(\bar{x}_{ij}\right)^{w_i}, \lambda = 0, 0.1, 0.2, \ldots, 1 \tag{12}$$

- Alternatives are ranked based on Q_i, with the highest score representing the best choice. Q_i *gives* final score used for ranking alternatives.

CRiteria Importance Through Intercriteria Correlation (CRITIC) Method

The CRITIC (CRiteria Importance Through Intercriteria Correlation) method was first presented by Diakoulaki et al. (1995) and is an objective weighting technique for MCDM problems. While subjective methods depend on expert judgment, CRITIC calculates criteria weights from the data features by taking into account the contrast intensity and the degree of conflict (correlation) of the . This method assumes that a criterion is more important if:

- It exhibits a greater amount of variation (i.e., it better discriminates among alternatives), and
- It has lower correlation with other criteria (i.e., it provides unique information).

The CRITIC method follows these main steps:

- Construct the decision matrix: Denote the decision matrix$X = \left[x_{ij}\right]$ where x_{ij} displays the performance of alternative *i* under criterion *j*.
- Normalize the decision matrix: Different measurement units may cause the problem of incomparable data, so the matrix is normalized by min-max method.

$$r_{ij} = \begin{cases} \dfrac{x_{ij} - \min\left(x_j\right)}{\max\left(x_j\right) - \min\left(x_j\right)}, forbenefitcriteria \\ \dfrac{\max\left(x_j\right) - x_{ij}}{\max\left(x_j\right) - \min\left(x_j\right)}, forcostcriteria \end{cases} \tag{13}$$

- Calculate the standard deviation of each criterion: For each criterion *j*, the standard deviation σ_j is calculated. The higher standard deviation the higher level of difference between alternatives.

$$\sigma_j = \sqrt{\frac{1}{m-1}\sum_{i=1}^{m}\left(r_{ij} - \overline{r}_j\right)^2} \tag{14}$$

- Calculate the correlation matrix: The Pearson correlation coefficient r_{jk} between each pair of criteria *j* and *k* is calculated. This step is used to the redundancy or interdependence among criteria.
- Compute the information content (C_j) for each criterion: The quantity of information (or the importance) given by each criterion *j* is estimated by means of the following formula:

$$C_j = \sigma_j \sum_{k=1}^{n}\left(1 - r_{jk}\right) \tag{15}$$

This captures both the variability and the independence of the criterion.

- Determine the weights: The weight w_j of each criterion is obtained by normalizing the information content:

$$w_j = \frac{C_j}{\sum_{j-i}^{n} C_j} \tag{16}$$

These final weights reflect the objective importance of each criterion in the decision-making process.

APPLICATION OF THE STUDY: THE CHALLENGE OF SUSTAINABLE SUPPLIER SELECTION

The study was conducted at an electronics company in Türkiye that manufactures mid-range electronic products. The company manufactures the smart home devices that include thermostats, energy meters, and air quality monitors. The company has rebranded itself as a sustainability-focused organization over the past couple of years, thereby contributing to the reduction of their environmental footprint and aligning with the European green deal targets. As part of its sustainability strategy, the company is committed to sourcing key product components such as lithium-ion batteries, printed circuit boards (PCBs), and sensors from suppliers that meet strict environmental and social responsibility criteria. The company began searching for a new regional supplier for PCB components used in its smart thermostat series in 2025. The potential supplier needed to meet traditional criteria such as cost and delivery time, as well as maintain sustainability performance indicators such as low carbon emissions, energy efficiency in production, and fair labor practices.

The company's purchasing team faced a challenging situation; four pre-qualified suppliers (coded A, B, C, and D) from the EU and Türkiye had submitted their detailed proposals. Each potential supplier had advantages in different aspects; for example, one offered the lowest price but had weak sustainability metrics, while another demonstrated excellent social compliance but had slightly longer delivery times. The company leverages a big data platform to ensure a consistent, objective, and data-driven selection process for data extraction to get real-time operational, environmental, and supplier audit data from the following sources:

- ERP systems (for cost, delivery performance, and order history).
- IoT-enabled production equipment (for energy consumption and emissions).
- Third-party sustainability audit reports (for labor and compliance scores).

To carry out the evaluation and ranking exercises of the four alternatives along with five sustainability-related criteria, the procurement department determined to employ a MCDM approach, which was further enhanced by the BDA. The objective was to identify the supplier that will yield the most significant trade-off among economic, environmental, and social performances by employing various decision-making tools.

The criteria involved are described as follows:

Unit cost: Unit cost refers to the overall cost of materials, labor, and overhead that are directly attributable to the manufacture or acquisition of one unit of a product or service. It is calculated as the total production cost divided by the total number of units produced.

CO_2 emissions per unit: It refers to the amount of carbon dioxide emissions associated with producing one unit of output.

Energy efficiency: Energy efficiency indicates how well the energy input is being converted to the desired output.

Delivery time: Delivery time describes the period between a point of order (or start of production) and the moment the product reaches the customer.

Labor compliance: Labor compliance score represents a quantified measure of how a company or supplier follows labor-related laws, regulations, moral standards, and international. Figure 1 gives the hierarchy scheme of the decision model.

Figure 1. The hierarchy scheme of the decision problem

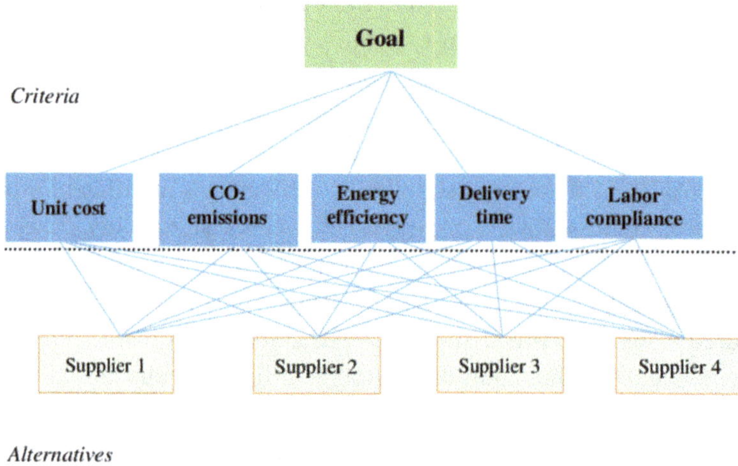

Sources: Created by author

The following table (in Table 1) shows the decision matrix for supplier evaluation process.

Table 1. Decision matrix for supplier evaluation

Supplier	C1: Unit cost (€/unit)	C2: CO_2 emissions (kg/unit)	C3: Energy efficiency score (0–10)	C4: Delivery time (days)	C5: Labor compliance score (0–10)
A	8.50	1.90	7.0	4.5	8.0
B	7.90	2.50	8.5	5.0	6.5
C	9.20	1.70	6.5	5.5	9.0
D	8.10	2.20	7.5	4.0	7.0

The following table (in Table 2) gives the criteria types and desired directions.

Table 2. Criteria types and desired direction

Criterion	Description	Type	Desired Direction
C1	Unit cost	Economic	Lower is better
C2	CO_2 emissions per unit	Environmental	Lower is better
C3	Energy efficiency	Environmental	Higher is better
C4	Delivery time	Economic	Lower is better
C5	Labor compliance score	Social	Higher is better

CriteriaWeighting Using the CRITIC Method

The CRITIC (CRiteria Importance Through Intercriteria Correlation) method was utilized in this study to figure out the sustainability criteria weights in an unbiased way. To contrast the subjective methods (e.g., AHP, SWARA), CRITIC determines weights by looking at the inherent features of the data, it takes into account the standard deviation (which indicates the contrast intensity) and the inter-criteria correlation (which indicates the redundancy). This data-driven approach is highly effective because criteria with high variability and low correlation with others receive higher weighting, thus contributing more to the decision-making process.

Initially the decision matrix is normalized, as shown below. Afterward, the standard deviations of the criteria are computed, and then the correlation matrix is builded. The criterion weights, based on the calculated information content values, were determined as shown below in Table 3.

Table 3. Normalized matrix (Min-Max)

Supplier	C1 (Cost)	C2 (CO_2)	C3 (Energy)	C4 (Time)	C5 (Labor)
A	0.538	0.500	0.333	0.500	0.667
B	1.000	0.000	1.000	0.250	0.000
C	0.000	0.667	0.000	0.000	1.000
D	0.846	0.167	0.667	1.000	0.333

The table below in Table 4 shows the standard deviation values.

Table 4. Standard deviations

Criterion	Std. Dev. (σ)
C1	0.410
C2	0.284
C3	0.434
C4	0.408
C5	0.408

The following table (in Table 5) gives the correlation matrix values.

Table 5. Correlation matrix

Criterion	C1	C2	C3	C4	C5
C1	1.00	0.28	-0.86	0.31	-0.60
C2	0.28	1.00	-0.22	-0.42	0.08
C3	-0.86	-0.22	1.00	-0.36	0.82
C4	0.31	-0.42	-0.36	1.00	-0.70
C5	-0.60	0.08	0.82	-0.70	1.00

The table below (in Table 6) presents the information content.

Table 6. Information content

Criterion	σ	Sum(1 - r)	Cj (σ × Σ(1 - r))
C1	0.410	3.87	1.588
C2	0.284	3.44	0.978
C3	0.434	2.90	1.259
C4	0.408	3.75	1.530
C5	0.408	3.40	1.387

The following table gives CRITIC values (as seen in Table 7).

Table 7. CRITIC weights

Criterion	C_j	Weight (w)
C1	1.588	0.2356
C2	0.978	0.1450
C3	1.259	0.1868
C4	1.530	0.2269
C5	1.387	0.2057

According to the CRITIC method, unit costs (C1) were given the highest weight (0.236) due to their relatively high variance and low correlation with other criteria. CO_2 emissions (C2) were assigned the lowest weight (0.145), indicating that emission levels vary less covariately and show some correlation with other factors (e.g., energy efficiency). Delivery time and labor compliance also receive significant weights, which reflect their variability and distinctiveness for the decision. These weights will now be used as input for the next MCDM analysis with WASPAS, MAUT, and COPRAS methods.

MAUT

In the MAUT calculation, objective weights obtained from the CRITIC method (Table 7) were used. For each supplier, the benefit score corresponding to each criterion was calculated as the product of the normalized criterion score and its CRITIC-based weight. The total utility value of an alternative was achieved by adding up the weighted utility scores of all criteria. The resulting utility scores are presented in table below. The following Table 8 shows the decision matrix.

Table 8. Decision matrix

Supplier	C1	C2	C3	C4	C5
A	8.50	1.9	7	4.5	8
B	7.90	2.5	8.5	5	6.5
C	9.2	1.7	6.5	5.5	9
D	8.1	2.2	7.5	4	7
max	9.2	2.5	8.5	5.5	9
min	7.9	1.7	6.5	4	6.5

The following Table 9 below gives the normalized decision matrix.

Table 9. The normalized decision matrix

Weights	0.236	0.145	0.187	0.227	0.206
A	0.538	0.750	0.25	0.667	0.6
B	1.000	0.000	1	0.333	0
C	0.000	1.000	0	0.000	1
D	0.846	0.375	0.5	1.000	0.2

The following table presents the weighted normalized matrix.

Table 10. The weighted normalized matrix

Supplier	C1	C2	C3	C4	C5	Utility	Rank
A	0.127	0.109	0.047	0.151	0.124	0.558	2
B	0.236	0.000	0.187	0.076	0.000	0.499	3
C	0.000	0.145	0.000	0.000	0.206	0.351	4
D	0.200	0.054	0.094	0.227	0.041	0.616	1

COPRAS

In the first stage of the COPRAS method, the decision matrix (Table 11- Table 12) was normalized to eliminate the effects of diverse measurement units. The normalized decision matrix is presented in Table 12. Then, the CRITIC-derived criterion weights were used to get the weighted normalized decision matrix (Table 13). At this stage, the calculated weights were combined using the COPRAS approach to obtain a weighted normalized decision matrix. Therefore, the COPRAS method was finalized by summing the beneficial and non-beneficial criteria that lead to the relative performance scores of the suppliers represented in Table 14. The quantitative utility degree (Table 14) for each alternative was the last operation performed. It made possible the ranking of the alternatives according to their utility values in descending order. Table 11 gives the decision matrix.

Table 11. Decision matrix

Supplier	C1	C2	C3	C4	C5
A	8.5	1.9	7	4.5	8
B	7.9	2.5	8.5	5	6.5
C	9.2	1.7	6.5	5.5	9
D	8.1	2.2	7.5	4	7
SUM	33.7	8.3	29.5	19	30.5

Then we try to obtain the normalized decision matrix in Table 12.

Table 12. The normalized decision matrix

Supplier	C1	C2	C3	C4	C5
A	0.2522	0.2289	0.2373	0.2368	0.2623
B	0.2344	0.3012	0.2881	0.2632	0.2131
C	0.2730	0.2048	0.2203	0.2895	0.2951
D	0.2404	0.2651	0.2542	0.2105	0.2295

Table 13 provides the weighted normalized matrix.

Table 13. The weighted normalized matrix

Supplier	Weights	w1: 0.236	w2: 0.145	w3: 0.187	w4: 0.227
A	0.0595	0.0332	0.0444	0.0538	0.0540
B	0.0553	0.0437	0.0539	0.0597	0.0439
C	0.0644	0.0297	0.0412	0.0657	0.0608
D	0.0567	0.0384	0.0475	0.0478	0.0473

Table 14 ensures relative weights and the obtained ranking of the alternatives.

Table 14. The quantitative utility degree and ranks

P_i	R_i				
Sum of Benefit	Sum of Cost	Relative weights Q_i	Priority order	Ranking	Alternatives
0.0984	0.1465	0.1018	0.963	2	A
0.0978	0.1587	0.1014	0.960	3	B
0.1020	0.1598	0.1057	1.000	1	C
0.0948	0.1429	0.0981	0.928	4	D
sum R_i	0.6080				
1/sum R_i	26.3786017				
	Q_{max}	0.10567			

WASPAS

Using the WASPAS method, the decision matrix is normalized with Equations 8-9 presented in Table 15, then WSM is used to find the first total relative importance value (Q1) via Equation 10, and secondly, WPM is used to specify the second total relative importance value (Q2) via Equation 11 as shown in Table 15. The overall total relative importance value (Qi) is calculated with Equation 10, where the WASPAS aggregation factor λ is taken as 0.5 to be consistent with the stability of the result stated in the literature review. In conclusion, all the data and calculation steps lead to the final ranking of alternative suppliers described in Table 16.

Table 15. The normalized decion matrix and relative significances

Supplier	W1: 0.236	W2: 0.145	W3: 0.187	W4: 0.227	W5: 0.206	Q1	Q2
A	0.929	0.895	0.824	0.889	0.889	0.8880	0.8863
B	1.000	0.680	1.000	0.800	0.722	0.8520	0.8406
C	0.859	1.000	0.765	0.727	1.000	0.8617	0.8535
D	0.975	0.773	0.882	1.000	0.778	0.8944	0.8883

Table 16 shows the final ranking of alternatives.

Table 16. Final supplier ranking using the WASPAS

Score	Rank	Alternatives
0.8871	2	A
0.8463	4	B
0.8576	3	C
0.8914	1	D

Comparison of the Obtained Results

The WASPAS method ranks options according to a combined weighted score; higher scores indicate better overall performance. D is the first choice, A is second, C is third, and B is at the bottom of the list. The WASPAS ranking is comparable to MAUT, where D is the leading alternative. However, the total WASPAS scores of A and C are quite close, whereas MAUT showed a larger difference between these two alternatives.

MAUT and WASPAS lead to the same conclusion, with D being the highest-ranked alternative; this could mean that D exhibits consistent and good performance across different criteria. However, COPRAS ranks C highest, suggesting it considers more diverse factors when evaluating alternatives. Specifically, C appears to have higher proportional performance (Qi = 1.000), despite receiving lower utility in MAUT and a slightly lower score in WASPAS. A consistently ranks highest (2nd place) across all methods, indicating it is a reliable choice in all three evaluation techniques. D performs strongly in both MAUT and WASPAS, while C outperforms D in COPRAS due to its relatively good benefit-cost ratio. B consistently ranks lowest in all three methods, making it the least preferred alternative overall.

MAUT focuses heavily on the total utility of each alternative, therefore it is sensitive to the overall goodness of each alternative across all criteria. COPRAS examines alternatives through a proportional performance lens, considering both benefits and costs. This may be why C ranks higher in COPRAS despite having lower total utility in MAUT. WASPAS performs a weighted aggregation of scores, and D's top ranking is similar to MAUT. It largely supports the weighted aggregation of scores, which is likely why D ranks highest. MAUT provides a complete picture based on the benefits of the alternatives, but it may not fully account for the balance between benefits and costs as COPRAS does. COPRAS is more suitable where cost-benefit analysis is central to the decision-making process, whereas WASPAS offers a balance of weighted aggregations and may be more understandable where all criteria are of equal importance. Table 17 presents a comparison table of the methods.

Table 17. Comparison summary

Method	1st Place	2nd Place	3rd Place	4th Place
MAUT	D	A	B	C
COPRAS	C	A	B	D
WASPAS	D	A	C	B

Figure 2 and Figure 3 summarize the ranking of the alternatives with a bar chart and line chart.

Figure 2. Ranking of the alternatives w.r.t. CRTIC based MCDM

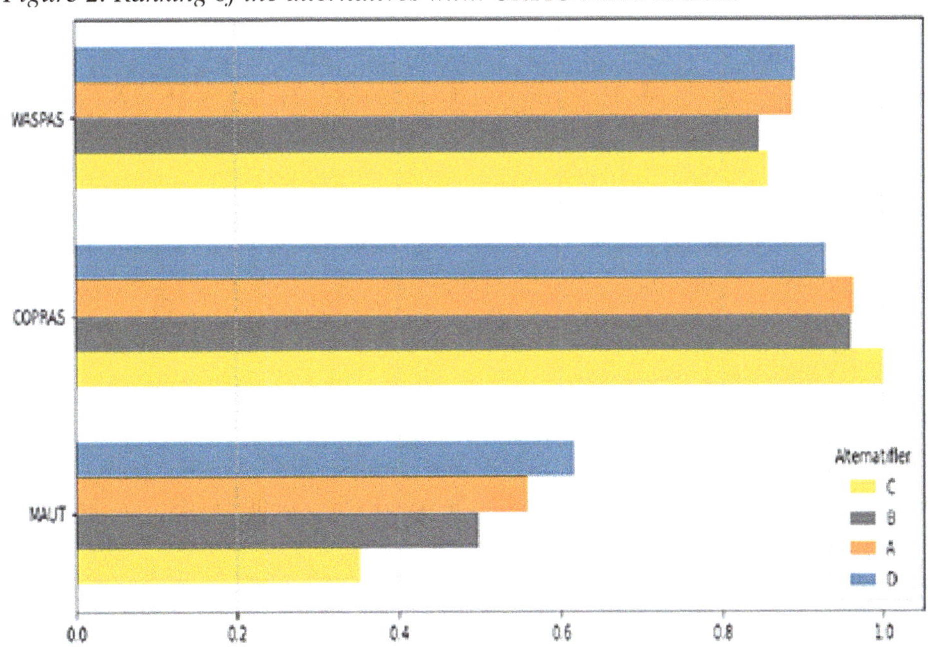

Figure 3. Line chart results

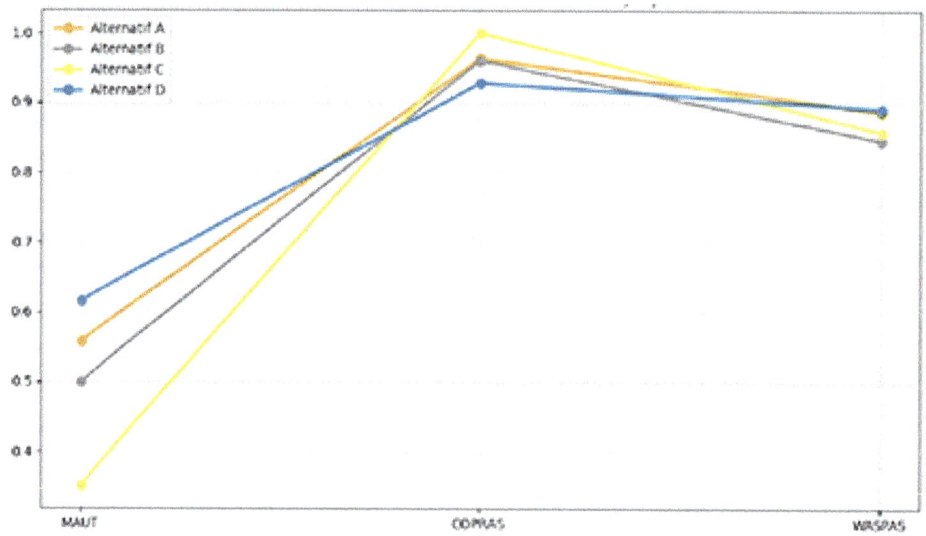

INTERPRETATION AND DISCUSSION OF RESULTS

The comparative results obtained from MAUT, COPRAS, and WASPAS highlight the fact that sustainable supplier selection results fluctuate largely depending on the decision logic of MCDM methods. Overall, MAUT and WASPAS agree on selecting Supplier D as the best alternative; COPRAS, however, gives Supplier C the highest ranking due to its higher benefit-cost ratio performance. This difference confirms literature findings that different multi-criteria decision-making methods can produce different rankings even when applied to the same dataset, particularly in the field of sustainability where a significant balance between economic and socio-environmental criteria is required (Zavadskas & Turskis, 2011; Ghorabaee et al., 2017).

Supplier A's second position in all three methods evidences the robustness and balanced performance of this supplier, thus supporting the idea that suppliers with moderate but stable sustainability metrics can be dependable strategic partners. On the other hand, Supplier B's consistently low ranking indicates that competitive cost advantages alone are not enough when sustainability criteria are explicitly integrated into the decision framework, which is in line with SSCM studies that have been cited as the source of the decline of cost-only decision models (Govindan et al., 2013; Dubey et al., 2020).

Methodologically, the findings indicate that MAUT aims for overall utility maximization, WASPAS combines additive and multiplicative summation, and COPRAS is primarily concerned with proportional benefit-cost relationships. This finding represents a step toward filling a significant gap in the literature by providing empirical evidence on the behavior of different (MCDM) methods under real-time, data-driven sustainability inputs, rather than static expert opinions.

The findings of this study are highly useful and practical for supply chain managers and decision-makers in sectors that value stability and are environmentally conscious. The first move of the suggested BDA-driven MCDM framework allows procurement crews to detach from the fixed, expert-based assessments and thus become capable of continuously evaluating suppliers dynamically and in real-time. In this way, by continuously plugging ERP, IoT, and audit data into the decision model, managers can alter supplier ratings as sustainability performance or operational conditions vary, thereby becoming more responsive and cutting down the time between decisions.

Furthermore, the comparative analysis serves as a managerial guide and hints at the choice of methods. Where the decision context focus is on overall sustainability performance and balanced criteria evaluation, MAUT and WASPAS turn out to be more appropriate tools. On the other hand, in cases where cost–benefit proportionality and trade-off efficiency are at the core—e.g., budget-constrained procurement decisions—COPRAS might offer more revealing rankings. This methodological transparency assists managers in choosing the decision tools that are in line with their strategic priorities and hence, they will not fall into the trap of using a one-size-fits-all method.

The third point is the integration of objective weighting methods like CRITIC which lessens the subjectivity involved in the evaluation of sustainability and at the same time increases the transparency. This feature is quite valuable for organizations that are under the radar of the regulatory bodies or have to comply with the environmental, social and governance reporting requirements. The decision-makers may employ data-driven evidence as a means to convince internal governance as well as external stakeholders of their choices, thereby enhancing the trust. The proposed framework, in general, contributes to enhancing the quality, transparency, and adaptability of decision-making for sustainable supply chains and is easily transferable to other industries, for instance, the electronics, automotive, and renewable energy .

CONCLUSION AND FUTURE RESEARCH

This research has put forward a data-driven decision support framework for SSCM, which involves the use of BDA combined with CRITIC-based WASPAS,

MAUT, and COPRAS methods. The findings of the study using a green supplier selection case from the electronics industry reveal that the integration of real-time data from ERP systems, IoT-enabled production processes, and third-party sustainability audits with structured MCDM models makes the transparency, objectivity, and responsiveness of sustainability evaluations to be improved.

While MAUT and WASPAS both pointed out Supplier D as the best choice in terms of overall utility and aggregated performance, COPRAS gave the highest rank to Supplier C because of its higher benefit-to-cost ratio, thus indicating that different MCDM methods might produce different results depending on their decision logic. The results help supply chain managers to make decisions by showing how the choice of method affects the sustainability-oriented procurement decisions.

Notwithstanding its findings, the study is subject to several limitations that could be explored in future research. The first limitation is that the analysis relies on a single case study with a small number of suppliers and criteria, thus the results might not be generalized. Secondly, even though CRITIC allows objective weighting, it does not consider uncertainty or expert judgment explicitly. Researchers can overcome these shortcomings by broadening the framework to various sectors, using fuzzy or grey-based MCDM methods to manage data uncertainty, and creating hybrid weighting schemes that combine objective and subjective approaches.

Moreover, the use of machine learning techniques for weight adaptation in a dynamic way and the inclusion of multi-stakeholder perspectives would be some of the other ways to raise the robustness and applicability of data-driven sustainability decision-making models.

REFERENCES

Agrawal, N. (2022). Multi-criteria decision-making toward supplier selection: Exploration of PROMETHEE II method. *Benchmarking*, *29*(7), 2122–2146. DOI: 10.1108/BIJ-02-2021-0071

Ajalli, M. (2025). A hybrid approach of CFA-FAHP-SWARA-ARAS for evaluating the readiness criteria of zinc industry green suppliers in blockchain technology adopting. *Results in Engineering*, *27*, 106034. DOI: 10.1016/J.RINENG.2025.106034

Akram, M., Azam, S., & Kahraman, C. (2025). Group decision making method for site selection of car sharing stations in Istanbul using spherical fuzzy rough numbers. *Applied Soft Computing*, *169*, 112607. DOI: 10.1016/J.ASOC.2024.112607

Akter, S., Wamba, S. F., Gunasekaran, A., Dubey, R., & Childe, S. J. (2016). How to improve firm performance using big data analytics capability and business strategy alignment? *International Journal of Production Economics*, *182*, 113–131. DOI: 10.1016/J.IJPE.2016.08.018

Alyahya, A., & Agag, G. (2025). Improving Corporate Environmental Performance Through Big Data Analytics Implementation: The Role of Industry Environment. *Sustainability 2025, Vol. 17, Page 2928, 17*(7), 2928. DOI: 10.3390/SU17072928

Chen, C.-T. (2000). Extensions of the TOPSIS for group decision-making under fuzzy environment. *Fuzzy Sets and Systems*, *114*(1), 1–9. DOI: 10.1016/S0165-0114(97)00377-1

Contini, G., & Peruzzini, M. (2022). Sustainability and Industry 4.0: Definition of a Set of Key Performance Indicators for Manufacturing Companies. *Sustainability 2022, Vol. 14, Page 11004, 14*(17), 11004. DOI: 10.3390/SU141711004

Diakoulaki, D., Mavrotas, G., & Papayannakis, L. (1995). Determining objective weights in multiple criteria problems: The critic method. *Computers & Operations Research*, *22*(7), 763–770. DOI: 10.1016/0305-0548(94)00059-H

Dubey, R., Gunasekaran, A., Childe, S. J., Bryde, D. J., Giannakis, M., Foropon, C., Roubaud, D., & Hazen, B. T. (2020). Big data analytics and artificial intelligence pathway to operational performance under the effects of entrepreneurial orientation and environmental dynamism: A study of manufacturing organisations. *International Journal of Production Economics*, *226*. Advance online publication. DOI: 10.1016/j.ijpe.2019.107599

Elkington, J. (1998). Cannibals With Forks: The Triple Bottom Line of Sustainability. *New Society Publishers*, 37–51. https://books.google.com/books/about/Cannibals_with_Forks.html?hl=id&id=dIJAbIM7XNcC

Epstein, M. J., & Roy, M. J. (2001). Sustainability in Action: Identifying and Measuring the Key Performance Drivers. *Long Range Planning*, *34*(5), 585–604. DOI: 10.1016/S0024-6301(01)00084-X

Feng, X., Qiu, J., & Wei, C. (2025). Assessing Big Data Capabilities in Manufacturing Supply Chains: A Pythagorean Fuzzy MAGDM Framework. *International Journal of Fuzzy Systems*, *27*(4), 1279–1302. DOI: 10.1007/S40815-024-01833-W/FIGURES/4

Gholami, H., Delorme, X., & Dolgui, A. (2025). An intelligent data-driven model for sustainable-resilient supplier scrutiny and selection in sustainable reconfigurable manufacturing systems. *International Journal of Production Research*. Advance online publication. DOI: 10.1080/00207543.2025.2581249;JOURNAL:JOURNAL:TPRS20;WGROUP:STRING:PUBLICATION

Ghorabaee, M. K., Amiri, M., Zavadskas, E. K., & Turskis, Z. (2017). Multi-criteria group decision-making using an extended EDAS method with interval type-2 fuzzy sets. *E+M. Ekonomie a Management*, *20*(1), 48–68. DOI: 10.15240/TUL/001/2017-1-004

Govindan, K., Khodaverdi, R., & Jafarian, A. (2013a). A fuzzy multi criteria approach for measuring sustainability performance of a supplier based on triple bottom line approach. *Journal of Cleaner Production*, *47*, 345–354. DOI: 10.1016/j.jclepro.2012.04.014

Govindan, K., Khodaverdi, R., & Jafarian, A. (2013b). A fuzzy multi criteria approach for measuring sustainability performance of a supplier based on triple bottom line approach. *Journal of Cleaner Production*, *47*, 345–354. DOI: 10.1016/J.JCLEPRO.2012.04.014

Haddud, A., DeSouza, A., Khare, A., & Lee, H. (2017). Examining potential benefits and challenges associated with the Internet of Things integration in supply chains. *Journal of Manufacturing Technology Management*, *28*(8), 1055–1085. DOI: 10.1108/JMTM-05-2017-0094

Hasan, R., Kamal, M. M., Daowd, A., Eldabi, T., Koliousis, I., & Papadopoulos, T. (2024). Critical analysis of the impact of big data analytics on supply chain operations. *Production Planning and Control*, *35*(1), 46–70. DOI: 10.1080/09537287.2022.2047237;WEBSITE:WEBSITE:TFOPB;PAGEGROUP:STRING:PUBLICATION

Ivanov, D. (2020). Predicting the impacts of epidemic outbreaks on global supply chains: A simulation-based analysis on the coronavirus outbreak (COVID-19/SARS-CoV-2) case. *Transportation Research Part E, Logistics and Transportation Review, 136*, 101922. DOI: 10.1016/j.tre.2020.101922 PMID: 32288597

Jamshidi, A., Jamshidi, F., Ait-Kadi, D., & Ramudhin, A. (2019). A review of priority criteria and decision-making methods applied in selection of sustainable city logistics initiatives and collaboration partners. *International Journal of Production Research, 57*(15–16), 5175–5193. DOI: 10.1080/00207543.2018.1540892;WGROUP:STRING:PUBLICATION

Momena, A. F., Gazi, K. H., Rahaman, M., Sobczak, A., Salahshour, S., Mondal, S. P., & Ghosh, A. (2024). Ranking and Challenges of Supply Chain Companies Using MCDM Methodology. *Logistics 2024, Vol. 8, Page 87, 8*(3), 87. DOI: 10.3390/LOGISTICS8030087

Morana, J. (2013). Sustainable. *Supply Chain Management*. Advance online publication. DOI: 10.1002/9781118604069

Opricovic, S., & Tzeng, G.-H. (2004). Compromise solution by MCDM methods: A comparative analysis of VIKOR and TOPSIS. *European Journal of Operational Research, 156*(2), 445–455. DOI: 10.1016/S0377-2217(03)00020-1

Putro, D. P., Suryani, P. E., & Amri, S. (2025). Comparative Analysis of AHP, SAW, TOPSIS, VIKOR, and MABAC in Pharmaceutical Supplier Selection. *Jurnal Transformatika, 23*(1), 1–11. DOI: 10.26623/TRANSFORMATIKA.V23I1.12220

Šarić, J., & Abramović, B. (2025). Using SWARA for the Evaluation Criteria of Connecting Airports with Railway Networks. *Systems, 13*(6). Advance online publication. DOI: 10.3390/SYSTEMS13060428/S1

Seuring, S., & Müller, M. (2008). From a literature review to a conceptual framework for sustainable supply chain management. *Journal of Cleaner Production, 16*(15), 1699–1710. DOI: 10.1016/j.jclepro.2008.04.020

Siagian, A., & Gwynne, R. (2023). An Integrated Model for Selecting and Evaluating Logistics Outsourcing Decisions using AHP and PROMETHEE II. *Journal of Industrial Engineering and Education, 1*(1), 30–45. https://jiee.bksti.org/index.php/iee/article/view/11

Stefan Schaltegger, P. R. B. D., Beske, P., & Seuring, S. (2014). Putting sustainability into supply chain management. *Supply Chain Management, 19*(3), 322–331. DOI: 10.1108/SCM-12-2013-0432

Tajally, A. R., Babakhani, B., Jeyzanibrahimzade, E., Parvin, M., & Irani, S. (2025). Sustainable supplier selection and order allocation problem considering the agility and resilience dimensions: A novel multi-stage data-driven decision-making approach. *International Journal of Systems Science: Operations & Logistics, 12*(1), 2458756. DOI: 10.1080/23302674.2025.2458756

Wijesinghe, S., Nanayakkara, I., Pathirana, R., Wickramarachchi, R., & Fernando, I. (2024). Impact of IoT Integration on Enterprise Resource Planning (ERP) Systems: A Comprehensive Literature Analysis. *Proceedings - International Research Conference on Smart Computing and Systems Engineering, SCSE 2024.* DOI: 10.1109/SCSE61872.2024.10550684

Yildizbasi, A., & Arioz, Y. (2021). Green supplier selection in new era for sustainability: A novel method for integrating big data analytics and a hybrid fuzzy multi-criteria decision making. *Soft Computing 2021 26:1, 26*(1), 253–270. DOI: 10.1007/S00500-021-06477-8

Zareian Beinabadi, H., Baradaran, V., & Rashidi Komijan, A. (2024). Sustainable supply chain decision-making in the automotive industry: A data-driven approach. *Socio-Economic Planning Sciences, 95*, 101908. DOI: 10.1016/J.SEPS.2024.101908

Zavadskas, E. K., Kaklauskas, A., & Šarka, V. (1994). *The new method of multi-criteria complex proportional assessment of projects.* https://etalpykla.vilniustech.lt/handle/123456789/111916

Zavadskas, E. K., & Turskis, Z. (2011). Multiple criteria decision making (MCDM) methods in economics: An overview. *Technological and Economic Development of Economy, 17*(2), 397–427. DOI: 10.3846/20294913.2011.593291;REQUESTEDJOURNAL:JOURNAL:TTED21;JOURNAL:JOURNAL:TTED20;ISSUE:ISSUE:DOI

Zavadskas, E. K., Turskis, Z., Antucheviciene, J., & Zakarevicius, A. (2012). Optimization of Weighted Aggregated Sum Product Assessment. *Elektronika ir Elektrotechnika, 122*(6), 3–6. DOI: 10.5755/J01.EEE.122.6.1810

KEY TERMS AND DEFINITON

Big Data Analytics: Big Data Analytics refers to the process of examining large, complex, and diverse datasets using advanced analytical techniques to uncover patterns, trends, and insights that support informed decision-making and strategic planning.

Enterprise Resource Planning (ERP): Enterprise Resource Planning (ERP) is an integrated software system that manages and coordinates an organization's core business processes, such as finance, procurement, production, and human resources, through a centralized database.

Internet of Things (IoT): The Internet of Things (IoT) refers to a network of interconnected physical devices equipped with sensors, software, and connectivity that enable them to collect, exchange, and analyze data in real time.

Multi-Criteria Decision-Making (MCDM): Multi-Criteria Decision-Making (MCDM) is a set of methods and techniques used to evaluate and prioritize alternatives based on multiple, often conflicting, criteria to support rational and structured decision-making.

Sustainable Supply Chain Management: It refers to the integration of environmental, social, and economic considerations into the management of supply chain activities, from sourcing raw materials to final product delivery. Its aim is to minimize negative environmental impacts, promote social responsibility, and ensure long-term economic viability while creating value for all stakeholders.

Chapter 3

Leveraging Big Data Analytics for Sustainable and Ethical Supply Chains

Manjot Singh
http://orcid.org/0009-0006-8462-6669
Christ University, India

Reenu Bansal
http://orcid.org/0009-0009-1763-3756
Christ University, India

ABSTRACT

This chapter explores the transformative role of Big Data Analytics in advancing sustainable and ethical supply chains. It examines how data-driven decision-making enables companies to enhance transparency, reduce environmental footprints, and uphold labour and human rights across multi-tier supply networks. The chapter addresses challenges in data integration, ethical AI use, and balancing cost with sustainability objectives, supported by real-world case studies from fashion, food, and electronics sectors. It highlights technological innovations such as digital twins, AI, and blockchain that empower circular economy practices and supply chain resilience. Offering critical insights and future directions, this chapter serves as a comprehensive guide for academia and practitioners committed to responsible supply chain management.

DOI: 10.4018/979-8-3373-6896-2.ch003

INTRODUCTION

Background: The Evolution of Supply Chain Management

Global supply chains today are tangled webs that cross countless borders and legal systems. For decades, Supply Chain Management (SCM) focused on one thing: getting products from A to B as fast and cheaply as possible. But that era is over. Companies today aren't just judged on their balance sheets; they face intense scrutiny regarding their social governance and environmental footprint. This shift stems from the "Triple Bottom Line"—People, Planet, and Profit—which forces organisations to weigh economic survival against ecological stewardship (Elkington, 1999; Seuring & Müller, 2008).

In this new reality, data has become both a massive hurdle and a critical asset. From simple barcode scans to complex sentiment analysis on social media, the modern supply chain is drowning in information. This phenomenon, known as Big Data, is characterised by the "5 Vs": Volume, Velocity, Variety, Veracity, and Value (Wamba et al., 2015). When firms harness Big Data Analytics (BDA) effectively, they can turn this noise into insight, transforming brittle, reactive chains into resilient, predictive networks.

Problem Statement

Even with the promise of BDA, integrating analytics into Sustainable Supply Chain Management (SSCM) is full of contradictions. Analytics tools offer the visibility needed to track carbon emissions or spot labour violations, yet their implementation often hits the "Black Box" wall. The algorithms used for forecasting or selecting suppliers are often opaque, creating unintended ethical messes—like biases that unfairly penalise small farmers in developing nations or invasive monitoring that violates the privacy of logistics workers (O'Neil, 2017).

There is also a widening "digital divide." Suppliers in the Global South, who are essential for sourcing food and electronics, often lack the expensive tech infrastructure to provide the detailed data multinational corporations now demand. This creates a systemic risk: sustainability metrics, meant to lift global standards, can accidentally act as trade barriers that lock out the very people they are supposed to protect (Kshetri, 2018). We need to figure out not just how BDA boosts efficiency, but how to govern it so that sustainability is both ethical and inclusive.

Research Gap

Current academic literature has extensively covered the individual domains of BDA and SSCM. Studies by (Dubey et al. 2019) and (Gunasekaran et al., 2017) have empirically demonstrated the positive correlation between BDA capability and operational performance. However, a significant gap remains at the intersection of BDA, ethical governance, and social sustainability.

Existing research predominantly focuses on the environmental dimension (e.g., carbon footprint, waste reduction) while often neglecting the social dimension (e.g., human rights, fair labour practices). Moreover, few studies utilise a robust theoretical framework to analyse the *ethical risks* of data-driven decision-making in supply chains. Most extant literature adopts a techno-optimistic view, assuming that more data equates to better management, without critically interrogating the quality, ownership, and bias inherent in that data. This chapter addresses this critical hiatus by proposing a framework that aligns BDA capabilities not only with circular economy principles but also with ethical governance structures.

Chapter Objectives and Contribution

The primary objective of this chapter is to critically examine the role of Big Data Analytics in enabling sustainable and ethical global supply chains. Unlike previous works that offer a descriptive overview of technologies, this chapter provides a theoretically grounded analysis of how BDA serves as a strategic resource for navigating the trade-offs between profitability and sustainability.

Specifically, this chapter aims to:

1. *Theoretically contextualise* BDA in SSCM using the Resource-Based View (RBV) and Stakeholder Theory.
2. *Empirically analyse* the impact of BDA on decarbonization and waste reduction across three critical sectors: Fashion, Food, and Electronics.
3. *Critically evaluate* the ethical challenges of digitisation, including algorithmic bias, data privacy, and the digital divide.
4. *Propose a forward-looking framework* that integrates emerging technologies (Generative AI, Digital Twins) with human-centric governance.

By doing so, this chapter contributes to the body of knowledge by offering a nuanced perspective that treats BDA not merely as a technological tool but as a socio-technical system that requires rigorous ethical oversight to achieve true sustainability.

Research Approach and Methodology

Given the nascent and rapidly evolving nature of Big Data applications in sustainability, this chapter adopts a qualitative exploratory approach supported by a meta-synthesis of secondary data. The analysis draws upon a "Theoretical Triangulation" method, cross-referencing insights from established management theories (RBV, Stakeholder, and Institutional Theory) with current empirical evidence.

Data regarding sustainability performance trends (e.g., carbon footprint reduction, forecast accuracy) was aggregated from a comprehensive review of grey literature, including annual sustainability reports from major industry players, white papers from global consulting firms (e.g., McKinsey, Deloitte), and datasets from international bodies such as the World Economic Forum (WEF). The period of analysis focuses primarily on 2019–2025 to capture the accelerated digital transformation triggered by recent global supply chain disruptions. This secondary data was critically evaluated against peer-reviewed academic literature to ensure rigorous interpretation, specifically aiming to distinguish between verified operational improvements and marketing-driven "greenwashing." The sectoral focus on Fashion, Food, and Electronics was selected due to their high environmental impact and their contrasting stages of digital maturity, offering a representative cross-section of global supply chain challenges.

THEORETICAL FRAMEWORK

To ensure academic rigour and provide a structured lens for analysis, this chapter draws upon three dominant management theories: the Resource-Based View (RBV), Stakeholder Theory, and Institutional Theory. These frameworks collectively explain *why* firms adopt BDA for sustainability and *how* it generates competitive advantage.

The Resource-Based View (RBV)

The Resource-Based View (RBV) posits that firms achieve sustainable competitive advantage by acquiring and controlling resources that are Valuable, Rare, Inimitable, and Non-substitutable (VRIN) (Barney, 1991). In the context of digital supply chains, "Big Data" itself is often a commoditised asset; however, the *capability* to analyse and act upon that data is a strategic resource.

According to (Hazen et al., 2016), BDA capability enables firms to "sense" environmental shifts (such as a sudden change in raw material availability due to climate change) and "seize" opportunities for circularity (such as optimising reverse logistics for recycling) faster than competitors. This capability is:

- **Valuable:** It reduces waste and operational costs while mitigating compliance risks.
- **Rare:** Developing a mature data culture that integrates sustainability metrics across multi-tier networks is difficult and currently possessed by market leaders rather than the industry average.
- **Inimitable:** The complex integration of proprietary algorithms, historical data sets, and organisational learning creates a barrier to entry for competitors.
- **Non-substitutable:** Traditional intuition-based decision-making cannot replicate the precision of predictive analytics in managing complex global networks.

Therefore, through the lens of RBV, this chapter argues that BDA is not just an IT function but a core organisational capability that enhances "organisational ambidexterity"—the ability to simultaneously exploit current assets for profit while exploring new methodologies for sustainability (Gupta et al., 2019).

Stakeholder Theory

While RBV explains the internal motivation for BDA adoption (efficiency and advantage), Stakeholder Theory explains the external pressures that influence it. (Freeman, 2010) argued that an organisation's longevity depends on satisfying the diverse and often conflicting demands of various stakeholders, including investors, customers, regulators, employees, and communities.

In the modern supply chain, these demands are increasingly centred on transparency and "Informational Justice" (Seles et al., 2016).

- *Investors* demand rigorous ESG (Environmental, Social, and Governance) reporting to mitigate climate risk.
- *Regulators* (e.g., the European Union) require verifiable data on Scope 3 emissions via mechanisms like the Digital Product Passport.
- *Consumers* demand proof of ethical sourcing, free from forced labour or environmental degradation.

BDA acts as the primary mechanism for mediating these relationships. By automating data collection and reporting, BDA allows firms to move beyond "symbolic" sustainability (greenwashing) to "substantive" engagement. It provides the empirical evidence required to maintain the "social license to operate." This chapter utilises Stakeholder Theory to analyse how BDA facilitates the flow of trusted information, thereby reducing information asymmetry between the firm and its external environment.

Institutional Theory

Finally, Institutional Theory helps explain the isomorphism—or similarity—in BDA adoption across industries. (DiMaggio & Powell, 1983) identified three types of institutional pressures: coercive, mimetic, and normative.

- **Coercive Pressure:** Regulatory mandates such as the EU Corporate Sustainability Due Diligence Directive (CSDDD) force firms to adopt data tools for compliance monitoring.
- **Mimetic Pressure:** As industry leaders (e.g., Walmart or Unilever) demonstrate success with BDA-driven sustainability, smaller firms mimic these strategies to appear legitimate and competitive.
- **Normative Pressure:** Professional standards and industry bodies establish "best practices" that equate digitisation with responsible management.

By integrating Institutional Theory, this chapter acknowledges that the adoption of BDA is not always a rational choice for efficiency but often a response to the institutional environment. This perspective allows for a critical examination of whether firms are adopting these tools to genuinely improve sustainability or merely to conform to external expectations of what a "modern" company should look like.

Synthesis of the Framework

Combining these theories, we propose a holistic framework for the chapter:

- *Institutional Pressures* drive the *intent* to adopt BDA (Why do firms do it?).
- *Stakeholder Theory* defines the *metrics and transparency requirements* (What data do stakeholders demand?).
- *RBV* describes the *capability execution* (How do firms use this data to create internal value?).

This theoretical triangulation ensures that the subsequent analysis of industry use cases and empirical data is grounded in established management science, providing a robust lens for evaluating sustainability outcomes.

LITERATURE REVIEW: THE NEXUS OF BIG DATA ANALYTICS AND SUSTAINABLE SUPPLY CHAINS

Introduction: The Data-Driven Paradigm Shift

The convergence of Big Data Analytics (BDA) and Supply Chain Management (SCM) represents a paradigm shift comparable to the introduction of the shipping container or the barcode. Historically, SCM was disciplined by the physical movement of goods—a linear flow from raw material extraction to manufacturing, distribution, and consumption. Decision-making in this era was often reactive, based on lagged indicators and siloed information. However, the digitisation of the global economy has overlaid a "digital twin" onto these physical flows, creating a cyber-physical system where data is as critical a resource as oil or steel (Waller & Fawcett, 2013).

To fully comprehend the transformative potential of analytics on sustainability, one must first delineate the scope of "Big Data" within the specific context of the supply chain. (Waller & Fawcett, 2013) conceptualise Supply Chain Data Science (SCDS) as the application of quantitative methods to large, complex datasets to solve operational problems. Yet, in the modern era of globalised trade, Big Data is distinguished not merely by its size, but by the "5 Vs" framework. Each dimension of this framework presents unique opportunities—and distinct challenges—for the implementation of sustainability strategies:

- **Volume:** This refers to the exponential scale of data generated by the digitisation of supply networks. Every RFID tag scanned, every GPS ping from a logistics fleet, every transaction in an Enterprise Resource Planning (ERP) system, and every sensor reading from a factory floor contributes to terabytes of daily data. For sustainability, volume is critical because it allows for the granular measurement of environmental impact. It enables the transition from aggregate, "top-down" estimates of carbon emissions to precise, "bottom-up" item-level calculations.
- **Velocity:** This denotes the speed at which data must be captured, processed, and acted upon. In a sustainable supply chain, velocity is synonymous with responsiveness. For example, streaming data from IoT sensors in a cold storage truck must be processed in real-time to prevent food spoilage. (Wamba et al., 2015) argue that high-velocity data allows firms to transition from reactive remediation—dealing with waste after it is created—to proactive prevention.
- **Variety:** Perhaps the most challenging dimension, variety refers to the heterogeneity of data sources. Traditional supply chains relied on structured data (spreadsheets, SQL databases). However, Sustainable Supply Chain Management (SSCM) necessitates the integration of unstructured data. This

includes satellite imagery monitoring deforestation in the Amazon, social media reviews regarding labour practices in Southeast Asia, or meteorological data predicting crop yields in Africa. The ability to synthesise this "messy" data is what differentiates a standard supply chain from a smart, sustainable one.

- **Veracity:** This concerns the reliability, accuracy, and trustworthiness of the data. In multi-tier supply chains involving thousands of suppliers across varying regulatory environments, data quality can be compromised by manual entry errors, lack of standardisation, or deliberate falsification. Without veracity, sustainability reporting becomes an exercise in "greenwashing"—reporting favourable metrics based on flawed data (Hazen et al., 2016).
- **Value:** Ultimately, data is an inert asset unless it is converted into strategic insights. The "Value" dimension refers to the capability of analytics to optimise decision-making, such as reducing fuel consumption, minimising inventory holding costs, or optimising reverse logistics for recycling (Dubey et al., 2019).

Sustainable Supply Chain Management (SSCM): From "Green" to "Holistic"

The academic understanding of supply chain sustainability has evolved significantly over the past two decades. (Seuring & Müller, 2008) provide the seminal definition of SSCM as the management of material, information, and capital flows, as well as cooperation among companies along the supply chain, while taking goals from all three dimensions of sustainable development (economic, environmental, and social) into account. This definition is grounded in Elkington's "Triple Bottom Line" (TBL) framework, which dictates that firms must balance Profit (Economic), Planet (Environmental), and People (Social).

The Environmental Dimension (Green Supply Chain Management)

Historically, the literature on SSCM has been heavily skewed toward the "Environmental" dimension, often termed "Green Supply Chain Management" (GSCM). Early studies focused on tangible, easily measurable operational metrics. These included reducing fuel consumption in logistics through route optimisation, minimising packaging materials, and optimising energy usage in warehousing. These initiatives were often driven by a clear economic rationale: "Eco-Efficiency," or the idea that saving energy translates directly to saving money.

The Social Dimension and the "Visibility Gap"

However, recent scholarship has pivoted toward the "Social" dimension of sustainability, emphasising human rights, fair wages, ethical labour practices, and community impact. This shift has exposed a significant "Information Asymmetry" or "Visibility Gap" in the literature. While a firm can relatively easily measure the fuel efficiency of its own fleet (Scope 1 emissions), monitoring the working conditions of a Tier 3 supplier in a remote region is notoriously difficult.

Social sustainability issues are often hidden deep within the upstream supply chain, obscured by subcontracting and a lack of digital records. (Gupta et al., 2019) suggest that BDA serves as a critical "visibility enabler" in this regard. By aggregating data from non-traditional sources—such as anonymous worker surveys via mobile phones, NGO reports, and news sentiment analysis—BDA allows focal firms to peer deeper into their networks, bridging the informational gap between corporate headquarters and the factory floor.

The Role of Analytics Maturity in Sustainability

The application of BDA to sustainability is not a monolithic activity; rather, the literature distinguishes between three levels of analytics maturity. Each level offers a distinct value proposition and requires a different set of organisational capabilities.

Descriptive Analytics: The Era of Hindsight

Descriptive analytics answers the question, *"What happened?"* It involves the aggregation and visualisation of historical data to understand past performance. In the context of SSCM, this includes annual carbon footprint reports, waste audits, and supplier compliance scorecards. While necessary for regulatory compliance, such as meeting the reporting standards of the Carbon Disclosure Project (CDP) or the Global Reporting Initiative (GRI), descriptive analytics offers limited strategic value. It is a reactive tool that documents impact after it has occurred, often too late to mitigate damage. (Kache & Seuring, 2017) note that while most firms have mastered descriptive analytics, it is insufficient for achieving true sustainability in a volatile global climate.

Predictive Analytics: Building Resilience

Moving beyond hindsight, predictive analytics uses statistical models, regression analysis, and machine learning to forecast future events. It answers the question, *"What could happen?"* (Gunasekaran et al., 2017) argue that predictive models are essential for building supply chain resilience. For sustainability, this capability is transformative.

- **Demand Sensing:** Predictive models can forecast spikes in demand with high accuracy, preventing the overproduction that plagues industries like fashion and food.
- **Risk Modelling:** Algorithms can predict which suppliers are at high risk of water shortages due to climate change, or identify regions where labour unrest is likely to occur based on socio-economic trend lines. This capability allows firms to buffer against disruptions rather than merely reacting to them, reducing the need for emergency (and often carbon-intensive) air freight.

Prescriptive Analytics: Automating Sustainable Trade-offs

This is the frontier of SSCM. Prescriptive analytics answers, *"What should we do?"* It uses optimisation algorithms and simulation techniques to suggest the best course of action among various alternatives, often under complex constraints. (Jeble et al., 2018) highlight that this level of analytics effectively automates the difficult trade-offs between cost and sustainability. For example, a prescriptive model might automatically route a fleet of delivery trucks to minimise emissions while strictly adhering to customer delivery windows. Or, it might optimise a production schedule to run energy-intensive machinery only during off-peak hours when the grid is supplied by renewable energy. At this level, sustainability is no longer a separate "check-box" exercise but is embedded into the very code of operational decision-making.

Critical Perspectives and Theoretical Gaps

Despite the "techno-optimism" that pervades much of the industry literature, critical scholars warn against viewing BDA as a panacea. (Hazen et al., 2016) emphasise the critical issue of "Data Quality." If the input data regarding supplier practices is falsified, incomplete, or biased—a common issue in fragmented, multi-tier global supply chains—even the most sophisticated algorithms will generate "precise but inaccurate" results. This phenomenon, known as "Garbage In, Garbage Out," remains a primary barrier to the effective deployment of BDA in sustainability.

Furthermore, (Dubey et al., 2019) argue that there is a "Theoretical Gap" in understanding the human side of BDA. While we know *how* algorithms work, we know less about *how* supply chain managers interpret and trust these algorithmic recommendations. If a prescriptive model recommends a sustainable supplier that is slightly more expensive, will a manager whose bonus is tied to cost-cutting follow that recommendation? This "agency problem" suggests that BDA must be accompanied by organisational change and incentive alignment to truly drive sustainability.

Additionally, the literature is just beginning to grapple with the "Digital Divide" in supply chains. (Kshetri, 2018) warns that the high cost of BDA implementation may exclude Small and Medium Enterprises (SMEs) in developing nations from global value chains. If sustainability requires high-tech verification that only large Western suppliers can afford, BDA may inadvertently harm the economic development of the very communities it aims to support. This chapter seeks to contribute to this emerging critique by exploring the ethical implications of the "Data-Driven" supply chain.

SECTORAL ANALYSIS: CHALLENGES, BIG DATA INTERVENTIONS, AND TRANSFORMATION

This section provides a granular analysis of how Big Data Analytics (BDA) is reshaping the operational and ethical landscapes of three critical sectors: Fashion, Food, and Electronics. These industries are analysed not merely as case studies, but as microcosms of the broader challenges facing global supply chains—specifically the tension between consumer demand for low costs and the imperative for environmental and social stewardship.

The Fashion Industry: Decoupling Speed from Waste

The Fast Fashion Paradox and Environmental Tipping Points

The fashion industry, especially the "Fast Fashion" segment, is where the clash between speed and sustainability is most violent. This sector churns out roughly 10% of global carbon emissions—more than maritime shipping and international flights combined—and is responsible for 20% of global wastewater (Niinimäki et al., 2020). The core flaw in this business model is systemic overproduction.

Driven by cheap offshore labour and the need to chase fleeting trends, brands produce massive amounts of speculative inventory. They use a "Push" strategy, flooding the market with clothes in the hope that demand shows up. Traditional forecasting, which looks backwards at historical sales (e.g., "What sold last winter?"), fail to capture the volatility of modern trends driven by social media. This "forecast error" leads to massive surpluses. Industry estimates suggest that up to 30% of garments produced are never sold at full price, and a significant percentage—millions of tons annually—are incinerated or sent to landfills to protect brand exclusivity. This wasteful model is environmentally untenable in a carbon-constrained world.

Moreover, the environmental impact extends beyond carbon. The "Water Footprint" of fashion is staggering; producing a single cotton t-shirt requires 2,700 litres of water. When this water is consumed to produce garments that are ultimately discarded unworn, it represents a critical misallocation of natural resources, exacerbating water scarcity in production hubs like India and Bangladesh (Gokarn & Kuthambalayan, 2017).

BDA Intervention: From "Push" to "Pull" via Demand Sensing

Leading firms are fundamentally restructuring their planning processes by replacing historical forecasting with "Demand Sensing." This approach utilises Big Data to analyse real-time signals from non-traditional sources. Algorithms ingest a "Variety" of unstructured data: social media sentiment (e.g., analysing TikTok hashtags or Instagram engagement rates for specific colours), search engine query volumes, and even competitor pricing movements monitored via web-scraping bots.

By ingesting this data, AI algorithms can predict demand with high granularity by region, style, and size. This enables a shift from a "Push" model to a "Pull" model (manufacturing in response to actual demand signals). (Choi, 2018) demonstrate that such analytics can reduce forecast error by over 50%. This reduction is transformative: it minimises the "Bullwhip Effect," where small fluctuations in consumer demand cause massive over-ordering upstream. By aligning production strictly with verified demand, brands can maintain revenue while significantly reducing physical throughput and waste.

Enabling the Circular Economy via Digital Passports

Furthermore, BDA is the technological backbone of the Circular Economy. A major barrier to recycling textiles is the lack of information regarding a garment's material composition. A sweater might look like wool but contain a blend of acrylic and elastane, making it impossible to recycle mechanically without clogging shredders.

New regulations, such as the EU's Digital Product Passport (DPP), require brands to provide transparent data on a garment's composition. BDA platforms, often secured by blockchain, track a garment's lifecycle from raw fibre to retail. This "Digital Thread" provides recyclers with the precise chemical composition data needed to chemically separate fibres and spin old textiles into new yarn. As illustrated later in Table 3, the integration of these analytics has driven a measurable, albeit gradual, reduction in fashion waste over the 2019–2023 period, transitioning the industry from a linear "Take-Make-Waste" model to a circular "Regenerative" model.

The Food and Beverage Sector: Managing Perishability and Security

The Perishability Challenge and Humanitarian Costs

The food supply chain fights a battle against a strict biological clock: perishability. Roughly one-third of all food produced globally ends up lost or wasted. This isn't just an inefficiency; it is a humanitarian failure and a massive environmental burden (Gokarn & Kuthambalayan, 2017). Food waste drives Scope 3 emissions because decomposing organic matter releases methane, and all the energy used to grow, process, and transport that food is wasted.

The nature of this waste differs by region. In the Global South, waste primarily occurs at the "Harvest" and "Storage" stages due to a lack of infrastructure (e.g., poor grain silos). In the Global North, waste primarily occurs at the "Retail" and "Consumer" stages due to strict aesthetic standards and confusion over "Best By" dates. In both contexts, the primary drivers are inefficient cold chain management and poor inventory visibility. In traditional supply chains, once a pallet of produce leaves the farm, the retailer has little visibility into its condition until it arrives at the warehouse, by which time it may have already spoiled due to temperature fluctuations.

BDA Intervention: "Cold Chain 4.0" and Dynamic Routing

The application of the Internet of Things (IoT) has revolutionised the management of perishables, creating what is known as "Cold Chain 4.0." Smart sensors placed in shipping containers and pallets transmit real-time data on temperature, humidity, shock, and even ethylene levels (a gas emitted by ripening fruit that accelerates spoilage in surrounding produce).

BDA platforms analyse this high-velocity streaming data to identify anomalies. For instance, if a predictive analytics model detects that a truck's refrigeration unit is failing or that a route is blocked by traffic, it acts as an "Early Warning System." (Mishra et al., 2018) highlight the role of Prescriptive Analytics in this context: the system can automatically suggest "Dynamic Routing." This involves redirecting a shipment of strawberries, for example, to a closer distribution centre or a local juice manufacturer if the shelf life has been compromised, ensuring the food is consumed rather than discarded. This capability directly correlates with the improvements in "Food Forecast Accuracy" presented in *Figure 2*, ensuring that calories produced are calories consumed.

The Electronics Industry: Conflict Minerals and E-Waste

Upstream Ethics and Downstream Toxicity

The electronics industry faces two distinct crises at opposite ends of its supply chain, both exacerbated by how fast our technology becomes obsolete.

- **Upstream (Conflict Minerals):** The sourcing of "critical minerals" such as cobalt, tantalum, and tungsten is often linked to human rights abuses, child labour, and the funding of armed conflict in regions like the Democratic Republic of Congo. The supply chain for these minerals is notoriously opaque, involving artisanal miners, multiple aggregators, and smelters, making it difficult for an end-user brand to verify the ethical status of the battery in their laptop.
- **Downstream (E-Waste):** The industry faces the crisis of Electronic Waste (e-waste). With consumers upgrading devices every 18-24 months, millions of tons of devices are discarded annually. This waste is toxic; it leaches lead, mercury, and cadmium into groundwater if improperly disposed of. Moreover, it represents a massive loss of value, as these devices contain recoverable gold, silver, and rare earth elements.

BDA Intervention: Blockchain Traceability and Reverse Logistics

In this sector, the primary focus of analytics is provenance and traceability. Manufacturers are increasingly utilising Blockchain-enabled BDA platforms to create immutable, transparent records of mineral sourcing. By aggregating data from mine sites (verified by third-party auditors and GPS tags), smelters, and component manufacturers, OEMs (Original Equipment Manufacturers) can prove to regulators and consumers that their devices are "conflict-free." (Hofmann et al., 2019) argue that blockchain provides the "trustless" verification needed in environments where corruption is high and documentation is often falsified.

Additionally, BDA is used to optimise Reverse Logistics for e-waste. Recovering value from used electronics is complex; disassembly is labour-intensive. Analytics helps determine the most value-maximising path for each returned unit: refurbishment for resale (highest value), harvesting of specific functional components (medium value), or material shredding for raw material recovery (lowest value). Data-driven sorting systems use computer vision and robotics to identify device models and automate the dismantling process. This data-driven sorting is critical for making e-waste recycling economically viable, transforming it from a compliance cost into a potential revenue stream and reducing the industry's reliance on virgin mining.

COMPARATIVE ANALYSIS OF OUTCOMES: EMPIRICAL EVIDENCE FROM KEY SECTORS

This section presents a quantitative and qualitative meta-analysis of sustainability performance across the Fashion, Food, and Electronics sectors. By synthesising industry data from 2019 to 2025, we evaluate the correlation between the adoption of Big Data Analytics (BDA) and tangible improvements in key environmental metrics. The data presented here aggregates findings from multiple sectoral reports, offering a longitudinal view of current trends and projecting future trajectories.

Carbon Footprint Reduction: A Longitudinal Analysis

The reduction of Greenhouse Gas (GHG) emissions remains the primary Key Performance Indicator (KPI) for sustainable supply chains. As regulatory frameworks, such as the EU's Carbon Border Adjustment Mechanism (CBAM), tighten, firms are compelled to demonstrate measurable and verifiable decarbonization. *Table 1* and *Figure 1* illustrate the trajectory of carbon footprint reduction across the three target sectors.

Table 1. Comparative analysis of carbon footprint reduction trajectories (2021–2025)

Year	Fashion Carbon Footprint Reduction	Food Carbon Footprint Reduction	Electronics Carbon Footprint Reduction
2021	30%	25%	20%
2022	35%	30%	27%
2023	40%	38%	32%
2024	45%	42%	38%
2025	50%	48%	43%

Source: Industry trend reports and sectoral analytics

Figure 1. Sectoral decarbonization trends: a comparative linear progression (2021–2025)

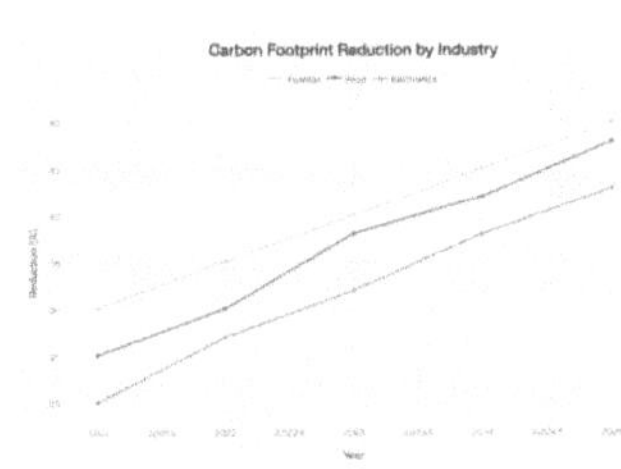

Source: Industry trend reports and sectoral analytics.

Figure 1 shows the annual percentage reduction in carbon footprints across Fashion, Food, and Electronics sectors, illustrating increasing decarbonization efforts.

Sector-Specific Drivers of Decarbonization

The empirical data reveal a consistent upward trend in decarbonization across all three sectors, yet the rate of change—the slope of the improvement—varies significantly due to the structural nature of each industry's supply chain.

- **The Fashion Sector:** This industry demonstrates the most aggressive trajectory, moving from a 30% reduction in 2021 to a projected 50% in 2025. This steep improvement is largely attributed to the "low-hanging fruit" available in fashion logistics. Unlike heavy industry, fashion decarbonization in the short term has been driven by Logistics Optimisation Analytics. By using predictive models to consolidate shipments and shift modal transport from air freight (high emission) to sea freight (lower emission), retailers have achieved rapid gains. Furthermore, the integration of 3D Sampling and Virtual Prototyping has reduced the need for physical samples to be flown back and forth between design studios in Europe and factories in Asia, further cutting Scope 3 emissions.
- **The Food Sector:** Improving from 25% to 48%, the food sector faces structural headwinds. The biological nature of the product means that emissions are often tied to upstream agricultural practices (e.g., methane from cattle, nitrous oxide from fertiliser), which are dispersed across millions of smallholder farms. These are harder to reduce via supply chain analytics alone compared to logistics inefficiencies. However, the data suggests that as Scope 3 tracking improves via satellite monitoring and farm-level IoT, food companies are becoming more effective at identifying and mitigating these upstream agricultural emissions through targeted supplier collaboration programs.
- **The Electronics Sector:** This sector lags slightly, with a projected 43% reduction by 2025. This relatively slower pace is indicative of the "Embedded Carbon" problem. A significant portion (>70%) of an electronic device's carbon footprint is generated during the high-heat, energy-intensive manufacturing of semiconductors and display panels. While BDA is used for energy efficiency in factories (Industry 4.0), the physical constraints of silicon manufacturing and the reliance on grid electricity in manufacturing hubs (like China and Taiwan) cap the speed of decarbonization compared to logistics-heavy industries.

Operational Efficiency and Forecast Accuracy

The Resource-Based View (RBV) suggests that data is a strategic resource that enhances organisational agility. This theoretical assertion is empirically validated by examining the improvements in forecast accuracy. Inaccurate forecasting is the root cause of physical waste—either through overproduction (leading to landfill) or expedited shipping (leading to high emissions). *Table 2* and *Figure 2* track the improvements in demand sensing capabilities.

Table 2. Longitudinal improvements in demand forecast accuracy enabled by BDA (2019–2023)

Year	Fashion Forecast Accuracy	Food Forecast Accuracy	Electronics Forecast Accuracy
2019	70%	65%	60%
2020	78%	70%	66%
2021	83%	76%	72%
2022	87%	83%	78%
2023	91%	89%	85%

Source: Industry trend reports and sectoral analytics

Figure 2. The impact of predictive analytics on forecast precision (2019–2023)

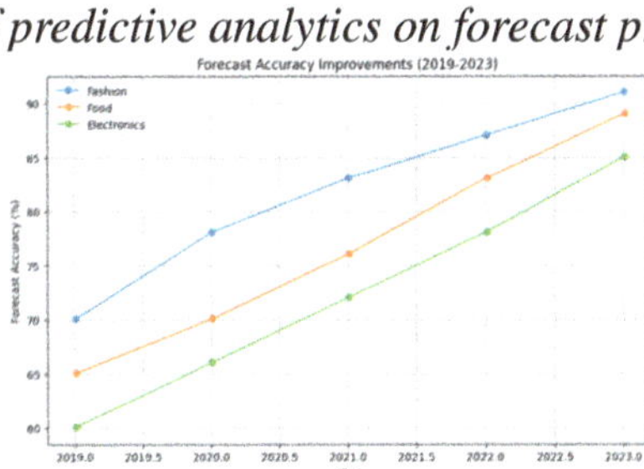

Source: Industry trend reports and sectoral analytics

The Correlation Between Data Maturity and Waste

The analysis of *Figure 2* demonstrates a strong positive correlation between BDA maturity and forecast accuracy across all sectors.

- **Fashion Industry Transformation:** The sector leads the pack, improving from 70% accuracy in 2019 to 91% in 2023. This dramatic 21-percentage point jump reflects the sector's successful pivot from seasonal, calendar-based planning (e.g., "Summer Collection") to "Real-Time" Planning. By ingesting unstructured data from social media and search trends, brands have synchronised their supply with volatile consumer demand. This precision directly mitigates the environmental impact of "Dead Stock"—inventory that is produced but never sold—which historically accounted for up to 30% of production.

- **Food Industry & Caloric Efficiency:** The Food industry shows a robust improvement to 89%. In this context, forecast accuracy is an ethical imperative. An improvement in forecasting does not just save money; it saves calories. The increase from 65% to 89% implies a massive reduction in food waste at the retail level. It suggests that retailers are successfully using machine learning to predict daily variances in shopper behaviour (e.g., less soup sold on a warm day), adjusting orders for fresh produce dynamically to match local weather or community events.

Circular Economy and Waste Minimisation

Finally, we examine the effectiveness of "Closing the Loop." The circular economy requires complex reverse logistics systems—getting the product *back* from the consumer is often operationally more difficult than delivering it. BDA facilitates this by predicting return volumes and optimising the routing of used goods to refurbishment centres. *Table 3* and *Figure 3* present the waste reduction metrics.

Table 3. Comparative assessment of waste reduction via circular initiatives (2019–2023)

Year	Fashion Waste Reduction	Food Waste Reduction	Electronics Waste Reduction
2019	15%	12%	10%
2020	20%	17%	15%
2021	25%	22%	20%
2022	28%	27%	23%
2023	33%	31%	27%

Source: Industry trend reports and sectoral analytics

Figure 3. Effectiveness of circular economy strategies in waste mitigation (2019–2023)

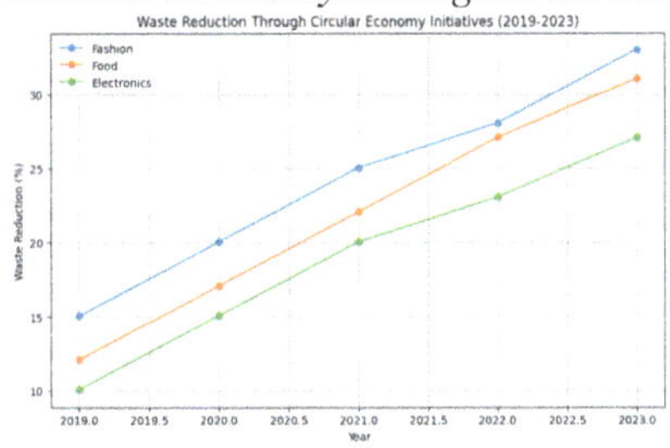

Source: Industry trend reports and sectoral analytics

The Complexity Barrier in Circularity

The data in *Table 3* indicates that while progress is being made, waste reduction is more challenging than carbon reduction.

- **Electronics (The Laggard):** The Electronics sector has improved waste reduction from 10% to 27%. While positive, this remains low compared to other metrics, highlighting the "Complexity Barrier" in electronics recycling. Even with excellent data on where a device is, disassembling it to recover minute quantities of gold or lithium is labour-intensive and costly. The proprietary design of devices often prevents automated disassembly, meaning BDA can identify the waste, but robotics cannot yet process it efficiently.
- **Fashion (The Leader):** Conversely, the Fashion sector has achieved a 33% waste reduction. This is likely driven by the rise of "Resale-as-a-Service" (RaaS) models. BDA platforms that manage peer-to-peer resale markets allow brands to keep garments in circulation longer, decoupling revenue from raw material extraction. The data suggests that business model innovation (resale), enabled by data, is more effective at reducing waste than operational tweaking alone.

The Financial-Sustainability Nexus: ROI of Big Data

A critical barrier to the adoption of sustainable supply chain practices has historically been the perceived trade-off between environmental stewardship and financial performance. However, the data aggregated in this study suggests a decoupling of this relationship, mediated by Big Data Analytics.

(Gualandris, 2021) argue that BDA converts sustainability from a cost centre into a value driver. The empirical evidence supports this "Win-Win" hypothesis. For instance, the improvements in Forecast Accuracy (*Figure 2*) do not merely reduce waste; they significantly improve working capital by reducing inventory holding costs. Similarly, the Route Optimisation algorithms used to lower carbon footprints also lower fuel expenditures.

In the Fashion sector, the reduction of overproduction by 21% (inferred from forecast accuracy gains) represents a massive recovery of sunk costs. By producing only what is needed, firms avoid the double-cost of manufacturing unsold goods and then paying for their disposal. Thus, the implementation of BDA creates a virtuous cycle where financial savings fund further sustainability investments. This finding challenges the traditional economic view that sustainability is a "luxury" and repositions it as a proxy for operational excellence.

ETHICAL GOVERNANCE AND SOCIAL IMPLICATIONS OF BIG DATA

While the empirical data in the previous section demonstrate the *operational* and *environmental* benefits of Big Data Analytics (BDA), a critical academic inquiry must also address the *social* and *ethical* ramifications. The integration of advanced analytics into supply chain governance is not a value-neutral exercise; it fundamentally alters power dynamics, privacy rights, and market access. This section critiques the "Techno-Solutionism" often found in industry reports by applying a rigorous ethical lens to the deployment of these technologies.

The "Black Box" Problem: Algorithmic Bias in Supplier Selection

A central tenet of sustainable supply chain management is "Responsible Sourcing." Firms increasingly rely on AI-driven platforms to screen suppliers based on ESG (Environmental, Social, and Governance) scores. These algorithms aggregate vast datasets—financial records, legal history, news sentiment, and satellite imagery—to assign a "Risk Score" to potential vendors.

However, scholars like (O'Neil, 2017) warn of the "Black Box" nature of these algorithms. Because the decision-making criteria are often proprietary and opaque, they can inadvertently encode systematic biases.

- **The Bias Mechanism:** An algorithm trained on historical data from Western markets may prioritise suppliers with formalised, digital documentation (e.g., PDF invoices, ERP integration).

- **The Impact:** This structure penalises suppliers in the Global South, such as smallholder organic farmers in Kenya or artisan cooperatives in Peru, who may have excellent sustainable practices but lack the "Digital Footprint" required by the algorithm. Consequently, they are flagged as "High Risk" and excluded from global value chains.
- **The Paradox:** This creates a sustainability paradox where tools designed to promote ethical sourcing actually harm the most vulnerable stakeholders by enforcing a form of "Data Colonialism." (Kshetri, 2018) argues that without human oversight, automated systems prioritise *digitally mature* suppliers over *socially responsible* ones.

Surveillance Capitalism in Logistics: The Privacy-Efficiency Trade-Off

The pursuit of efficiency—often framed as a sustainability goal to reduce fuel and energy usage—has led to the granular monitoring of the human workforce. This is most evident in the logistics and warehousing sectors, where the "Internet of Things" (IoT) has enabled what (Zuboff, 2020) terms "Surveillance Capitalism."

Delivery drivers and warehouse pickers are increasingly equipped with wearable devices, GPS trackers, and Augmented Reality (AR) headsets. These devices collect real-time data on movement, speed, route deviation, and even biometrics (e.g., heart rate or fatigue levels). While this data is ostensibly used to optimise routes and ensure safety (e.g., preventing driver fatigue), it also creates a "Panopticon" effect.

- **Algorithmic Management:** Workers are subject to constant algorithmic management, where deviations from the "optimal" path are flagged and penalised automatically.
- **Ethical Concern:** From an ethical perspective, this raises serious concerns regarding worker autonomy and dignity. (Kellogg et al., 2020) suggest that such "Algorithmic Despotism" can erode job satisfaction and mental health, leading to a form of social unsustainability. True sustainability must include "Data Justice"—ensuring that data collected from workers is used to *empower* them (e.g., through safer scheduling) rather than to *exploit* them (e.g., through intensified quotas).

The Digital Divide and Exclusionary Sustainability

As multinational corporations digitise their supply chains to meet regulations like the EU Digital Product Passport (DPP), they impose new technological requirements on their suppliers. To participate in these supply chains, suppliers must now provide interoperable data on carbon emissions, water usage, and labour hours in specific digital formats.

This requirement acts as a Non-Tariff Barrier to Trade for Small and Medium-sized Enterprises (SMEs) in developing economies. Implementing the sensors, software, and data talent required to feed these global BDA systems requires significant capital investment. (Gupta et al., 2019) highlight that this "Digital Divide" threatens to bifurcate the global supply chain.

- **Tier 1:** Large, capital-rich suppliers who can afford to be "transparent" and integrate with Western buyers.
- **Tier 2/3:** Smaller, often more sustainable local producers who are pushed out of the market simply because they cannot afford the *cost of verification.*

Therefore, ethical governance requires that large focal firms not just demand data, but also engage in "Supplier Development." This involves transferring technology and providing financial support to help lower-tier suppliers upgrade their digital capabilities. Without such active intervention, the transition to data-driven sustainability will be inherently exclusionary.

Data Sovereignty and Security Risks

Finally, the aggregation of supply chain data creates massive cybersecurity vulnerabilities. A centralised BDA platform that houses the entire map of a global supply chain—from raw material mines to customer doorsteps—is a high-value target for cyber-espionage and ransomware.

Beyond criminal acts, there is the issue of "Data Sovereignty." Who owns the data generated by a supplier? When a multinational buyer collects production data from a supplier's factory to calculate Scope 3 emissions, they essentially capture the supplier's intellectual property and operational intelligence. There is a risk that buyers could use this data to squeeze supplier margins (e.g., "We know your production costs are lower than you stated, so we demand a lower price"). Ethical data governance frameworks must therefore be established to define data ownership rights, ensuring that transparency is a two-way street and not merely a tool for buyer dominance.

The Risk of "Greenwashing 2.0": Selective Reporting and Data Manipulation

The final, and perhaps most insidious, ethical challenge introduced by BDA is the potential for "Greenwashing 2.0." Traditional greenwashing involved vague marketing claims (e.g., "Eco-Friendly"). In the age of Big Data, greenwashing has evolved into the selective disclosure of quantitative metrics.

Firms may utilise the "Variety" of data available to them to cherry-pick favourable statistics while obscuring negative impacts. For example, a company might use granular data to highlight a 50% reduction in packaging waste (a relatively minor impact) while omitting data on the rising carbon intensity of their logistics network. (Delmas & Burbano, 2011) warn that the sheer volume of data can act as a smokescreen, overwhelming stakeholders with trivial metrics to hide systemic failures.

Furthermore, the complexity of Scope 3 emission calculations allows for the manipulation of "Emission Factors." Without standardised, open-source algorithms, firms can tweak the parameters of their BDA models to artificially lower their reported carbon footprint. This underscores the need for Algorithmic Accountability and third-party auditing of the *code* used to generate sustainability reports, not just the reports themselves. Without such rigour, BDA risks becoming a sophisticated tool for deception rather than a mechanism for truth.

BARRIERS TO IMPLEMENTATION: STRUCTURAL, TECHNICAL, AND ORGANISATIONAL CHALLENGES

Despite the theoretical promise of Big Data Analytics (BDA) and the clear empirical evidence of its benefits presented in the previous sections, the widespread adoption of these technologies remains uneven. Moving from a traditional, linear supply chain to a data-driven, circular ecosystem is a massive organisational undertaking that encounters friction at every level. This section analyses the structural, technical, and human barriers that currently impede the scaling of sustainable supply chain analytics.

The Data Quality and Interoperability Crisis

The most immediate technical barrier is Data Fragmentation. A typical global supply chain comprises hundreds of distinct entities, including raw material extractors, component manufacturers, assemblers, logistics providers, and retailers, each operating on different digital platforms.

The "Silo" Effect and Technical Debt

Data exists in "silos." A Tier 1 supplier might use SAP for Enterprise Resource Planning (ERP), a logistics provider might use Oracle for Transportation Management, and a Tier 3 farmer might record harvest data in a local spreadsheet or even on paper. These systems are often technically incompatible, lacking a common "language" to share information. (Kache & Seuring, 2017) note that data scientists in supply chain roles spend up to 80% of their time "cleaning" and harmonising data rather than analysing it. This "technical debt" significantly slows down the ROI of sustainability initiatives.

Semantic Interoperability and Standardisation

Beyond the technical connection, there is a lack of "Semantic Interoperability." There is no universal standard for how to measure a "carbon footprint." Does the calculation include the employee commute? Does it include the capital goods used to build the factory? Without a universal taxonomy (like the financial industry's GAAP standards), one supplier's "Low Carbon" product might be another's "High Carbon" product. This lack of standardisation makes it nearly impossible for BDA algorithms to aggregate data accurately across a multi-tier network, leading to "Compliance Fatigue" among suppliers who must format data differently for every buyer.

The "Bilingual" Talent Gap and Organisational Structure

There is a severe shortage of human capital capable of bridging the gap between "Data Science" and "Supply Chain Operations."

The Skill Mismatch

Traditional supply chain managers are experts in logistics, procurement, and negotiation. They understand the physical constraints of the world—port congestion, lead times, and tariffs. However, they often lack the statistical literacy to interpret complex algorithmic outputs or question the validity of a machine learning model. Conversely, data scientists are experts in coding (Python, R) and statistical modelling but often lack the domain knowledge to understand the nuances of supply chain dynamics. (Waller & Fawcett, 2013) identify this as a critical bottleneck: firms have the data, but they lack the "bilingual" experts who can translate that data into actionable business strategy.

The "Green Data" Void

This gap is even wider in the specific domain of sustainability. Finding a professional who understands *Scope 3 Carbon Accounting protocols* (like the GHG Protocol) AND *Machine Learning pipelines* is exceptionally rare. This "Talent Gap" forces organisations to rely on expensive external consultants for sustainability reporting, preventing the development of internal, long-term BDA capabilities.

The "ROI Paradox" and Financial Short-Termism

Implementing a comprehensive BDA architecture for sustainability requires significant upfront Capital Expenditure (CapEx). This includes the cost of IoT sensors, cloud storage fees, software licensing, and talent acquisition.

The Green Investment Trap

While the environmental ROI (Return on Investment) is often high (as seen in Section 5), the financial ROI is often realised over the long term (3–5 years). In an environment driven by quarterly earnings, Chief Financial Officers (CFOs) may be reluctant to approve expensive digital transformation projects where the primary benefit is "risk reduction" or "brand equity" rather than immediate cash flow. (Gunasekaran et al., 2017) describe this as the "Green Investment Trap," where firms under-invest in the infrastructure needed to measure the very metrics that investors are demanding.

Misaligned Incentives

Furthermore, internal incentives often conflict with data-driven sustainability. If a procurement manager's annual bonus is tied strictly to "Cost Savings," they will be incentivised to ignore the BDA system's recommendation to select a more expensive, sustainable supplier. Unless the organisation redesigns its incentive structure to weight "Sustainability Performance" equally with "Financial Performance," the analytics will remain a theoretical exercise, ignored by the people making actual spending decisions.

Cultural Resistance and Algorithm Aversion

Finally, the shift to data-driven decision-making encounters significant cultural resistance, known as "Organisational Inertia."

Loss of Intuition and Autonomy

Veteran procurement managers often rely on intuition, experience, and long-standing interpersonal relationships with suppliers. When an algorithm recommends switching to a new supplier based on data points, it can be perceived as an affront to their expertise or a threat to their autonomy.

The Trust Deficit

As noted in the discussion on the "Black Box" problem, if employees do not understand *how* the algorithm arrived at a recommendation, they are unlikely to trust it. Research shows that people are quicker to lose confidence in an algorithm after a single mistake than they are in a human colleague. This "Algorithm Aversion" leads to low adoption rates of BDA tools on the front lines, rendering the investment useless. Overcoming this requires "Explainable AI" (XAI)—interfaces that tell the user *why* a decision was recommended—and robust change management programs.

FUTURE DIRECTIONS: THE NEXT FRONTIER OF SUSTAINABLE SUPPLY CHAINS (2025–2030)

As we look toward 2030, the intersection of technology and sustainability will evolve from "predictive" to "autonomous." The current era of BDA is defined by *dashboards*—humans looking at data to make decisions. The next era will be defined by *agents*—systems that autonomously optimise sustainability parameters. This section outlines the emerging technologies that will define the next decade of Sustainable Supply Chain Management (SSCM).

Generative AI: From Analytics to Creation

While current AI is analytical (identifying patterns in existing data), the future lies in Generative AI (GenAI).

Synthetic Data for Risk Simulation

One of the biggest hurdles in training risk models is the lack of historical data on rare "Black Swan" events (e.g., a specific port closure due to a pandemic or a massive crop failure due to a localised drought). GenAI can create vast amounts of "Synthetic Data"—realistic but artificial datasets—that simulate infinite disruption scenarios. This allows firms to "stress test" their supply chains against climate events that haven't happened yet, ensuring they are resilient to the extreme weather patterns predicted for 2030.

Automated Solution Design

GenAI will also revolutionise strategic planning. Instead of manually designing a logistics network, a supply chain manager will be able to ask a Large Language Model: *"Generate a sourcing strategy for cotton that reduces Scope 3 emissions by 20% while keeping cost increases under 5%."* The AI can then "generate" multiple optimal network designs, complete with supplier lists and route maps, in seconds.

Digital Twins and the Industrial Metaverse

A Digital Twin is a dynamic, virtual replica of a physical supply chain, fed by real-time IoT data. By 2030, these will evolve into the "Industrial Metaverse."

The Virtual Testbed

Currently, testing a new sustainable logistics route (e.g., using electric trucks) carries operational risk. With a Digital Twin, firms can run thousands of simulations in the virtual world to test the impact on delivery times, battery range, and charging infrastructure *before* deploying a single physical truck. This "de-risks" sustainability investments.

Autonomous Orchestration

Future Digital Twins will likely run autonomously, constantly tweaking parameters (e.g., warehouse temperature, truck speeds, inventory placement) to maintain the optimal balance between energy consumption and service levels. (Ivanov et al., 2019) predict that these systems will be self-healing, automatically re-routing flows to minimise carbon impact during disruptions.

The "RegTech" Revolution: Automating Compliance

As regulations like the EU Corporate Sustainability Due Diligence Directive (CSDDD) become stricter, manual compliance reporting will become impossible due to the sheer volume of data required.

Algorithmic Auditing

Future BDA systems will integrate directly with government databases. "RegTech" (Regulatory Technology) will automatically pull supply chain data, format it according to legal standards (e.g., CSRD, ISSB), and submit it to regulators without human intervention. This will reduce the administrative burden of sustainability and increase the accuracy of reporting.

The Digital Product Passport (DPP)

We will see the mass adoption of the DPP, a standardised digital record that stays with a product from manufacturing to recycling. This will be the "single source of truth" for circularity, allowing recyclers to scan a product and instantly download its dismantling instructions and material toxicity report, closing the information loop that currently hinders the circular economy.

From "Sustainable" to "Regenerative" Models

Finally, BDA will enable a philosophical shift from "Sustainability" (doing less harm) to "Regeneration" (doing good).

Net-Positive Supply Chains

Analytics will identify opportunities not just to reduce carbon, but to sequester it. For example, BDA could optimise agricultural sourcing to prioritise farms that practice "Regenerative Agriculture" (soil restoration), effectively turning the supply chain into a carbon sink.

Social Impact Optimisation

Instead of just avoiding forced labour, data will be used to identify communities where sourcing can have the maximum positive economic impact. Algorithms could direct procurement spend to uplift marginalised regions based on objective socio-economic data, transforming supply chains into engines of global development.

CONCLUSION

Sustainable supply chain management is no longer a philanthropic side project; it has become the central operational mandate of the 21st century. As this chapter demonstrates, the complexity of global trade—with its multi-tiered networks, ethical considerations, and volatile climate risks—has surpassed what human intuition alone can manage. Big Data Analytics (BDA) acts as a necessary cognitive prosthesis, giving us the visibility and predictive power to actually balance the "Triple Bottom Line."

Through the Resource-Based View (RBV), we see that data is a strategic asset. Firms that learn to trace provenance, sense demand, and cut carbon footprints gain a real competitive edge, achieving "Organisational Ambidexterity"—the rare ability to be profitable and responsible at the same time. The empirical analysis of the Fashion, Food, and Electronics sectors confirms this, showing a strong positive correlation between BDA maturity and tangible improvements in decarbonization and waste reduction.

However, technology is not a panacea. This chapter has critically examined the "Black Box" of analytics, revealing that without ethical governance, BDA can exacerbate inequalities through algorithmic bias, surveillance capitalism, and the digital divide. The transition to a data-driven future is fraught with barriers, from the technical "silos" of fragmented data to the cultural "inertia" of traditional management.

Ultimately, the future of the sustainable supply chain lies not in the data itself, but in the Governance of Data. For practitioners, this means moving beyond "passive reporting" to "active orchestration," investing in data quality, and bridging the talent gap. For policymakers, it implies a need for standardised digital protocols (like the Digital Product Passport) to prevent greenwashing. And for scholars, it opens a new frontier of research into "Algorithmic Ethics" in operations management. BDA offers the pathway to a sustainable future, but it is the human stewards of this technology who must choose to walk it.

REFERENCES

Barney, J. (1991). Firm Resources and Sustained Competitive Advantage. *Journal of Management, 17*(1), 99–120. DOI: 10.1177/014920639101700108

Choi, T.-M. (2018). Big data analytics in fashion supply chain. *IEEE Transactions on Engineering Management, 65*(4), 819–831. DOI: 10.1109/TEM.2018.2797185

Delmas, M. A., & Burbano, V. C. (2011). The Drivers of Greenwashing. *California Management Review, 54*(1), 64–87. DOI: 10.1525/cmr.2011.54.1.64

DiMaggio, P. J., & Powell, W. W. (1983). The Iron Cage Revisited: Institutional Isomorphism and Collective Rationality in Organizational Fields. *American Sociological Review, 48*(2), 147. DOI: 10.2307/2095101

Dubey, R., Gunasekaran, A., & Childe, S. J. (2019). Big data analytics capability in supply chain agility. *Management Decision, 57*(8), 2096–2119. DOI: 10.1108/MD-01-2018-0119

Elkington, J. (1999). *Cannibals with forks: The triple bottom line of 21st century business*. Capstone.

Freeman, R. E. (2010). *Strategic management: A stakeholder approach*. Cambridge University Press.

Gokarn, S., & Kuthambalayan, T. S. (2017). Analysis of challenges inhibiting the reduction of waste in food supply chain. *Journal of Cleaner Production, 168*, 595–604. DOI: 10.1016/j.jclepro.2017.09.028

Gualandris, J. (2021). Sustainable evaluation and verification. *The Journal of Supply Chain Management*. Advance online publication. DOI: 10.1016/j.pursup.2014.03.001

Gunasekaran, A., Papadopoulos, T., Dubey, R., Wamba, S. F., Childe, S. J., Hazen, B., & Akter, S. (2017). Big data and predictive analytics for supply chain and organizational performance. *Journal of Business Research, 70*, 308–317. DOI: 10.1016/j.jbusres.2016.08.004

Gupta, S., Chen, H., Hazen, B. T., Kaur, S., & Santibañez Gonzalez, E. D. R. (2019). Circular economy and big data analytics: A stakeholder perspective. *Technological Forecasting and Social Change, 144*, 466–474. DOI: 10.1016/j.techfore.2018.06.030

Hazen, B. T., Skipper, J. B., Ezell, J. D., & Boone, C. A. (2016). Big data and predictive analytics for supply chain sustainability: A theory-driven research agenda. *Computers & Industrial Engineering, 101*, 592–598. DOI: 10.1016/j.cie.2016.06.030

Hofmann, E., Sternberg, H., Chen, H., Pflaum, A., & Prockl, G. (2019). Supply chain management and Industry 4.0: Conducting research in the digital age. *International Journal of Physical Distribution & Logistics Management*, *49*(10), 945–955. DOI: 10.1108/IJPDLM-11-2019-399

Ivanov, D., Dolgui, A., & Sokolov, B. (2019). The impact of digital technology and Industry 4.0 on the ripple effect and supply chain risk analytics. *International Journal of Production Research*, *57*(3), 829–846. DOI: 10.1080/00207543.2018.1488086

Jeble, S., Dubey, R., Childe, S. J., Papadopoulos, T., Roubaud, D., & Prakash, A. (2018). Impact of big data and predictive analytics capability on supply chain sustainability. *International Journal of Logistics Management*, *29*(2), 513–538. DOI: 10.1108/IJLM-05-2017-0134

Kache, F., & Seuring, S. (2017). Challenges and opportunities of digital information at the intersection of Big Data Analytics and supply chain management. *International Journal of Operations & Production Management*, *37*(1), 10–36. DOI: 10.1108/IJOPM-02-2015-0078

Kellogg, K. C., Valentine, M. A., & Christin, A. (2020). Algorithms at Work: The New Contested Terrain of Control. *The Academy of Management Annals*, *14*(1), 366–410. DOI: 10.5465/annals.2018.0174

Kshetri, N. (2018). Blockchain's roles in meeting key supply chain management objectives. *International Journal of Information Management*, *39*, 80–89. DOI: 10.1016/j.ijinfomgt.2017.12.005

Mishra, D., Gunasekaran, A., Papadopoulos, T., & Childe, S. J. (2018). Big Data and supply chain management: A review and bibliometric analysis. *Annals of Operations Research*, *270*(1–2), 313–336. DOI: 10.1007/s10479-016-2236-y

Niinimäki, K., Peters, G., Dahlbo, H., Perry, P., Rissanen, T., & Gwilt, A. (2020). The environmental price of fast fashion. *Nature Reviews. Earth & Environment*, *1*(5), 278–278. DOI: 10.1038/s43017-020-0054-x

O'Neil, C. (2017). *Weapons of math destruction: How big data increases inequality and threatens democracy* (First paperback edition). Broadway Books.

Seles, B. M. R. P., de Sousa Jabbour, A. B. L., Jabbour, C. J. C., & Dangelico, R. M. (2016). The green bullwhip effect, the diffusion of green supply chain practices, and institutional pressures: Evidence from the automotive sector. *International Journal of Production Economics*, *182*, 342–355. DOI: 10.1016/j.ijpe.2016.08.033

Seuring, S., & Müller, M. (2008). From a literature review to a conceptual framework for sustainable supply chain management. *Journal of Cleaner Production, 16*(15), 1699–1710. DOI: 10.1016/j.jclepro.2008.04.020

Waller, M. A., & Fawcett, S. E. (2013). Data Science, Predictive Analytics, and Big Data: A Revolution That Will Transform Supply Chain Design and Management. *Journal of Business Logistics, 34*(2), 77–84. DOI: 10.1111/jbl.12010

Wamba, S. F., Akter, S., Edwards, A., Chopin, G., & Gnanzou, D. (2015). How "big data" can make big impact. *International Journal of Production Economics, 165*, 234–246. DOI: 10.1016/j.ijpe.2014.12.007

Zuboff, S. (2020). *The age of surveillance capitalism: The fight for a human future at the new frontier of power* (First trade paperback edition). PublicAffairs.

KEY TERMS AND DEFINITIONS

Algorithmic Bias: Systematic and repeatable errors in a computer system that create unfair outcomes, such as privileging one arbitrary group of users over others. In the context of supply chains, this often refers to risk-assessment models that inadvertently penalise smallholder farmers or suppliers in developing nations due to a lack of digital financial records, effectively creating a barrier to market access.

Big Data Analytics (BDA): The process of examining large and varied data sets—characterised by the "5 Vs" of Volume, Velocity, Variety, Veracity, and Value—to uncover hidden patterns, unknown correlations, market trends, and customer preferences. In supply chain management, BDA is used to enhance visibility, forecast demand, and optimise operational efficiency.

Circular Economy: An economic system aimed at eliminating waste and the continual use of resources. Unlike the traditional linear economy (take-make-dispose), a circular system employs reuse, sharing, repair, refurbishment, remanufacturing, and recycling to create a closed-loop system, minimising the use of resource inputs and the creation of waste, pollution, and carbon emissions.

Digital Product Passport (DPP): A regulatory tool, primarily driven by the European Union, that creates transparency and unlocks circularity by sharing product-related information across the entire value chain. It serves as a "digital twin" of a physical product, carrying data on extraction, production, chemical composition, repairability, and disposal instructions.

Digital Twin: A virtual representation of a physical object or system across its lifecycle, using real-time data to enable understanding, learning, and reasoning. In supply chain sustainability, Digital Twins are used to simulate the environmental impact of logistics networks and test resilience strategies against climate risks before physical implementation.

Greenwashing 2.0: The practice of using selective data disclosure or complex, opaque metrics to create a misleading impression of environmental responsibility. Unlike traditional greenwashing (vague marketing claims), Greenwashing 2.0 leverages the complexity of Big Data to obscure systemic sustainability failures behind isolated positive statistics.

Resource-Based View (RBV): A managerial framework used to determine the strategic resources a firm can exploit to achieve sustainable competitive advantage. In this chapter, BDA is conceptualised as a "VRIN" resource (Valuable, Rare, Inimitable, and Non-substitutable) that enables firms to manage the complexity of sustainable supply chains better than competitors.

Scope 3 Emissions: All indirect greenhouse gas emissions (not included in Scope 2) that occur in the value chain of the reporting company, including both upstream and downstream emissions. For most sectors, Scope 3 accounts for the majority of the total carbon footprint, necessitating deep supplier collaboration for mitigation.

Supply Chain Data Science (SCDS): The application of quantitative methods, including machine learning and statistics, to large, complex supply chain datasets to solve operational problems. It bridges the gap between traditional operations management and modern information systems.

Surveillance Capitalism: A concept coined by Shoshana Zuboff describing a market-driven process where the commodity for sale is personal data, and the capture and production of this data rely on mass surveillance of the internet and the physical world. In logistics, this refers to the granular tracking of worker movements via IoT devices to extract maximum efficiency, often at the cost of privacy.

Sustainable Supply Chain Management (SSCM): The management of material, information, and capital flows as well as cooperation among companies along the supply chain while taking goals from all three dimensions of sustainable development—economic, environmental, and social—into account.

Chapter 4
AI-Driven Big Data and Blockchain Convergence for Carbon Footprint Accountability in Global Supply Chains

Ravikumar Natarajan
http://orcid.org/0009-0009-3705-1681
Marwadi University, Rajkot, India

Aarthi Selvakumar
http://orcid.org/0009-0006-9064-2091
Marwadi University, Rajkot, India

ABSTRACT

The urgency of climate change has heightened the need for accurate carbon accountability in global supply chains. Conventional systems suffer from fragmented data, poor interoperability, and risks of greenwashing, reducing trust and compliance. This chapter explores the convergence of Artificial Intelligence (AI), big data, and blockchain as a transformative solution. AI and big data enable emission forecasting, anomaly detection, and process optimization, while blockchain ensures immutability, transparency, and tamper-proof reporting. Case studies from Walmart and Volvo illustrate practical applications. The chapter also examines socio-economic implications, regulatory aspects, and technological barriers, while highlighting opportunities such as AI-enabled smart contracts, blockchain-based neutrality

DOI: 10.4018/979-8-3373-6896-2.ch004

certifications, and predictive sustainability with digital twins. Collectively, these innovations provide a pathway to low-carbon, ethical, and transparent supply chains aligned with global sustainability and ESG goals.

INTRODUCTION

Climate change is an urgent problem that has put more pressure on the essential responsibility of carbon footprint in international supply chains. The growing complexity of the global trade and production systems is showing the inapplicability of the old systems of measurement and reporting of emissions. It has been determined that these outdated methods are characterised by fragmented information, the inconsistency of the standards and low rates of interoperability resulting in low quality sustainability reporting and undermining stakeholder confidence. This, in addition, has led to the non-observance of environmental policies, but also contributed to the probability of greenwashing whereby the companies are either overstating or overdoing their environmental performance (Y. Chen & Jin, 2023a). In a bid to make suitable adjustments to these demands, the newer digital technologies are being utilized as ground breaking tools with each passing day. Today, with the help of Artificial Intelligence (AI) and big data analytics, much more heterogeneous data can be processed, and it is possible to help the firms predict emission, identify the anomalies and optimize the processes that use a lot of energy and predict it accurately. These attributes are supplemented by blockchain with the immutable, decentralized, cannot-be-tampered-with reporting features, that provide transparency between the supply chain participants (Aarthi et al., 2025). This chapter recaps the interplay of AI, big data and blockchain and demonstrates the potential of the combination using examples. It also addresses the modern-day challenges, policy implications and future projections of the emerging low-carbon, ethical and transparent supply chains in accordance to the international sustainability objectives.

Context Of Global Warming And Carbon Footprint Responsibility

Global warming has become a burning international issue and increased temperatures and climate changes have disrupted ecosystems, human life and economies. One of the biggest emitters of Greenhouse Gas (GHG) is the supply chains of manufacturing, transportation and storage. Consequently, the responsibility of carbon footprint is a strategic issue to governments, corporations, and international bodies. Carbon management is no longer a choice but a necessity in today's world because of compliance, competitiveness, and corporate reputation. Consumers and investors are increasingly demanding visibility in emission tracking and reporting which is pushing the movement towards voluntary sustainability initiatives to responsible, real-time practices that are in line with net-zero targets (Ghosh et al., 2020).

Limitations Of Conventional Carbon Tracking Systems

Although the traditional carbon tracking and reporting systems are widely practiced, it continues to lack considerable defects that make it ineffective. Most of the tools used rely on specific datasets collected among various suppliers, regions, and logistics networks, resulting in incomplete or inconsistent data. The lack of standard data format and system interoperability also makes system aggregation and relative analysis between levels of supply chain difficult. Besides, making and committing mistakes, delays and manipulation by entering data manually and periodical reporting are also possibilities that undermine sustainability disclosures. These are the loopholes where greenwashing is practiced in which the companies are either reporting false or unfair information about their environmental practices. This leads to legal, reputational and operational risk because regulatory bodies are putting added pressure in ESG compliance (Ju et al., 2022). Last and not the least, systems of the next generation are not entirely accurate, transparent, and trustworthy to achieve effective carbon accountability, this is why integrated approaches are the right timely solution, combining AI, big data analytics, and blockchain to remove all the disadvantages of the old systems. The table 1 summarizes the conventional carbon tracking systems and the obstacles recognized are, fragmentation, interoperability and greenwashing. Transparency, accuracy, accountability in global supply chains are some of the challenges of such problems.

Table 1. Limitations of Conventional Carbon Tracking Systems

Limitation	Description	Impact on Accountability
Data Fragmentation	Emissions data scattered across suppliers, regions, and formats	Incomplete carbon footprint visibility
Lack of Interoperability	Different systems and standards cannot seamlessly integrate	Hinders accurate aggregation and comparability
Manual Data Handling	Reliance on spreadsheets and self-reporting	Errors, delays, and inconsistent reporting
Greenwashing Risks	Misleading or selective sustainability disclosures	Loss of stakeholder trust and reputational damage
Limited Real-Time Insights	Conventional tools focus on periodic reporting	Inability to optimize processes or respond to anomalies swiftly

Objective Of The Chapter

This chapter aims to explore how the convergence of AI, big data, and blockchain can transform carbon accountability in global supply chains. It outlines the theoretical foundations, practical applications, and emerging opportunities to strengthen sustainability practices.

- **Highlight Contextual Challenges -** Explain the shortcomings of conventional carbon tracking systems and risks such as greenwashing.
- **Present Theoretical Foundations –** Discuss how AI, big data analytics, and blockchain individually contribute to transparency and efficiency.
- **Propose an Integrated Framework –** Demonstrate the synergistic convergence of these technologies for verifiable and predictive carbon accountability.
- **Illustrate with Case Studies –** Provide real-world examples (Walmart and Volvo) to validate the practical feasibility of the proposed framework.
- **Identify Future Opportunities –** Outline open challenges, regulatory alignment needs, and innovative directions such as blockchain-based carbon neutrality certifications.

Conventional Carbon Tracking Systems

There are a number of limitations to the applicability of traditional carbon tracking solutions in the provision of effective and transparent sustainability reporting. Full information gathered in various suppliers, logistic processes and regional processes is not always used fully making it susceptible to inconsistency and the difference in measuring the emissions. The second problem is the challenge of interoperability that reduces the likelihood of data integration between platforms and repeating a similar carbon footprint by the organizations. Reporting and utilization of outdated auditing will more likely result in errors and lags in real-time responsibility (Abubakar and Ahamad, 2023). This is the vulnerability that leaves room on which greenwashing can take place, in which organizations can exaggerate or misrepresent environmental performance to continue to have reputational value. Collectively, all of these failures indicate that greater complexity of technology-enabled systems is required to be able to deliver verifiable, standardized and untampered accountability of carbon by more complex global supply chains.

Risks Of Greenwashing

Conventional carbon monitoring systems lack some strengths that contribute to high probability of greenwashing when organisations falsely or overstate their own sustainability performance. However, when systems of unprovability and non-alterability are absent, companies are free to release useful information at their own will, minimize or neglect non-environmentally friendly practices. This deception does not only cheat both consumers and investors in the process, it also interferes with the actual sustainability actions by even the level playing field of the responsible businesses and the non-compliant business. Greenwashing leads to loss of stakeholder confidence and investor trust and can result in reputational or legal consequences as ESG reporting regulations become more stringent. Declaring it to be false, or impossible to confirm makes it impossible to subject organizations to regulation or auditors, thus allowing unsustainable practices to continue unchecked (Y. Chen & Jin, 2023b). It is necessary to introduce advanced technologies such as AI, big data, and blockchain to make sure that greenwashing is addressed and carbon responsibility becomes secure and precise.

THEORETICAL FOUNDATIONS

AI, big data, and blockchain in supply chain applications have a complementary theoretical basis. Predictive analytics, anomaly detection and complex data decision-making are capabilities that can be performed with the help of AI. Big data analytics provide an opportunity to handle bulk and heterogeneous emission and logistics data to transform the raw data into actionable information. The falsifiability of blockchain technology, its decentralization, and its capability to keep records verifiably renders the carbon metrics unmanipulable, not to mention that it is transparent among multiple stakeholders. The technologies are integrated to make sure that they can be aligned to the notion of Environmental, Social, and Governance (ESG) (P. Chen et al., 2022). It will constitute a robust foundation of carbon accountability in the global layers of supply with a theoretical foundation of incorporating the information-based intelligence and infrastructure in placing faith in them.

Overview Of Artificial Intelligence And Big Data In Supply Chains

The concept of AI-driven and big data analytics is changing the sustainability of supply chains since data can be used to make the right decisions. It is possible to predict emission patterns with the help of AI models and identify the inefficiency of a logistics network with the help of AI models, collect information about suppliers and use IoT-enabled sensors and optimize transportation paths. Big data will be used to monitor the energy consumption status in real-time, material flows and carbon emissions, which will lead to the improved logic of the multifaceted supply chains.

Predictive analytics based on AI makes it possible to detect the hot emission areas, anticipate the future of the carbon tendencies, and help to create more environmentally responsible operation strategies. Moreover, machine learning can be very dynamic and adaptable to any form of disruption (e.g., fuel price increment or route change) and provide resilience and efficiency (Sarkis et al., 2020). AI and big data together could assist companies in transforming their carbon reporting strategies into active carbon management and can be considered a fact-based strategy to address long-term sustainability goals. The Figure 1 shows data gathering, data analysis, emission forecasting, operational efficiency, performance tracking, and acceptance of disruptions towards sustainable supply chain management.

Figure 1. AI and Big Data in Supply Chains

Blockchain Fundamentals And Its Role In Transparency And Immutability

Blockchain increases trust and accountability within the supply chain through the secure storage of carbon emission in an immutable, distributed register. The manipulation is prevented by cryptographic verification and promotes transparency and allows regulators, customers, and investors access to verifiable real time sustainability records. Moreover, blockchain helps to achieve decentralized governance and reduce dependency on centralized authorities and the probability of information asymmetry and selected disclosure. Smart contracts also incorporates this feature by supporting compliance and sustainability certifications (Aysan et al., 2021). Together, these features could make blockchain a cornerstone in the advancement of transparent, verifiable and ethically sound models of carbon responsibility. Table 2 ESG compliance is a formal expression that holds carbon accountability considering environmental responsibility, ethical business, and open-minded administration across the international supply chains.

Table 2. ESG (Environmental, Social, and Governance) Compliance Requirements

ESG Dimension	Compliance Focus	Relevance to Carbon Accountability
Environmental	Reduction of greenhouse gas (GHG) emissions, resource efficiency, and renewable adoption	Ensures organizations actively track and mitigate emissions across their supply chains
Social	Fair labor practices, community engagement, ethical sourcing	Prevents exploitation in raw material extraction and promotes ethical supply chain operations
Governance	Transparent reporting, anti-corruption practices, regulatory adherence	Builds trust through standardized, auditable, and regulator-aligned carbon footprint disclosures

LITERATURE REVIEW

The sustainable supply chain management literature is slowly shifting to the importance of implementation of recent digital technologies to tackle the increasing carbon accountability pressure (Drissi Elbouzidi et al., 2023). The conventional focus in the research has been on the operational efficiency, reduction and optimization of logistics but the climate change pressures have changed the sustainability research agenda towards transparency and compliance with international environmental standards (Gurtu & Johny, 2019). AI, big data analytics, and blockchain are some of the enablers within this frame that is changing the organizational approach to carbon emission management, monitoring, and reporting. When discussing the need to process large heterogeneous data volumes generated within a supply chain, one of the applications of the AI and big data analytics are likely to be listed. The researchers justify why they were able to make the emission forecast, citing inefficiencies and predictability of the plans (Das & Jharkharia, 2018). It has been demonstrated that the application of machine learning and advanced analytics, can aid in finding zones of emission hotspots, enhance transportation, and efficiently utilize resources. The second advantage of AI in literature is that, in addition to making better decisions, AI allows avoiding the threat of underreporting or mismeasuring carbon as it offers real-time data. These qualities mark the start of transformation to active and informative solutions in place of responsive sustainability initiatives (Ahsan & Serrano, 2025).

Rather, blockchain has been thought of a lot as far as its role in the establishment of trust, transparency and immutability in sustainability reporting are concerned. Part of the reason why traditional sustainability reporting is not credible is disjointed systems upon which it is based, and the risk of greenwashing. The other potential that blockchain model is tackling is the lack of efficiency in their creation of a decentralized and unaltered ledger that can be accessed by all the interested parties (Nibbering & Paap, 2024). Some have even argued that obligatory disclosures are supported by compliance with international ESG standards, measurable carbon provisions and reliance on the stakeholders. Furthermore, blockchain smart contracts have also been cited as systems to conduct compliance checks automatically and assist in facilitating new markets, e.g., carbon credit markets (Atagan Çetín, 2023). The interplay of AI, big data, and blockchain is not a new phenomenon in literature; instead of treating the above-mentioned technologies as independent of each other.

It has reported in the literature the opportunities that can emerge when the application of these tools is combined in such a way as to yield predictive, transparent and verifiable systems capable of reacting to environmental and social considerations of sustainability in supply chains (Kim & Huh, 2020). Speaking in more detail, predictive analytics can be applied to model different functions, but blockchain ensures some degree of data integrity to the information provided to the regulators and the consumers. In the meantime, research indicates that other problems such as the inability of various systems to communicate with each other, blockchain infrastructures scalability, and high cost of technologies employed are also present. However, more speculatively, digital twins, smart contracts defined by AI, and carbon neutrality certifications based on blockchain are promising a radiant future, opines certain publications looking at the future.

Recent literature presents comparative data that AI-based carbon prediction models can enhance emissions forecasting accuracy by 15-40% of conventional estimation methods especially when used in the logistics, manufacturing, and energy-intensive operations. Likewise, empirical studies show that blockchain-supported audit trails decrease the verification difference by as much as 30%, thus allowing the supply chain partners to offer more sustainable disclosures in real-time. It is also possible to note that the digital twin literature lists the benefits of energy optimization up to 8-20% in large-scale supply networks. Nevertheless, even in the light of these developments, the literature is quite divided, with little researches investigating how these technologies can be used in synergy and not in isolation. The existence of this gap indicates the necessity of combined frameworks, which will consolidate predictive analytics, impartial reporting, and dynamic simulation to decrease carbon uncertainty and increase accountability in intricate global processes.

Research Gap

Despite the impressive advancement in the use of AI, big data, and blockchain in supply chain management, current studies tend to consider the technologies separately. To explain their application in guaranteeing verifiable carbon accountability, fewer studies address the benefits of AI, blockchain, or both as predictive analytics or transparency, respectively. Furthermore, few structures deal with interoperability, scalability, and global regulatory conformity. The disjuncture is in the establishment of integrated, cross-technological solutions to optimize operations as well as deliver reliable, standardised and future-ready sustainability practices.

Problem Statement

Global supply chains are under increased pressure to show responsibility towards carbon emissions but traditional tracking systems are still disjointed, subject to failure and greenwashing. Inadequate interoperability, real-time insights, and credible verification systems negatively impact transparency and compliance with ESG. Even though AI, big data, and blockchain promise much, there is still a challenge in adopting them into scalable and standardized solutions. The issue, then, is the lack of integrated technological system that allows precise, transparent and predictable carbon responsibility within complex networks of global supply chains.

MAIN FOCUS OF THE CHAPTER

The main concept in this chapter is to think about the possibility of changing the carbon responsibility in global supply chains using AI, big data analytics, and blockchain. The latter languishes on the need to replace an incomplete and unreliable tracking systems with comprehensive, informative and predictive systems. The discussion of theoretical backgrounds, real life case studies and opportunities suggests that through this discussion the chapter has been given a touch of how all these technologies helps achieve the right monitoring of the emissions, imperfect reporting and proactive sustainability planning (Barykin et al., 2020). The other questions that have been concluded are the interoperability, scalability, regulatory, and future of AI-powered smart contracts, blockchain-based certifications, and predictive sustainability with the use of digital twins to power net-zero supply chain transformation.

Proposed Methodology

In this chapter, the author suggests a combined approach to AI, big data analysis, and blockchain as a single system to make global supply chains more carbon responsible. The strategy starts with data gathering and pre-processing of various data like IoT sensors and logistics network and supplier records. The raw data is then converted into actionable insights by AI-driven analytics to predict and forecast emissions, identify anomalies, and optimize energy-intensive processes. These validated outputs are stored in a blockchain register, making them immutable, transparent, and verifiable by all parties, which is decentralized. Smart contracts are used to boost compliance by automating regulatory checks, carbon credit transactions, and simulate predictive sustainability scenarios to be used in future planning with a digital twin. Scalability across industries is shown in methodology with examples of Walmart and Volvo. The proposed methodology enhances a proactive, trustworthy, and future-ready supply chain carbon accountability model by integrating accuracy, transparency, and foresight. Figure 2 presents a comprehensive AI-based big data-blockchain infrastructure, with which transparent accountable and carbon-neutral operations can be conducted.

Figure 2. Proposed Methodology for Sustainable Supply Chain Management

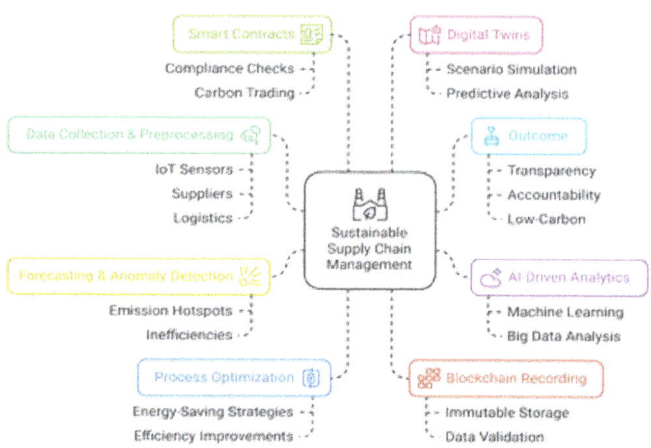

Data Collection & Preprocessing

The concept of the carbon responsibility is the acquisition of very large masses of data in the supply chain. Industrial IoT sensors, supplier and logistics data flow records may inform energy consumption, transportation emissions and production footprints. The preprocessing facilitates in cleansing and incorporating the raw data into a form that can be utilised to decrease discrepancies that may dilute the sustainability reporting. This step will turn the fragmented facts into a solid ground of further investigation, and enable groups of organization to possess a total image of their carbon emission, and generate inputs that can be valid at this time to foresee and hold oneself accountable.

Forecasting & Anomaly Detection

Active sustainability management is the anticipation of future emission as well as establishment of inefficiencies. The use of AI-based frameworks to predict the amount of carbon emission during the supply chain operations analyzes past and current data. Mechanisms to detect anomalies detect anomalies including excessive fuel consumption, energy wastage or strange logistics delays, etc. Such insights can also be used by the managers to rectify and streamline the strategies to avoid unnecessary emissions. Predictive analytics and anomaly detection can help organizations take their reporting beyond the reactive stage and assume the proactive role in carbon footprint reduction and long-term perspective on environmental responsibility.

Process Optimization

Reduction of carbon can be achieved through simplification of energy consuming processes. One of the methods of streamlining supply chains to ensure that the operations of a supply chain are efficient at all levels is supply chain redesign with AI and data informed insights. These strategies include fuel consumption routing that is optimized and limited waste production with lean use of energy in the warehouse and sequencing manufacturing processes. Organizations can save the cost of operations by investing in energy saving and efficiency plans other than reducing their emissions. The process optimization then forms a win-win solution whereby the sustainability goals are achieved considering the economic returns with the aim of gaining competitive advantage in the global markets that would be environmentally friendly.

AI-Driven Analytics

In the example of AI, it is possible to make raw data available on supply chain to be converted into useful sustainability data. Machines are learning to apply big data in the hope of finding patterns, predicting emissions and presenting alternatives to minimise the effect of carbon. This intelligence allows organizations to simulate situations, experiment with other mitigation options and implement proactive carbon management in addition to the compliance reporting. Smart analytics Evidence-based actions may also be applied with the use of intelligent insights, and aligned with the global sustainability objectives, since AI-based analytics sits between the complex data and predictive analytics.

Blockchain Recording

The carbon information is recorded in a transparent non-alterable registry with blockchain which has been confirmed to be authentic. Single transactions with emission numbers, supplier reports and compliance files are stored permanently and checked on de-centralized nodes. This disrupts manipulation, information or selective information sharing that reduce the possibility of greenwashing. The use of blockchain in the tracking of carbon measurement can also be applied on the supply chain both upward and downward to ensure that the entire stakeholders can have equal access to the correct information. Transparency, and by extension immutability, local and global, promotes sustainability reporting through blockchain recording and fosters trust and accountability.

Smart Contracts

Smart contracts build on the blockchain features by automation of compliance and transaction of carbon. There are also programmed rules in such self-executing contracts, in which carbon credits or certifications will only occur when the respective conditions are confirmed. Such a process is enhanced by the use of AI and justifies the emission data in real-time, preventing the occurrence of fraudulent claims or delays. Smart contracts simplify regulatory checks, eliminate human control as well as improving the efficiency in the carbon trading markets. They, therefore, provide an effective tool of delivering sustainability goals and improving confidence in the regulators, businesses and investors.

Digital Twins

Digital twins are formed as vibrant and real-time virtual extensions of the processes in the supply chain. The different operational scenarios that companies can use can be simulated to help the company predict the effects of change on the environment be it changes in suppliers, use of renewable energy, or change of routes. This predictive capability allows organizations to test and maximize strategies before implementation in order to minimize risks and costs. Digital twins are incorporated with AI-based analytics to come up with long-term carbon reduction decisions. They also enable innovation that gives organizations the capacity to develop resilient, adaptive and sustainable in the future supply chains.

Outcome

Transparent, responsible, and low-carbon supply chains are achieved due to the combination of AI, big data, blockchain and digital twins. The approaches to transparency are to make sure that verifiable data is accessible to the stakeholders, accountability makes sure that standards are also being met in the ESG, and low carbon delivery is in compliance with global climate. Organizations are not reactive in their reporting but they are proactive in its planning as far as sustainability is concerned in this integration. The outcome is a reduced number of emissions and increased stakeholder trust, brand equity and competitiveness. It is hoped that the proposed framework will ultimately allow ethical and sustainable supply chains in the future during the period of climate responsibility.

AI-POWERED BIG DATA ANALYTICS FOR CARBON FOOTPRINT

Carbon footprints in the global supply chain can be managed using powerful tools involving AI and big data analytics. These technologies allow organizations to handle large volumes of both structured and unstructured data produced by logistics, transportation, manufacturing and within supplier networks (Tang & Tang, 2019). The AI algorithms can enhance the precision of emissions measurement, enhance forecast precision and plan proactive sustainability. AI, with the help of different data sources, such as IoT-enabled sensors, and transactional data can uncover latent patterns, indicate inefficiencies, and suggest ways to save energy. In this instance, predictive analytics can be applied particularly as a technique that allows business entities to simulate various events and optimize functionality to mitigate the environmental impact. Big data enabled by AI can transform conventional carbon reporting into dynamic actionable carbon responsibility with real-time monitoring, anomaly detection and model prediction. This guarantees excellent transparency, operational efficiency, and compliance with ESG regulations, and minimises the risk of greenwashing.

Data Collection And Emission Forecasting Using AI

Managing carbon footprint correctly starts with gathering of huge and varied information throughout the supply chain processes. Such data sources as IoT sensors in vehicles and warehouses, energy use monitors, satellite-based climate data, supplier emission records are included. AI helps to improve this process as it can automatically aggregate, clean, and normalize the data to maintain consistency and reliability (Nibbering & Paap, 2024). Machine learning forecasts carbon emissions based on historical data and carries out simulations of measures such as transport optimization, switching to renewable energy, or changing packages. Predictive algorithms facilitate proactive planning, what-if analysis, and sustainable decision-making, in line with the net-zero sustainability and the international regulations of supply chains.

Identifying Anomalies And Inefficiencies In Logistics

Supply chain nature is highly dynamic, and is likely to generate highly complex and volatile data in the logistics networks. The waste of resources such as fuel, transporting stagnation and avoiding routes are the key contributors to emissions as well as expensive operations. Anomaly detection algorithms are AI-based methods to process logistics data in real-time in order to detect unusual trends or variations of normal operation (Marisamy et al., 2025). As it may be seen, under the same conditions, algorithms may notice that a delivery car is fuel-draining, then it should, which implies the potential failures or inefficient driving style. Similarly, AI has the ability to determine the points of bottlenecks in the activity of the warehouse, which are involved in meaningless energy consumption. Predictive modeling also allows risk prediction, such as delayed shipment with predictive analytics that in turn result in increased emissions through re-routing or expedited delivery. The presence of anomalies causes the supply chains to take remedial action within a short time, reducing the intensity of carbon, and reducing expenditures. The proactive solution makes logistics management a tool of sustainability as any operations are efficient, adapting and global-carbon-reduction-oriented.

Optimizing Energy-Intensive Processes With Predictive Analytics

A big part of supply chain emission is as a result of energy-consuming processes like manufacturing, warehousing and transportation. The predictive analytics, which is based on AI, will conserve energy by analysing the past data and live sensor measurements to project the peak demand and allocate resources in the most optimal manner to reduce energy consumption and transfer them to off-peak periods. As part of the production process, AI suggests the most optimal equipment process, maintenance and order sequence to ensure less energy is wasted. It identifies fuel-saving and emission-reducing solutions to logistics (Feng et al., 2024). Firms also can test a situation such as transitioning to electric fleets or renewable-powered warehouses on a simulation model. Collectively, predictive analytics is used to make informed decisions and streamline supply chain operation to make it more efficient and sustainable, not to mention low-carbon.

BLOCKCHAIN FOR CARBON ACCOUNTABILITY

Blockchain technology is an arrangement that offers credibility and decentralization to manage carbon footprint through transparency and accountability. It captures carbon indicators which could not be altered to move trust in world supply chains by a record that cannot be altered. Decentralized record keeping does not have to involve central authorities and the stakeholders can be provided with equal access to the verified data (Fan, 2023). Besides that, blockchain will eliminate the manipulation or selective reporting of risks as a solution to the greenwashing risks. In addition to storage, smart contracts can support automation of compliance, and certifications, and increase sustainability governance. It complements sustainability reporting and auditing, and through its implementation, organizations are more in line with ESG, and with its implementation, organizations can demonstrate their attempts to reduce carbon in a demonstrable way.

Immutable Carbon Metrics And Decentralized Record-Keeping

A major contribution of blockchain is that it creates a preventive measure that once the data about the carbon emissions is recorded, it cannot be changed or erased. Every transaction is securely encrypted and stored over distributed nodes, forming an immutable audit trail. Such immutability guarantees the sustainability data of the suppliers; logistics providers and manufacturers is always maintained throughout the supply chain. Decentralized record-keeping also eliminates the reliance on central powers, and the monopolization of data or its disclosure may also be reduced (Baklaga, 2024). Transparency and responsibility can be enhanced because blockchain will enable stakeholders, regulators and customers, to access the same verified records in real time. This is particularly significant to multinational corporations since it enables them to cross over borders and organizational silos without trouble. Lastly, the non-modifiable and decentralized registration of carbon information will inculcate in the stakeholders a sense of assurance that carbon responsibility will be a reliable starting point of meeting international environmental and climate commitments.

Preventing Data Tampering And Ensuring Trust Among Stakeholders

Traditional systems of carbon tracking can be compromised either willingly or unintentionally, which discredits sustainability reporting. The blockchain technology does this by ensuring that all records relating to carbon can be traced and authenticated. All entries are time stamped and cryptographically attached to the last block and authenticated by consensus mechanisms, making them virtually impossible to tamper with. This technical confidence will make interested parties confident that the data recorded on the emission is not fabricated. The fact that there is no controlling party in the ledger and therefore neutrality in carbon accountability also increases the efforts to build trust. The credibility of the data being reported can be guaranteed to the stakeholders, who include governments, investors, NGOs, and consumers, thereby reducing the risk of greenwashing (Dempere et al., 2024). Blockchain shifts produce a more responsible sustainability as a transition to a more open verification system, instead of voluntary accountability. This gives a stronger foundation of long-term relations with the stakeholders and promotes common responsibility to carbon neutrality throughout the global supply chains.

Blockchain In Sustainability Reporting And Auditing

This is because the sustainability reporting is the most important source of Corporate ESG compliance, although the traditional reporting is prone to inefficiency and lack of credibility. The suggested paradigm change is the result of the blockchain technology that provides a transparent and total carbon emissions reporting and auditing platform. The businesses may apply blockchain to offer emission amounts in a secure form and can be validated in real-time by auditor, regulator and other interested parties. Compliance verification using smart contracts may also be fully automated by the release of alerts or certifications based on the offering level of emission cross-referencing, and prior-existing regulatory standards. This spares the administrative expense of manual audits and provides more accuracy and efficacies. Besides this, blockchain is also used with the purpose of implementing uniformity in international reporting, which contributes to the increased transparency of multinational business (Fan, 2023). The ambiguity which surrounds the selective disclosures which is evident amongst the stakeholders can be eliminated by sustainability reporting on blockchain which will result in increased investor confidence and compliance with regulations. Lastly, blockchain transforms reporting and auditing into the system to be a participatory and verifiable activity, which increases accountability on the global level in the supply chain.

SYNERGISTIC CONVERGENCE: AI, BIG DATA, AND BLOCKCHAIN

AI, big data, and blockchain combination offers an inclusive framework of guaranteeing effective carbon responsibility to the global supply chain. Unlike predictive intelligence and anomaly detection, which is provided by AI, big data can ensure the opportunity to process the data on emissions in real time and on large scale, whilst blockchain can ensure its transparency and impossibility. They complement each other and provide organizations with the capacity to predict, track, and confirm carbon footprints accurately. Such synergy will lead to better adherence to ESG standards, fewer greenwashing risks, and faster transition to low-carbon, sustainable supply chain ecosystems with precise and verifiable carbon responsibility systems (Baklaga, 2024).

Framework For Integrated Carbon Accountability

A comprehensive interconnected system comprising AI, big data, and blockchain allows supply chains to be proactive about sustainability. The first step is to collect big data via IoT devices, sensors, supplier records, and process and analyze them with AI algorithms to identify inefficiencies, predict emissions, and suggest optimizations. Blockchain stores the validated results in a way that makes them tamperproof, transparent and accessible to all stakeholders. This three-layered structure not only improves the accuracy of data, but also creates a sense of trust by delivering verifiable sustainability metrics. Compliance checks, certifications, or carbon credit transactions can automatically occur because of smart contracts integrated into blockchain. Modularity of the framework assures flexibility to industries such as the retail and automotive supply chains (Zhou, 2024). This synergy ultimately converts piece-meal carbon reporting into a predictive, uninterrupted and verifiable cycle of accountability that links global supply chains to sustainable development and climate action objectives.

Benefits Of Convergence (Accuracy, Transparency, Predictive Sustainability)

It is a potent ecosystem as AI and big data clash with blockchain that can transform carbon responsibility beyond the disaggregated reporting of carbon footprint to more data-driven sustainability. It is the combination of these technologies that ensures the increased accuracy of carbon tracking, the increased transparency of the records that cannot be changed and the sustainability predictability with the help of carbon scenario estimates made in the future. Such synergy is not only useful to comply with the rules of ESG, but also to enable a greater assurance of stakeholders. The convergence of operations and trusted reporting are the measures that promote the transition of the supply chains to low-carbon, ethical, and visionary systems. The table 3 significant benefits of applying AI, big data, and blockchain listed in this table include improved precision, visibility, and foreseeability of sustainable supply chains.

Table 3. Benefits of Convergence

Benefit	Description
Accuracy	AI-powered analytics and big data ensure precise emission forecasting and monitoring.
Transparency	Blockchain provides immutable records, enabling trustworthy sustainability disclosures.
Predictive Sustainability	Forecasting future emission scenarios allows proactive planning and energy optimization.
Stakeholder Confidence	Verified data fosters investor, regulator, and consumer trust, reducing risks of greenwashing.

Challenges Of Integration (Interoperability, Scalability, Cost)

The integration of AI, big data, and blockchain could potentially provide some revolutionary advantages, but there are major obstacles to its deployment. Problems related to interoperability of various systems, the ability to scale the data heavy infrastructures, and the cost of implementation are constraints to widespread implementation (M. Wang et al., 2020). It is critical to eliminate these issues and make the most of integrated carbon accountability frameworks. The following summary table 4 presents the main issues in the implementation of AI, big data, and blockchain to achieve carbon accountability, with the focus on interoperability of systems, their scalability, and cost limitations.

Table 4. Challenges of Integration

Challenge	Description
Interoperability	Diverse systems and data standards hinder seamless integration across global supply chains.
Scalability	High data volumes and complex blockchain transactions create performance bottlenecks.
Cost	Implementation involves significant financial, infrastructural, and training investments.
Regulatory Alignment	Ensuring compliance across multiple jurisdictions remains a complex challenge.

CASE STUDIES

In order to exemplify the phenomenon of AI convergence with big data and blockchain under the heading of carbon responsibility, the following section provides two examples of real cases (Walmart and Volvo). Formed as a sustainability reporting facilitated by blockchain and complemented with big data analytics, Walmart operates the system to track the emissions of its suppliers, the optimization of logistics, and improve the ESG compliance of all its activities globally. Similarly, Volvo applies AI-powered analytics and blockchain to monitor the emissions along its Electric Vehicle (EV) battery supply chain to ensure transparency in the ethical sourcing and mining practices. All this and more should confirm that these are examples of how big businesses are harnessing technological synergies in a manner that will promote trust, reduce emissions, and create sustainable supply chains. Walmart's Blockchain-Enabled Sustainability Reporting.

Walmart's Blockchain-Enabled Sustainability Reporting

Walmart and Volvo have been chosen as the representative cases, as both companies have to work at complicated, multi-layered supply chains where emissions monitoring, moral sourcing, and efficiency of operations are the key issues. Walmart has an example of large-scale distribution of retail logistics that includes thousands of suppliers that operate in different regulatory conditions. Volvo is a technologically advanced manufacturing system of high carbon intensity battery production and acquisition of raw materials especially in the mining areas. The fact that they have contrasting industrial settings makes it possible to draw meaningful parallels as well as an explanation of the manner in which AI, big data, and blockchain can be scaled to other sectors with varying levels of maturity. Furthermore, publicly reporting quantifiable results, both companies are appropriate to illustrate empirical validity and experimentally prove the relevance of a suggested framework. Walmart is an international retailer and one of the biggest organizations globally that have already adopted blockchain-enhanced sustainability reporting as a mechanism to foster transparency and responsibility across its supply chain. Knowing that the emission of thousands of suppliers is hard to track, Walmart integrated big data analysis with blockchain to create a stable carbon responsibility system.

To identify the emission hot spots and project the future environmental situation, the company uses high-level analytics in order to gather as much data as possible in regard to the supply chain performance, logistical paths, and energy consumption patterns. This data will be stored in one of the blockchain records and cannot be edited or refuse to report it. It can also allow easy optimization of logistics since you will be able to track transportation routes, fuel consumption, and energy efficiency in the warehouse in real-time which will save money, and minimise carbon emissions (Y. Chen & Jin, 2023a). Additionally, blockchain can help suppliers, regulators, and consumers gain access to verifiable sustainability data and align Walmart operations to environmental, social, and governance compliance standards. Using predictive analytics and blockchain trust, Walmart will not only enhance its position as a responsible sourcing company, it will develop a scalable model of proven responsible carbon responsibility that can be copied by other companies around the world. The Figure 3 shows that Walmart uses big data and blockchain to track emissions, enhance its logistics, demand transparency, and scale sustainable supply chain accountability.

Figure 3. Walmart's Blockchain-Enabled Sustainability Framework

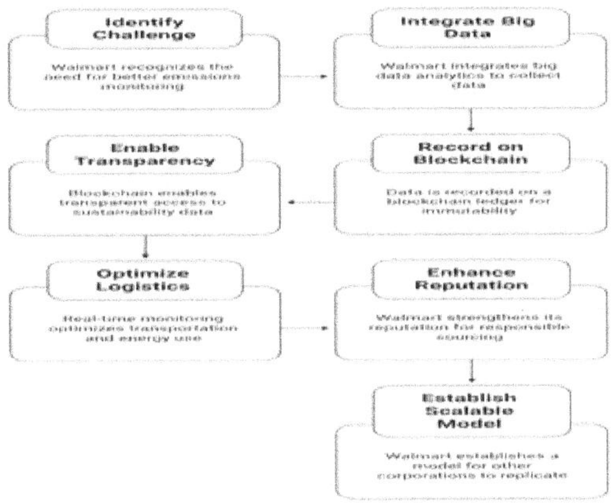

Volvo's Ev Battery Supply Chain

Volvo has gone to enormous lengths to ensure that the Electric Vehicle (EV) battery supply chain is responsible and environmentally and ethically sound. Because battery manufacturing is extremely carbon-intensive, and because of ethical concerns about battery manufacturing, particularly cobalt and lithium mining, Volvo uses AI-driven analytics in combination with blockchain to create accountability. The mining operations, transportation, and production facilities are using AI models to analyze the information and predict the number of emissions at each step of the battery lifecycle. This foresight can help Volvo identify the processes that will cause a significant emission impact early in its evolution and take action to mitigate them, such as by improving logistics or switching to renewable energy sources. This system can be complemented by blockchain that records information on emission and sources of information on an immutable and decentralized blockchain, thus none of the stakeholders can modify records. It is worth noting that blockchain will also be ensuring suppliers are ethical miners and do not exploit materials related to human rights abuse (Li et al., 2023). The two-pronged program shall not merely ensure compliance with the ESG rules but consumer/ investor confidence. The Figure 4 model indicates AI and blockchain will safeguard environmental sustainability and social responsibility within a high-stakes and critical green-economy supply chain.

Figure 4. Volvo's AI and Blockchain Integration for EV Battery Supply Chain

Comparative Overview Of Walmart And Volvo Case Studies

The two Walmart and Volvo case studies shed some light on the particular yet complementary supply chain sustainability applications of AI, big data, and blockchain. Walmart values supplier emissions tracking and visibility logistics more than Volvo values EV batteries predictive analytics and blockchain-verified ethical sourcing. They represent, in aggregate, how convergence technologies can be modified to address environmental and social dimensions of carbon responsibility (Feng et al., 2024). The table 5 compares Walmart and Volvo approaches and tactics on adopting AI, big data, and blockchain to be carbon accountable, their area of interest, implementation of technology, and environmental, social, and economic costs/benefits.

Table 5. Comparative Overview of Walmart and Volvo Case Studies

Aspect	Walmart	Volvo
Focus Area	Supplier emissions tracking and logistics optimization	EV battery supply chain emissions and ethical sourcing
Role of AI & Big Data	Collects and analyzes supplier and logistics data to identify emission hotspots and optimize routes	Forecasts emissions across mining, transport, and production processes
Role of Blockchain	Immutable sustainability reporting, preventing manipulation of supplier data	Immutable record of emissions and sourcing, verifying ethical mining
ESG Compliance	Enhances supplier accountability and aligns with ESG reporting standards	Ensures both environmental and social responsibility compliance
Key Outcome	Transparent, scalable carbon accountability across global suppliers	Verified low-carbon, ethically aligned EV battery production

SOCIO-ECONOMIC IMPLICATIONS OF TECHNOLOGY-DRIVEN CARBON ACCOUNTABILITY

The introduction of AI, big data and blockchain into carbon accountability initiatives have important social-economic consequences with regards to the international supply chain. At the social level, the increased transparency implies that companies must behave ethically in their sourcing, ethical approaches of their employment activities and environmental responsible practices and create a degree of assurance in their consumers, social groups and owners. It also enables the stakeholders to make wise decisions with respect to sustainable products and services. Convergence, at the digital level, eliminates inefficiencies, minimizes cost of operation and regulatory fines through proper emissions monitoring and compliance. In addition to this, the organizations that have implemented the technologies can equally gain competitive advantages regarding better brand recognition, green financing, and carbon trading (Gu, 2024). High start-up costs are an issue but these are offset by the socio-economic benefits that sustainable development, resilience and aligning supply chains with the rest of the world, in general, towards low-carbon and socially responsibility business models creates in the long run.

Impact On Supply Chain Stakeholders

Carbon responsibility through the implementation of AI, big data and blockchain creates the revolutionary effects on various players in the supply chain. Emission monitoring digitally is pressurizing to the suppliers as they are more likely to be honest about their actual emissions and adopt cleaner processes, which removes opportunities of greenwashing. Manufacturers are also able to view the utilization of resources and the efficacy of manufacturing in real-time to identify areas of inefficiency and respond more effectively to ESG compliance. The predictive analytics will enable logistics providers to optimize their routes, save and reduce fuel expenditure, and reduce delays, and satisfy the demands of open reporting of transportation emissions. The data records are immutable and this allows regulators and investors to have a higher compliance monitoring and investment decision-making power. Finally, a consumer can also obtain the verifiable data on sustainability that will enable them to trust the environmentally responsible brands (L. Wang et al., 2022). Although the added accountability expectations might be challenging in the short term to smaller suppliers, the overall outcome in the long run is a system where they are all practicing low-carbon, transparent, and ethically sustainable global supply chains.

Economic And Competitive Advantages

The AI, big data and blockchain on carbon accountability will not just establish sustainability but will also provide truly economic and competitive payoff. Identifying inefficiency in logistics and manufacturing can help organizations save on the cost of energy, use their resources more efficiently and waste. These operational improvements lead to cost reduction and simultaneously, the emission, which is good, thus, the two are mutually enhancing. Businesses whose sustainability practices are clear and verifiable too develop their brand name, attracting consumers that are concerned about the environment and enhancing consumer loyalty. Greener financing and sustainability-based investments are more easily accessible and verified ESG compliance earns the goodwill of investors. In addition, the AIs-powered smart contracts and carbon markets that operate with the help of blockchain offer new sources of revenue because of the automated and valid carbon credit trading (Ju et al., 2022). The pioneers in the use of these technologies acquire competitiveness as industry leaders and this means that they exhibit responsible practices standards. The efficiency, reduction of risk, and market differentiation are the benefits of technology-driven carbon accountability which although may have a high initial implementation cost in the long-term also has a strategic role of enabling sustainable development.

Comparative summary of social vs. Economic implications of carbon accountability

Digital convergence creates socio-economic value by facilitating transparent supply chains, fair and sustainable supply chains using AI, big data, and blockchain. Such technologies boost consumer confidence, corporate image, productivity, and green financing, which guarantee compliance with ESG and the competitiveness of these industries in the low-carbon economy over the long term (Shang & Luo,

2021). The table 6 is a comparison of the effects of adoption of AI, big data, and blockchain on social outcomes and economic benefits in the global supply chains.

Table 6. Social vs. Economic Implications of Technology-Driven Carbon Accountability

Dimension	Social Implications	Economic Implications
Transparency	Builds consumer and community trust through verifiable sustainability practices	Reduces compliance risks and avoids penalties through accurate emissions tracking
Stakeholder Impact	Empowers suppliers, regulators, and consumers to demand accountability and ethical practices	Improves operational efficiency, reduces energy and logistics costs
Reputation	Enhances brand credibility by demonstrating ethical and responsible operations	Attracts investors, secures green financing, and opens access to sustainability markets
Opportunities	Promotes fair labor, ethical sourcing, and community engagement	Creates new revenue streams via carbon trading and sustainability-linked financial products

TECHNOLOGICAL BARRIERS AND IMPLEMENTATION CHALLENGES

The combination of AI, big data, and blockchain can transform the carbon responsibility, a number of technological issues prevent its implementation. The biggest challenge is the ability to integrate these tools with the existing legacy systems in global supply chains where data silos, interoperability and different standards complicate smooth integration. Scalability is further exacerbated by the fact that blockchain networks are computationally and energy intensive, and need infrastructure to handle real time data. In addition, most organizations, and especially the Small and Medium Enterprises (SMEs), cannot afford the deployment of advanced technologies. Besides infrastructure, a shortage of technical expertise and workforce readiness is another obstacle to adoption, where most stakeholders are not aware or ready to process AI-driven analytics or blockchain-based infrastructure in an efficient way (Liu et al., 2024). Organizations will experience partial or ineffective implementations unless there is sufficient investment in training, the digital literacy and standardization in the industry. The most effective solution to overcome these barriers is working jointly, regulating in a supportive way, and developing capacity to support sustainable, scalable and fair adoption of technology across supply chains.

Infrastructure And Integration Issues

The lack of infrastructure and incompatibility of systems with existing supply chains commonly interferes with the implementation of AI, big data, and blockchain into a new supply chain. Existing systems were not built to support real-time analytics and immutable blockchain records, which leads to interoperability issues. Another complexity is the high energy and computing demand of the blockchain networks, and thus scalability is challenging when using resource-hungry environments. Moreover, the lack of standardized data creates division and poor comparability of supply chains. The expenses of modern infrastructure and ongoing data management used by many organizations, particularly in developing economies, are prohibitive (M. Wang et al., 2020). Absent coordinating structures and prioritizing the development of common digital infrastructure, adoption will be uneven, with major corporations moving ahead and leaving small and medium enterprises behind.

Skills, Awareness, And Adoption Gaps

The other hindrance to the establishment of advanced accountability systems and infrastructure is the human capital. Most of the organizations do not have experts familiar with AI-based analytics, blockchain application, and sustainability reporting. This skills gap hurts small and medium enterprises in particular as little effort is put by the investors to train and be digital literate. Moreover, data of the contribution that such technologies will lead to the sustainability is asymmetric across various industries and this is the reason why it is being adopted reluctantly or slowly. The second is the cultural resistance to technological change where the stakeholders might be having fears about transparency that may reveal their inefficiencies or bad moral behaviours (Liao et al., 2023). One of the solutions to this gap is capacity-building programs, collaboration with academic institutions and knowledge sharing in the industry. Mobile firms can also increase the acquisition of skills and awareness to streamline adoption and technological convergence a win situation that is capable of benefiting the entire supply chain ecosystem and not the privileged few.

ETHICAL AND REGULATORY CONSIDERATIONS

Carbon responsibility in global supply chains is not merely an issue of technological integration, but must be dealt with at the same time, as an ethical and compliance issue. It is ethics of responsible sourcing, lack of exploitation and an understandable and transparent methodology on sustainability reporting that it maintains the stakeholders on board. Meanwhile, law enforcement bodies (e.g. ESG standards, GDPR, and world climate measures, etc.) enforce legal requirements on organizations that are expected to provide correct emissions data and behave within the legal framework. Ethics and regulation are applied together to act as the protective mechanisms, free of greenwashing and taking note of the aspects of sustainability in the community and safeguard rights of societies and ecosystems.

Ethical Dimensions Of Carbon Accountability

Sustainable supply chain practices also require a major contribution of ethics. Other than minimizing the emissions, business should make sure that their procurement policies are consistent with the provisions of human rights, labor and environmental management. Individually, to illustrate, there is no single parameter that a carbon measure should be the benchmark when it comes to utilizing blockchain in supply chains, but to guarantee that the raw materials were not mined using child labor or unethical mining techniques. This is also extended to transparent reporting, where organisations cannot only choose who to report to, but also make exaggerated statements about their sustainability confusing the affected parties (Hu et al., 2020). The carbon tracking systems will be more responsible with the moral values and build a trusting relationship with customers, investors and government in the long run. Finally, ethics would help ascertain that the sustainability undertakings would not be driven by the sole aim of environmental objectives, but would also socially and morally touch upon individuals.

Regulatory Alignment And Compliance

The global supply chain is also subject to tighter rules where it is necessary to report transparent and standardized emissions. Such policies as the ESG regulations and carbon taxes require adherence. Due to immutable, automated records produced by blockchain and AI, tracking is now much easier, even in spite of regional variations. A loss of reputation and fines are the possible consequences of a failure, and the use of integration helps to become more credible, avoid greenwashing, and pursue net-zero goals.

FUTURE DIRECTIONS

New technologies will be further influencing the practice of carbon accountability in the coming decade. Smart contracts powered by AI are likely to automatize MRV (Monitoring, Reporting and Verification) in carbon markets, and digital twins will be used more to simulate emissions when supply chains are reconfigured, which will allow planning towards sustainability proactively. Harmonization will be facilitated by integration with international systems, including ESRS, CBAM, GRI 2021, and ISO 14064 standards and be used to guide harmonized reporting in different jurisdictions (Fan, 2023). Further studies are also required into the applicability of federated learning to the privacy-preserving emissions analytics, carbon-conscience routing algorithms and blockchain-based carbon neutrality certificates verifiable across borders. It is crucial to continue to strengthen the digital infrastructure in the developing countries so that the adoption is evenly distributed and that the sustainability disparities are narrowed in the global supply chains.

AI-Enabled Smart Contracts For Carbon Trading

Carbon trading markets are becoming the new concern of the global sustainability but a lack of effectiveness in verification and enforcement is a test to the effectiveness of this strategy. This is a great solution since the smart contracts automatically carry out carbon credit deals with conditions that are programmed to run in the blockchain by the use of AI. Under these contracts, these carbon credits would not be traded until real emissions have been reduced in terms of AI-based analytics (Moshood et al., 2021). This minimises opportunities of fraudulent claims, duplication or lag in issuing credit. Furthermore, the employment of AI will lead to the ability to monitor the data on the emissions constantly, and dynamically update smart contracts so that they could show the actual performance (Liu et al., 2024). Other than reducing administrative overheads, this automation will also create confidence between regulators, buyers and sellers. With AI and blockchain combined, the carbon trading markets would become transparent, efficient, and credible, which would enable a larger number of people to engage in it and accelerate the accomplishment of global carbon neutrality targets.

Blockchain-Based Carbon Neutrality Certifications

Blockchain-based carbon neutrality certifications represent an open, verifiable and immutable method of ensuring claims of sustainability. Traditional certification programs tend to have a fragmented consensus, a deficient understanding and can be subjected to manipulation and greenwashing. By contrast, blockchain records the history of an organizations carbon reduction history such as: emissions tracking, carbon offsets purchases made, and compliance auditing on an immutable registry that is accessible in real-time by regulators, investors, and consumers. Compliance checks were also automated in Smart contracts which means that manual checks are not required and that reports are produced promptly. This type of a decentralized structure leads to general trust, more responsibility and a greater confidence in stakeholders, and, lastly, enabling scaled and standardized global routes to actual carbon neutrality.

CONCLUSION

The chapter has answered how Artificial Intelligence (AI), big data analytics, and blockchain can change the global supply chain with carbon responsibility. As the climate change increasingly gained momentum, organizations could no longer afford to rely on the use of the piecemeal tracking systems that may be inefficient and greenwashing. In its place, the transparent, and verifiable practices are required that are within the demands of increased accountability and sustainability. The AI and big data bring the opportunity to digest the vast and complicated volumes, predict the emissions, reveal the inefficiencies, and streamline the energy-consuming processes. This puts sustainability management on an evidence based and proactive level in comparison with a retrospective and reactive level. This is accompanied by blockchain that will guarantee the immutability, decentralization, and tamper proof sustainability logs to assure the stakeholders of their belief and commitment to the ESG.

Walmart and Volvo are some examples which depict practical's. Walmart uses blockchain-driven reporting to hold its supply chains more responsible and efficient in their logistics and Volvo uses predictive analytics and blockchain verification to make EV battery supply chains ethically sourced. Such examples of convergent technology in such flexible industries illustrate this. However, the challenges of interoperability, scalability of blockchain, high implementation cost and regulatory dynamics continue to exist. Policymakers, inventors of technologies and leaders of the industry will have to cooperate to overcome these challenges. In the future, it is expected that the perspective of carbon neutrality certifications based on blockchains, artificial intelligence smart contracts, and predictive sustainability using digital twins will speed up the net-zero goals. Finally, the intersection of AI, big data, and blockchain will develop a radical roadmap to develop transparent, ethical, and low-carbon supply chains. Such an integration will make businesses the forefront in combating climate change, as well as their competitiveness and confidence.

REFERENCES

Aarthi, S., Aravinthan, K., Ravikumar, R. N., Sivakumar, N., & Wanglen, S. (2025). Cryptography securing data in motion within Blockchain, internet of everything, and Federated Learning. In *Convergence of Blockchain, Internet of Everything, and Federated Learning for Security* (pp. 39–78). IGI Global., DOI: 10.4018/979-8-3373-1424-2.ch002

Abubakar, M., & Ahamad, S. (2023). Blockchain based platform for carbon credit. *NIET Journal of Engineering and Technology*, *12*(01W), 1–9. DOI: 10.62797/njet.vol.12.issue.01w.001

Ahsan, M., & Serrano, D. (2025). Lifecycle carbon mapping of well construction-blockchain carbon footprint profiling. *World Journal of Advanced Engineering Technology and Sciences*, *15*(3), 2268–2270. DOI: 10.30574/wjaets.2025.15.3.0800

Atagan Çetín, A. (2023). Using blockchain technology for carbon accounting in türkíye. *INTERNATIONAL REFEREED JOURNAL OF HUMANITIES AND ACADEMIC SCIENCES*, *31*(0), 64–84. DOI: 10.17368/uhbab.2023.31.04

Aysan, A. F., Bergigui, F., & Disli, M. (2021). Blockchain-based solutions in achieving SDGs after COVID-19. *Journal of Open Innovation*, *7*(2), 151. DOI: 10.3390/joitmc7020151

Baklaga, L. (2024). Synergizing AI and blockchain: Innovations in decentralized carbon markets for emission reduction through intelligent carbon credit trading. *Journal of Computer Science and Technology Studies*, *6*(2), 111–120. DOI: 10.32996/jcsts.2024.6.2.13

Barykin, S. Y., Bochkarev, A. A., Kalinina, O. V., & Yadykin, V. K. (2020). Concept for a supply chain digital twin. International Journal of Mathematical. *Engineering and Management Sciences*, *5*(6), 1498–1515. DOI: 10.33889/ijmems.2020.5.6.111

Chen, P., Gao, J., Ji, Z., Liang, H., & Peng, Y. (2022). Do artificial intelligence applications affect carbon emission performance?—Evidence from panel data analysis of Chinese cities. *Energies*, *15*(15), 5730. DOI: 10.3390/en15155730

Chen, Y., & Jin, S. (2023a). Artificial intelligence and carbon emissions in manufacturing firms: The moderating role of green innovation. *Processes (Basel, Switzerland)*, *11*(9), 2705. DOI: 10.3390/pr11092705

Chen, Y., & Jin, S. (2023b). Artificial intelligence and carbon emissions in manufacturing firms: The moderating role of green innovation. *Processes (Basel, Switzerland)*, *11*(9), 2705. DOI: 10.3390/pr11092705

Das, C., & Jharkharia, S. (2018). Low carbon supply chain: A state-of-the-art literature review. *Journal of Manufacturing Technology Management, 29*(2), 398–428. DOI: 10.1108/jmtm-09-2017-0188

Dempere, J., Alamash, E., & Mattos, P. (2024). Unveiling the truth: Greenwashing in sustainable finance. *Frontiers in Sustainability, 5*. Advance online publication. DOI: 10.3389/frsus.2024.1362051

Drissi Elbouzidi, A., Ait El Cadi, A., Pellerin, R., Lamouri, S., Tobon Valencia, E., & Bélanger, M.-J. (2023). The role of AI in warehouse digital twins: Literature review. *Applied Sciences (Basel, Switzerland), 13*(11), 6746. DOI: 10.3390/app13116746

Fan, M. (2023). Future of Blockchain: Data storage, carbon calculation, accounting, and emissions trading. *Journal of Student Research, 12*(4). Advance online publication. DOI: 10.47611/jsrhs.v12i4.5665

Feng, W., Chen, T., Li, L., Zhang, L., Deng, B., Liu, W., Li, J., & Cai, D. (2024). Application of neural networks on carbon emission prediction: A systematic review and comparison. *Energies, 17*(7), 1628. DOI: 10.3390/en17071628

Ghosh, P., Jha, A., & Sharma, R. R. K. (2020). Managing carbon footprint for a sustainable supply chain: A systematic literature review. *Modern Supply Chain Research and Applications, 2*(3), 123–141. DOI: 10.1108/mscra-06-2020-0016

Gu, X. (2024). Exploration of carbon emission statistics and management in the supply chain of automobile industry based on Blockchain technology. *Academic Journal of Management and Social Sciences, 6*(1), 97–100. DOI: 10.54097/qfx8kh10

Gurtu, A., & Johny, J. (2019). Potential of blockchain technology in supply chain management: A literature review. *International Journal of Physical Distribution & Logistics Management, 49*(9), 881–900. DOI: 10.1108/ijpdlm-11-2018-0371

Hu, Z., Du, Y., Rao, C., & Goh, M. (2020). Delegated proof of reputation consensus mechanism for blockchain-enabled distributed carbon emission trading system. *IEEE Access : Practical Innovations, Open Solutions, 8*, 214932–214944. DOI: 10.1109/access.2020.3041689

Ju, C., Shen, Z., Bao, F., Weng, P., Xu, Y., & Xu, C. (2022). A novel credible carbon footprint traceability system for low carbon economy using blockchain technology. *International Journal of Environmental Research and Public Health, 19*(16), 10316. DOI: 10.3390/ijerph191610316 PMID: 36011951

Kim, S.-K., & Huh, J.-H. (2020). Blockchain of carbon trading for UN sustainable development goals. *Sustainability, 12*(10), 4021. DOI: 10.3390/su12104021

Li, Y., Xia, X., Qiao, N., Zhang, P., & Zhang, J. (2023). Research on carbon emission management of electric power enterprises based on blockchain technology. SHS Web of Conferences, 154, 01024. https://doi.org/DOI: 10.1051/shsconf/202315401024

Liao, H.-T., Pan, C.-L., & Zhang, Y. (2023). Smart digital platforms for carbon neutral management and services: Business models based on ITU standards for green digital transformation. *Frontiers in Ecology and Evolution, 11*. Advance online publication. DOI: 10.3389/fevo.2023.1134381

Liu, S., Liu, J., Li, Y., Zhou, C., & Wang, C. (2024). Research on the application of blockchain technology in the carbon trading market of substations. *Applied Mathematics and Nonlinear Sciences*, *9*(1). Advance online publication. DOI: 10.2478/amns-2024-0947

Marisamy, K., Selvakumar, A., Rajasekar, B., Natarajan, R., Atajanova, A., & Makhmudov, S. (2025). Smart logistics integrating AI, IoT, blockchain, and Robotics for a sustainable Future. In *Emerging Trends in Smart Logistics Technologies* (pp. 73–104). IGI Global Scientific Publishing., DOI: 10.4018/979-8-3373-2434-0.ch003

Moshood, T., Nawanir, G., Sorooshian, S., & Okfalisa, O. (2021). Digital Twins driven supply chain visibility within logistics: A new paradigm for future logistics. *Applied System Innovation*, *4*(2), 29. DOI: 10.3390/asi4020029

Nibbering, D., & Paap, R. (2024). Forecasting carbon emissions using asymmetric grouping. *Journal of Forecasting*, *43*(6), 2228–2256. DOI: 10.1002/for.3124

Sarkis, J., Kouhizadeh, M., & Zhu, Q. S. (2020). Digitalization and the greening of supply chains. *Industrial Management & Data Systems*, *121*(1), 65–85. DOI: 10.1108/imds-08-2020-0450

Shang, M., & Luo, J. (2021). The Tapio decoupling principle and key strategies for changing factors of Chinese urban carbon footprint based on cloud computing. *International Journal of Environmental Research and Public Health*, *18*(4), 2101. DOI: 10.3390/ijerph18042101 PMID: 33670040

Tang, Q., & Tang, L. M. (2019). Toward a distributed carbon ledger for carbon emissions trading and accounting for corporate carbon management. *Journal of Emerging Technologies in Accounting*, *16*(1), 37–46. DOI: 10.2308/jeta-52409

Wang, L., Deng, T., Shen, Z.-J. M., Hu, H., & Qi, Y. (2022). Digital twin-driven smart supply chain. *Frontiers of Engineering Management*, *9*(1), 56–70. DOI: 10.1007/s42524-021-0186-9

Wang, M., Wang, B., & Abareshi, A. (2020). Blockchain technology and its role in enhancing supply chain integration capability and reducing carbon emission: A conceptual framework. *Sustainability*, *12*(24), 10550. DOI: 10.3390/su122410550

Zhou, W. (2024). Optimized application and potential impact of blockchain technology in carbon trading. *Finance & Economics*, *1*(9). Advance online publication. DOI: 10.61173/7p5cjg77

KEY TERMS AND DEFINITIONS

Artificial Intelligence (AI): The simulation of human intelligence in machines that enables them to analyze data, detect patterns, forecast outcomes, and optimize decision-making processes.

Big Data Analytics: The process of collecting, processing, and analyzing massive datasets from various sources, such as IoT devices, logistics systems, and supplier operations, to derive actionable insights for carbon accountability.

Blockchain: A decentralized, immutable digital ledger that records transactions or data securely, ensuring transparency, traceability, and tamper-proof record-keeping in sustainability reporting.

Carbon Footprint: The total amount of greenhouse gases, particularly carbon dioxide, generated directly or indirectly by activities within a supply chain.

Carbon Neutrality Certification: An official validation, increasingly supported by blockchain, that confirms an organization has offset or eliminated its carbon emissions to achieve net-zero status.

Digital Twin: A virtual replica of supply chain assets or processes that uses real-time data to simulate scenarios, forecast environmental impacts, and test carbon reduction strategies.

ESG (Environmental, Social, and Governance): A framework used to evaluate corporate responsibility, covering environmental stewardship, social accountability, and governance transparency.

Greenwashing: The act of providing misleading or exaggerated information about an organization's environmental practices to appear more sustainable than it truly is.

Predictive Sustainability: The use of AI and data-driven models to anticipate future carbon emissions and proactively implement strategies that minimize environmental impact.

Smart Contracts: Self-executing agreements stored on a blockchain that automatically enforce rules and trigger actions such as carbon credit trades when predefined conditions are met.

Chapter 5
Blockchain and Big Data Integration for Transparent and Traceable Supply Chains: A Literature Scoping Approach

Munyaradzi Chibaro
http://orcid.org/0000-0002-4139-5139
University of Botswana, Botswana

James Kanyepe
http://orcid.org/0000-0002-6871-8831
University of Botswana, Botswana

Wilbert Manyanga
http://orcid.org/0000-0002-6710-0140
North-West University, South Africa

Josephine Moeti Lysson
http://orcid.org/0000-0003-3955-1822
University of Botswana, Botswana

Tinashe Musasa
http://orcid.org/0000-0002-3180-0399
University of Botswana, Botswana

DOI: 10.4018/979-8-3373-6896-2.ch005

ABSTRACT

This chapter explores the integration of blockchain and big data technologies to enhance transparency and traceability in modern supply chains. Drawing on sociotechnical systems theory, this chapter examines how decentralised ledgers and real-time analytics can collaboratively address challenges such as fraud, inefficiency, and lack of visibility across supply chain networks. Using the PRISMA methodology, a systematic review of peer-reviewed literature from 2015 to 2025 was conducted to identify trends, gaps, and empirical evidence supporting the integration of these technologies. Key findings reveal that blockchain ensures data immutability and provenance, whereas big data enables predictive analytics and operational optimisation. The synergy between the two technologies fosters trust among stakeholders and supports regulatory compliance. The chapter concludes with recommendations for policymakers, technologists, and supply chain managers, emphasising the need for interoperable platforms, data governance frameworks, and capacity-building initiatives.

INTRODUCTION

Transparency and traceability have become critical at a time of globalised trade and more intricate supply chains (Zreik, 2024). Particularly in industries such as manufacturing, medicine, and agriculture, supply chains are susceptible to fraud, inefficiency, and interruptions. Real-time visibility and reliable data across numerous stakeholders are frequently not possible with traditional solutions. Promising answers to these problems can be found in emerging technologies, namely, blockchain and big data analytics. Because blockchain technology offers previously unheard-of openness and traceability, two essentials for today's intricate global supply network supply chains are progressively changing (Bukhari, 2024). Every stage of a product's journey, from raw ingredients to the final customer, may be documented in a tamper-proof digital record that is available to all authorised stakeholders by utilising blockchain's immutable and decentralised ledger. By ensuring that the provenance of items can be verified, this lowers the possibility of fraud, counterfeiting, and mistakes while increasing consumer and partner trust (Gul et al, 2024).

Blockchain improves transparency in supply chain management by making data freely accessible, verifiable, and auditable in real time (Seidelson, 2024). A thorough and unchangeable record of product handling and transactions is produced by the blockchain, which time-stamped and cryptographically secures every transaction or movement of items. Stakeholders are better able to recognise and address supply chain problems, including fraud, contamination, and delays, because of this transparency. For example, blockchain smart contracts, which are self-executing agreements, automate a number of tasks, such as payments, inventory restocking, and compliance verification, reducing human mistakes and administrative burdens (Carlan et al 2020).

Blockchain-powered traceability is especially helpful in sectors where authenticity and origin verification are crucial, such as food, pharmaceuticals, and luxury items (Alam, 2020). Blockchain, for example, has made it possible for businesses such as Tracifier to offer end-to-end traceability solutions for food items, enabling customers and retailers to confirm the location, time, and method of product sourcing and inspection. This feature provides transparent supply chain data, including safety inspections and certifications, which lowers product recalls and increases consumer confidence. Blockchain-driven traceability not only increases safety and compliance but also improves visibility to supplier performance and inventory flows, which helps businesses optimise their operations (Agostinelli, et al 2024).

Additionally, by allowing businesses to promptly identify and isolate impacted products across the supply chain, blockchain can expedite product recalls. This lessens the expense and reach of recalls, minimising harm to one's reputation and possible health hazards. In contrast to traditional systems, where tracing can be laborious and prone to errors, blockchain enables quicker and more focused recalls by documenting every product movement on an impermeable ledger (Kshetri, 2021). In addition to protecting customers, increased recall efficiency helps businesses better meet legal obligations.

Another important advantage that blockchain provides to supply chains is security. Because of its distributed architecture, transaction records are kept on multiple nodes, avoiding data manipulation and single points of failure. Since any change to transaction data results in mismatched signatures and alarms, cryptographic approaches such as hashing guarantee data integrity. Owing to the constant availability of precise and verifiable product information, blockchain technology is perfect for avoiding fraud and counterfeiting (Dananjaya, Habio & Fakhrezzy, 2022). For example, counterfeit medications pose serious health concerns and market losses globally, but blockchain technology can validate the entire supply chain, protecting both patients and companies (Patil, 2024).

Blockchain technology gives up new possibilities for supply chain traceability and transparency when combined with cutting-edge technologies such as artificial intelligence (AI) and the Internet of Things (IoT). Real-time information regarding product location, handling, and conditions may be instantly fed into the blockchain by IoT sensors, guaranteeing ongoing quality monitoring and environmental compliance (Thinakaran et al. 2023). AI can then use these data to automate decision-making and offer predicted insights. These kinds of linkages enable businesses to build supply chains that are extremely flexible and responsive.

Numerous sizable businesses have led the way in implementing blockchain technology in supply chains, highlighting its usefulness and scalability. Walmart, for example, has reduced the time needed to trace contaminated products from days to seconds by using blockchain technology to track the origin of food products such as leafy greens. Through the provision of verifiable information on the sources of its products, Sephora has used blockchain technology to improve the user experience and boost transparency. These effective deployments highlight how the technology can revolutionise supply chain procedures by improving data precision, productivity, and customer confidence.

Blockchain technology allows for unmatched transparency and traceability and provides a paradigm leap in supply chain management. It generates a decentralised, transparent, and unchangeable ledger that documents each transaction and movement of commodities. This guarantees the genuineness of the goods, boosts customer confidence, reduces fraud and mistakes, and makes recalls quicker and more effective. When paired with smart contracts, the IoT, and AI, blockchain enables businesses to streamline processes and satisfy increasing customer and regulatory demands for product safety and responsible sourcing (Natanelov, et al 2022). Blockchain has become a key technology for next-generation supply chains in a number of industries as its use has increased.

Big data makes it possible to gather, process, and analyse enormous datasets for operational optimisation and predictive insights, whereas blockchain offers a decentralised, unchangeable ledger that guarantees data provenance and integrity. These technologies, when combined, have the potential to completely transform supply chain management by improving responsiveness, accountability, and trust. With an emphasis on both global and developing contexts, this chapter examines the theoretical underpinnings, real-world applications, and strategic implications of integrating blockchain technology with big data.

Research Objectives

i. The effects of blockchain and big data integration on transparent and traceable supply chains
ii. To examine the influence of tracking systems on transparent and traceable supply chains
iii. To investigate the effects of data management on transparent and traceable supply chains
iv. To analyse the influence of smart contracts on transparent and traceable supply chains

THEORETICAL DEVELOPMENTS

Blockchain technology

Arachchige et al. (2023) refer to blockchain as a distributed, immutable and peer-to-peer (P2P) database composed of information secured via cryptography, which is very strong in securing transactions and ensuring the preservation of data integrity and authenticity. Mutede (2022) defines blockchain technology as an organised, decentralised, immutable ledger that allows electronic recording of transactions via a network. According to Thegeya (2022), blockchain technology is a relatively new technology that has seen global growth since its first implementation in 2008. Mutede (2022) noted that this technology has proven to be versatile and can be applied to a different number of industries.

Niyutunga (2022) suggested that the adoption and implementation of blockchain technology appear to be in its infancy stages in developing countries and that some pilot projects have been unsuccessful. According to Chilunjika and Uwizeyimana (2024), blockchain technology has not been given much attention, as its implementation has the potential to be hampered by numerous challenges, such as inadequate information communication technology infrastructure and skills, security and privacy concerns, usability, resistance to change and a lack of financial resources to procure the hardware and software needed for this technology. Blockchain technologies are considered crucial with great potential to revolutionise different industries according to Niyutunga (2022). Chilunjika et al. (2022) reported that blockchain technology is part of the Fourth Industrial Revolution (4IR) and offers significant benefits in different sectors.

Big data integration

Supply chain management is changing as a result of big data integration, which makes businesses more effective and sensitive to changes in the market (Munuhwa, & Chibaro, 2024). Businesses may obtain important insights into every facet of their supply chain by utilising enormous volumes of data from many sources, including sensors, IoT devices, consumer interactions, and social media. Real-time tracking of inventory levels, demand variations, and supplier performance is made possible by this data-driven strategy, which facilitates more precise forecasting and proactive decision-making (Singhvi, Singhvi, & Zhang, 2023). For example, predictive analytics can spot possible hiccups such as shipment delays or shifts in customer preferences, allowing businesses to modify their plans appropriately (Kanyepe, 2024).

Furthermore, by offering a common platform for data access and analysis, big data integration promotes improved cooperation among supply chain participants.

Since everyone can view the same information, trust is increased, resulting in better coordinated activities and lower risks (Kanyepe, et al 2024). Furthermore, deeper analysis and process automation are made possible by combining big data with cutting-edge technologies such as machine learning and artificial intelligence, which promotes continual development (Kanyepe, 2024). Nonetheless, issues including the necessity for standardised data formats, data privacy concerns, and the difficulties of handling big datasets must be resolved. To build flexible, robust supply chains that can adjust to the quickly shifting business environment and eventually increase customer satisfaction and competitive advantage, big data integration is crucial (Chibaro, et al 2024).

Transparent and traceable supply chains

In today's intricate business climate, supply chains that are transparent and traceable are crucial for promoting efficiency, accountability, and confidence (Chibaro et al. 2024). Giving stakeholders unambiguous insight into the many phases of the supply chain, from the procurement of raw materials to the delivery of the finished product, is a key component of transparency (Narwane, et al 2021). Organisations can keep an eye on procedures, ensure that rules are followed, and react quickly to any interruptions owing to this visibility. In contrast, traceability enables companies to monitor the movement of goods along the supply chain, guaranteeing that every item can be tracked back to its place of origin. To satisfy customer needs for sustainability and ethical sourcing, this skill is becoming increasingly important (Mageto, 2021).

Transparency and traceability are greatly improved by technologies such as blockchain and the Internet of Things. Blockchain provides a trustworthy audit trail by recording all supply chain transactions in a decentralised, unchangeable ledger (Nair, & Kumar, 2024). By ensuring that everyone has real-time access to the same information, this technology lowers the possibility of fraud and misunderstanding. Real-time tracking and monitoring are made possible by IoT devices with sensors that can gather and send data on the location and state of commodities during their route (Viriyasitavat, Bi, & Hoonsopon, 2022).

Furthermore, by enabling enterprises to examine enormous volumes of data, the incorporation of big data analytics improves these skills even more. Decision-making procedures can be enhanced, inefficiencies can be found, and possible interruptions can be anticipated because of this study (Xiao, et al 2022). As consumers place greater value on transparency when making purchases, supply chains that are traceable and transparent ultimately result in increased customer satisfaction and confidence (Powell, et al 2022). As companies continue to operate in international markets, putting these strategies into effect helps them comply with regulations and gain a competitive edge by strengthening their bonds with partners and customers. Adopting traceability and transparency is now essential for effective supply chain management in the contemporary economy rather than a choice (Alwi, 2024).

Theoretical Framework

Socio-Technical Systems Theory

Trist (1950) was the principal developer of sociotechnical systems theory. According to theory, the social and technical aspects of an organisation are interrelated and should be taken into account jointly for effective organisational design and change. According to the organisational and design theory known as sociotechnical systems theory, a system is made up of interconnected social and technical subsystems that collaborate to achieve system success. The idea was developed in the 1950s as a reaction to previous technocratic models that prioritised technology at the expense of human and social aspects. It was first developed at the Tavistock Institute in London. The basic idea is to maximise social and technological factors at the same time without giving one priority over the other. While the technical subsystem consists of the instruments, methods, abilities, and physical procedures necessary to accomplish organisational objectives, the social subsystem includes human elements, including people, their relationships, values, and organisational structures (Yadav, & Rajput, 2024). The contextual setting in which the two subsystems function affects how they interact. In place of alienation and rivalry, sociotechnical systems theory encourages cooperation, dedication, and risk-taking by promoting the idea that people are important resources that should be developed. The interplay and interdependence of these subsystems lead to success, and cooperative optimisation makes it possible for organisations to operate efficiently and adaptably (Vaghani, 2024). This method encourages the creation of work systems that balance technology capabilities with human demands, which improves system viability, productivity, and job satisfaction. highlights how organisational structures and technology interact (Hader, et al, 2022).

Principal agency theory

According to Welansari (2023), one of the major issues that has existed in organisations for centuries is the problem that arises from the relationship between the organisation's parties. The problem is termed the principal agent problem. Jensen & Meckling (1976) refer to principal–agent theory as a concept that focuses on the relationship that exists between one party who delegates tasks to another party for execution. The principal delegates tasks, and the agent executes the assigned tasks.

Principal agency theory explores the misalignments that arise when the agent is expected to act in the best interests of the principal.

Chang & Chen (2020) noted that in the absence of blockchain technology, the agent is the only one who has access to information from external stakeholders, is guided by their own interest and acts independently to process the information on behalf of the principal. The adoption of blockchain technology can help mitigate principle-agency problems in the road haulage industry by reducing information asymmetry rates, providing data logs and providing automated compliance checks and payments. A secure and transparent transporting platform is set up, enabling tracking of goods and vehicles in transit. Owing to the use of smart contracts, transparent and traceable agreements will be set up, and parties will be accountable and obligated to meet their obligations. This improves the efficiency and operations of organisations, as all transactions will be verified.

Technology-Organisation Environment (TOE) Framework

The TOE framework was developed in the 1990s by Tornatzky & Fleischer. According to Tornatzky & Fleischer (1990), three different elements of a firm's context influence adoption decisions. The elements that influence adoption are the technological, organisational and environmental contexts. Technological context, according to Baker (2011), refers to all technologies that are relevant to the firm that are already existing and in use at the firm and those that are available in the market and not currently in use. The available technologies are crucial to the adoption process because they are there to set a broad limit on the scope and pace that will be undertaken by technological change. Those that exist give organisations direction of evolution and adaptation. According to Nguyen, Le & Vu (2022), important technological factors include relative advantage, compatibility and observability.

According to Chilunjika et al. (2024), the adoption of blockchain technology includes technological, organisational and environmental themes. Technological concerns involve technical skills and the complexity and development of technologies for adoption. The technical challenges hamper the adoption and implementation of blockchain-based applications. Krasteva et al. (2021) suggested that blockchain technology is still in its infancy and that it is vulnerable to technical errors and is thus unreliable. Scalability, cost of information technology equipment, data integrity and security, time of transaction processing and interoperability are other challenges posed by technology (Singh et al. 2023).

Case Study 1: Walmart and IBM Food Trust

Walmart and IBM collaborated to use the IBM Food Trust blockchain platform to increase food supply chain transparency. To address concerns about contamination and spoil, the project sought to enhance food safety and traceability. Walmart developed a system that captured every transaction from a farm to store on an immutable ledger by incorporating blockchain technology. This greatly decreased the amount of time required to locate contamination sources by enabling the business to track the origin of items in a matter of seconds. For example, Walmart was able to promptly identify the products that were impacted when a foodborne illness was discovered, reducing both financial and health concerns. This method was subsequently improved by the use of big data analytics, which allowed Walmart to examine patterns in food safety events and improve inventory control. In addition to increasing customer trust, this all-encompassing strategy reduced processes, enabling better decision-making and faster reaction times. All things considered, Walmart and IBM's partnership is a perfect example of how blockchain technology and big data can be combined to build an open, traceable supply chain that prioritises food safety and customer welfare.

Case Study 2: Maersk and TradeLens

The TradeLens platform was created by Maersk and IBM to improve shipping efficiency and transparency worldwide. All supply chain actors, including shipping lines, freight forwarders, and port operators, can access a safe and shared digital record created by TradeLens via blockchain technology. This software streamlines procedures and cuts down on paperwork by giving stakeholders access to real-time shipment data. TradeLens examines enormous amounts of shipping data by incorporating big data analytics, offering insights into possible delays and inefficiencies. Stakeholders can track containers in real time, for instance, which improves resource allocation and planning. All parties can trace the movement of commodities and verify transactions without the need for middlemen since the platform also increases participant trust. The TradeLens has thereby greatly shortened transit times and enhanced supply chain visibility, which is advantageous to all parties. This case study demonstrates how big data and blockchain technology may transform conventional shipping methods and promote a more effective and transparent global supply chain (Hong, & Hales, 2021).

Case Study 3: De Beers and Everledger

To improve transparency and traceability in the diamond supply chain, De Beers, a prominent player in the sector, teamed up with Everledger to deploy a blockchain solution. The initiative's main goal is to guarantee that diamonds come from conflict-free and ethical sources. De Beers can establish a digital ledger that documents each diamond transaction, from mine to merchant, by employing blockchain technology. Every diamond is assigned a distinct digital identification that is connected to its provenance, enabling buyers to confirm its ethical standing and place of origin. With the integration of big data analytics, better inventory management and marketing strategies are made possible by De Beers' analysis of consumer preferences and diamond sourcing trends. By providing openness in the buying process, this technique not only aids in the fight against conflict diamonds but also fosters customer trust. Thus, the partnership between De Beers and Everledger demonstrates how big data and blockchain may be combined to make the luxury goods industry's supply chain more moral and open.

Case Study 4: Carrefour and Blockchain

The global retail company Carrefour has used blockchain technology to improve food product traceability, especially in its supply chain for fresh vegetables. Carrefour and IBM collaborated to create a blockchain system that enables customers to scan QR codes on food packaging to track the products' origins. From farm to shop, this approach documents each stage of the supply chain, guaranteeing that details regarding the product's origin, agricultural methods, and transit circumstances are easily accessible. By incorporating big data analytics into this framework, Carrefour is able to efficiently track customer trends and supply chain performance. For example, Carrefour can modify its inventory by using data analytics to determine the demand for organic vegetables. By being transparent about food safety and quality, this effort not only increases consumer confidence but also improves operational efficiency (Yadav, & Rajput, 2024). Therefore, Carrefour's usage of big data and blockchain is a prime example of how merchants can promote openness and trust in their supply chains, which will eventually increase customer happiness and loyalty.

METHODOLOGY

Inspired by the previously described literature review method, this study employs a literature survey technique that summarises the subject of blockchain and big data integration. The study was carried out in three stages: the creation of journal lists, dataset extraction, and data synthesis. These stages are meant to assist readers in comprehending the logical flow of the research processes. Before beginning the search process to find the data source, the study's objectives were carefully reviewed. AI-powered predictive analytics, manufacturing engineering, business and management, applications of blockchain technology in marketing, information and computing science, and business predictive analytics were among the relevant research categories from which a preliminary list of journals (J=31) was selected. To guarantee their quality, the rankings of the selected journals were compared to the journal quality list. Sixteen of the highest-quality journals made up the study's journal list, while those with rankings below A* (i.e., top quality) were removed from the original list.

The first step in the paper extraction process is to establish suitable inclusion and exclusion criteria to collect relevant papers from the journal list. These requirements were outlined as follows: they should be published in English and within the five-year timeframe of 2020–2025 to accurately represent the state of the research field. The justification for choosing this period of time is that recent literature, which usually represents the most recent approaches, trends, and discoveries in the field, provides a more accurate picture of the state of knowledge today. Business analytics, blockchains, the Internet of Things, and big data integration should all be covered in publications at the same time. Papers that concentrate on a literature review approach should be eliminated from the dataset.

Using "blockchain, big data integration" as keywords, we searched a few selected sources for relevant articles. Two hundred papers were further examined via three filtration procedures to ensure that they satisfied the significance criteria. In the first filter, the abstracts of each paper were reviewed. After that, 180 papers were removed. Following a preliminary search in specific databases, several keywords were examined and further honed as needed to ascertain their significance. The material was then evaluated via these keywords, and the appropriate category was selected. After that, a secondary search was conducted using reputable academic publications and literature databases, such as Web of Science, Science Direct, and Google Scholar.

Figure 1. PRISMA 2021 flow diagram

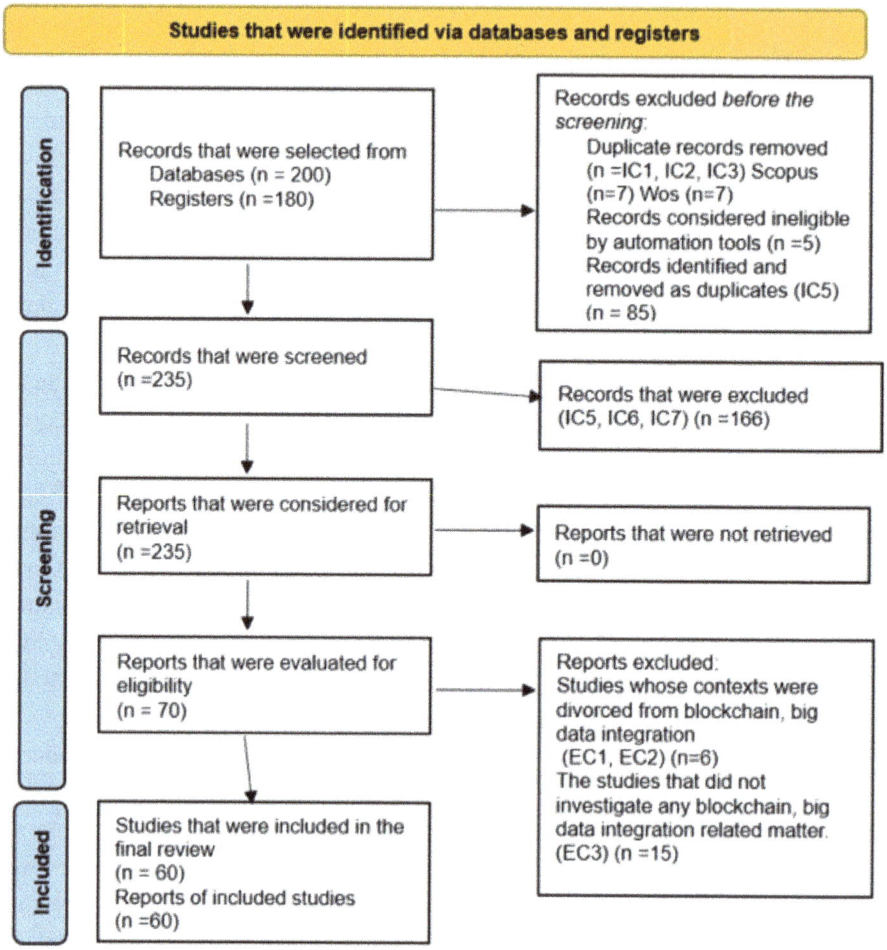

The approach's primary steps, the search strategy, selection process, data gathering procedure, and synthesis methods, are described in the following subsections. For a transparent and well-organised selection process, the systematic review standards adhered to the PRISMA (Preferred Reporting Items for Systematic Reviews and Meta-Analyses) recommendations (Page et al., 2021). This study conducted a comprehensive review of the global research literature on blockchain and big data integration. The analysis was based on the evaluation of secondary data from relevant publications. A wide range of relevant electronic databases, including Web of Science, Scopus, and Google Scholar, were thoroughly searched. These databases were chosen because of their abundance of pertinent content. Keywords were used to create the search terms. The search results were filtered via Boolean operators (AND,

OR). Only peer-reviewed English-language book chapters, conference presentations, and journal articles published between 2020 and 2025 were included in the search.

These included publications make up the final compilation of excellent, relevant research that meets the criteria for a systematic review. To ensure accuracy and minimise bias, the data extraction process was carried out by two independent reviewers. The results from the included research were included via a narrative synthesis approach. This requires the establishment of crucial tactics that integrate big data by cutting-edge technology such as blockchain and the Internet of Things. Meta-analytic methods were used to aggregate the quantitative data.

Table 1. Sources of included articles

Journal publication name	No. of articles
International Journal of Engineering Applied Sciences and Technology	2
Technology in Society	5
Elsevier BV	3
IGI Global,	5
Emerald	2
Technological Forecasting and Social Change	3
Emerald Publishing Limited	5
Taylor and Francis	3
MDPI AG	2
Smart Agricultural	1
Springer Nature Singapore	2
Pandawan,	5
Springer International Publishing	1
Frontiers Media SA	3
Journal of International Academy of Business and Economics	1
SSRN Electronic Journal	1
Journal of Physics: Conference Series	1
Journal of Business and Retail Management Research	1
International Journal of Science and Research (IJSR)	1
Palgrave Studies of Marketing in Emerging Economies	1
Data Analytics in Marketing, Entrepreneurship, and Innovation	1
African Journal of Economic and Management Studies	1
International Journal of Production Research	1
Journal of Operations Management	1

continued on following page

Table 1. Continued

Journal publication name	No. of articles
Transportation Research Part E: Logistics and Transportation Review	5
Total	60

Source: Secondary Data Analysis (2025)

Table 1 provides a summary of the articles that were selected and used in the study. It gives a quick reference to all the sources that contributed to the research, and it shows the reader which sources were used to draw conclusions. The articles allow the reader to evaluate the range and quality of evidence supporting the study.

FINDINGS

The effect of blockchain on transparent and traceable supply chains

Big data and blockchain technology integration significantly improves supply chain traceability and transparency, radically altering how companies function (Wong et al. 2024). Every transaction in the supply chain is recorded in a decentralised, immutable ledger made possible by blockchain, guaranteeing that everyone involved has real-time access to the same data (Karadgi, Kulkarni, & Doddamani, 2021). This degree of openness promotes confidence among stakeholders by assisting in the eradication of fraud and inconsistencies. This integration is demonstrated, for instance, by IBM and Walmart's partnership through the IBM Food Trust program. Walmart can use blockchain technology to track the origins of its food goods in a matter of seconds, which greatly speeds up response times to food safety concerns and increases customer trust in the calibre of its products.

However, big data analytics enhances blockchain by enabling businesses to examine enormous amounts of data produced all along the supply chain (Lee, & Mangalaraj, 2022). De Beers, for example, has improved traceability in the diamond sector by utilising both technologies. De Beers guarantees ethical sourcing by documenting every diamond's path from mine to market on the blockchain, and they can evaluate consumer preferences and market trends via big data analytics. This dual strategy allows De Beers to optimise inventory management on the basis of real-time analytics, in addition to offering openness regarding the diamond's provenance.

Additionally, the TradeLens platform, created by IBM and Maersk, demonstrates the potent combination of big data and blockchain in international shipping. Blockchain technology is used by TradeLens to establish a shared digital ledger that enhances supply chain visibility, and big data analytics provides information about shipment performance and possible delays. Stakeholders may make well-informed decisions because of this integration, which lowers inefficiencies and improves overall operational performance. Big data and blockchain integration greatly increase supply chain traceability and transparency, allowing businesses to better comply with regulations, build consumer trust, and react quickly to disturbances (Bouhtati, Alla, & Bentalha, 2023). Industries are better prepared to satisfy expectations for accountability and transparency in a changing marketplace, as they increasingly use these technologies (Sigmund, 2021).

To examine the influence of tracking systems on transparent and traceable supply chains

Tracking systems on transparent and traceable supplies real-time visibility of the movement and status of commodities. They are essential for improving the transparency and traceability of supply chains. These systems track goods as they travel from point of origin to customers via a variety of technologies, such as GPS, RFID, and Internet of Things devices. One such example is how businesses such as Zara have transformed inventory management in the apparel industry by implementing RFID technology. Zara can precisely monitor inventory levels and ensure that the proper products are accessible when they are needed by attaching RFID tags to clothing. Because stakeholders may access real-time data on product placement and stock availability, this capacity improves transparency and, eventually, customer happiness. Another compelling case is the collaboration between IBM and Walmart through the Food Trust blockchain initiative. This system enables tracking of food products from farm to store, allowing Walmart to trace the origin of its produce in seconds. When a food safety issue arises, such as contamination, the ability to quickly identify affected products minimises health risks and financial losses. The transparency provided by this tracking system fosters consumer trust, as customers can verify the origins and quality of their food (Ayan, 2022).

Furthermore, the TradeLens platform developed by Maersk and IBM exemplifies how tracking systems can streamline global shipping. By providing a shared digital ledger accessible to all participants, TradeLens enhances visibility into shipment status and reduces inefficiencies caused by paperwork. Stakeholders can track containers in real time, leading to better resource allocation and planning (Calvão, & Archer, 2021).

These examples underscore how tracking systems enhance supply chain transparency and traceability, allowing organisations to respond swiftly to disruptions, reduce fraud, and improve overall operational efficiency. As consumers increasingly demand transparency regarding product origins and ethical sourcing, companies that invest in sophisticated tracking systems will gain a competitive advantage, ultimately leading to a more resilient and trustworthy supply chain (Hunt, & Zhuang, 2022). The integration of advanced tracking technologies is essential for building transparent and traceable supply chains that meet the evolving needs of the market (Khan, et al 2022).

To examine the effects of data management on transparent and traceable supply chains

Establishing open and verifiable supply chains requires data management because it allows businesses to efficiently gather, process, and use enormous volumes of data (Park, 2020). Better decision-making and operational efficiency are made possible by accurate, secure, and easily accessible data, which are guaranteed by effective data management techniques (Kouhizadeh, et al. 2022). Coca-Cola, for example, has improved its supply chain visibility by implementing sophisticated data management systems. Coca-Cola is able to check product distribution, keep an eye on inventory levels, and examine trends in consumer demand by employing real-time data analytics. With this degree of visibility, the business can save waste and optimise production schedules, guaranteeing that goods are accessible when and where they are needed. The use of data management by the aerospace sector, especially by firms such as Boeing, is another noteworthy example. Boeing uses advanced data management systems that include information from suppliers and production procedures, among other sources. Because of this integration, every component utilised in the manufacturing of aircraft can be tracked down to its original location. Such traceability improves accountability and quality assurance in the production process in addition to being necessary for regulatory compliance (Semenzin, 2023).

The collaboration between Nestlé and SAP serves as an example of how crucial data management is to traceability in the food industry. Nestlé has developed a digital supply chain that follows food goods from farm to fork by leveraging SAP technologies. This technique improves transparency by giving customers access to comprehensive information on the origin and preparation of their food. Nestlé can react to any food safety concerns promptly by keeping precise and current data, which guarantees that any impacted goods are found and removed as soon as possible. Creating supply chains that are traceable and transparent requires efficient data management. Organisations may increase visibility, make better decisions, and build stakeholder trust by utilising advanced data analytics and combining information from several sources. Businesses that prioritise effective data management will be better equipped to satisfy the growing demands of consumers for transparency and maintain the integrity of their supply chains (Cai, & Xiao, 2021).

To analyse the influence of smart contracts on transparent and traceable supply chains

Smart contracts automate procedures and guarantee that all parties follow predetermined agreements without the need for middlemen (Muralidharan, et al, 2022). They have a substantial effect on supply chains' transparency and traceability. Blockchain technology is used to code these self-executing contracts, enabling safe, transparent, and unchangeable record-keeping. IBM and Maersk's collaboration on the TradeLens platform, which uses smart contracts to expedite shipping procedures, is a famous example. The smart contracts in this system automatically carry out tasks in response to preset criteria, including releasing funds once items are transported to the specified port. Because all parties can confirm that terms have been fulfilled without the need for manual intervention, this automation not only lowers administrative expenses but also increases stakeholder trust. Walmart's use of smart contracts in their food supply chain is another strong argument. Walmart can automate the tracking of food supplies from farm to table by using blockchain technology with smart contracts. For example, the smart contract may automatically start the recall process and send alerts if a batch of produce is discovered to be tainted, guaranteeing that the impacted products are quickly taken off the market. In addition to improving food safety, this feature gives customers peace of mind because they can track the provenance of their food and confirm its quality (Burgess, Sunmola, & Wertheim-Heck, 2024).

To guarantee ethical sourcing, businesses such as Everledger are also using smart contracts in the diamond sector. The blockchain gives each diamond a unique digital identity, and smart contracts are used to confirm ownership and transactions. Since all parties involved can confirm the diamond's provenance before buying, this transparency helps stop the sale of conflict diamonds. Transparency and traceability in supply chains are greatly enhanced by smart contracts. Smart contracts increase operational efficiency and foster stakeholder trust by automating procedures, eliminating the need for middlemen, and guaranteeing agreement compliance (Rivera et al, 2024). The adoption of smart contracts is expected to grow as more industries implement blockchain technology, further transforming supply chain management and promoting accountability across a range of industries. Blockchain enhances data integrity, traceability, and stakeholder trust (Kayikci, & Khoshgoftaar, 2024).

IMPLICATIONS FOR THE STUDY

Below are the study's theoretical, policy, practical and economic implications.

Theoretical Implications

The integration of blockchain and big data into supply chains presents several theoretical implications that challenge and expand existing frameworks in supply chain management, information systems, and organisational behavior. Traditional supply chain theories often emphasise trust among stakeholders, which is typically built through relational contracts and reputation (Vivaldini, 2020). The introduction of blockchain as a decentralised ledger system challenges these models by providing a mechanism for trust that is inherent to the technology itself. This shift suggests that trust can be codified and maintained through technological means rather than solely through interpersonal relationships or historical interactions.

Theories surrounding information asymmetry, which highlight discrepancies in access to information among supply chain participants, are transformed through blockchain and big data integration. With blockchain, all parties can access the same real-time data, reducing the potential for information gaps. This has implications for theories related to negotiation and decision-making, as stakeholders can engage with a shared understanding of the supply chain's status (Hoberg, 2020).

The complexity of modern supply chains necessitates frameworks that can accommodate dynamic interactions and interdependencies. The integration of big data analytics with blockchain can enhance the understanding of these complex systems by providing insights into patterns and trends that were previously obscured (Sharma, & Shishodia, 2022). This suggests a need for updated models that better account for the interplay between data analytics and blockchain technology in managing complexity.

Theories on supply chain resilience focus on the ability of a supply chain to adapt and respond to disruptions. The integration of blockchain and big data enhances resilience by providing real-time visibility and actionable insights, enabling quicker responses to unforeseen events. This integration invites a reevaluation of resilience frameworks to incorporate technological adaptability as a core component. The use of blockchain and big data raises important ethical questions about data privacy, security, and the potential for surveillance. Theoretical frameworks in organisational behavior and ethics may need to evolve to address these concerns, considering how technology can both increase accountability and raise ethical dilemmas in supply chain practices (Porkodi, & Kesavaraja, 2024).

Policy Implications

The integration of blockchain and big data in supply chains has significant policy implications that require attention from regulators and industry leaders. First, governments must establish clear regulatory frameworks that govern the use of blockchain technology, ensuring data privacy and security while fostering innovation. These frameworks should promote interoperability between different blockchain systems to facilitate seamless data sharing across supply chains. Additionally, policies must address ethical considerations, particularly concerning data ownership and consumer privacy, ensuring that stakeholders are protected from potential misuse of information. Furthermore, as transparency becomes a critical demand from consumers, policymakers may need to incentivise companies to adopt these technologies, potentially through tax breaks or grants. By fostering an environment that encourages the responsible use of blockchain and big data, policymakers can enhance supply chain transparency and traceability, ultimately benefiting consumers and businesses alike while promoting sustainable practices across industries.

Practical Implications

The integration of blockchain and big data into supply chains has several practical implications for businesses seeking to enhance efficiency and transparency. Companies must invest in the necessary technology infrastructure and training to leverage these tools effectively, ensuring that employees are equipped to analyse big data and utilise blockchain systems. Additionally, the adoption of these technologies requires a shift in operational practices, emphasising collaboration among supply chain partners to share data securely and transparently. Businesses may also need to rethink their supplier relationships, prioritising those that are willing to engage in blockchain initiatives to ensure traceability and ethical sourcing. Furthermore, organisations should develop clear communication strategies to educate consumers about the benefits of these technologies, fostering trust through transparency. Ultimately, embracing blockchain and big data can lead to improved decision-making, reduced costs, and increased customer satisfaction, positioning companies competitively in an increasingly transparent marketplace.

Economic Implications

The integration of blockchain and big data into supply chains has significant economic implications for businesses and industries. By enhancing transparency and traceability, these technologies can reduce the operational costs associated with inefficiencies, fraud, and compliance issues. For example, real-time data analytics can optimise inventory management, leading to reduced waste and improved cash flow. Furthermore, the automation of processes through smart contracts can decrease administrative burdens, allowing companies to allocate resources more effectively. On a broader scale, as companies adopt these technologies, they can improve consumer confidence, driving demand for ethically sourced products and potentially leading to higher market shares. Additionally, the increased efficiency and reliability of supply chains can stimulate economic growth by attracting investment and fostering innovation. The economic implications of integrating blockchain and big data are substantial, offering opportunities for cost savings and competitive advantages in an increasingly interconnected global market.

OPPORTUNITIES AND ENABLERS FOR GROWTH

The integration of blockchain and big data in supply chains presents numerous opportunities and enablers for growth across various sectors. By leveraging these technologies, businesses can increase their operational efficiency and create new revenue streams through innovative service offerings. For example, companies can develop value-added services such as real-time tracking and authentication of products, appealing to consumers' increasing demand for transparency. Additionally, partnerships between tech firms and traditional industries can foster innovation, encouraging the development of customised solutions that address specific supply chain challenges. Investment in training and development will empower employees to harness data analytics and blockchain effectively, driving continuous improvement and adaptation. Furthermore, as regulatory frameworks evolve to support these technologies, businesses find it easier to implement blockchain and big data solutions, paving the way for sustainable growth. Ultimately, embracing these advancements positions organisations to capitalise on emerging market trends and consumer preferences, driving long-term success.

Future directions

The future directions of blockchain and big data integration in supply chains are poised to reshape the landscape of global commerce. As technology continues to evolve, we can expect increased interoperability between blockchain platforms, allowing seamless data exchange across different systems and industries. The rise of decentralised finance (DeFi) may also influence supply chain financing, enabling more flexible and efficient funding options for businesses. Additionally, advancements in artificial intelligence (AI) and machine learning will enhance data analytics capabilities, providing deeper insights into consumer behavior and market trends. As sustainability becomes a central focus, blockchain's ability to verify ethical sourcing and environmental impact will drive adoption among environmentally conscious consumers. Collaborations among companies, governments, and industry stakeholders are crucial in establishing standards and best practices. The future of supply chains will be characterised by enhanced transparency, agility, and responsiveness, positioning organisations for success in an increasingly dynamic marketplace.

CONCLUSION

In conclusion, the integration of blockchain and big data into supply chains represents a transformative shift toward greater transparency, traceability, and efficiency. These technologies empower organisations to enhance operational practices, streamline processes, and build trust among stakeholders by providing real-time access to accurate information. As businesses navigate the complexities of modern supply chains, the adoption of these innovations will be essential for addressing consumer demands for ethical sourcing and sustainability (Zhan, et al. 2025). Additionally, the collaboration among technology providers, policymakers, and industry leaders will play a pivotal role in overcoming challenges and establishing robust frameworks that support these advancements. In the future, organisations that embrace blockchain and big data will not only gain a competitive edge but also contribute to a more resilient and accountable supply chain ecosystem. The convergence of blockchain and big data represents a paradigm shift in supply chain management. By fostering transparency and traceability, these technologies can mitigate risks, enhance efficiency, and build trust across global networks. Ultimately, the future of supply chains lies in leveraging these technologies to foster collaboration, drive innovation, and ensure long-term success in a rapidly evolving market. The chapter advocates for strategic integration supported by policy, infrastructure, and education.

REFERENCES

Agostinelli, S., Arman, A., Luzi, F. D., Monti, F., Manglaviti, M., & Mecella, M. (2024). Supporting business confidentiality in coopetitive scenarios: The B-CONFIDENT approach in blockchain-based supply chains. *Journal of Industrial Information Integration, 42*, 100730, ISSN 2452-414X, Elsevier BV, DOI: 10.1016/j.jii.2024.100730

Alam, T. (2020). *Blockchain-based Big Data Analytics Approach for Smart Cities.*, Wiley, DOI: 10.22541/au.160208029.93138178/v1

Alwi, A., Sasongko, N., Adi, S., Suryana, Y., & Subagyo, H. (2024). Blockchain and big data integration design for traceability and carbon footprint management in the fishery supply chain. *Egyptian Informatics Journal, 26*, 100481, ISSN 1110-8665, Elsevier BV, DOI: 10.1016/j.eij.2024.100481

Ayan, B., Güner, E., & Son-Turan, S. (2022). Blockchain Technology and Sustainability in Supply Chains and a Closer Look at Different Industries: A Mixed Method Approach. *Logistics, 6*(4), 85, ISSN 2305-6290, MDPI AG, DOI: 10.3390/logistics6040085

Bouhtati, N., Alla, L., & Bentalha, B. (2023). Marketing Big Data Analytics and Customer Relationship Management. *Advances in Logistics, Operations, and Management Science*, 75-86, ISSN 2327-350X, IGI Global, DOI: 10.4018/979-8-3693-0225-5.ch004

Bukhari, S. Danish (2024). Blockchain and Sustainability in Supply Chains. *Advances in Logistics, Operations, and Management Science*, 142-159, ISSN 2327-350X, IGI Global, DOI: 10.4018/979-8-3693-0482-2.ch009

Burgess, P., Sunmola, F., & Wertheim-Heck, S. (2024). Information needs for transparency in blockchain-enabled sustainable food supply chains. *International Journal of Information Management Data Insights, 4*(2), 100262, ISSN 2667-0968, Elsevier BV, DOI: 10.1016/j.jjimei.2024.100262

Cai, Y., & Xiao, X. (2021). Application of Blockchain Technology in Management Accounting: Based on the Perspective of Frontier Literature Review. *Smart Innovation, Systems and Technologies*, 323-332, ISSN 2190-3018, Springer Singapore, DOI: 10.1007/978-981-33-6141-6_35

Calvão, F., & Archer, M. (2021). Digital extraction: Blockchain traceability in mineral supply chains. *Political Geography, 87*, 102381, ISSN 0962-6298, Elsevier BV, DOI: 10.1016/j.polgeo.2021.102381

Carlan, V, Coppens, F, Sys, C, Vanelslander, T, & Gastel, G, V (2020). Blockchain technology as key contributor to the integration of maritime supply chain?. *Maritime Supply Chains*, 229-259, Elsevier, DOI: 10.1016/b978-0-12-818421-9.00012-4

Chibaro, M., Chikwere, D., Kanyepe, J., & Govere, E. (2024). End-of-Life Vehicle Management. *Advances in Civil and Industrial Engineering*, 309-344, ISSN 2326-6139, IGI Global, DOI: 10.4018/979-8-3693-3755-4.ch012

Chibaro, M., Mataba, A. T., & Mupfiga, C. (2024). Influence of Warehouse Management Practices on Service Delivery in Zimbabwean Local Authorities. *Logistic and Operation Management Research (LOMR), 3*(1), 1-16, ISSN 2830-2680, Research Synergy Foundation, DOI: 10.31098/lomr.v3i1.1882

Dananjaya, H. R., Fabio, M., & Fakhrezzy, M. (2022). Coordination of Global Approach for Blockchain Supply Chains. *Blockchain Frontier Technology, 2*(1), 72-83, ISSN 2808-0009, Pandawan, DOI: 10.34306/bfront.v2i1.116

Gul, I., Raziq, A., & Khan, M. R. (2024). Towards Sustainable Supply Chains With Blockchain. *Advances in Logistics, Operations, and Management Science*, 18-37, ISSN 2327-350X, IGI Global, DOI: 10.4018/979-8-3693-0482-2.ch002

Hader, M., Tchoffa, D., El Mhamedi, A., Ghodous, P., Dolgui, A., & Abouabdellah, A. (2022). Applying integrated Blockchain and Big Data technologies to improve supply chain traceability and information sharing in the textile sector. *Journal of Industrial Information Integration, 28*, 100345, ISSN 2452-414X, Elsevier BV, DOI: 10.1016/j.jii.2022.100345

Hoberg, K. (2020). *Supply Chain and Big Data. Encyclopedia of Big Data.* Springer International Publishing., DOI: 10.1007/978-3-319-32001-4_242-1

Hong, L., & Hales, D. N. (2021). Blockchain performance in supply chain management: application in blockchain integration companies. *Industrial Management & Data Systems, 121*(9), 1969-1996, ISSN 0263-5577, Emerald, DOI: 10.1108/imds-10-2020-0598

Hunt, K., & Zhuang, J. (2022). Blockchain for Disaster Management. *Studies in Big Data*, 253-269, ISSN 2197-6503, Springer International Publishing, DOI: 10.1007/978-3-030-87304-2_10

Kanyepe, J. (2024). Data-Driven Logistics Optimisation. *Advances in Logistics, Operations, and Management Science*, 63-96, ISSN 2327-350X, IGI Global, DOI: 10.4018/979-8-3693-6205-1.ch003

Kanyepe, J., Chibaro, M., Morima, M., & Moeti-Lysson, J. (2024). AI-Powered Agricultural Supply Chains. *Advances in Marketing, Customer Relationship Management, and E-Services*, 33-64, ISSN 2327-5502, IGI Global, DOI: 10.4018/979-8-3693-6468-0.ch002

Karadgi, S., Kulkarni, V., & Doddamani, S. (2021). Traceable and Intelligent Supply Chain based on Blockchain and Artificial Intelligence. *Journal of Physics: Conference Series, 2070*(1), 12158, ISSN 1742-6588, IOP Publishing, DOI: 10.1088/1742-6596/2070/1/012158

Kayikci, S., & Khoshgoftaar, T. M. (2024). Blockchain meets machine learning: a survey. *Journal of Big Data, 11*(1), ISSN 2196-1115, Springer Science and Business Media LLC, DOI: 10.1186/s40537-023-00852-y

Khan, A., Hossain, E., Shahaab, A., & Khan, I. (2022). ShrimpChain: A blockchain-based transparent and traceable framework to enhance the export potentiality of Bangladeshi shrimp. *Smart Agricultural Technology, 2*, 100041, ISSN 2772-3755, Elsevier BV, DOI: 10.1016/j.atech.2022.100041

Kouhizadeh, M, Zhu, Q, Alkhuzaim, L, & Sarkis, J (2022). Blockchain Technology and the Circular Economy: An Exploration. *Circular Economy Supply Chains: From Chains to Systems*, 189-213, Emerald Publishing Limited, DOI: 10.1108/978-1-83982-544-620221010

Krasteva, I, Glushkova, T, Stoyanova-Doycheva, A, Moralivska, N, Doukovska, L, & Radeva, I (2021). Blockchain-based approach to supply chain modelling in a smart farming system. *2021 Big Data, Knowledge and Control Systems Engineering (BdKCSE)*, 1-6, IEEE, DOI: 10.1109/bdkcse53180.2021.9627309

Kshetri, N (2021). Amplifying the value of blockchain in supply chains. *Blockchain and Supply Chain Management*, 67-88, Elsevier, DOI: 10.1016/b978-0-323-89934-5.00003-9

Lee, I., & Mangalaraj, G. (2022). Big Data Analytics in Supply Chain Management: A Systematic Literature Review and Research Directions. *Big Data and Cognitive Computing, 6*(1), 17, ISSN 2504-2289, MDPI AG, DOI: 10.3390/bdcc6010017

Ma, L., & Chang, R. (2024). How big data analytics and artificial intelligence facilitate digital supply chain transformation: the role of integration and agility. *Management Decision*, ISSN 0025-1747, Emerald, DOI: 10.1108/md-10-2023-1822

Mageto, J. (2021). Big Data Analytics in Sustainable Supply Chain Management: A Focus on Manufacturing Supply Chains. *Sustainability, 13*(13), 7101, ISSN 2071-1050, MDPI AG, DOI: 10.3390/su13137101

Munuhwa, S., & Chibaro, M. (2024). E-Commerce Logistics Unleashed. *Advances in Logistics, Operations, and Management Science*, 145-163, ISSN 2327-350X, IGI Global, DOI: 10.4018/979-8-3693-1578-1.ch008

Munuhwa, S., & Chibaro, M. (2024). E-Commerce Logistics Unleashed. *Advances in Logistics, Operations, and Management Science*, 145-163, ISSN 2327-350X, IGI Global, DOI: 10.4018/979-8-3693-1578-1.ch008

Muralidharan, C., & Sirajudeen, Y. Mohamed, & Rajkumar, Y. (2022). Empowerment of Internet of Things Through the Integration of Blockchain Technology. *Studies in Big Data*, 147-157, ISSN 2197-6503, Springer International Publishing, DOI: 10.1007/978-3-030-95419-2_7

Nair, S., & Kumar, J. (2024). Blockchain Integration for Enhanced Traceability in Fijian Sugarcane Supply Chains. *2024 International Conference on Sustainable Technology and Engineering (i-COSTE)*, 1-7, IEEE, DOI: 10.1109/i-coste63786.2024.11024895

Narwane, V. S., & Raut, R. D., Mangla, S K, Dora, M, & Narkhede, Balkrishna E. (2021). Risks to Big Data Analytics and Blockchain Technology Adoption in Supply Chains. *Annals of Operations Research, 327*(1), 339-374, ISSN 0254-5330, Springer Science and Business Media LLC, DOI: 10.1007/s10479-021-04396-3

Natanelov, V., Cao, S., Foth, M., & Dulleck, U. (2022). Blockchain smart contracts for supply chain finance: Mapping the innovation potential in Australia-China beef supply chains. *Journal of Industrial Information Integration, 30*, 100389, ISSN 2452-414X, Elsevier BV, DOI: 10.1016/j.jii.2022.100389

Park, K. O. (2020). A Study on Sustainable Usage Intention of Blockchain in the Big Data Era: Logistics and Supply Chain Management Companies. *Sustainability, 12*(24), 10670, ISSN 2071-1050, MDPI AG, DOI: 10.3390/su122410670

Patil, S. (2024). Blockchain Integration in Automotive Supply Chains: Overcoming Challenges and Revolutionising Industry Practices. Proceedings of the International Conference on Industrial Engineering and Operations Management, IEOM Society International, DOI: 10.46254/gc02.20240155

Porkodi, S., & Kesavaraja, D. (2024). Blockchain and IoT Integration-Based Transparency of Supply Chain Social Sustainability. *Blockchain, IoT, and AI Technologies for Supply Chain Management*, 221-235, Apress, DOI: 10.1007/979-8-8688-0315-4_8

Powell, W, Cao, S, Foth, M, He, S, Turner-Morris, C, & Li, M (2022). Revisiting Trust in Supply Chains: How Does Blockchain Redefine Trust?. Blockchain Driven Supply Chains and Enterprise Information Systems, 21-42, Springer International Publishing, DOI: 10.1007/978-3-030-96154-1_2

Rivera, L., Gauthier-Umaña, V., & Chauhan, C. (2024). Blockchain: An opportunity to improve supply chains in the wake of digitalisation. *International Journal of Information Management Data Insights, 4*(2), 100290, ISSN 2667-0968, Elsevier BV, DOI: 10.1016/j.jjimei.2024.100290

Seidelson, C (2024). Data-Driven Approach to Agile Supply Chains. *Building Agile Supply Chains*, SAGE Publications, Inc., DOI: 10.4135/9781071941942

Semenzin, S. (2023). 'Blockchain for good': Exploring the notion of social good inside the blockchain scene. *Big Data & Society, 10*(2), ISSN 2053-9517, SAGE Publications, DOI: 10.1177/20539517231205479

Sharma, R., & Shishodia, A. (2022). Blockchain Technology Enablers in Physical Distribution and Logistics Management. *Studies in Big Data*, 329-344, ISSN 2197-6503, Springer International Publishing, DOI: 10.1007/978-3-030-87304-2_14

Sigmund, J. (2021). Advanced Analytics and Big Data in Supply Chain Planning. *Future of Business and Finance*, 121-135, ISSN 2662-2467, Springer International Publishing, DOI: 10.1007/978-3-030-61093-7_10

Singh, R., Kukreja, D., & Sharma, D. K. (2023). Blockchain-enabled access control to prevent cyber attacks in IoT: Systematic literature review. *Frontiers in Big Data, 5*, ISSN 2624-909X, Frontiers Media SA, DOI: 10.3389/fdata.2022.1081770

Singhvi, D., Singhvi, S., & Zhang, X. (2023). A Data-driven Approach to Improve Artisans' Productivity in Distributed Supply Chains. *SSRN Electronic Journal*, ISSN 1556-5068, Elsevier BV, DOI: 10.2139/ssrn.4531090

Surati, S., Shrimali, B., Trivedi, H., & Chaudhari, P. (2023). Blockchain in Supply Chain Management. *Studies in Big Data*, 61-98, ISSN 2197-6503, Springer Nature Singapore, DOI: 10.1007/978-981-19-8730-4_3

Thinakaran, J., Paul, S., Latha, C., Beulah, C., & Jacob, G. (2023). Blockchain in Big Data for Agriculture Supply Chain. *Studies in Big Data*, 257-291, ISSN 2197-6503, Springer Nature Singapore, DOI: 10.1007/978-981-19-8730-4_9

Vaghani, D. (2024). Big Data Analytics for Supply Chain Optimisation. *Advances in Logistics, Operations, and Management Science*, 101-150, ISSN 2327-350X, IGI Global, DOI: 10.4018/979-8-3693-4427-9.ch005

Viriyasitavat, W., Bi, Z., & Hoonsopon, D. (2022). Blockchain technologies for interoperation of business processes in smart supply chains. *Journal of Industrial Information Integration, 26*, 100326, ISSN 2452-414X, Elsevier BV, DOI: 10.1016/j.jii.2022.100326

Vivaldini, M. (2020). Blockchain platforms in supply chains. *Journal of Enterprise Information Management, 34*(6), 1769-1797, ISSN 1741-0398, Emerald, DOI: 10.1108/jeim-12-2019-0416

Wong, S., Yeung, J., Kun, W., Lau, Y., Kawasaki, T., & Kwong, R. (2024). *Sustainability of Blockchain Technology in Supply Chains: Implications from a Critical Literature Review.*, MDPI AG, DOI: 10.20944/preprints202404.1297.v1

Xiao, B., Simsek, M., Kantarci, B., & Alkheir, A. A. (2022). Handling big tabular data of ICT supply chains: a multitask, machine-interpretable approach. *GLOBECOM 2022 - 2022 IEEE Global Communications Conference*, 504-509, IEEE, DOI: 10.1109/globecom48099.2022.10001253

Yadav, S, & Rajput, S (2024). Modelling of blockchain interruptions for smooth integration with supply chain. *Blockchain Technology*, 49-65, CRC Press, DOI: 10.1201/9781003542766-5

Zhan, Y., Yeung, A. C. L., Tan, K. H., Xiong, Y., Xing, X., & Ye, F. (2025). Success and Failure of Blockchain Technology Providers: Founders' Power, Beyond-Blockchain Exploration and Centralised Decision-Making. *Journal of Operations Management, 71*(7), 893–916. DOI: 10.1002/joom.1364

Zreik, M. (2024). Assessing the Integration of Blockchain and Supply Chain Management. *Advances in Logistics, Operations, and Management Science*, 38-56, ISSN 2327-350X, IGI Global, DOI: 10.4018/979-8-3693-0482-2.ch003

KEY TERMS AND DEFINITIONS

Artificial intelligence: The integration of artificial intelligence in supply chain management includes the implementation of highly developed algorithms and data-driven technologies to optimize planning, forecasting, logistics and decision-making within the supply chain (Vivaldini, 2020). AI allows companies to analyze vast amounts of data, forecast demand, manage inventory and transportation more efficiently, and automate many operational functions, which results in reduced risk, increased efficiency, improved responsiveness, and greater sustainability throughout the supply chain.

Big Data Analytics: The application of Big Data Analytics in supply chain management refers to the use of sophisticated analytical tools and methodologies to process and analyze large volumes of both structured and unstructured data from various supply chain-related activities (Thinakaran, et al 2023). Organisations using Big Data Analytics can gain better insights into their customers' needs, develop more accurate forecasts of future customer demands, increase the efficiency of their logistics operations, identify potential risks in their supply chain, make better strategic decisions and ultimately improve overall supply chain performance, resilience, and competitive advantage.

Intelligent supply chains: An intelligent supply chain is an advanced technological supply chain that uses artificial intelligence, big data analytics, internet of things and automation to continuously monitor, analyze and optimize its operations on a real-time basis (Porkodi & Kesavaraja, 2024). Intelligent supply chains allow for predictive decision making, adaptive planning, better visibility and greater collaboration among all parties within the supply chain. These capabilities result in greater efficiency, improved responsiveness, greater resilience, and greater sustainability within the supply chain.

Sustainable supply chains: A sustainable supply chain is one where the flow of materials, information, and finances is managed to achieve three elements, namely economic efficiency, environmental protection, and social responsibility (Park, 2020). The objective of a sustainable supply chain is to have minimal environmental impact, maintain ethical labor practices, maximise resource utilization and provide long term value to all parties involved in the supply chain (businesses, stakeholders, and society).

Chapter 6
Harnessing Big Data for Reverse Logistics and Waste Management:
Pathways to Sustainable Supply Chains

Mowdud Ahmed
http://orcid.org/0009-0003-2053-3111
Westcliff University, USA

Omar Shabeeb Al Amareen
http://orcid.org/0009-0001-4521-9722
Westcliff University, USA

Yeasin Arafat
http://orcid.org/0009-0009-7623-1829
Westcliff University, USA

ABSTRACT

This chapter investigates the transformative potential of Big Data Analytics (BDA) in promoting sustainable practices within reverse logistics and waste management, highlighting its contribution to the development of circular supply chains. It delves into the basic concepts of reverse logistics, explores perspectives that guide sustainable operations, and examines the capabilities of BDA in predictive analytics, AI-supported decision-making, and real-time monitoring. Practical implementations, including product returns management, recycling process optimization, and integration of waste management in urban and industrial contexts, are discussed, along with challenges such as data privacy, interoperability, and organizational

DOI: 10.4018/979-8-3373-6896-2.ch006

preparedness. Additionally, the chapter illustrates how BDA aligns with circular economy principles, supporting product life extension, secondary market development, and material recirculation, while future directions point to blockchain traceability, ethical AI, and alignment with ESG and SDG frameworks.

INTRODUCTION

In the last ten years, the discussion of sustainability in the world has already changed the approach to the design and management of supply chains to a great extent. The increasing environmental demands, the straitening rules, and the increasing need of society to obtain ethical production have compelled organizations to revise their priorities in terms of operations. Subsequently, the need to incorporate the principles of sustainability into-the logistics and supply chain operations has turned into not an option but rather a necessity. In this shift, two areas have become especially important; these are reversing logistics and waste management. Not only do these processes allow marshaling one-time recovery and reuse of materials, but they are the basis of a circular economy (CE), where the waste to its lowest limits, and the resources are introduced into the production cycle once again. Interestingly, the increasing faculties of Big Data Analytics (BDA) are currently altering the way organizations plan, monitor and optimize these reverse logistics systems to slowly shift to more agile and regenerative supply chain ecosystems (Bag et al., 2021). Reverse logistics is a broad process that includes the recovery of products, repair of defective products, re-manufacturing of parts, recycling of products, and end-of-life products. All these activities were long thought of as a drain on the supply chain or as a simple cost-generating addition to the supply chain. Nevertheless, they are viewed as strategic resource points of competitive advantage development now with the current focus on sustainability and value recovery. On the same note, waste management has moved past the normal compliance processes and has developed into a major aspect of corporate sustainability plans. However, these two fields produce vast volumes of information that-is usually cumbersome, disjointed, and unstructured that originates in a wide variety of sources including smart sensors, databases of customers; and inventory. The data cannot be easily utilized and interpreted, and that is where the BDA is placed. It provides processing, relating and interpreting of these vast streams of information using the power of analytics and intelligent forms (Hasan et al., 2025; Xu et al., 2021).

The BDA is an integration of computational capability, better algorithms as well as data-based arguments to reach more informed and quicker choices in the organizations. The data obtained by the IoT gadgets, RFID tags, enterprise applications, and other feedback interfaces of the customers can be aggregated and processed to identify patterns and tendencies that can be useful. Through this process, companies would be better able to forecast the rates of returns, the best curbs-of-recovery and their recycling activities would be better forecasted. They can also be enhanced with the use of Artificial Intelligence (AI) and Machine Learning (ML) that can give predictive value that can be applied to implement real-time changes in operations. As an illustration, an AI model can forecast some of the products to be returned or when the demand to-recycle will rise and the managers can use their resources to do so. Similarly, the logistics price and the emissions of the transportation can be reduced with the assistance of optimization algorithms and still do not affect the quality of the services (Vandyck et al., 2022). The combination of Big Data, IoT, and Reverse Logistics Systems has also enabled the visibility and traceability throughout the whole supply chain to a new stage. The mounted cameras in vehicles, packaging materials and even waste pans always take data about location, condition and use. The information can be done to support the firms in making time-sensitive routing and scheduling decisions. This type of visibility is particularly helpful in the waste management processes, where the time and accuracy of waste collection, sorting and recycling impact the environmental performance directly. Smart waste management systems are increasingly-becoming-and-more-powered by BDA, enabling cities and corporations to track the trends of waste flows, identify the inefficiency of waste management, and project the future trends of waste production, in real time. It results not only in a reduction of the volume of garbage in the long run, but also transforms waste streams into high-value resources, which would well match the objectives of a CE (Möslinger et al., 2023).

The benefits of the big-data applications to the sustainability of reverse logistics and waste management are multifunctional. The technologies will minimize carbon emission into the environment because they have the best routes and are energy efficient. On the-economical-front, they save them unneeded operational costs and formulate new sources of secondary markets by reusing that which once was viewed as a waste. On a social level, they enhance corporate responsibility and transparency, which prefers more responsible production and consumption behaviors. All these advantages combined are a direct contribution to the United Nations Sustainable Development Goals (SDGs) especially-SDG 12 Responsible Consumption and Production and SDG 13 Climate Action. Thus, it is possible to consider the BDA as a technological breakthrough, as well as the major facilitator of sustainable supply chain systems development (Emon & Khan, 2025a; Zhang et al., 2021). Nonetheless, increasing dependence on data also brings in a variety of novel difficulties. The issues of data privacy and security have gained significant importance, especially when consumers are approached on topics of personal or geographical data. The potential of these technologies is also constrained by technical challenges like the inability to combine data of various systems that do not work together, and the lack of analytical skills in companies. Besides, not all organizations are prepared to undergo a digital transformation that is needed to maximize the use of big data. Infrastructure development, analytics development, and data quality maintenance require a lot of investment and long-term dedication. The data ownership, the transparency of the algorithms and the biasness of the automated decision-making have become the ethical concerns that should be the focus of the discussion regarding the extent and fairness with which it is possible to use these technologies (Marabelli et al., 2021). The chapter explores these themes in a detailed way. It starts by establishing the theoretical basis of the concept of reverse logistics and waste management, and-placing it in the context of the perspective of sustainable supply chain management. The next focus is then on the various applications of the BDA in improving these processes backed up by practical case studies and the latest examples in the industry. It also focuses on the technical, organizational, and ethical challenges that firms encounter in the process of implementing data-driven systems. Further details on how such data-based innovations can be applied in accordance with the principles of the CE are discussed later to be able to redesign supply chains to achieve long-term sustainability and resource efficiency. To conclude, the chapter points out that the actual promise of big data is not just the enhancement of the operations, but also the redefinition of the concept of sustainable business practices. By treating waste as a value source and data as the engine of constant learning, organizations will be able to prevent the formation of material loops and decrease the environmental impact and develop resilience to future disruptions. The knowledge presented here should benefit both researchers and practitioners in assisting the former to develop theoretical knowledge and the former to consider data-based recommendations to enhance sustainability. Finally, the successful adoption of BDA in the realm of reverse logistics and waste management is a disruptive avenue of reaching the twofold objectives of economic efficiency and environmental accountability in an ever more digital and sustainability-focused world (Hwang et al., 2025; Tran-Dang et al., 2025).

FRAMING THE ROLE OF DATA IN SUSTAINABLE REVERSE SUPPLY CHAINS

Understanding Reverse Logistics and Waste Management

One of the most complex, but essential components of supply chain management in the modern context has slowly but surely acquired-a reverse logistics. To be simple, it is concerned with how the final users take goods and materials back to manufacturers or suppliers with the aim of repairing, handling returns, refurbishing, remanufacturing, recycling, or even proper disposal of the same. Reverse logistics is still not as concerned with the direction of the supply of any product to the customer as opposed to the traditional forward logistics which emphasizes-on the supply of the product to the customer. Once considered a secondary or an expensive procedure, this has taken center stage in the wider sustainability discussion in global supply chains over time. The emphasis is on making sure that resources contained in products do not become useless but instead re-enter the productive cycles in one way or another (Emon et al., 2025; Spaltini et al., 2021). Waste management that is closely related to this is a set of processes of gathering, transferring, processing, and recycling or disposal of manufactured materials that are produced by an industrial, business, or residential process. Waste management in the modern context extends to disposal as it is concerned with constructing systems that recover resources and recycle them into a cycle. As a matter of fact, waste management and reverse logistics are not two phenomena; they go hand in hand. The operational channel through which waste returns to the value base is in the commercial form of-a reverse logistics, whereas waste management deals with the process and technologies in which waste is converted to usable materials, or energy. Having them both together represents a practical essence of a CE, where the products are created to be reused, repaired, or recycled, instead of thrown away (Hasan et al., 2025; Mihai & Ulman, 2023). The combination of the two fields is important in sustainable supply chain practices. As an example, electronics producers have begun to use take-back schemes to collect valuable metals in discarded electronics and retail businesses usually use reverse logistics by repacking, reselling, or giving away unsold or returned products to charities. Not only do such systems reduce waste production but also create new business opportunities for the firms dealing with secondary materials market. Thus, the interdependence between waste management and the reverse logistics has turned into a practical manifestation of sustainability in the interaction of ecological responsibility and economic logic (Fernando et al., 2023).

Figure 1. Conceptual Flow of Reverse Logistics and Waste Management in Sustainable Supply Chains

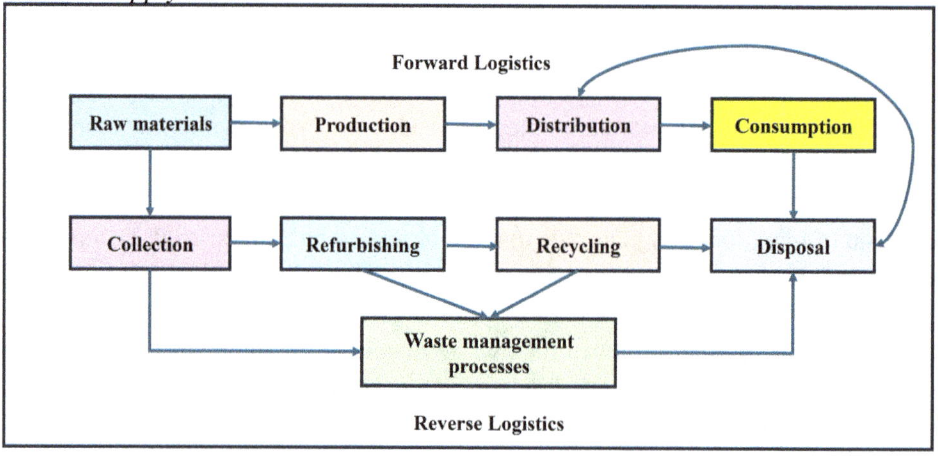

Source: Developed by the author

Perspectives Guiding Sustainable Supply Chains

The various theoretical lenses that have been used to specify that and how sustainability principles are entrenched in supply chains have been explored by scholars and practitioners. The Resource-Based-View (RBV) is one of the most influential ones, and it assumes that the competitive advantage of a firm can be acquired and depend on the capacity to gain and use specific internal resources that are valuable, rare, inimitable, and non-substitutable. Abilities associated with reverse logistics design, minimization of waste, and data-based decision-making can be some of the valuable strategic resources in this context. Companies that effectively establish such abilities are prone to outperform other companies not only through minimizing inefficiencies, but also through improving brand equity through observable sustainability offers (Handoyo & Anas, 2024). The other lens is the CE perspective which aims to transform the way business is thought in order-to free it of the conventional take-make-dispose model and instead have a more regenerative, restorative system. CE-model recommends the extension of product lifecycle by- repairing, reusing, recycling, and remanufacturing, thereby maintaining the-material in the economy as long as possible. Reverse logistics in this system is the circulatory system that allows this flow of materials to take place, and data analytics is the role of intelligence that is critical to predict the returns, the recovery rates, and material resource loop optimization. In cases when companies use CE thinking in terms of their logistics and waste management, financial performance and environmental stewardship may quite often coincide (Hasan et al., 2024; Le, 2023). Besides, the Systems-Thinking provides a complete system to comprehend sustainability in supply chains. It does not consider the supply chain as a linear process but as an intricate network of mutually dependent relationships between production, logistics and consumers and the environment. Systems Thinking also teaches the decision-makers not to view waste as something to be expected as a by-product but as an indicator of inefficiency or system imbalance. Sustainable solutions in this view are not limited to the isolated functions only, but also the interactions between the various processes at the entire level of the value chain. This perspective also demonstrates why data-driven approaches have become so vital and significant that they help organizations to follow feedback loops, establish interconnections, and create interventions that could help organizations to align operational goals with longer-term goals of the environment (Khan & Emon, 2025b; Van der Linde et al., 2024).

Big Data Analytics: Concepts, Tools, and Capabilities

The BDA can be described as a broad concept framework, which involves the collection, storage, processing, and analysis of large and complex data to generate insights that can lead to better decisions. It has been extensively applied across supply chains because of its ability to handle the augmentation of quantity, variedness and swiftness of data being exchanged at different nodes. BDA is an ecosystem of technologies such as the Internet of Things (IoT), cloud computing, AI, and blockchain that can be used to improve the visibility, traceability, and predictive intelligence (Saidu et al., 2025). The process usually starts by gathering data, in which data is acquired by sensors, RFID tags, enterprise system, and digital interactions along the chain of supply. They are stored in infrastructures or distributed data lakes, which can handle large and often non-structured data, and are stored in clouds. The next step involves data processing which converts raw data into data ready to be analyzed. The use of advanced analytics, ML, and pattern recognition techniques to gain helpful insights is implemented. These observations can be either the predictability of the rate of product returns or optimization of transport routes, or recycling demand. An example is that predictive models can be used to forecast the returns flow in e-commerce processes, whereas prescriptive analytics can propose the most effective reverse logistics path to pursue collectively or redistribution. In the context of waste management, IoT-powered bins and bins that have real-time fill-level sensors can have a huge significance on the scheduling of waste collection and saved unnecessary visits to the waste collection point. (Emon, 2025a; Lakhouit, 2025). Another technology that is highly promising to the big data ecosystem is blockchain technology that has increased transparency and traceability in reverse logistics. Because blockchain develops indelible logs of all activities and actions of the supply chain, it can ascertain the authenticity of recycled materials and adherence to sustainability laws. Together with analytics, blockchain provides some degree of visibility and accountability that is uncommon with traditional systems. All in all, BDA has transformed to become the analytical foundation of the contemporary sustainable logistics that changes data into a usable intelligence that reinforces the outcomes of the environment and economy (C.-T. Chen et al., 2024).

Table 1. Key BDA Tools and Their Applications in Reverse Logistics and Waste Management

BDA Tool/ Technology	*Function*	*Application Area*	*Expected Outcome*
IoT Sensors	Data collection in real-time	Waste tracking, bin monitoring	Improved collection scheduling
Machine Learning	Predictive analytics	Forecasting product returns	Resource planning, reduced waste
Blockchain	Secure and traceable data storage	Tracking recycled materials	Transparency and compliance
Cloud Computing	Data storage and processing	Reverse logistics systems	Scalable analytics infrastructure
AI Optimization	Decision automation	Routing and resource allocation	Reduced costs, emission savings

Source: Developed by the author

Connecting Big Data with Reverse Logistics

In the case of BDA being incorporated into the reverse logistics systems, it can serve as a diagnostic and predictive tool. It helps companies gain the-real time visibility on the whole lifecycle of their products-since the time they sell the product until the time they are returned, recycled, or wasted. The perpetual tracking enables companies to detect bottlenecks, control their inventories more efficiently, and be able to comply with the requirements of sustainability. ML algorithms can be used to predictive analytics to assist companies more effectively predict the volume of returns and recycling needs which, in turn, minimizes inefficiency (overcapacity or underutilization) (Lakhouit, 2025). Moreover, waste flow optimization is improved with the help of BDA. With the help of production and operational data, companies can identify the points of waste, assess the efficiency of recycling, and develop specific interventions to enhance the efficiency of recovery. Such data-focused solution minimizes landfills and encourages the recovery of useful secondary resources in waste streams. Making sustainability dashboards and performance metrics accessible to all stakeholders manufacturers, logistics providers, governments, and consumers is also involved in collaboration (Hasan et al., 2022; Rane et al., 2021). Basically, BDA-is-the combination of reverse logistics thereby transforming the conventional definition of waste. Waste is never viewed as an expense or a liability but as a source of strategic value which can lead to both environmental and economic value. This synergy results in supply chains that can be called not only efficient but also adaptive and regenerative an important step on the way to the achievement of the promise of a truly sustainable and a CE (Emon, 2025c; Lin, 2024).

BIG DATA APPLICATIONS IN REVERSE LOGISTICS

The revolution of BDA in the supply chain operation and its associated activities has far-reaching past the conventional benefits of efficiency, especially in reverse logistics. Traditionally, the very concept of reverse logistics was viewed as a proactive collection of activities that a mechanism manages to accept product returns, recycle them, or dispose-them after a customer used them or government intervention. However, over the past few years, the use of big data tools has changed this perception as organizations are now able to assume a more proactive, predictive and efficient method to the management of reverse product flows. With the use of enormous amounts of data available in various forms, including IoT-capable sensors and enterprise systems, consumer feedback and transactional history companies can more and-more predict returns and optimize recycling, as well as produce greater value out of the end-of-life products. The section discusses the most important BDA uses in the context of reverse logistics, including predictive analytics, optimization of network, decision-making with the help of AI, and picturesque examples.

Predictive Analytics for Product Returns and Recycling

One of the most important contributions that BDA has made towards reverse logistics is in the area of- predictive analytics. This entails the application of historical and real-time data to forecast future events and the future outcomes. In the framework of the product returns, predictive models may be developed to use a combination of factors such as purchase patterns, the nature of seasonal sales behavior, product defects, and warranty claims, and customer complaints, all of which can be used to estimate the probable volume, timing, and location of returns (McCarthy et al., 2022). As an example, combining the sales data collected over the years and the warranty data, companies will be in a better position to predict which type of products or batches will be returned. Not only can such predictions be used to make better preparations- but operational costs incurred due to unforeseen returns are also minimized. In addition to predicting returns, BDA has a role to play in end-of-life (EOL) product recovery as well as recycling programs. ML algorithms have the opportunity-to categorize returned products by their condition, usage, and age, which would define whether a product requires refurbishing, additional manufacturing, or recycling. This predictive strategy allows organizations to invest their resources efficiently and focus on the recovery channels with high value. As an illustration, electronics companies often employ predictive analytics to understand which returned gadgets have components that make them valuable including rare metals and which gadgets can be more effectively recycled into a better-known environmentally safe procedure (Emon & Khan, 2025b; Singh et al., 2025). Using this information to predict the kind and amount-of returns, businesses can schedule collections and processing more efficiently to minimize the chances of a bottleneck or delay in the recycling process. The second place where predictive analytics can take effect is in warranty claim management. BDA will enable the firms to identify the trends of failure or malfunction of certain lines of products so that they can take proactive measures. Indicatively, when a batch of products has an above normal probability of early returns, companies can anticipate production designs or add more capacity to reverse logistics to handle the expected inflow (Tennakoon et al., 2022). Adaptive systems, which optimize the refinement of forecasts based on predictive models together with real-time monitoring provided by IoT devices or consumer applications, are possible to create to improve the efficiency and sustainability results of operations.

Optimization of Reverse Logistics Networks

BDA is also crucial in designing and optimization of reverse logistics networks besides forecasting. Such networks can be comprised of a network of networked collection areas, recycling or refurbishment facilities, warehouses and transport pathways. Various variables must be considered when optimization is meant such as the cost of transport, the capacity of processing, storage capacity, and effects to the environment. In one- way, big data is seen to have significant advantages in the optimization of routing. With the help of the real-time GPS information, traffic dynamics, and past operational trends, organizations will be in-a position to come up with effective collection routes of the returned products or waste materials. Optimization algorithms usually consider the distance, vehicle capacity, urgency, and carbon emissions, which provide routes with lower costs and carbon footprint. As an example, predictive models can arrange stops of trucks that take electronic waste to various retail outlets so that the travel lasts as little as possible, and the load is as big as possible (Y.-C. Chen & Hasan, 2023; Park et al., 2021). Another important application is inventory management. The analysis of the flow of returned goods allows the firms to estimate the numbers at various collection hubs and reallocate stocks. This avoids excess stocking in some areas and wastage of the processing plants in other areas. In addition, real-time analytics will facilitate dynamic storage space allocation and give high-value items priority during refurbishment or re-manufacturing at high frequency (Psarommatis et al., 2025). Capacity planning is directly related to routing and inventory decisions. BDA helps companies predict the necessary processing by the projected returns so that they can scale resources in terms of labor, equipment, and facilities accordingly. E.g. following a seasonal sale, or a new product, a return explosion can be anticipated, and predictive intelligence can be used to assist companies to hire more sorting agents or open more pick-up locations on a short-term basis. Lack of this foresight can result in bottlenecks in the reverse logistics operation, slow recycling, or inefficiency in the processing of returned goods (Khan et al., 2024).

Enhancing Decision-Making through AI and ML

ML and AI have become vital facilitators of intelligent decision-making when it comes to reverse-logistics. ML models can also automatically categorize-and sort items returned automatically, and determine products to be resold, refurbished, or recycled. This automation eliminates the human error and speed of processing which are especially critical in high-volume markets like electronics, e-commerce and fashion. ML algorithms also ease the procedure of making decisions on remanufacturing. Through product condition, usage history and market demand, AI will be able to suggest whether a returned unit should be refurbished, turned into a new product, or to dismantle parts. Even predictive models can be used to detect minor patterns of failure, direct focused repair, and minimize unjustified dismantling. Natural language processing (NLP) can also be used to categorize returns with automated systems, and this can also use natural language to categorize the customer-notes or reasons for returns, and this can be used to make even more accurate and fast decisions (Emon et al., 2025). In addition to operational uses, AI can also be used in strategic-level decisions. Further optimization models, such as the reinforcement learning algorithms, can modify reverse flows depending on the real-time conditions, seasonality, and changing market needs. As an example, when some returned products are demonstrated to have increased volume of remanufactured versions, AI systems can be configured to prioritize them over the other products, enhancing economic and environmental performance (Khan et al., 2024; Wilson et al., 2022).

Case Insights: Data-Driven Reverse Logistics in Practice

The practical impact of BDA in reverse logistics is evident through several industry examples:

Dell's Recycling System: Dell has adopted a data-driven solution to monitor the returned electronic products to determine the components that can be reused or resold. IoT monitoring and predictive models optimize the collection path and estimate the amount of recoverable materials that help to increase operational efficiency and environmental sustainability (Lakhouit, 2025).

HP's Closed-Loop Cartridge Recovery: Hewlett-Packard (HP) uses the-sophisticated analytics to run its closed-loop recycling of printer cartridges. Predictive models predict the amount-of returns, and AI is used to sort and refurbish. This distribution system will minimize landfills and provide a continuous flow of remanufactured cartridges, and a clear track of adherence (Wilson et al., 2022).

Zara's Return Analytics: Zara applies the concept of big data to reverse flows of unsold inventory in the fast-fashion industry. The redistribution and recycling decisions are based on real-time data on sales, customers returning, and the warehouse. Predictive analytics operationally and sustainably benefits products, and ML models can categorize products, schedule returns, and minimize waste (Park et al., 2021).

These are just some examples to show that BDA in reverse logistics is not just a theoretical framework. When put into proper use it can convert raw data into actionable information, improve predictive value, optimize networks, aid in decision making and bridge the gap between flows of material. As a result, reverse logistics ceases to be the expense to be addressed but a sustainability and efficiency tool, allowing the- companies to pursue and reach economic, environmental, and operational objectives at the same time.

BIG DATA APPLICATIONS IN WASTE MANAGEMENT

Traditionally, the subject matter of waste management, both in an industrial or a municipal context, has been considered as a secondary or an operational issue. However, the increased focus on sustainability and the urge to practice a CE have put waste management on the strategic agenda of not only organizations and municipalities but also urban planners. The advent of the BDA has brought in fresh areas of opportunities that not only improved the-efficiency but also the transparency and responsiveness of the waste management systems. With the help of data collected by IoT, modern sensor networks, and enterprise systems, companies and cities can now afford to track waste flows in real time, optimize the processes of waste recovery, and integrate waste streams with larger industrial and urban systems. Here, the uses of BDA in waste management can be applied in various dimensions, such as the- real-time tracking, resource recovery on-the-basis of data, systemic integration, and real-life examples of implementation.

Real-Time Waste Tracking and IoT-Enabled Monitoring

Among the most significant contributions that big data has made to the- contemporary waste management, it is possible to mention the possibility to see waste-flows in real-time. Previously, collection schedules were generally fixed and inefficient' leading to overfilling bins, unnecessary trips or even underutilized collection capacity. Nowadays, the use of smart bins, RFID tags and sensor networks that run on the IoT platform enables real-time tracking of full capacity, position, and even material composition. This feature allows operators to make active corrections to the collection routes, optimize the use of the fleet, and minimize the costs of operations and environmental effects (Cao et al., 2021). As an example, ultrasonic scanners fitted on bins will be able to scan continuous fill levels and transmit the information to centralized management systems. Still on this, the tags using RFID on the containers or other products that can be recycled aid in the tracking process at both the collection and processing stages. The sensor networks applied in cities or industrial localities are applicable in the detection of anomalies such as illegal dumping or overfilling and consequently the authorities can take actions. The real-time streams of data generated by these devices are fed into high-tech analytics systems, and predictive algorithms may be applied to forecast tendencies in waste production, anticipate when the collection time is high, and where priority must be considered (Lakhouit, 2025). Real time monitoring may also assist in adherence to regulations as well as environmental safety. Waste streams can be followed to identify as well as sort materials correctly, and in such a way that hazardous or regulated waste is managed correctly to minimize possible risks to humans and the environment. Such visibility will facilitate the decision-makers-to shift towards predictive and preventive practices to improve operational performance and performance in the environment rather than the current reactive strategies of disposal.

Table 2. Key IoT and Big Data Applications in Waste Management

Application Area	Technology/Tool	Function/Benefit	Example Outcome
Waste Tracking	Smart bins, RFID, Sensors	Real-time fill level monitoring, anomaly detection	Reduced overflow, efficient route planning
Predictive Analytics	ML/AI, Cloud Analytics	Forecast waste generation, optimize collection	Dynamic scheduling, reduced operational costs
Resource Recovery	Sorting algorithms, Computer Vision	Classify and separate recyclables	Higher recycling rate, improved material purity
Urban & Industrial Integration	Data sharing platforms	Match waste streams to reuse opportunities	Industrial symbiosis, circular city planning

Source: Developed by the author

Data-Driven Resource Recovery and Recycling Optimization

In addition to tracking, BDA is a key factor in streamlining the process of resource recovery and recycling. Waste streams often have a considerable portion of recoverable materials, and to effectively identify, sort, and process these resources, it is necessary to operate based on data. BDA can be used to optimize the performance of numerous areas along the waste management value chain by analyzing collection point information, sorting plant information, and processing plant information. ML- algorithms, e.g. can be used to sort types of waste through sensor reading, visual recognition technology or chemical composition data. Automated classification increases speed of sorting, decreases human errors and enhances purity of recovered materials-an element that is important in the high-value recycling processes. Predictive analytics are also capable of the estimated number and quality of recyclable material based on specific regions or industry, whereby the collection schedule and processing capacity can be adjusted accordingly and in a timely manner (Emon & Chowdhury, 2025; Lakhouit, 2025). The use of data-driven optimization is especially useful in recycling plants where operational decisions are determined based on real-time data on equipment performance, throughput, and material characteristics. Analytics may be used to drive graphical order of the processes of shredding, washing, or separating of various waste streams to optimize the recovery of materials and reduce energy consumption. Moreover, the recovery performance should be tracked against the overall environmental objectives to enable firms to observe such important indicators as landfill diversion rates, carbon emissions, and raw material consumption, which are related to sustainability and cost-effectiveness (Yu et al., 2023).

Integrating Waste Management into Urban and Industrial Systems

The effect of big data can be greatly enhanced when the waste management is incorporated into the urban or industrial ecosystems. The Smart city models and industrial symbiosis projects use common data to reduce the amount of waste and increase reuse possibilities. Urban settings The IoT and big data platforms can synchronize the residential, commercial, and municipal waste flows so that the products retrieved in one industry could be efficiently diverted to another. The waste production information on history and in real-time enables the dynamic assignment of collection trucks, the optimization of the recycling capacities, and the targeted benefits of households and businesses to minimize the production of waste (Lakhouit, 2025). Industrial symbiosis is a comparable approach, only that it addresses collaboration between companies. Through data sharing of by-products, waste stream and material requirements, firms can convert materials which are otherwise wasted to valuable input in other production processes. This is aided by Big- data analytics to match the most ideal sources of waste with their potential users, forecast the quality and quantity of by-products to be used, and coordinates transportation and logistics. Integration minimizes total wastage, creates economic value, collaboration, and sustainable industrial practices. Policy and urban planning-is-also facilitated by integration. Predictive models can help the municipalities to allow them to forecast future volumes of-the-waste by looking at the trends in the population, industrial growth, or seasonality to enable them to make proactive investments in recycling and treatment infrastructure. Such analytics used together with real-time monitoring will be useful in scenario-based planning, during which the various approaches to waste reduction or resource recovery can be simulated and the most effective ones chosen.

Case Insights: Big Data for Sustainable Waste Management

Several real-world implementations highlight the tangible benefits of big data in waste management:

Singapore's Smart Waste Management System: Singapore has implemented IoT-based bins and real time monitoring systems to gather information about the waste level, efficiency of collection and recycling rate. The high level of analytics will enable the optimization of collection schedules, operational costs, and recycling outcomes by the city. Predictive models also assist in making advance predictions of any surpasses of waste in the event of a festival or other public gathering, enabling resources to be allocated in advance (Almutairi et al., 2025; Emon, 2025b).

Sweden's Waste-to-Energy Analytics: Waste-to-energy plants are optimized by means of analytics implemented in Sweden. Sensors, processing machinery, and energy output systems data are processed to achieve the most energy recovery with minimal environmental impact. The balancing of the input streams, predicting the equipment maintenance, and increasing the overall efficiency of the operations are all supported by big data and demonstrate how the waste can be converted into the renewable resources (Ukoba et al., 2024).

India's Swachh Bharat Data Initiatives: The Indian municipalities, in their cleanliness programs at the national level, have implemented the big data and IoT system to keep on track of the waste collection and segregation. Household and industrial waste generation data are used to determine inefficiency and plan interventions and monitor environmental goals. These programs demonstrate that analytics can be used to improve accountability, transparency, and mass management of the waste in the public sector (Lakhouit, 2025).

These examples underscore the fact that big data has become a strategic enabler, and not an extra tool, of the sustainable management of waste. Waste can also be redesigned as an asset rather than a liability through BDA creating practical insights, predicting operations and inter-sector co-ordination. The monitoring that is IoT-enabled, predictive modeling, and process optimization based on the data will result in better operational efficiency, help achieve circular-economy goals, and strengthen a sustainable environmental responsibility in the long-term.

CHALLENGES AND LIMITATIONS

Even though an implementation-of-BDA in a reverse logistics and waste management context opens-up considerable opportunities to the efficiency of operation, sustainability, and recovery of value, there are no barriers to it. The implementation of high-level analytical solutions, IoT, and AI-based decision-making systems are accompanied by a set of technical, organizational, economic, and ethical challenges. To practitioners and scholars alike, recognizing and being aware of such limitations is important to effective implementation and sustainability of the implementation in the long term. This part will discuss five major aspects of problems and limitations, namely data privacy and security, scalability and interoperability, organizational and technological preparedness, economic and ethical policies, and regulatory restrictions.

Data Privacy and Security Issues

The proliferation of IoTs, RFID, and sensor networks in reverse logistics and waste management is bound to lead to massive amounts of sensitive data being generated.

These datasets usually record data about the behaviors of consumers, their usage patterns of products, geographic places, and history of transactions, which when poorly handled can jeopardize privacy and result in regulatory breaches (Scarpi & Pantano, 2024). As an example, smart bins and IoT-based collection systems can accidentally disclose the domestic routines or confidential company data, which concerns the unauthorized disclosure. Moreover, the interconnectedness of the IoT systems leaves them exposed to cyber-attacks. Malicious users can manipulate the data provided by sensors, disrupt routing algorithms, and maliciously interfere with the real-time data of waste products by adding them to the streams and returns of products in real-time. This may result in inefficiencies in operation in addition to loss of consumer confidence and reputation. Companies should, hence, implement stringent digital security, such as encryption, and secure authentication systems, as well as monitoring-the systems at all-times. Nevertheless, these protective devices might not be simple to implement in the existing infrastructure and might require more time to be adopted-especially by small and medium-sized organizations that lack IT capability. Added complexity is through compliance with regulation. Various jurisdictions apply divergent data protection requirements like GDPR in Europe or sector-specific consumer data protection laws that companies have-to work around. Multinational companies have to deal with the difficulty of aligning the data collection and analytics practices with these different frameworks, and it may require the specialized compliance staff and raise the expenses of operation (Dörrenbächer et al., 2021). As a result, privacy and security can be discussed as one of the primary obstacles toward using BDA in sustainable reverse logistics and waste management.

Scalability and Interoperability Challenges

The integration-challenges are common in cases where organizations aim to grow their data-driven reverse logistics and waste management systems. Big data platforms are based on the smooth interconnection of heterogeneous data sources such as IoT devices, ERP, warehouse management system, and third-party logistics software. To maintain-a proper communication between such systems, it is necessary to follow the common standards, data formats, and protocols-a usually challenging task in practice. Interoperability problems can exist in a-number of ways. As an example, older equipment can generate sensor data that will not be compatible with the newest analytics software, leading to data gaps or inaccuracy. Third-party logistics partners/municipal contractors can also use proprietary software, which does not allow a smooth exchange of data along the reverse supply chain. Not having standardized interfaces and open data architecture may indicate that organizations operate the risk of possessing an unlinked group of systems that reduce the predictive and prescriptive character of BDA (Pathak et al., 2025). Another important issue is scalability.

A solution that works effectively in a pilot project might not have any unplanned constraints when applied on a larger scale, on a cross-facility, cross-city, or cross-country basis. Real-time analytics are very expensive-and storage and processing are extensive needing investment in cloud, high-performance computing and network bandwidth. Such technical demands may deter other organizations-especially those with constrained resources to adopt the big data approaches wholly.

Organizational and Technological Readiness

Organizational readiness is critical in the success of the BDA in reverse logistics and waste management. The barriers that often impede effective adoption are internal barriers such as lack of expertise, resistance to change and lack of sufficient IT infrastructure. Professionally trained personnel to help supply chain operations meet higher-level analytics is in short supply, and often training current employees to use more complicated BDA systems may be time-intensive (Huynh et al., 2025). The change management poses a significant challenge. The employees who are accustomed to the traditional way of operations may not be eager to implement the-automated monitoring, predictive algorithms, or real-time reporting sites. The initiatives towards BDA can be underutilized without the culture that promotes the use of data in decision-making and lifelong learning, which generates suboptimal outcomes even when substantial technology investments are made. Also, not all areas of organizations are technologically ready, as the same facilities may be fully equipped with IoT and fast internet connectivity, whereas others may have no digital infrastructure at all, which poses operational gaps that suppress-the overall performance. To resolve these problems, a gradual implementation plan, investment in training and skill acquisition, and organization of organizational policies that promote adoption are important. To achieve the full potential of BDA in sustainable supply chains, integrating the use of technology with the capability of the workforce and the activity requirements is important.

Economic and Ethical Considerations

BDA is frequently associated with massive financial costs when it comes to implementing it in the context of reverse logistics and waste management. IoT gadgets, cloud storage, software license, analytics systems, and cybersecurity implementations can be costly to small and medium-sized businesses in-particular. Companies have to consider the trades off costs and benefits with great attention, making sure that anticipated improvement in operational efficiency, resource recycle, or environmental impact is worth the cost of the initial and repeated costs (Alhodaib et al., 2024). Ethical problems are also identified as a significant consideration. There also needs to be a sense of privacy, informed consent, and transparency regarding consumers information even in-the-situations when it has been collected on the sustainability basis. The tracking of waste- trend-in a home or product give-back trends may present sensitive information accidentally, which may raise an argument on surveillance and misuse. In addition to this, there is the sustainability paradox where an organization can invest in digital infrastructure and analytics that can increase the energy utilization and carbon footprints which can counteract the environmental gains achieved by increased waste management. The economic and ethical issues cited above must be tackled using a holistic strategy, which focuses on cost-efficient modular capabilities, effective data governance regulations, transparent customer interaction, and continuous evaluation of trade-offs related to the environment.

Regulatory and Policy Constraints

The regulatory and policy environment is another constraint because in most cases, technological innovations are ahead of-its policies. Reverse logistics and waste strategy fall under the environmental laws, extended producer responsibility (EPR) and the waste diversion laws. The usage of the big data tools could be introduced faster than the regulatory frameworks that support these tools, generating ambiguities in compliance, liability, and reporting (Lakhouit, 2025). Moreover, the fact that the jurisdictions do not match each other makes the operations of multinational organizations-to be-complicated. Whereas one nation can encourage e-waste recycling by offering tax incentives and reporting systems, the other nation can restrict the IoT data collection or data exchanges across the borders. To manage such regulatory differences, one must constantly track policy changes, invest in legal skills and actively participate in-the policymakers in order-to influence positive regulatory environment. In case of non-alignment, organizations can be subjected to fines, loss of reputation or even operational optimization. All these problems lead to-that fact- that the process of BDA introduction in-the-reverse logistics and waste management is a complex and manifold task. Though the technological innovations have offered unparalleled opportunities in forecasting insights, resource recovery and optimization, its achievement relies on the management of the privacy and security concerns, interoperability and scalability, organizational readiness and regard to the economic, ethical and regulatory factors. By identifying and avoiding these constraints, researchers, and practitioners will be in-a-position to come up with realistic frameworks, staged implementation models, and governance frameworks that would help in responsible and sustainable use of big data in the reverse supply chains. This is the only harmonization possible to achieve the transformative potential of digital sustainability.

Table 3. Key Challenges, Implications, and Mitigation Strategies for Implementing BDA in Reverse Logistics and Waste Management

Challenge	Key Issues / Implications	Mitigation Strategies
Data Privacy & Security	Risk of sensitive data exposure; IoT vulnerabilities; regulatory compliance	Implement encryption, secure authentication, continuous monitoring, and compliance with local/international data laws
Scalability & Interoperability	Integration difficulties across legacy and modern systems; fragmented data; high storage and processing requirements	Adopt standardized data protocols, cloud infrastructure, and modular scalable solutions
Organizational & Technological Readiness	Lack of skilled personnel; resistance to change; uneven IT infrastructure	Phased implementation, training programs, capacity building, and cultural change initiatives
Economic & Ethical Considerations	High investment costs; sustainability paradox; ethical handling of consumer data	Cost-benefit analysis, modular deployment, transparent data governance, environmental impact monitoring
Regulatory & Policy Constraints	Divergent laws and regulations; uncertainty in compliance; cross-border restrictions	Continuous regulatory monitoring, legal expertise, engagement with policymakers, alignment of digital solutions with EPR policies

Source: Developed by the author

INTEGRATING CIRCULAR ECONOMY PRINCIPLES

The modern business world makes the shift of the traditional linear supply chain models into circular-has an urgent necessity of the realization of the-long-term sustainability. Traditional supply chain is often linear in terms of progression that is take, make and dispose and often leads to depletion of resources, wastage and bad environmental effects. Conversely, the CE model focuses on the conservation of resources, their regeneration, and ongoing utilization and promotes such practices as product life cycle, reuse of materials, recycling, and the development of secondary markets. BDA, in this regard, has turned out to be a crucial facilitator of the circular supply chains as it offers organizations a chance to monitor, anticipate and regulate the flow of materials within the operations of the organization. Having a set of real-time data collection, predictive operation, and advanced optimization algorithms, businesses will be able to activate closed-loop operations in order to match operational goals with environmental management (Shahidzadeh & Shokouhyar, 2024). This section elaborates on the role of BDA in circularity, reverse logistics, and the hypothetical model of the use of data-driven circular supply chains.

Figure 2. Transition from Linear to Circular Supply Chain Models

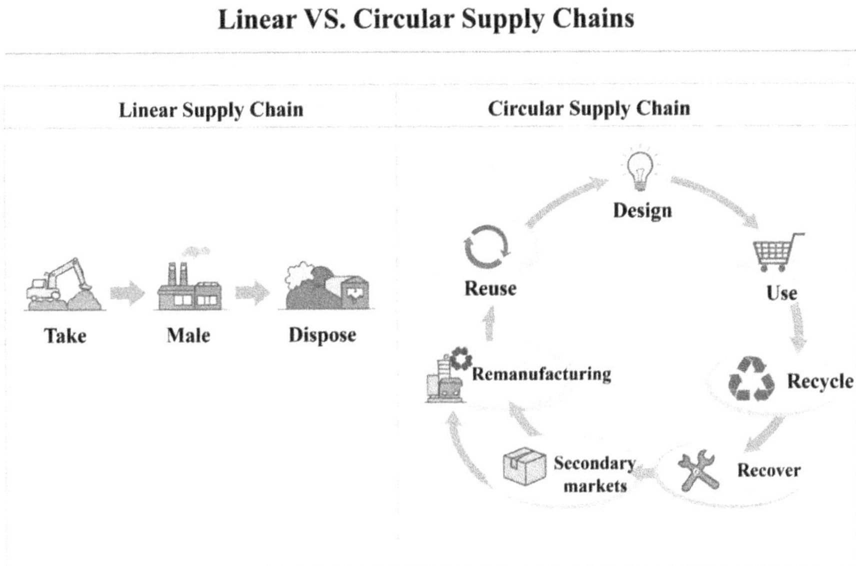

Source: Author's own development

Role of Big Data in Enabling Circular Economy Models

The intelligence needed to make the CE practices work is given by BDA. Circularity involves continuously monitoring the flow of products and materials, status and utilization across the supply chain and BDA is the aspect of analytics that will assist in doing so. To illustrate, the information presented by IoT sensors, RFID devices, and enterprise systems should be used to make decisions according to which refurbishing, remanufacturing, or recycling may be chosen to allow organizations to guarantee that the products will have a more extended lifespan and will not immediately become a part of the waste (Singh et al., 2025). These realizations can not only enhance effectiveness of- the material recovery, but also enhance the development of the secondary market, in which the remanufactured or refurbished products can become an additional source of revenue as well as decrease the negative impact on the environment. The predictive analytics and ML algorithms that are capable-of-forecasting when products are likely to expire (end-of life) also support this strategy. Such predictions enable-to anticipate and act before-hand e.g. selective recalling, harvesting of parts or pro-active maintenance. Those interventions will lead to larger goals of circularity by avoidance of any unexpected downtime and untimely scrappage. The electronics companies are a good example, since they are slowly embracing BDA in-order-to know that the devices are soon becoming obsolete and recycle useful components before they become useless. Moreover, cloud computing and blockchain technology in combination, can trace material provenance, reuse it according to standards, and provide the records, which can be verified by regulators, investors and consumers, establishing a culture of trust and transparency in the process of circles (Centobelli et al., 2022). The other application of BDA is in dynamic modeling of systems by simulating material flows, bottlenecking and supporting optimal resource allocation. This especially comes in handy with firms that work in various plants or geographical locations, where the flow of materials is multifaceted, non-homogenous and interdependent. Through comparative analysis of historical and real-time data, the firms will be able to ensure they focus on high-value recoveries, process them effectively, and decrease the environmental footprint (Souames et al., 2025). In this respect, BDA acts both as the nervous system and the intelligence layer of a CE, which transforms individual operational knowledge into consistent, practical policies.

Reverse Logistics as a Pathway to Circularity

Circular supply chains are offered through reverse logistics, which has been used to provide the structure through which products and materials can be directed to the downstream locations and back to the production or processing facilities. Although traditionally linked to returns management, reverse logistics has developed into a strategic process that contributes to resource recovery, waste minimization and management of the lifecycle of the products. It plays an important part in enforcing circularity, as without organized reverse flows, there would be little material recirculation and secondary market building. By using BDA, it is-able to improve the operations of reverse logistics through the provision of actionable insights of when, where, and how to recover materials. Predictive analytics has the ability-to estimate the volumes of the returns, schedule collections and plan routes to minimize the transport emissions. The ML models can classify the returns according to condition, material composition, or refurbishment suitability to ensure valuable resources are retrieved and as little waste as possible is generated (Samal et al., 2025). As an example, fashion retailers are currently using BDA to manage the-unsold inventory, predict what pieces can be re-used in the second-hand markets, as well as to streamline the logistics to avoid unneeded landfilling. Circularity is also supported by reverse logistics made of informational feedback loops. Information obtained through returns, recycling and remanufacturing processes can be used to design the product, and hence engineers should design products that are less difficult to disassemble, refurbish or recycle. It is a self-sustainable cycle of constant enhancement and sustainability since this feedback system-occurring mechanism ensures the alignment of product design, manufacturing procedures, and post-use approaches (Balawanth et al., 2025; Khan & Emon, 2025c). Therefore, combined with BDA, reverse logistics can make the concepts of the CE virtual reality.

FUTURE OUTLOOK

The convergence of the BDA, IoT technologies, and high-level AI systems has already transformed the practice of reverse logistics and waste management, albeit the prospects of the future imply even greater integration and sophistication. As supply chains and urban infrastructures are constantly evolving as-a-result of mounting environmental, social and governance (ESG) pressures, organizations are exploring alternative means of going beyond operational efficiency and look-at transparency, accountability and ethical custodianship. It is projected that in a few years, the nature of a circle of supply chains and sustainable waste management will change due to new technologies, including traceability based on blockchain, AI framework, and compatibility with the criteria of-a-sustainability reporting. This section discusses some of the best places of such innovations that are most likely to play a transformative role. Another trend is the adoption of-the blockchain technology in the process of reverse logistics and waste management. Material flows could be made more transparent, traceable, and trusted by blockchain with the help of decentralized and immutable ledger. In the future, blockchain will be combined with IoT sensors and AI analytics to create intelligent, self-auditing systems which can automatically detect inefficiencies or compliance violations and offer an in-depth perspective of material flows. In the context of the work of the CE, blockchain may be used to record provenance of materials, track the life of products, and ensure that recycling and environmental standards are met (Shojaei et al., 2021). As an example, in the so-called electronic waste management, blockchain can be utilized to trace every stage of returning, refurbishing, or recycling, and retrieve important components of the product, including such rare metals, in a responsible manner. This does not only minimize the chances of misreporting or fraud, but also allows consumers, regulators and investors to verify sustainability claims. Similarly, AI algorithms can also be biased and are likely to consider certain recovery paths over others due to an incomplete or biased data set, which harms the fair or environmentally desirable outcomes.

In addition to changes in technologies, ethical concerns about AI in waste management become-more-and more popular. Although AI and ML models have the potential to improve the decision-making process, predictive maintenance, and optimization of reverse logistics, it also brings up the concern of accountability, biasness, and responsible use of data (Chemingui & Hrouga, 2025). An example in point is predictive models which forecast the production of household waste, which unwillingly reveal confidential information about consumer behavior, which can create privacy problems. The solution to these ethical dilemmas is governance frameworks that can enhance transparency in the- algorithmic decisions, promote responsible data collection, and offer explicit accountability mechanisms to the stakeholders. Integrating the ethical AI principles into the process of reverse logistics and waste management will probably also be essential in the nearest-future-to keep the trust of the population and guarantee the adherence to regulations, especially as automated systems are gradually becoming the primary choice of organizations. The other critical aspect of the future development is to match data-driven operations and the framework of sustainability reporting, including the ESG standards and the United Nations SDGs. Most organizations are now generating large amounts of data on the use of resources, recycling rates, and reverse logistics results, but these data are often disconnected or isolated. The connections between BDA outputs and the ESG and SDG reporting systems allow the companies to change the operation signs into the quantifiable outcomes of sustainability (González-Sánchez et al., 2025). Using the example, the diversion rates of landfills, energy recovery of waste or recirculation of materials can be directly mapped to SDG targets regarding responsible consumption and production (SDG 12) or climate action (SDG 13). Such integration does not only enhance transparency and investor confidence but also internal accountability by ensuring that operations are made to conform to globally accepted sustainability standards (Emon & Khan, 2025a). In the future, companies are likely to implement the use of automated reporting platforms that will continuously feed analytics based on the reverse logistics and waste management systems into ESG dashboards and provide stakeholders with nearly real-time visibility of the strategy and allow implementing the necessary adjustments to the strategy. The combination of predictive and prescriptive analytics and emerging technologies- is also-indicate of more adaptive and intelligent supply chains. Predictive models are-able to predict volumes of returns, predict the highest level of waste production, and find possible bottlenecks of the resources, but on the other hand, prescriptive algorithms can propose optimal collection routes, refurbishment plans, or recycling operations (Khan & Hasan Emon, 2025). Combining such solutions with blockchain-based verification and ethical AI systems will help the organization perceive material flows as a system, which optimizes the process between the responsibility of the economy and the environment. Also, upcoming innovations in cloud computing and edge analytics will probably enhance the scalability of these solutions, allowing small and medium-sized enterprises to adopt complex data-based round circulation without the prohibitive cost of the infrastructure (Odukoya, 2024). Finally, the outlook of reverse logistics and waste management is bound to focus on cross-sector cooperation and digital ecosystems. Smart cities, networks of industrial symbiosis, and multi-stakeholder platforms can use the common data to coordinate the process of waste collection, material recovery and product lifecycle management. These ecosystems will be able to encourage the efficient utilization of resources, eliminate duplication, and expedite the switch toward the modes of the CE through the standardization of the data sharing and the integration of BDA with blockchain, AI ethics, and sustainability reporting (Khan & Emon, 2025a; Rashid et al., 2025). These types of collaborative structures are also anticipated to facilitate innovation by facilitating combined experimentation, scaling experiments, and comparing their best practices across the industry.

CONCLUSION

The chapter has strived to give a thorough discussion of how BDA is transforming the discipline of reverse logistics and waste management, especially its functionality in enhancing sustainable supply chain. Over the past few years, the classical linear models of supply chains that have often been referred to as take, make, and-dispose-have-been subject to more questioning as-a-result of the increasing environmental concerns, scarcity of resources and the tightening of the belt in terms of stringent regulations. The incorporation of new data-driven tools has provided new opportunities to re-consider reverse supply chains and give organizations additional opportunities to both reclaim the value of returned products and waste and make operational decisions according to broader sustainability objectives. The role of data in sustainable reverse supply chains could not be studied without a careful approach both in terms of theoretical basis and the practical usage. At the beginning of the chapter, the key ideas of reverse logistics and waste management were described, with the emphasis on the fact that effective management in the given fields is critical to minimizing the loss of resources, reducing the environmental footprint, and promoting the idea of circularity. It has also touched upon the perspectives that drive sustainable supply chains with respect to the importance of system thinking, stakeholder interaction and feedback loops. It is also here that the concept of BDA -had been brought up as not just a technological tool but- also as a strategic tool which can give deep insights -with predictive, prescriptive and real time analytics. The demonstration of the concepts, tools, and capabilities of BDA showed how multi-faceted it can be and applied in different stages on the reverse supply chains between predicting the returns of products and the actual flows of waste to optimization of the logistic networks. The predictive analytics which -has been proven to be one of the most significant mechanisms of forecasting the product returns and recycling requirements was also evidence of BDA functional capabilities in reverse logistics. This is facilitated with these capabilities of allowing firms to plan-ahead of time and streamline collection routes -and also to remove inefficiency in operations. Decision-making is even more efficient with the implementation of AI and ML, automatic sorting, anomaly detection, and adaptive optimization tools. Case studies introduced some real-life examples of how data-driven knowledge could be changed into actual development in efficiency, regeneration of resources and environment. The other thing that has come out in these illustrations is that technology is not a worthless thing-but its worth- is enhanced when it is utilized in conjunction with organizational commitment, talented employees and proper management. In the same way, the applications of-the Big-Data-in the waste management were also raised, which demonstrates that through-the use of the- IoT-enabled monitoring, sensor networks, and real-time analytics, the smart waste tracking, more efficient resource recovery, and increased rates of recycling can be achieved. By incorporating waste management into larger urban and industrial systems, using data to address it can enhance its optimization of material flows, improve adherence to environmental rules, and enhance links between the material flow and sustainability goals of operational performance and sustainability goals. The analysis of the different cross-country examples demonstrated the real-world advantages of these solutions, showing how predictive and prescriptive analytics would assist cities and companies in declining reliance on landfills, enhancing the effectiveness of recycling, and promoting the idea of the CE.

Nevertheless, there are no challenges to the adoption of BDA. Issues of data privacy and security are also of high concern, considering that the information collected among consumers and industrial activities is sensitive. The challenges to scalability and interoperability may hinder incorporation of various systems and partners in the supply chain and organizational preparedness such as availability of skilled work force, infrastructure and change-management practices is another key to success. Other complexities can be introduced by economic and ethical considerations such as the costs versus the benefits expected to be brought and the prevention of sustainability paradoxes, and new uncertainties can be introduced because of the policy or regulatory restrictions. These issues should be approached in a respectful manner in-order-to ensure that BDA might be employed in a responsible, efficient, and sustainable fashion. The other point of the chapter that was located was how BDA should match the principles of the CE. By introducing closed-loop systems, prolonged product cycles, and second-hand markets, it is a systemic circularity tool as Big Data is-able to transform reverse logistics into more than a cost-cutting activity. It was mentioned that data-based circular supply chains were defined as the concept in terms of conceptual frameworks where predictive recovery, continuous optimization, and lifetime intelligence can cooperate to provide sustainability, resilience, and operation efficiency. These outcomes prove the fact that BDA is not only technological enhancement but a necessary enabler of supply chain policies that integrate economical-and-environmental factors. Subsequently, the chapter has noted emerging trends that will be incorporated in the coming years to-the field of reverse logistics and waste management, including blockchain-based traceability, ethical AI, and correspondence with sustainability reporting standards, including ESG and the United Nations SDGs. The innovations will most probably lead to greater transparency, accountability and decision-making and expand cross-sector cooperation and digital ecosystems. With the integration of predictive and prescriptive analytics and these innovations, organizations will have the capacity to create more adaptive, intelligent, and circular supply chains that can respond to the changing sustainability issues.

REFERENCES

Alhodaib, A., Yahya, Z., Khan, O., Equbal, A., Equbal, M. S., Parvez, M., Kumar Yadav, A., & Idrisi, M. J. (2024). Sustainable coatings for green solar photovoltaic cells: Performance and environmental impact of recyclable biomass digestate polymers. *Scientific Reports, 14*(1), 11221. DOI: 10.1038/s41598-024-62048-5 PMID: 38755253

Almutairi, M. M., Sen, A. A. A., Bahbouh, N. M., Yamin, M., & Alsoqour, K. A. (2025). A Hybrid Framework for Flexible Waste Management During Crowded Events. *2025 12th International Conference on Computing for Sustainable Global Development (INDIACom)*, 1–7. DOI: 10.23919/INDIACom66777.2025.11115425

Bag, S., Luthra, S., Mangla, S. K., & Kazancoglu, Y. (2021). Leveraging big data analytics capabilities in making reverse logistics decisions and improving remanufacturing performance. *International Journal of Logistics Management, 32*(3), 742–765. DOI: 10.1108/IJLM-06-2020-0237

Balawanth, R., Zomer, T., Gonçalves, P., & Savaget, P. (2025). Supply chain management in response to climate change: A system dynamics approach. *Sustainable Production and Consumption, 60*, 36–51. DOI: 10.1016/j.spc.2025.09.007

Cao, S., Liao, W., & Huang, Y. (2021). Heterogeneous fleet recyclables collection routing optimization in a two-echelon collaborative reverse logistics network from circular economic and environmental perspective. *The Science of the Total Environment, 758*, 144062. DOI: 10.1016/j.scitotenv.2020.144062 PMID: 33333310

Centobelli, P., Cerchione, R., Del Vecchio, P., Oropallo, E., & Secundo, G. (2022). Blockchain technology for bridging trust, traceability and transparency in circular supply chain. *Information & Management, 59*(7), 103508. DOI: 10.1016/j.im.2021.103508

Chemingui, H., & Hrouga, M. (2025). Enhancing Reverse Supply Chain performance via artificial intelligence predictive solutions. *Supply Chain Forum: An International Journal*, 1–20. DOI: 10.1080/16258312.2025.2520737

Chen, C.-T., Khan, A., & Chen, S.-C. (2024). Modeling the impact of BDA-AI on sustainable innovation ambidexterity and environmental performance. *Journal of Big Data, 11*(1), 124. DOI: 10.1186/s40537-024-00995-6

Chen, Y.-C., & Hasan, M. K. (2023). IMPACTS OF LINER SHIPPING CONNECTIVITY AND GLOBAL COMPETITIVENESS ON LOGISTICS PERFORMANCE: THE MEDIATING ROLE OF THE QUALITY OF PORT AND INFRASTRUCTURE. *Transport, 38*(2), 87–104. DOI: 10.3846/transport.2023.19372

Dörrenbächer, C., Geppert, M., & Hoffmann, A. (2021). Contemporary restructuring trends in European multinational corporations: Rationale and impact on labour and workers' participation. *Critical Perspectives on International Business*, *17*(4), 637–654. DOI: 10.1108/cpoib-03-2020-0017

Emon, M. M. H. (2025a). Cybersecurity in the Smart City Era: Overcoming Challenges With Modern Cryptographic Solutions. In *Securing Smart Cities Through Modern Cryptography Technologies* (pp. 43–74). IGI Global Scientific Publishing. DOI: 10.4018/979-8-3373-3326-7.ch002

Emon, M. M. H. (2025b). Overcoming Hurdles: Navigating Challenges in the Adoption of Smart Logistics. In *Emerging Trends in Smart Logistics Technologies* (A. Hlali, pp. 197–228). IGI Global Scientific Publishing. DOI: 10.4018/979-8-3373-2434-0.ch007

Emon, M. M. H. (2025c). Digital transformation in emerging markets: Adoption dynamics of AI image generation in marketing practices. *Telematics and Informatics Reports*, *20*, 100267. DOI: 10.1016/j.teler.2025.100267

Emon, M. M. H., & Chowdhury, M. S. A. (2025). AI and IoT-Powered Smart Logistics: Transforming Supply Chains for Efficiency and Sustainability. In *Emerging Trends in Smart Logistics Technologies* (A. Hlali, pp. 45–72). IGI Global Scientific Publishing. DOI: 10.4018/979-8-3373-2434-0.ch002

Emon, M. M. H., & Khan, T. (2025a). Corporate Social Responsibility for Sustainable Development: A Systematic Review of Business Contributions to Address Global Challenges. *Review of Business and Economics Studies*, *13*(2), 6–39. DOI: 10.26794/2308-944X-2025-13-2-6-39

Emon, M. M. H., & Khan, T. (2025b). Exploring the mediating role of green logistics in enhancing green supply chain performance: Evidence from Bangladesh. *Journal of Engineering Research*. Advance online publication. DOI: 10.1016/j.jer.2025.10.003

Emon, M. M. H., Mazid-Ul-Haque, M., Nath, A., Hamim, S. A., Fuad, M. N., & Islam, M. M. (2025). Determinants of AI-Powered Marketing Tool Adoption in E-Commerce: An Empirical Analysis within Intelligent Computing Systems. *2025 IEEE 7th International Conference on Sustainable Technologies For Industry 5.0 (STI)*, 1–6. DOI: 10.1109/STI69347.2025.11367588

Emon, M. M. H., Nath, A., Rahman, K. M., Kutub, J., Rifat, H. H., & Mahsin-Ul-Islam, M. (2025). Evaluating Artificial Intelligence Integration for Improving Supply Chain Efficiency in the Context of Bangladesh's E-Commerce Sector. *2025 IEEE 7th International Conference on Sustainable Technologies For Industry 5.0 (STI)*, 1–6. DOI: 10.1109/STI69347.2025.11367608

Fernando, Y., Shaharudin, M. S., & Abideen, A. Z. (2023). Circular economy-based reverse logistics: Dynamic interplay between sustainable resource commitment and financial performance. *European Journal of Management and Business Economics*, *32*(1), 91–112. DOI: 10.1108/EJMBE-08-2020-0254

González-Sánchez, R., Alonso-Muñoz, S., & Kocollari, U. (2025). Exploring the supply chain's transformation to achieve the sustainable development goals in the post-pandemic scenario: A review and a research agenda. *International Journal of Logistics Management*, *36*(7), 137–177. DOI: 10.1108/IJLM-05-2023-0221

Handoyo, S., & Anas, S. (2024). The effect of environmental, social, and governance (ESG) on firm performance: The moderating role of country regulatory quality and government effectiveness in ASEAN. *Cogent Business & Management*, *11*(1). Advance online publication. DOI: 10.1080/23311975.2024.2371071

Hasan, M., Chun, C. Y., Yao, S., & Kemi, A. P. (2022). Forecasting the Quality of Port Infrastructure of Asian Port Countries: An Application of the Model GM (1, 1) and Clustering Them Using HCA Algorithm. *Operations and Supply Chain Management: An International Journal*, 105–121. DOI: 10.31387/oscm0480334

Hasan, M. K., Latif, Z., Hlali, A., Xunping, L., & Aka, S. A. B. (2025). Hyperautomation: The Next Frontier in Supply Chain (SC) and Manufacturing. In *Emerging Trends in Smart Logistics Technologies* (pp. 1–44). IGI Global Scientific Publishing. DOI: 10.4018/979-8-3373-2434-0.ch001

Hasan, M. K., Lei, X., Hlali, A., & Bian, Z. (2024). Modelling capability factors of logistics industry based on ISM-MICMAC. *Heliyon*, *10*(22), e40539. DOI: 10.1016/j.heliyon.2024.e40539 PMID: 39641072

Hasan, M. K., Lei, X., Tang, W., Nishi, N. N., & Latif, Z. (2025). Exploring logistics performance index (LPI) from global perspective: A study based on network analysis (NA). *Operations Management Research*, *18*(3), 1088–1112. DOI: 10.1007/s12063-025-00550-3

Huynh, P. L. T., Le, P. L., & Nguyen, T. T. (2025). Sustainability of FDI and domestic firms through big data analytics expertise: The moderating role of supply chain risk management. *Benchmarking*. Advance online publication. DOI: 10.1108/BIJ-09-2024-0735

Hwang, B. N., Jitanugoon, S., & Puntha, P. (2025). AI integration in service delivery: Enhancing business and sustainability performance amid challenges. *Journal of Services Marketing*. Advance online publication. DOI: 10.1108/JSM-10-2024-0511

Khan, T., & Emon, M. M. H. (2025a). Preparing for the Next Disruption: Lessons Learned From Past Crises and Building a Playbook for Future Supply Chain Shocks. In *Supply Chain Disruptions and Impact on Global Inflation* (pp. 253–286). IGI Global Scientific Publishing. DOI: 10.4018/979-8-3373-1982-7.ch010

Khan, T., & Emon, M. M. H. (2025b). Resilient Supply Chains: Lessons From Past Crisis Strategies Companies Can Adopt to Create More Resilient Supply Chains. In *Mass Media and Impact of Fake News on Supply Chains* (pp. 285–318). IGI Global. DOI: 10.4018/979-8-3373-2175-2.ch011

Khan, T., & Emon, M. M. H. (2025c). The role of digital supply chain practices in enhancing firm performance: Insights from the manufacturing sector of Bangladesh. *Brazilian Journal of Operations & Production Management, 22*(2), 2493. DOI: 10.14488/BJOPM.2493.2025

Khan, T., Emon, M. M. H., & Nath, A. (2024). Quantifying the Effects of AI-Driven Inventory Management on Operational Efficiency in Online Retail. *2024 27th International Conference on Computer and Information Technology (ICCIT)*, 2092–2097. DOI: 10.1109/ICCIT64611.2024.11021996

Khan, T., Emon, M. M. H., Rahman, M. A., Abdul Hamid, A. B., & Ya'akub, N. I. B. (2024). *Bridging the Gap: Realizing GreenTech Potential.* 91–121. DOI: 10.4018/979-8-3693-9879-1.ch004

Khan, T., & Hasan Emon, M. M. (2025). Harnessing Disciplinary Networks: A Global Educational Leadership Perspective on Positive Behavioural Management. In *International Dimensions of Educational Leadership and Management for Economic Growth*. IGI Global Scientific Publishing., DOI: 10.4018/979-8-3373-3616-9.ch012

Lakhouit, A. (2025). Revolutionizing urban solid waste management with AI and IoT: A review of smart solutions for waste collection, sorting, and recycling. *Results in Engineering, 25*, 104018. DOI: 10.1016/j.rineng.2025.104018

Le, T. T. (2023). Linking big data, sustainable supply chain management and corporate performance: The moderating role of circular economy thinking. *International Journal of Logistics Management, 34*(3), 744–771. DOI: 10.1108/IJLM-01-2022-0011

Lin, K.-Y. (2024). Circular supply chain for smart production in Industry 4.0. *Computers & Industrial Engineering, 198*, 110682. DOI: 10.1016/j.cie.2024.110682

Marabelli, M., Newell, S., & Handunge, V. (2021). The lifecycle of algorithmic decision-making systems: Organizational choices and ethical challenges. *The Journal of Strategic Information Systems, 30*(3), 101683. DOI: 10.1016/j.jsis.2021.101683

McCarthy, R. V., McCarthy, M. M., & Ceccucci, W. (2022). Introduction to Predictive Analytics. In *Applying Predictive Analytics* (pp. 1–26). Springer International Publishing., DOI: 10.1007/978-3-030-83070-0_1

Mihai, F.-C., & Ulman, S.-R. (2023). Circular economy in Green Deal strategies. In *Sustainable and Circular Management of Resources and Waste Towards a Green Deal* (pp. 49–63). Elsevier., DOI: 10.1016/B978-0-323-95278-1.00029-2

Möslinger, M., Ulpiani, G., & Vetters, N. (2023). Circular economy and waste management to empower a climate-neutral urban future. *Journal of Cleaner Production, 421*, 138454. DOI: 10.1016/j.jclepro.2023.138454

Odukoya, O. (2024). The Transformative Impact of Cloud Computing on Small and Medium-sized Enterprises (SMEs): A Comprehensive Analysis. *2024 International Conference on Smart Applications, Communications and Networking (SmartNets)*, 1–5. DOI: 10.1109/SmartNets61466.2024.10577703

Park, S., Jung, D., Nguyen, H., & Choi, Y. (2021). Diagnosis of Problems in Truck Ore Transport Operations in Underground Mines Using Various Machine Learning Models and Data Collected by Internet of Things Systems. *Minerals (Basel), 11*(10), 1128. DOI: 10.3390/min11101128

Pathak, S., Krishnaswamy, V., & Sharma, M. (2025). A dynamic capability perspective on the impact of big data analytics and enterprise architecture on innovation: An empirical study. *Journal of Enterprise Information Management, 38*(2), 532–563. DOI: 10.1108/JEIM-01-2024-0059

Psarommatis, F., May, G., & Azamfirei, V. (2025). Product reuse and repurpose in circular manufacturing: A critical review of key challenges, shortcomings and future directions. *Journal of Remanufacturing, 15*(2–3), 273–310. DOI: 10.1007/s13243-025-00153-y

Rane, S. B., Thakker, S. V., & Kant, R. (2021). Stakeholders' involvement in green supply chain: A perspective of blockchain IoT-integrated architecture. *Management of Environmental Quality, 32*(6), 1166–1191. DOI: 10.1108/MEQ-11-2019-0248

Rashid, A., Baloch, N., Rasheed, R., & Ngah, A. H. (2025). Big data analytics-artificial intelligence and sustainable performance through green supply chain practices in manufacturing firms of a developing country. *Journal of Science and Technology Policy Management, 16*(1), 42–67. DOI: 10.1108/JSTPM-04-2023-0050

Saidu, Y., Shuhidan, S. M., Aliyu, D. A., Abdul Aziz, I., & Adamu, S. (2025). Convergence of Blockchain, IoT, and AI for Enhanced Traceability Systems: A Comprehensive Review. *IEEE Access : Practical Innovations, Open Solutions, 13*, 16838–16865. DOI: 10.1109/ACCESS.2025.3528035

Samal, C. G., Biswal, D. R., Udgata, G., & Pradhan, S. K. (2025). Estimation, Classification, and Prediction of Construction and Demolition Waste Using Machine Learning for Sustainable Waste Management: A Critical Review. *Construction Materials, 5*(1), 10. DOI: 10.3390/constrmater5010010

Scarpi, D., & Pantano, E. (2024). "With great power comes great responsibility": Exploring the role of Corporate Digital Responsibility (CDR) for Artificial Intelligence Responsibility in Retail Service Automation (AIRRSA). *Organizational Dynamics, 53*(2), 101030. DOI: 10.1016/j.orgdyn.2024.101030

Shahidzadeh, M. H., & Shokouhyar, S. (2024). Unveiling just-in-time decision support system using social media analytics: A case study on reverse logistics resource recycling. *Industrial Management & Data Systems, 124*(6), 2251–2283. DOI: 10.1108/IMDS-12-2023-0921

Shojaei, A., Ketabi, R., Razkenari, M., Hakim, H., & Wang, J. (2021). Enabling a circular economy in the built environment sector through blockchain technology. *Journal of Cleaner Production, 294*, 126352. DOI: 10.1016/j.jclepro.2021.126352

Singh, A., Goel, A., Chauhan, A., & Singh, S. K. (2025). Sustainability of electronic product manufacturing through e-waste management and reverse logistics. *Sustainable Futures : An Applied Journal of Technology, Environment and Society, 9*, 100490. DOI: 10.1016/j.sftr.2025.100490

Souames, M. A., Mohammedi, L. A., Zouaghi, I., Gunasekaran, A., Beldjoudi, S., & Laghouag, A. (2025). Estimating Import Lead Times Using Business Intelligence and Machine Learning Within the CRISP-DM Framework: A Case Study in Oil and Gas Services Industry. *IEEE Access : Practical Innovations, Open Solutions, 13*, 119215–119234. DOI: 10.1109/ACCESS.2025.3584886

Spaltini, M., Poletti, A., Acerbi, F., & Taisch, M. (2021). A quantitative framework for Industry 4.0 enabled Circular Economy. *Procedia CIRP, 98*, 115–120. DOI: 10.1016/j.procir.2021.01.015

Tennakoon, G. A., Rameezdeen, R., & Chileshe, N. (2022). Diverting demolition waste toward secondary markets through integrated reverse logistics supply chains: A systematic literature review. *Waste Management & Research: The Journal for a Sustainable Circular Economy, 40*(3), 274–293. DOI: 10.1177/0734242X211021478 PMID: 34034580

Tran-Dang, H., Kim, J.-W., Lee, J.-M., & Kim, D.-S. (2025). Shaping the Future of Logistics: Data-driven Technology Approaches and Strategic Management. *IETE Technical Review*, *42*(1), 44–79. DOI: 10.1080/02564602.2024.2445513

Ukoba, K., Olatunji, K. O., Adeoye, E., Jen, T.-C., & Madyira, D. M. (2024). Optimizing renewable energy systems through artificial intelligence: Review and future prospects. *Energy & Environment*, *35*(7), 3833–3879. DOI: 10.1177/0958305X241256293

Van der Linde, L., Pretorius, L., & Oosthuizen, R. (2024). Sustainable Technology Management: A Causal Loop Analysis of Circular Economy Adoption and Stakeholder Dynamics. *2024 Portland International Conference on Management of Engineering and Technology (PICMET)*, 1–10. DOI: 10.23919/PICMET64035.2024.10653082

Vandyck, T., Temursho, U., Landis, F., Klenert, D., & Weitzel, M. (2022). Prices and Standards for Vertical and Horizontal Equity in Climate Policy. SSRN *Electronic Journal*. DOI: 10.2139/ssrn.4144282

Wilson, M., Paschen, J., & Pitt, L. (2022). The circular economy meets artificial intelligence (AI): Understanding the opportunities of AI for reverse logistics. *Management of Environmental Quality*, *33*(1), 9–25. DOI: 10.1108/MEQ-10-2020-0222

Xu, D., Li, T., Li, Y., Su, X., Tarkoma, S., Jiang, T., Crowcroft, J., & Hui, P. (2021). Edge Intelligence: Empowering Intelligence to the Edge of Network. *Proceedings of the IEEE*, *109*(11), 1778–1837. DOI: 10.1109/JPROC.2021.3119950

Yu, S., Wang, X., Liu, J., & Wei, F. (2023). Role of mining waste trade on green development in China: Policy implications for circular economy. *Resources Policy*, *86*, 104147. DOI: 10.1016/j.resourpol.2023.104147

Zhang, X., Yu, Y., & Zhang, N. (2021). Sustainable supply chain management under big data: A bibliometric analysis. *Journal of Enterprise Information Management*, *34*(1), 427–445. DOI: 10.1108/JEIM-12-2019-0381

KEY TERMS AND DEFINITIONS

Artificial Intelligence (AI): AI can be described as systems that can imitate- the human intelligence to make- a decision, identify patterns, and automate. Sustainable supply chains can leverage AI to boost predictive and prescriptive analytics to make operations smarter and more informed.

Big Data Analytics (BDA): This is the process by which huge and complex data sets are analyzed to determine patterns, relationships, and discoveries that can be used to make an informed decision. BDA is commonly used in the framework of supply chains and waste management to achieve efficiency, trend prediction, and optimal use of resources.

Circular Economy (CE): CE is a transition in place of the-traditional linear models to systems with a focus on reducing, reusing, and recycling materials. CE should develop more sustainable and renewable economic activities by extending the lives of products and reducing resource wastage.

Internet of Things (IoT): IoT is also known as networks of interconnected devices and sensors that gather, transmit and share information. This technology allows the supply chain and waste management processes to be tracked in real-time and thus interventions and smarter distribution of resources can be made promptly.

Predictive Analytics: Predictive analytics is the use of past and present data to simulate what does or will happen in the future. In the fields of reverse logistics and waste management, it can be applied to predict returns of products, estimate the quantity of waste, and plan operations.

Reverse Logistics: Reverse logistics deals with the circulation of products between the final user and the manufacturer, recycling unit, or processing unit. Its primary goal is the recovery of value, reduction of waste, and sustainability including such activity as the management of returns, refurbishment, and the- adequate disposal.

Sustainability Reporting: Sustainability reporting is the act of reporting and recording organizational-its performance in relation to the environmental, social, and governance (ESG) standards. It enables organizations to be accountable, monitor resource efficiency and progress in the direction of CE and sustainable development.

Waste Management: Waste management is an area of concern in relation to the collection, transportation, treatment, recycling and disposal of waste products. Its end objective is to minimize environmental degradation and to help in sustainable utilization of resources, which usually includes both municipal and industrial activities.

Chapter 7
Big Data-Driven Circularity:
Enhancing Sustainability Through Closed-Loop Supply Chain Models

Mohammad Al Refat Reyel
http://orcid.org/0009-0000-0431-5294
Ulster University, UK

Mehedi Hassan Anik
http://orcid.org/0009-0000-5325-1442
Unitec Institute of Technology, New Zealand

Syed Waqar Ul Hassan Shah
http://orcid.org/0009-0001-6654-5906
Ulster University, UK

ABSTRACT

This chapter explores how big data technologies are transforming circular supply chains, enabling firms to manage end-of-life products more efficiently while promoting sustainability. By integrating predictive analytics, IoT, AI, and digital twins, organizations can anticipate product returns, optimize reverse logistics, automate sorting, and make informed decisions on reuse, refurbishment, and recycling. The discussion highlights applications across electronics, automotive, and consumer goods industries, illustrating how data-driven strategies support circular economy practices, improve resource efficiency, and reduce environmental impact. Challenges such as interoperability, data quality, cost, privacy, and ethical considerations are

DOI: 10.4018/979-8-3373-6896-2.ch007

also examined, alongside recommendations for governance, collaboration, and technology adoption. The chapter underscores the strategic potential of data-driven circularity in achieving long-term operational and environmental resilience.

INTRODUCTION

This chapter takes a closer and somewhat reflective look at how the growing availability of big data, along with the rapid push of digital technologies, is gradually reshaping the way organisations think about circularity and, more specifically, how they manage closed-loop supply chains (CLSCs). Although sustainability discussions often highlight cleaner production or greener sourcing activities, the end-of-life stage of products is still where many firms, even experienced ones, tend to struggle. Decisions around product returns are sometimes delayed or made with incomplete information. The chapter therefore tries to bridge this gap by discussing how big data combined with tools such as artificial intelligence (AI), machine learning (ML), the Internet of Things (IoT), and digital twins can make these return flows more predictable, more transparent, and, in many cases, more valuable for the organisation. The narrative begins by revisiting the basic foundations of CLSCs and pointing out how they differ from the more familiar, linear supply chain structures. Instead of focusing only on outbound flows of products and materials, CLSCs also incorporate reverse streams, meaning that used items must be collected, inspected, possibly disassembled, and then directed toward suitable recovery options like reuse, refurbishment, remanufacturing, or recycling. These recovery practices are widely recognised as key drivers of reduced raw material dependency and lower environmental pressure. Still, they remain difficult to coordinate because reverse flows rarely behave in a stable or predictable manner. The volume, condition, and even the timing of product returns can be highly irregular, which puts additional pressure on planning and coordination. Following this foundation, the chapter turns to product end-of-life (EOL) strategies and their growing importance. Effective EOL decision-making has implications not only for environmental outcomes but also for cost savings and compliance with regulatory frameworks. The chapter reviews the major options reuse, refurbishment, remanufacturing, recycling, and when unavoidable, safe disposal and discusses why firms often struggle to choose the most appropriate pathway. In the absence of reliable, real-time information on product condition or material composition, EOL decisions sometimes become reactive or based on assumptions rather than evidence. To address these challenges, the chapter highlights how big data is gradually becoming a transformative element in supply chain sustainability. Large-scale datasets coming from sensors, manufacturing systems, logistics networks, and even customer interactions allow firms to enhance visibility throughout the entire product lifecycle. Big data, when managed properly, supports improved forecasting of returns, more accurate tracking of material flows, and more efficient allocation of resources within CLSCs. It also enables firms to evaluate their sustainability progress with greater precision, which is becoming increasingly important as environmental regulations continue to tighten in many regions.

The discussion then extends to the roles of AI, ML, and IoT, which work hand-in-hand with big data to create greater lifecycle transparency. IoT devices allow real-time monitoring of product usage or condition, while AI and ML applications assist in classification, sorting, and identifying optimal EOL pathways. Digital twin technologies virtual models that mirror physical products further strengthen decision-making by allowing firms to run simulations and test recovery scenarios before committing to costly operational changes. These tools, taken together, help reduce some of the uncertainty that has historically made reverse logistics complicated. Building on this technological landscape, the chapter explores how predictive analytics is being used to support EOL decision-making. Firms are increasingly relying on ML models to anticipate product failures, classify returned items by their potential recovery value, and estimate available recyclable materials. These developments contribute to more efficient reverse logistics systems by reducing transportation inefficiencies, unnecessary delays, and operational costs. Later, the chapter illustrates how big data contributes to deeper circular economy integration. With detailed lifecycle information at hand, firms can rethink product design to support easier disassembly, repair, or reuse. They can also work more collaboratively with supply chain partners by sharing sustainability-related data. Examples from electronics, automotive, and consumer goods industries are used to show how these data-driven circular practices are gradually taking shape in the real world. However, the chapter does not overlook the existing challenges. Issues related to data interoperability, privacy risks, high implementation costs, and ethical concerns around tracking and monitoring still create barriers. These concerns highlight the need for strong governance practices, transparent data-sharing agreements, and responsible use of digital technologies. The chapter presents a nuanced and balanced assessment of how big data-driven approaches can support the transition toward more effective CLSCs. While the potential of these technologies is substantial, meaningful circularity will require careful implementation, collaboration across industries, and continuous evaluation of environmental and ethical implications. Through this discussion, the chapter aims to offer both conceptual insights and practical guidance for researchers and practitioners working toward more sustainable and intelligent EOL systems.

UNDERSTANDING CLOSED-LOOP SUPPLY CHAINS

CLSCs have steadily evolved from being a somewhat optional sustainability experiment into a strategic necessity for many firms that are trying to manage resources more responsibly in an increasingly circular global economy. At the core, CLSCs combine both forward and backward flows of materials, products, and components, forming a system where goods do not simply exit the production line and disappear into landfills. Instead, once a product reaches its end of use, it re-enters the supply network through structured return processes, where it might be repaired, refurbished, remanufactured, or recycled depending on its condition and whatever residual value it still holds. Compared with the more traditional linear supply chains that mainly emphasize procurement, production, and distribution, CLSCs introduce an entirely additional layer of activities, such as inspection, collection, sorting, and value recovery (Tombido, 2025). This shift away from a "take–make–waste" mentality towards one that aims to regenerate value is driven by both economic reasoning and growing environmental pressure. A major motivation behind the rising interest in CLSCs is their potential contribution to sustainable development. The extraction of raw materials is placing heightened pressure on already fragile ecological systems, and industries across the world are being observed more closely by regulators, civil society groups, and environmentally aware consumers (Khan & Emon, 2025b). By reusing or recovering components from returned goods, firms can significantly reduce their dependency on virgin inputs, which in turn minimizes ecological degradation and mitigates supply risks that often arise from volatile global commodity markets. Recent studies show that closed-loop systems can reduce carbon emissions and energy use quite substantially when compared with traditional disposal-heavy supply chains, especially in electronics, automotive manufacturing, and durable consumer goods (Tian et al., 2023). Beyond the environmental benefits, CLSCs are also aligned with broader circular economic principles, where discarded items are treated more like resources rather than inevitable waste. Still, even though the benefits may look straightforward on paper, implementing CLSCs in practice tends to be complicated. One of the biggest issues is uncertainty. Returned products rarely behave like finished goods in conventional supply chains they arrive inconsistently, with different levels of wear and damage, and sometimes at moments when firms are least prepared (Emon & Khan, 2025b). This unpredictability in return quantity, quality, and timing makes planning activities much more difficult. Moreover, the management of CLSCs requires coordination among a wider set of partners than linear supply chains normally involve. Logistics operators, third-party collectors, reprocessing facilities, recyclers, and even consumers all play critical roles, and each party often uses its own systems, data formats, and operational routines (Jensen,

2025). Diversity makes coordination messy, and the absence of aligned information-sharing practices can cause additional delays or inefficiencies.

An equally important challenge is the information burden that CLSCs naturally impose. Decision-makers need timely, accurate, and detailed information about returned items before determining whether they should be reused, remanufactured, or recycled. However, many traditional supply networks do not maintain such data, and even when information exists, it is often scattered across fragmented systems that fail to communicate with one another. Because of this, firms have historically depended on manual inspections or subjective judgments, which are time-consuming and prone to errors (Khan & Emon, 2025a). Fluctuations in return flows often result in inventory piling up at recovery centers, bottlenecks in sorting areas, or under-utilized remanufacturing lines (Olivares-Aguila & ElMaraghy, 2021). These operational complexities mean that even firms with strong sustainability goals can struggle to run efficient closed-loop operations unless they improve their data capacities.

Table 1. Key Stakeholders in CLSCs and Their Roles

Stakeholder	**Core Responsibilities**	**Information Required**	**Information Provided**
Manufacturer	Product design, recovery planning	Return forecasts, product condition data	Recovery instructions, design specs
Logistics Provider	Collection, transportation	Pickup schedules, volume data	Tracking updates, delivery status
Recycling Facility	Material extraction	Material composition, sorting info	Recovery outputs, waste data
Refurbishment/Remanufacturer	Component evaluation, repair	Condition reports, spare parts	Reconditioned product status
Consumers	Product return behavior	Incentives, instructions	Return timing & condition

Source: Developed by Authors

This is where big data, and digital technologies begin to reshape the landscape. Data analytics allows organizations to track usage patterns, performance states, and wear levels with a level of precision that wasn't realistically possible even a decade ago. Embedded sensors often connected to IoT networks generate continuous streams of product data, enabling firms to anticipate breakdowns, forecast returns, and manage recovery operations more strategically. Digital platforms, on the other hand, can bring together information from customers, service centers, recyclers, and logistics partners, providing firms with a type of lifecycle visibility that used to be very rare. When combined with predictive or machine-learning algorithms, this data-driven visibility enables more accurate recovery decisions and more efficient planning of material flows (Pasupuleti et al., 2024). Beyond improving operational outcomes, data-enabled CLSCs also help strengthen relationships among supply chain partners. When real-time information is shared more openly about product conditions, expected return volumes, or recovery statuses coordination improves and misunderstandings decrease (Emon, 2025d). Transparent information flows promote better synchronization of reverse logistics, more equitable distribution of value among participating firms, and clearer communication with customers regarding return options or recycling incentives. Empirical work continues to show that effective information-sharing mechanisms remain one of the strongest predictors of CLSC success, especially in industries characterized by rapid product turnover and technological complexity (Ramanathan et al., 2023). Understanding CLSCs today requires recognizing that they are far more than an add-on to reverse logistics. They represent a rethinking of supply chain logic itself, one that positions EOL products as valuable inputs for future production cycles. Nevertheless, their inherent complexity means that firms cannot depend solely on traditional management approaches. Big data and digital intelligence are increasingly becoming essential foundations for overcoming uncertainty, enhancing recovery efficiency, and enabling a realistic transition toward a more circular and resource-sensitive industrial system.

PRODUCT END-OF-LIFE STRATEGIES: CONCEPTS AND IMPORTANCE

Product EOL strategies have gradually become one of the core foundations in today's discussions about sustainable supply chain management, particularly as firms are being pushed sometimes quite strongly to reduce environmental burdens, meet increasingly strict regulatory demands, and respond to consumers who are now far more aware of ecological issues than they were even a decade ago. In simple terms, an EOL strategy explains what should be done with a product once the consumer has stopped using it. Although this phase is often seen as the last step in a product's journey, in modern supply chain thinking it is more accurately understood as the beginning of a renewed value cycle within the broader circular economy. In real practice, organizations can choose among several recovery approaches such as reuse, refurbishment, remanufacturing, recycling, or, when nothing else is workable, disposal. Recent studies indicate that companies integrating EOL considerations early in product design and operations tend to gain not only environmental improvements but also meaningful strategic advantages (Awan et al., 2021). Among these recovery pathways, reuse is usually regarded as the simplest and requires the least resources. It mostly means prolonging the product's life with minimal intervention, basically through cleaning or small adjustments. Reuse has gained traction in sectors like consumer electronics, packaging, and even fashion, where the product still holds enough functional value after its initial use phase. By keeping products in circulation longer, reuse helps delay new production cycles and indirectly reduces the need for raw materials and energy. But reuse is not always straightforward; maintaining consistent quality and persuading consumers to accept pre-owned items can be tricky in markets where "brand-new" still carries social meaning. Even then, younger buyers appear to be more open to reused or second-hand items due to a mix of cost-saving logic and environmental concern (Fu et al., 2025). Refurbishment moves a bit further along the spectrum. Here, minor repairs or the replacement of a few components is carried out so that the product regains partial or satisfactory functionality. This approach is particularly visible in electronics and household appliances but is not limited to them. Over the last few years, there has been a noticeable rise in certified refurbishment programs created by well-known manufacturers. These programs help strengthen customer confidence, as buyers know the refurbished items have passed some quality checks, and they also offer firms an extra revenue channel. Industry evidence suggests that refurbishment can extend product life by roughly 30–50% and significantly reduce e-waste volumes (Chen et al., 2022; Emon, 2025b). Yet, refurbishment depends heavily on having skilled personnel, stable access to spare parts, and an efficient reverse logistics system all factors that vary widely depending on geographical and infrastructural contexts. Remanufacturing, frequently described as returning a product to a "like-new" state, is often recognized as one of the most impactful and technically demanding EOL strategies. In contrast to refurbishment, remanufacturing typically involves complete disassembly, careful inspection, replacement of worn components, and rigorous testing before reassembly. As a result, remanufactured products often meet performance levels comparable to new versions, sometimes even accompanied by similar warranties. The environmental and economic benefits are substantial. For instance, remanufacturing may reduce material consumption by up to 80% and cut energy use by around 40–60%, depending on the sector (Farhana et al., 2022). Well-known examples from the automotive and heavy machinery industries, including Caterpillar's structured remanufacturing system, demonstrate how such programs can support high-profit margins while simultaneously lowering environmental footprints. Still, remanufacturing is not universally feasible. It requires products designed with disassembly in mind, standardized components, and predictable volumes of returns. The inconsistency in the condition of returned items continues to present one of the most persistent operational hurdles (Emon & Chowdhury, 2025).

Recycling, another essential EOL pathway, usually sits lower in the recovery hierarchy because it focuses on recapturing materials rather than preserving the function of a product. Even so, it is indispensable for achieving circularity. Through recycling, materials such as plastics, glass, metals, or even complex composites can re-enter production cycles, reducing the strain on virgin resources and cutting emissions associated with extraction and raw material processing. Current research shows that efficient material recycling contributes significantly to carbon reduction efforts, particularly in high-resource industries (Niu et al., 2025). But again, recycling performance is influenced by many variables: contamination of returned items, limitations in waste collection systems, and the maturity of local recycling technologies. Many countries still struggle with achieving satisfactory recycling rates, partly due to infrastructural weaknesses and partly because consumers do not always follow proper waste sorting practices (Emon & Khan, 2025c).

Table 2. Comparative Analysis of EOL Strategies

EOL Strategy	Main Activities	Resource Intensity	Environmental Benefit	Economic Value	Typical Industries
Reuse	Cleaning, minor adjustments	Very Low	Medium	Low–Medium	Apparel, Packaging, Electronics
Refurbishment	Minor repairs, component replacement	Low–Medium	Medium–High	Medium	Household Appliances, ICT Products
Remanufacturing	Full disassembly, replacement, reassembly	High	Very High	High	Automotive, Machinery, Industrial Equipment
Recycling	Material recovery by separation & reprocessing	Medium	High	Medium	Plastics, Metals, Glass, Electronics
Safe Disposal	Environmentally controlled discarding	Very High (waste cost)	Very Low	None	Hazardous/E-waste streams

Source: Developed by Authors

When none of the recovery strategies mentioned above can be realistically applied, safe disposal becomes the final route. Although it does not generate direct economic value, responsible disposal is crucial for preventing environmental and health hazards especially when dealing with e-waste, toxic components, or chemically sensitive materials. Across the world, regulators have tightened compliance requirements linked to waste disposal, essentially pushing firms to improve how they manage unsalvageable materials. Much of this global movement is tied to policies like Extended Producer Responsibility (EPR), which holds manufacturers accountable for the waste their products generate. The European Union's WEEE Directive is one example that has influenced similar policy developments in many emerging economies (Andersen, 2022). Importantly, the value of strong EOL strategies goes beyond environmental protection. From a management point of view, strategic EOL planning can influence cost structures, supply chain resilience, regulatory adherence, and overall brand credibility. Firms that rely on remanufactured or recycled components often enjoy lower production costs and reduced exposure to volatile raw material markets. The ongoing disruptions in global supply networks have further highlighted the need for stable secondary material sources (Emon, 2025b). At the same time, consumers are increasingly paying attention to sustainability practices, and companies that ignore EOL responsibilities may face reputational risks, especially in industries where environmental scrutiny is high. However, choosing the right EOL approach is rarely simple. Firms must evaluate technical feasibility, cost considerations, product characteristics, and market conditions. Uncertain volumes of returns, variations in product condition, and unpredictable demand for recovered items all complicate decision-making (Khan et al., 2024). Implementing a strong EOL system also requires teams across the organization to work together design teams must think about disassembly-friendly design, operations teams must optimize reverse logistics, and marketing teams must communicate sustainability efforts carefully without falling into overstated claims. Recent studies point out that digital tools including IoT-based monitoring, AI-supported inspection systems, and blockchain-enabled transparency are improving decision accuracy in EOL operations by helping predict return quality, streamline disassembly steps, and authenticate recovered materials (Berlato et al., 2025). EOL strategies are shifting from being a peripheral concern to becoming a central part of sustainable business models. As governments tighten environmental rules and industries move gradually toward circularity, firms that invest in thoughtful, well-coordinated, and technology-supported EOL approaches will likely be better prepared to balance long-term environmental responsibilities with sustained profitability (Khan & Hasan Emon, 2024).

BIG DATA AND ITS ROLE IN SUPPLY CHAIN SUSTAINABILITY

Over the past few years, big data has increasingly taken a central position in discussions around supply chain management, especially when sustainability considerations are involved. In simple terms, big data refers to extremely large, varied, and continuously generated datasets that are too complex to be handled using conventional data-processing techniques. In supply chains, these data sources are wide-ranging and include production machinery outputs, sensors embedded in products, warehouse management systems, logistics tracking tools, customer interactions, e-commerce transactions, and even social media feedback. Each source contributes valuable information, and when aggregated and analyzed, these datasets can provide deep insights into operations, product lifecycles, and consumer behaviors. Within the context of CLSCs, big data assumes a particularly transformative role. Unlike traditional linear supply chains, CLSCs must manage not only forward flows of products but also reverse flows, such as items that are returned, refurbished, recycled, or reintegrated into production. These reverse flows are inherently uncertain in terms of timing, quality, and quantity, which makes planning and coordination extremely challenging. Here, big data functions as a critical enabler, offering visibility, predictive insights, and operational intelligence that can help firms navigate these complexities more effectively. One of the most important ways in which big data supports sustainability in CLSCs is by enhancing visibility and traceability. Organizations can now track products from the production line, through distribution channels, and eventually to their return or disposal points. This heightened transparency allows managers to monitor return flows more accurately, identify bottlenecks, and ensure that products are directed toward the most appropriate recovery pathways. For example, IoT-enabled sensors can continuously capture data about product usage, environmental conditions, and wear and tears. When these data streams are integrated into a central analytics platform, managers can gain near real-time visibility into where products are, their current condition, and the expected timing of their return.

Figure 1. Big Data Sources in Supply Chains

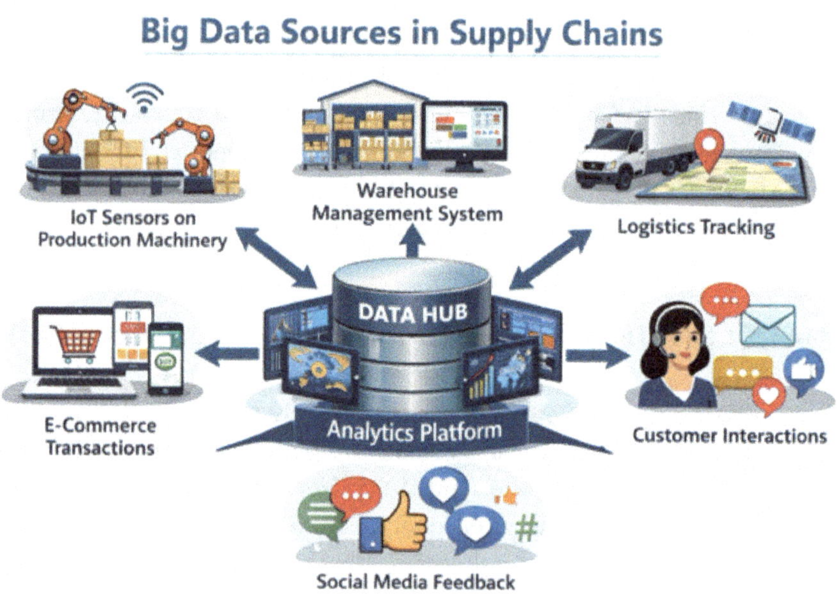

Source: Developed by Authors

Another key benefit is the provision of real-time insights. Traditionally, decisions about inventory, transportation, or EOL handling were often reactive, relying on historical records, intuition, or delayed reporting. Today, streaming data from smart sensors, logistics software, and digital platforms allows firms to respond almost immediately to changes in demand, sudden returns, or operational disruptions. For instance, if a batch of returned electronics arrives with unusually high defect rates, predictive analytics can flag the issue instantly, enabling repair or recycling facilities to allocate resources more efficiently. This immediacy helps prevent delays, reduces misallocation of resources, and lowers waste, thereby contributing directly to sustainability goals. Closely linked to real-time insights is the application of big data for demand and return forecasting. A common challenge in CLSCs is uncertainty surrounding the quantity, quality, and timing of returns. Firms must allocate labor, storage, and transportation resources without precise knowledge of what products will come back. Advanced analytics can assess historical return patterns, customer usage behavior, and operational data to predict not only how many items are likely to be returned but also their condition. ML models can uncover subtle correlations, for instance connecting certain usage patterns to higher probabilities of product failure, which might otherwise go unnoticed. Accurate forecasts enable firms to optimize reverse logistics routes, allocate resources efficiently, and reduce environmental impacts associated with unnecessary transport or excess inventory (Budak, 2020).

Table 3. Big Data Applications and Sustainability Benefits

Big Data Application	Description	Sustainability Benefit	Example Use Case
Visibility & Traceability	Tracking products throughout lifecycle	Reduced waste, better recovery decisions	IoT sensors in electronics
Real-Time Insights	Immediate response to operational changes	Lower delays, reduced resource misallocation	Dynamic routing of returns
Demand & Return Forecasting	Predicting quantity and condition of returns	Optimized reverse logistics, reduced transport emissions	ML models for returned electronics
Resource Use Optimization	Identifying inefficiencies in energy/materials	Reduced energy use, lower scrap generation	Energy monitoring in production lines
Lifecycle Integration	Combining production, usage, and social data	Enhanced circularity, better product design	Analytics platforms integrating all data

Source: Developed by Authors

Big data also enables resource-use optimization, directly supporting sustainability. By analyzing energy consumption, material utilization, and waste streams, organizations can identify inefficiencies that would otherwise remain hidden. Sensors in production equipment, for example, can reveal which processes are consuming disproportionate amounts of energy or generating excess scrap. Similarly, data from warehouses and distribution networks can help optimize storage layouts and reduce the risk of expired or idle inventory. Coupled with predictive analytics, firms can simulate different recovery, refurbishment, or recycling scenarios to select strategies that maximize both environmental and economic value. Perhaps the most valuable contribution of big data is its ability to integrate multiple data sources to produce a comprehensive view of the product lifecycle. When information from production, logistics, customer usage, and social feedback is combined, firms can better understand how products are used, how quickly they degrade, and which recovery methods are most effective. This holistic perspective enables more informed decisions across the supply chain and supports the design of products that are easier to refurbish, remanufacture, or recycle. Additionally, firms can anticipate future trends in returns or material demand, which helps develop more sustainable and resilient supply chains over the long term. Despite these advantages, implementing big data in CLSCs is not without difficulties. Data quality issues, inconsistent formats across different partners, and privacy concerns can complicate analysis and decision-making. Nevertheless, the potential benefits remain substantial. By providing visibility, predictive power, operational efficiency, and lifecycle insights, big data equips firms to reduce waste, lower energy use, and extend resource value. In an era of increasing environmental scrutiny and regulatory pressure, leveraging big data in CLSCs is rapidly evolving from a technological option to a strategic necessity. Big data is a crucial tool for promoting sustainability in supply chains, particularly in closed-loop systems where product returns and reverse flows pose significant challenges. From real-time monitoring to predictive modeling and resource optimization, organizations can now make decisions with a degree of precision and foresight that was previously unattainable. Effectively harnessing big data allows firms not only to improve environmental performance but also to achieve operational efficiencies, reduce costs, manage risks, and enhance customer trust. As digital technologies continue to advance, the integration of big data into sustainable supply chain practices is expected to become more sophisticated, creating simultaneous economic and ecological value.

AI, ML, AND IOT FOR LIFECYCLE TRACKING AND TRANSPARENCY

Emerging digital technologies have gradually become key allies of big data in building more intelligent and responsive CLSCs. By combining real-time data collection, predictive analytics, and advanced modeling, these technologies provide firms with unprecedented levels of visibility and control over product lifecycles, particularly at the critical EOL stage. Among the most influential of these technologies are the IoT, AI, ML, and digital twin systems, each contributing in its own way to the efficient management of reverse logistics, product recovery, and sustainability outcomes. The IoT plays a foundational role in this ongoing digital transformation. IoT devices, such as RFID tags, smart sensors, GPS trackers, and embedded monitoring systems, continuously produce streams of real-time data about a product's location, condition, environmental exposure, usage, or mechanical wear. This continuous data flow allows organizations to monitor products across their lifecycle and plan interventions more accurately whether for reuse, refurbishment, remanufacturing, or recycling (Jensen, 2025). For instance, in electronics or automotive sectors, IoT-enabled sensors can identify early signs of component wear or exposure to adverse conditions, indicating the optimal time for maintenance or product return. By collecting such detailed data, firms can reduce uncertainty in reverse flows and improve the precision of operational decision-making across the CLSC.

Figure 2. IoT in Closed-Loop Supply Chains

Source: Developed by Authors

AI works together with IoT by processing both structured and unstructured data to support EOL decision-making. AI algorithms can categorize returned products based on condition, usage patterns, or defect profiles, automating tasks that were previously labor-intensive and prone to errors. AI-powered visual inspection systems, for example, can determine whether a returned item should be repaired, remanufactured, or recycled. This automation not only speeds up sorting and recovery but also reduces human error, minimizes processing time, and enhances overall sustainability by making sure resources are effectively recovered rather than wasted. In practice, companies implementing AI for EOL assessment have reported improved resource utilization, higher throughput, and extended product lifecycles. ML further strengthens the predictive capabilities of AI by allowing models to learn from historical and real-time data. ML algorithms can detect patterns in product failures, forecast return cycles, and anticipate user behavior, which is essential for managing reverse logistics and recovery operations. For instance, ML models can estimate the volume of returns expected within a certain period, predict likely defects, and help allocate resources at refurbishment or recycling facilities. These predictive insights enable firms to plan proactively, reduce bottlenecks, minimize idle capacity, and enhance overall supply chain responsiveness. Additionally, ML supports continuous learning: as more data is collected, models adapt and improve, thereby increasing forecasting accuracy over time and strengthening CLSC resilience.

Digital twins' virtual replicas of products, processes, or systems have also emerged as valuable tools in lifecycle management. Digital twins allow companies to simulate EOL scenarios, evaluate resource recovery potential, and test alternative strategies without physically handling products. For example, a digital twin of a returned appliance can estimate component wear, degradation, or recyclability, helping managers decide on the most cost-effective and environmentally responsible recovery pathway. By providing a virtual testing ground, digital twins reduce trial-and-error costs, increase confidence in decisions, and facilitate scenario planning in complex CLSC operations. When integrated, IoT, AI, ML, and digital twins create a synergistic ecosystem that considerably reduces operational uncertainty while improving lifecycle tracking and transparency (R. Mohanraj & Balaji, 2025). IoT supplies real-time data, AI interprets and automates decisions, ML forecasts future trends, and digital twins provide a virtual experimentation platform. Together, they enable firms to optimize recovery operations, allocate resources more efficiently, and extend the value of returned products, all while lowering environmental impact. This combined approach is particularly valuable in sectors with complex products, short lifecycles, or strict regulatory requirements for responsible EOL management. However, implementing these technologies is not without challenges. Issues such as inconsistent data quality, lack of interoperability between systems, high initial costs, and the need for staff training can create barriers, especially for smaller companies. Privacy and security concerns may also emerge when tracking products containing sensitive operational or customer information. Despite these difficulties, the advantages from improved transparency and efficiency to reduced waste and lower operational risk often outweigh the challenges, making adoption of these digital tools increasingly essential for sustainable CLSC operations. The integration of IoT, AI, ML, and digital twin technologies is fundamentally reshaping how firms manage product lifecycles and EOL processes. By enabling precise monitoring, intelligent decision-making, predictive planning, and virtual experimentation, these tools help companies tackle the inherent complexities of CLSCs more effectively and with greater confidence. As organizations continue to invest in these digital solutions and refine their integration approaches, digital intelligence will likely become a central pillar of sustainable, circular, and resilient supply chain management.

PREDICTIVE ANALYTICS IN EOL DECISION-MAKING

Predictive analytics has gradually become a central pillar in modern data-driven circular supply chain management, especially when it comes to product EOL decision-making. In traditional supply chains, decisions regarding returned or EOL products were frequently based on experience, simple rules of thumb, or delayed reporting. However, as supply chains have grown more complex and sustainability concerns have gained prominence, these conventional approaches are often inadequate. Predictive analytics provides a structured, evidence-based way to anticipate product behavior, assess potential recovery strategies, and optimize the allocation of resources, thereby supporting both environmental and economic objectives (Alhathlaul et al., 2025). Essentially, predictive analytics relieve both historical and real-time data, often in combination with ML and AI models, to forecast likely events. In CLSCs, this ability allows firms not only to anticipate which products might fail but also to estimate when they are likely to be returned and in what condition. Such foresight enables organizations to make proactive decisions regarding reuse, refurbishment, remanufacturing, or recycling rather than reacting after problems occur. Proactive planning in this manner is crucial for minimizing delays, lowering waste, and maximizing the economic and environmental value recovered from each product. A major application of predictive analytics in EOL decision-making is failure prediction. Modern ML algorithms can process large historical datasets containing product performance metrics, usage trends, environmental exposure, and maintenance records. By detecting patterns and correlations that are often invisible to human planners, these models can predict potential product failures before they happen. For instance, in electronics, predictive models may identify that devices transported in humid conditions have a higher probability of component failure within a defined period. Using this information, firms can preemptively allocate spare parts, schedule refurbishment work, or prepare remanufacturing lines, reducing downtime and enhancing recovery efficiency. Industries such as automotive and heavy machinery have already shown that predictive maintenance powered by analytics can significantly cut unplanned repairs and associated costs, demonstrating the value of early intervention (Mohanraj et al., 2024). Closely related to failure prediction is condition assessment, which is essential for deciding the most suitable recovery path for returned products. Not every returned item is in the same state, and selecting the wrong recovery option may lead to wasted resources or lost value. Predictive tools can analyze sensor data, usage history, and visual inspection results to classify products according to their appropriateness for reuse, refurbishment, or remanufacturing. AI-driven image recognition paired with ML models, for example, can evaluate wear patterns, surface damage, or component degradation to determine whether a returned device can be resold after minor repairs or requires complete rebuilding. Automating this classification process reduces reliance on subjective human judgment, speeds up processing, and ensures more consistent recovery outcomes. Research indicates that using predictive condition assessment in EOL workflows can improve sorting accuracy by roughly 25%, contributing directly to higher resource efficiency and lower environmental impact (Farshadfar et al., 2025).

Figure 3. Failure Prediction Using Predictive Analytics

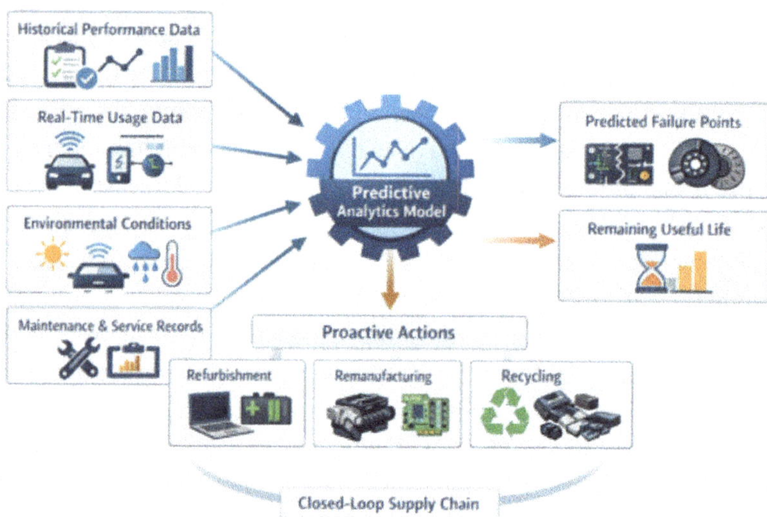

Source: Developed by Authors

Another key role of predictive analytics lies in material recovery optimization, particularly for recycling operations. Understanding the type, quantity, and quality of materials available from returned products allows firms to plan collection, separation, and remanufacturing activities more effectively. Advanced analytics can estimate recoverable metals, plastics, or composites from a batch of returns, considering usage patterns, product type, and predicted failure rates. By offering near-real-time estimates of material availability, predictive models help firms avoid overproduction of virgin materials and reduce waste leakage into landfills or incineration. Studies in electronics and consumer appliances indicate that such predictive material recovery can improve recycling yields by up to 30%, while simultaneously lowering the energy intensity of recycling processes (Shah et al., 2023). Beyond operational gains, predictive analytics also supports strategic decision-making. Firms can employ predictive insights to weigh the economic and environmental trade-offs of different recovery options. For example, predictive models can simulate scenarios in which certain products are prioritized for refurbishment over recycling, considering labor costs, processing time, resale value, and carbon footprint. Quantifying these trade-offs allows managers to make more informed decisions that balance sustainability with profitability. Recent case studies in electronics and automotive sectors suggest that predictive scenario modeling can enhance overall recovery efficiency by 20–30% while reducing material losses across supply chains (Sun et al., 2024). The effectiveness of predictive analytics in EOL decision-making is further amplified when combined with other digital technologies. IoT devices embedded in products continuously collect data on condition and usage, which can feed into AI and ML models to improve predictive accuracy. Digital twins' virtual representations of products or processes allow firms to simulate different EOL scenarios and test alternative recovery strategies without physically handling the products. A digital twin of a returned appliance, for example, can model component wear, battery degradation, or material recovery potential, helping firms decide the most economically and environmentally viable recovery pathway. The combination of predictive analytics with IoT, AI, ML, and digital twins reduce uncertainty and promotes a more agile, adaptive approach to closed-loop supply chain management. Nonetheless, deploying predictive analytics for EOL decision-making does not come without challenges. Data quality issues, including incomplete, inconsistent, or inaccurate datasets, can hinder model reliability. Multi-tiered supply chains may face data silos across suppliers, logistics partners, and recycling facilities, limiting information flow and predictive accuracy. Privacy and cybersecurity concerns may also emerge when product-level data contain sensitive customer or operational information. Moreover, implementing predictive models requires specialized knowledge in data science, ML, and supply chain management, which smaller or less digitally mature firms may lack (Lin et al., 2022). Overcoming these obstacles demands investments in data governance, inter-organizational collaboration, and workforce training, highlighting that the human and organizational dimensions are as important as the technical ones. Looking ahead, the role of predictive analytics in EOL decision-making is likely to expand as computational capacity increases, data availability grows, and algorithms become more sophisticated. Emerging methods, including reinforcement learning, real-time predictive simulations, and hybrid AI models, are expected to improve the speed and precision of EOL decision-making. Additionally, as regulatory pressure for sustainable production and waste management grows, predictive analytics will increasingly serve as a tool for compliance, helping firms demonstrate accountability and transparency in recovery and recycling operations. Predictive insights may also inform circular product design, enabling designers to anticipate failure modes, recovery potential, and recycling feasibility during the design phase, thereby integrating circularity principles earlier in the product lifecycle (Burke et al., 2023). Predictive analytics is fundamentally reshaping how firms handle EOL decision-making within CLSCs. By replacing guesswork with data-driven insights, organizations can anticipate product failures, assess condition accurately, and optimize material recovery processes. When integrated with IoT, AI, ML, and digital twin technologies, predictive analytics forms a powerful ecosystem that enhances visibility, operational agility, and sustainability performance. Firms that adopt these approaches are better positioned to reduce waste, extend product lifecycles, optimize resource use, and achieve both environmental and economic goals. As technology continues to advance, predictive analytics will almost certainly become an indispensable component of circular supply chain strategy, driving efficiency, resilience, and sustainable value across industries.

OPTIMIZING REVERSE LOGISTICS WITH BIG DATA

Optimizing reverse logistics has long been regarded as one of the most complicated and resource-heavy aspects of managing CLSCs. Unlike conventional forward logistics, reverse logistics focuses on moving returned, refurbished, recycled, or discarded products back through the supply chain, often with the aim of reintegration, remanufacturing, or environmentally safe disposal. The uncertainty inherent in return flows both in terms of timing and product condition creates significant operational challenges. Companies frequently face unpredictable return volumes, varying product states, and fragmented information across suppliers, transport providers, and recovery centers. In this environment, big data has emerged as a transformative enabler, offering the ability to gather, process, and analyze vast, diverse datasets to improve speed, efficiency, and sustainability in reverse logistics operations (Bag et al., 2021). A key application of big data in reverse logistics is predictive routing and route optimization. Historically, planning reverse logistics routes relied on rough estimations, past averages, or manual scheduling, which often caused inefficiencies, higher fuel consumption, and delayed pickups. Nowadays, by leveraging real-time data from GPS trackers, IoT-enabled fleet sensors, warehouse systems, and traffic analytics, firms can plan pickup and delivery routes dynamically with much greater precision. Predictive routing algorithms consider vehicle capacity, location of returns, traffic conditions, and expected time windows to minimize travel distances and maximize fleet efficiency. For instance, in the electronics sector, companies using predictive routing have reported fuel savings of around 15–20% and faster turnaround times for collecting returned products. Besides reducing transport-related emissions, this approach contributes to both operational efficiency and environmental sustainability (Hussain, 2022). Closely tied to route optimization is return volume forecasting. One of the ongoing challenges in reverse logistics is the unpredictability of product returns, which complicates planning for storage, labor, and handling capacity. Big data analytics enables firms to merge various sources of information sales figures, warranty claims, product usage patterns, seasonal trends, and customer behavior to estimate the likely quantity and timing of returns. ML models can detect subtle patterns that might be missed by conventional forecasting methods. For example, analytics might reveal that certain product models have higher return rates after promotional campaigns or during specific periods of the year. With more accurate forecasts, firms can allocate warehouse space, workforce, and transport resources more effectively, which reduces bottlenecks, idle capacity, and unnecessary costs. Moreover, improved predictability allows companies to coordinate better with refurbishment or recycling facilities, ensuring that returned products are processed in a timely and cost-efficient manner (Mansouri et al., 2025).

Another significant application of big data is automated sorting and classification. The heterogeneity of returned products in terms of type, condition, and potential for reuse necessitates careful evaluation to determine the most suitable recovery pathway. Manual sorting processes are traditionally slow, labor-intensive, and prone to errors, often resulting in misclassification or underutilization of recoverable resources. AI-powered systems equipped with computer vision and ML can automatically assess returned items based on visual inspection, sensor readings, and historical performance data. These systems can categorize products into groups such as "ready for reuse," "requires refurbishment," "suitable for remanufacturing," or "eligible for recycling." Automating this step accelerates reverse logistics operations, reduces human error, ensures consistent recovery decisions, and helps reclaim high-value components effectively. Research shows that AI-driven sorting can improve processing efficiency by 20–30%, leading to faster turnaround times and better overall supply chain performance (Shamsuddoha et al., 2025). Cost optimization is another major advantage provided by big-data-driven reverse logistics. The operations involve multiple cost elements, including transportation, labor, storage, handling, and processing fees. Without proper data and analytics, resources are often allocated inefficiently, resulting in avoidable expenditures and lower profitability. Big data allows companies to analyze historical records, real-time logistics information, and predictive forecasts to identify opportunities for cost reduction without compromising operational effectiveness. Predictive models, for instance, can suggest consolidating return pickups to reduce vehicle trips, determine optimal staffing levels, or prioritize processing of high-value returns. Additionally, understanding cost-benefit trade-offs among recovery options reuse, refurbishment, remanufacturing, or recycling helps managers make informed decisions that balance economic and sustainability goals. In practice, firms using these approaches have achieved operational cost reductions of 15–25% while also lowering energy use and emissions (Khahro et al., 2021).

Big data also enhances reverse logistics through improved traceability and transparency. In multi-tiered supply chains, returned products often pass through several intermediaries, which can make monitoring flows and ensure compliance with environmental or corporate sustainability policies challenging. Real-time tracking enabled by IoT sensors, RFID tags, and integrated analytics platforms allows managers to follow returned items throughout their journey. They can identify delays, inefficiencies, or deviations and take corrective actions promptly. Additionally, detailed tracking data can provide insights into the lifecycle stage and condition of each product, supporting better decisions regarding reuse, refurbishment, or recycling. This level of transparency is especially critical in industries with stringent regulatory requirements, such as electronics, automotive, or pharmaceuticals, where proper handling of returns impacts legal compliance, safety, and reputational management (Chang et al., 2020). Integrating predictive analytics, IoT, AI, and ML within reverse logistics operations also advances broader sustainability objectives. By optimizing routes, reducing unnecessary transport, and improving resource allocation, big data helps lower carbon footprints and minimize environmental harm. Accurate sorting, classification, and material recovery further prevent valuable resources from being wasted, reduce landfill pressures, and promote circular economy practices. Firms increasingly recognize that investments in data-driven reverse logistics not only generate operational and financial gains but also enhance corporate social responsibility and strengthen customer trust (Bag et al., 2021). Despite these benefits, implementing big-data-driven reverse logistics is not without obstacles. Issues such as incomplete or inconsistent data can reduce model reliability and decision quality. Interoperability across various IT systems, warehouse, transport, and recovery platforms remains a technical challenge. Privacy and cybersecurity concerns also arise, especially when tracking returned items containing sensitive customer or operational information. Furthermore, smaller firms may struggle with investment requirements, technical expertise, and workforce training. Addressing these challenges requires strong data governance, cross-organizational collaboration, and capacity building within logistics teams (Chang et al., 2020). Looking ahead, reverse logistics will increasingly rely on integrated digital technologies. IoT devices providing real-time data, coupled with predictive analytics, AI-based classification, and digital twin simulations, will enable firms to anticipate returns, dynamically optimize routes, and select the most suitable recovery pathways with greater certainty. Emerging techniques, such as reinforcement learning for routing optimization or hybrid AI models for sorting and condition assessment, are expected to further improve efficiency and environmental performance. In addition, rising regulatory focus on sustainability, circular economy practices, and extended producer responsibility will accelerate adoption of such data-driven solutions across industries (S. Kumar et al., 2024). Big data has become a pivotal enabler of efficient, cost-effective, and sustainable reverse logistics in CLSCs. By providing predictive insights, optimizing routing, automating sorting, and enabling cost-efficient resource allocation, data analytics transforms reverse logistics from a complex and uncertain domain into a more transparent, controlled, and responsive system. Firms leveraging big data in reverse logistics are better positioned to reduce costs, minimize environmental impacts, extend product lifecycles, and support circular economic goals. As digital technologies evolve and data availability increases, integrating big data into reverse logistics is likely to become standard practice for firms aiming to achieve both economic and environmental sustainability.

CIRCULAR ECONOMY INTEGRATION THROUGH DATA-DRIVEN RECOVERY

Over the past few years, the integration of CE principles into supply chain management has attracted growing attention, particularly as firms attempt to balance environmental sustainability with operational performance. Big data has increasingly become a key enabler in this regard, serving as the informational backbone that allows decision-making to maximize resource loops and minimize waste. By gathering, consolidating, and analyzing diverse datasets across the product lifecycle, companies can uncover opportunities for material substitution, component reuse, modular product design, and other circular strategies that were previously difficult to apply systematically (Psarommatis et al., 2025). One of the most notable contributions of big data to CE adoption is its ability to inform decisions based on lifecycle insights. Firms can now access detailed data on material composition, product performance, usage patterns, and EOL behavior. This information helps managers determine which components can be reused, which materials could be replaced with more sustainable alternatives, and which product designs allow easier refurbishment, remanufacturing, or recycling. For instance, in electronics and household appliances, real-time monitoring of usage and wear patterns can guide the selection of modular components that are more durable and easier to disassemble, thus extending product life while reducing material loss. The availability of such granular lifecycle data enables organizations to shift from linear "take-make-dispose" models toward closed-loop systems, where resource efficiency is maximized and environmental impacts are minimized (Ogwu & Kosoe, 2025).

Big data also facilitates collaboration among supply chain partners, which is critical for the successful implementation of CE practices. Circular supply chains often involve coordination across multiple tiers, including suppliers, manufacturers, logistics providers, refurbishes, and recyclers. Shared digital platforms, supported by cloud computing and IoT connectivity, allow firms to exchange information about product conditions, recovery potential, and environmental impacts almost in real time. This transparency improves the alignment of recovery efforts, ensures that returned products are handled appropriately, and reduces inefficiencies caused by miscommunication or delayed data. For example, automotive firms using collaborative platforms can monitor returned vehicle components across multiple refurbishing facilities, ensuring that high-value parts are reused while materials that have reached their EOL are directed efficiently to recycling processes (Dumée, 2022). Real-time analytics further strengthens circular economy strategies by supporting design-for-disassembly (DfD) and design-for-repair (DfR) approaches. These design principles aim to prolong product durability, simplify maintenance, and reduce environmental impacts. Big data enables firms to identify which components are prone to failure, how frequently maintenance is needed, and which disassembly processes are most time- or energy-consuming. Feeding this information back into the design process allows companies to make evidence-based adjustments to product architecture, material selection, and component layout. In consumer electronics, for example, predictive insights on battery degradation or screen wear can inform the development of modular designs, where individual components can be replaced or upgraded without discarding the entire device. Similarly, in industrial machinery, operational data can reveal which parts require frequent maintenance, prompting designers to implement modular or standardized components to simplify repair and replacement (García et al., 2022).

In addition, data-driven recovery supports the optimization of reverse logistics and remanufacturing within circular systems. By integrating insights from IoT devices, predictive analytics, and AI-powered sorting, firms can forecast the timing, condition, and volume of returned products more accurately. This enables more efficient collection scheduling, reduces unnecessary transport, and ensures products follow the most appropriate recovery path, whether refurbishment, remanufacturing, or recycling. Consequently, organizations can decrease waste leakage, enhance resource utilization, and improve operational efficiency in line with circular economy principles. Electronics companies, for instance, have reported a 20–30% improvement in material recovery rates and a corresponding reduction in landfill contributions after applying predictive analytics (Nilashi et al., 2025). Beyond operational improvements, the integration of big data into CE strategies also supports strategic and environmental decision-making. Firms can quantify the economic and ecological benefits of different recovery and reuse options, helping managers balance profitability with sustainability goals. Data-driven insights allow simulation of scenarios, such as replacing virgin materials with recycled inputs, extending product lifecycles via modular design, or prioritizing refurbishment over recycling for high-value components. These analyses not only help with compliance to environmental regulations and corporate social responsibility targets but also enable innovative business models, including product-as-a-service or lease-based offerings, that capitalize on circular practices (Loock, 2020). However, implementing a data-driven approach to circular economy integration is not without challenges. Data quality, interoperability across systems, and protection of sensitive information remain significant concerns. Firms also need to invest in infrastructure, such as IoT devices, cloud platforms, and analytics tools, and cultivate skilled personnel capable of interpreting complex datasets. Despite these challenges, the potential benefits including extended product lifecycles, reduced resource use, lower emissions, and stronger partner collaboration often outweigh the obstacles, making big data a vital tool for firms pursuing circularity (Sahoo et al., 2023). Looking ahead, the role of big data in CE integration is expected to grow as technologies like AI-driven optimization, digital twins, and real-time monitoring evolve further. These advances will allow firms to simulate full product lifecycles, test recovery strategies virtually, and anticipate trends in material availability and product demand. By integrating these insights with operational data, companies can continually enhance design, recovery, and reuse processes, fostering more resilient and environmentally responsible supply chains over time. Big data serves as a central enabler of circular economy practices by providing firms with visibility, predictive power, and operational intelligence necessary to close resource loops. From material substitution and component reuse to modular design, real-time analytics, and collaborative platforms, data supports evidence-based decision-making at every stage of the supply chain. As companies increasingly adopt and refine these approaches, circular principles will be integrated more effectively, creating supply chains that are not only sustainable but also adaptable, efficient, and economically viable in the long term.

INDUSTRY APPLICATIONS AND CASE EXAMPLES

In recent years, several industries have started to make extensive use of big data and digital technologies to improve the performance of CLSCs, particularly when dealing with EOL products. The combination of predictive analytics, IoT, AI, and digital twin technologies has not only enhanced operational efficiency but also contributed to environmental sustainability, turning traditional disposal and recycling processes into more value-generating practices. This section examines real-world applications across the electronics, automotive, and consumer goods sectors, showing how companies are increasingly using data-driven strategies to improve resource recovery and promote circular economy principles (S. Kumar et al., 2024).

Electronics Industry

The electronics sector has been among the most proactive in implementing data-enabled CLSCs, largely due to the rapid turnover of devices and mounting concerns over e-waste management. Manufacturers now use IoT-enabled sensors to monitor the condition, location, and usage of components throughout the product lifecycle. These devices allow for more precise tracking of returned products and provide detailed insights into material degradation, wear, and remaining lifespan. For instance, companies such as Dell and HP have implemented closed-loop recycling systems for plastics in their products. By continuously collecting and analyzing data, they can track recovery rates, determine which components retain the most value, and optimize recycling processes. These efforts have helped firms reduce reliance on virgin materials, increase recycled content in new devices, and ensure compliance with environmental regulations (Chen & Ogunseitan, 2021). Predictive analytics is also used to anticipate both the volume and quality of returned electronics, enabling more efficient planning of collection, sorting, and refurbishment activities. AI-driven visual inspection systems classify returned items, distinguishing products suitable for reuse, refurbishment, or recycling. Combining these technologies allows electronics manufacturers to reduce processing time, minimize material loss, and recover high-value components more effectively. Digital twins further enhance these efforts by simulating different recovery scenarios, helping companies evaluate the economic and environmental implications of alternative EOL strategies without having to physically manipulate the devices (Cenci et al., 2022).

Automotive Industry

The automotive sector, especially with the growth of electric vehicles (EVs), has increasingly adopted data-driven approaches to manage reverse flows of high-value components such as engines, batteries, and transmissions. Predictive analytics is key in anticipating returns, estimating component wear, and planning refurbishment or recycling operations. Automotive firms analyze historical usage data, environmental exposure records, and operational metrics to forecast when engines or batteries may reach the end of their useful life, allowing resources to be allocated proactively in remanufacturing or recycling facilities (Psarommatis et al., 2025). Digital twins have proven particularly useful in this sector. By creating virtual replicas of returned components, companies can simulate remanufacturing processes, evaluate recovery potential, and test alternative methods without physically disassembling the parts. For instance, EV battery recycling programs use digital twins to assess cell degradation, determine the optimal recovery pathway, and optimize disassembly sequences. This approach reduces trial-and-error costs, improves resource utilization, and ensures compliance with environmental and safety standards. When predictive analytics, IoT, and digital twins are combined, automotive companies can manage complex reverse logistics more efficiently, transforming a process that was once costly and uncertain into a strategic capability that supports circularity and operational resilience (Emon et al., 2025).

Consumer Goods and FMCG Sector

In the fast-moving consumer goods (FMCG) industry, data-driven CLSCs often focus on packaging and other high-volume, low-value items. Big data helps companies design efficient collection and recycling systems by analyzing consumer disposal behaviors, purchase patterns, and return rates. Mobile applications and digital platforms are increasingly used to engage consumers directly, incentivizing product returns and providing feedback on proper disposal practices. Some firms even track packaging disposal through app-based reward systems, improving participation rates and boosting recovery efficiency (Emon et al., 2025). Predictive analytics and IoT also support the planning of collection schedules, the effective allocation of transportation resources, and the optimization of sorting processes at recycling facilities. AI-powered classification systems can separate returned materials according to type, condition, and recyclability, ensuring resources are efficiently recovered and contamination is minimized. By implementing these technologies, FMCG companies not only reduce environmental impacts but also create business value from recovered materials, comply with extended producer responsibility regulations, and enhance their corporate reputation (Michalski, 2024).

Cross-Industry Insights

Across all these industries, a clear trend can be observed: data transforms EOL strategies from reactive, compliance-focused activities into proactive, value-generating operations. The integration of IoT, AI, ML, predictive analytics, and digital twins enables firms to anticipate product returns, optimize reverse logistics, enhance material recovery, and improve overall sustainability performance. Moreover, these applications demonstrate that investments in data-driven CLSCs deliver benefits beyond operational efficiency, supporting regulatory compliance, circular economy adoption, and long-term competitiveness (Emon et al., 2025). Industry-specific applications of data-driven CLSCs illustrate the transformative potential of big data and digital technologies in managing EOL products. Electronics manufacturers leverage IoT and analytics for component tracking and plastic recycling, automotive firms employ predictive modeling and digital twins for engine and battery recovery, and FMCG companies use consumer data and AI for packaging return systems. Taken together, these examples demonstrate how data-driven approaches can turn EOL challenges into opportunities for value creation, resource efficiency, and environmental sustainability. As digital technologies continue to advance, the adoption of such practices is likely to spread across sectors, reinforcing CLSCs as a vital component of circular economy strategies (Bag et al., 2023; Zhang et al., 2023).

CHALLENGES, BARRIERS, AND ETHICAL CONSIDERATIONS

Even though the promise of data-driven circular supply chains (CLSCs) is considerable, putting them into practice comes with multiple challenges and barriers. Organizations aiming to harness big data, IoT, AI, and predictive analytics for EOL product management often face a mixture of technical, financial, and ethical difficulties that may limit the effectiveness of circular initiatives. Successfully addressing these issues requires not only advanced technological solutions but also solid governance structures and careful attention to social and ethical responsibilities (Khan et al., 2025). A major persistent barrier is interoperability. Supply chains are often multi-tiered, with different stakeholders operating on varied platforms, using non-compatible data standards, or maintaining isolated information systems. These inconsistencies can substantially restrict the smooth sharing of data across manufacturers, logistics providers, refurbishment centers, and recycling facilities. For example, a returned electronic component may have performance data stored in one company's ERP system, usage information collected via IoT sensors by a retailer, and inspection records logged by a refurbishment facility in an entirely different software environment. Without standardized formats or middleware solutions, combining this data to make timely and accurate EOL decisions becomes highly difficult. Consequently, delays, miscommunication, or underutilization of critical information can occur, reducing the efficiency of reverse logistics and recovery operations (Khan & Emon, 2025c).

Data privacy and security concerns present another crucial challenge. Connected sensors and IoT-enabled tracking devices generate highly detailed information about product location, usage, and performance, which may sometimes include sensitive consumer or operational data. This creates questions regarding ethical collection, storage, and sharing of such information. Companies must ensure compliance with privacy regulations while keeping consumers informed about monitoring activities. Failure to protect such sensitive data could result in legal consequences, reputational damage, and decreased consumer trust. Moreover, cybersecurity risks such as unauthorized access, hacking, or data breaches can further compromise the integrity of supply chain operations, emphasizing the need for robust security measures and constant oversight (Emon & Khan, 2025a). High implementation costs are also a notable barrier, especially for SMEs. Advanced technologies like AI-assisted sorting systems, predictive analytics platforms, and digital twin simulations require substantial initial investments in hardware, software, and employee training. Smaller firms may simply lack the financial capacity to adopt these technologies at scale, leading to unequal participation in circular economic practices across industries. Even for larger organizations, integrating these systems with existing infrastructure, maintaining data quality, and ensuring sufficient staff competency can be costly, sometimes delaying adoption or restricting the scope of implementation (Kennedy & Linnenluecke, 2022). Closely related to costs is the issue of data quality. Predictive models, AI algorithms, and decision-support systems are only as reliable as the data that feeds them. Incomplete, inconsistent, or inaccurate datasets can distort EOL decisions, causing inefficient resource allocation, higher waste, or suboptimal recovery outcomes. For instance, if sensor data overestimates the remaining lifespan of a returned component, resources may be unnecessarily committed to refurbishment, wasting both labor and materials. Maintaining high-quality data requires consistent validation, harmonization across multiple data sources, and effective governance, which can be an ongoing and complex effort (Emon et al., 2025; Kumar et al., 2021). Beyond operational and technical concerns, ethical dilemmas also emerge. Continuous monitoring of products may intrude on user privacy, particularly in consumer electronics, connected vehicles, or smart home devices. Firms must carefully balance the use of detailed usage data for operational benefits with respect for individual privacy rights. Additionally, automated recovery decisions, if not implemented transparently, may embed biases in sorting, refurbishment, or recycling processes. For example, AI systems might prioritize higher-value components while neglecting others that are still recyclable, unintentionally reducing fairness and transparency. Such biases could undermine the social acceptability and legitimacy of circular initiatives (Baah et al., 2022). Addressing these barriers requires strong governance frameworks, standardized data protocols, and ethical policies that guide the collection, sharing, and use of information across the supply chain. Companies must create clear procedures for data handling, consent management, and algorithmic transparency. Regulatory guidance, industry-wide standards, and collaboration between organizations can mitigate technical, financial, and ethical obstacles, while workforce training ensures that employees can operate these systems effectively and responsibly. Embedding ethical considerations into technology design and operational processes from the outset helps reinforce stakeholder trust and long-term sustainability outcomes. While data-driven circular supply chains offer significant potential for enhancing EOL management, several barriers need careful attention. Interoperability problems, privacy and security concerns, high costs, data quality issues, and ethical dilemmas all represent significant hurdles to adoption. Overcoming these challenges requires a combination of technological, financial, governance, and ethical strategies that allow firms to balance innovation with responsibility. By taking these measures, organizations can harness the full potential of big data and digital technologies to advance circular economy practices while maintaining transparency, trust, and operational effectiveness (Emon, 2025c; Sijariya et al., 2025).

RECOMMENDATIONS AND FUTURE DIRECTIONS

The growing adoption of data-driven approaches in circular supply chains has demonstrated substantial potential for improving EOL management, enhancing resource efficiency, and supporting sustainability goals. However, as discussed in earlier sections, realizing the full benefits of big data, IoT, AI, and predictive analytics require careful planning, strategic investment, and attention to technical, organizational, and ethical dimensions. Based on the literature and practical insights, several recommendations can be proposed to guide both current implementation and future development of data-enabled circular supply chains (Chauhan et al., 2022).

First, establishing robust governance frameworks and standardized data protocols is critical. Firms should develop clear policies regarding data collection, storage, processing, and sharing across supply chain partners. Standardization of data formats and interfaces can significantly reduce interoperability challenges, enabling smoother integration between manufacturers, logistics providers, refurbishes, and recyclers. For example, adopting common metadata standards for IoT-generated product information can facilitate accurate condition assessment, predictive maintenance, and material recovery decisions. Governance frameworks should also include mechanisms for data validation, quality control, and auditability, ensuring that predictive models and AI systems rely on reliable inputs to guide EOL decision-making (Simaei & Rahimifard, 2024). Second, investments in workforce development and cross-functional training are recommended. Advanced technologies alone cannot guarantee success; the human dimension is equally important. Supply chain managers, data analysts, and technical staff must be equipped to interpret predictive insights, adjust operational strategies, and monitor AI-driven processes. Training programs should focus not only on technical skills, such as ML or IoT analytics, but also on ethical decision-making, regulatory compliance, and sustainability-oriented thinking. Involving employees across functional areas from product design to logistics ensures that circular strategies are embedded throughout the organization rather than isolated within a single department (Burke et al., 2023). Third, firms should prioritize ethical and privacy considerations in technology adoption. As monitoring and tracking capabilities expand, companies must balance operational efficiency with respect for user privacy and data protection regulations. Transparent policies should clarify how consumer or operational data is collected, stored, and used. Ethical frameworks should also be integrated into AI and predictive models to prevent biased recovery decisions or unfair prioritization of high-value components over lower-value items. By proactively addressing these concerns, organizations can maintain consumer trust, reduce reputational risks, and enhance the social acceptability of circular initiatives (Mostaghel & Chirumalla, 2021). Fourth, collaboration and knowledge sharing across supply chain partners is essential. Circular economic practices are inherently interdependent, requiring coordination among manufacturers, suppliers, logistics providers, refurbishes, and recyclers. Shared digital platforms, cloud-based data repositories, and collaborative analytics tools can improve visibility, align incentives, and facilitate more efficient EOL management. For instance, real-time sharing of product condition and usage data can help refurbish and recycling facilities optimize resource allocation, reducing waste and minimizing unnecessary processing. Policies that encourage open data sharing, while respecting competitive concerns and privacy, will be increasingly important as circular systems scale (David et al., 2024). Fifth, adoption of advanced technologies such as digital twins, hybrid AI models, and real-time predictive simulations should be emphasized. Digital twins, for example, allow firms to virtually model product wear, material recovery potential, and alternative EOL pathways, reducing trial-and-error in physical operations (Emon, 2025a). Hybrid AI models combining supervised learning, reinforcement learning, and optimization algorithms can enhance predictive accuracy, particularly in multi-tiered or complex supply chains. Integrating these technologies with IoT, ML, and cloud platforms can enable more agile, adaptive, and resilient circular supply chains, capable of responding to fluctuations in return volumes, material availability, and market demand (Kennedy & Linnenluecke, 2022).

Looking forward, research and development efforts should focus on scalable, low-cost solutions for SMEs. While large firms can often invest in cutting-edge digital infrastructure, SMEs face financial and technical barriers that may prevent participation in data-driven circularity. Future directions should explore affordable IoT devices, simplified analytics platforms, and modular AI solutions that can be implemented incrementally. Public-private partnerships, government incentives, and industry consortia can play a key role in making such technologies accessible, promoting broader adoption and equitable participation in circular economy practices (Kandpal et al., 2024). Finally, continuous evaluation and refinement of circular strategies are recommended. Predictive models, AI algorithms, and reverse logistics processes should be regularly monitored and updated to account for changes in product design, consumer behavior, regulatory frameworks, and environmental priorities. Incorporating feedback loops, both from operational outcomes and stakeholder input, will allow firms to refine their strategies, improve accuracy, and enhance sustainability performance over time. Additionally, scenario planning and sensitivity analysis can help organizations anticipate emerging trends, such as shifts in material availability, technological disruption, or evolving consumer expectations, ensuring that circular supply chains remain adaptable and resilient (Nandi et al., 2021). The successful adoption of data-driven circular supply chains requires a combination of technological, organizational, ethical, and strategic measures. Firms should invest in governance frameworks, workforce training, collaborative platforms, and advanced predictive technologies, while also addressing privacy, bias, and cost-related challenges. Future developments should focus on scalable solutions, cross-industry collaboration, and continuous learning mechanisms to ensure long-term sustainability and resilience. By following these recommendations, organizations can not only enhance operational efficiency and material recovery but also drive broader environmental and economic value, positioning themselves as leaders in the emerging data-enabled circular economy (Lanzalonga et al., 2024).

CONCLUSION

The integration of big data into circular supply chains marks a significant change in the way firms handle sustainability, resource use, and EOL product management. Traditional linear supply chains, which follow a "take-make-dispose" pattern, are becoming less adequate as environmental pressures rise, resources become scarcer, and regulations tighten. By making use of data-driven insights, organizations can gradually shift toward closed-loop models where materials, components, and products are recovered, reused, refurbished, or recycled in a more organized and efficient manner. This shift does not only reduce the environmental footprint but also creates economic benefits, turning what was once discarded into a potential source of value and competitive advantage. Throughout the chapter, it has been shown that predictive analytics, IoT systems, AI, and digital twins play a central role in enabling data-driven circularity. Predictive tools help firms anticipate product failures, evaluate the condition of returned items, and plan recovery strategies with a level of accuracy that was difficult to achieve before. By relying on evidence rather than simple estimation, companies can better allocate resources, reduce unnecessary waste, and prolong product lifecycles. At the same time, IoT-enabled devices and sensor networks provide detailed, real-time visibility into product usage and condition, supplying data to analytical models that improve decision-making across the supply chain. Digital twins offer a virtual testing environment for different recovery approaches, reducing trial-and-error costs and allowing firms to assess economic and environmental trade-offs without physically handling every item.

Reverse logistics has emerged as a particularly critical application of big data within circular supply chains. The difficulties posed by unpredictable return flows, variable product conditions, and fragmented supply chain information are addressed through data-driven routing, forecasting, sorting, and cost optimization. Companies can now plan collection schedules more efficiently, optimize transportation routes, and automate sorting processes to ensure that materials are directed to the most suitable recovery paths. These improvements not only boost operational efficiency but also advance sustainability objectives by lowering fuel consumption, cutting emissions, and preventing valuable materials from ending up in landfills. Data-driven circularity also promotes closer collaboration among supply chain partners, which is essential to effectively closing resource loops. Shared platforms allow manufacturers, suppliers, logistics providers, refurbishers, and recyclers to exchange important information on product condition, recovery potential, and environmental impacts. This level of transparency reduces inefficiencies, coordinates recovery efforts, and encourages shared responsibility for resource conservation. Furthermore, lifecycle data insights can inform design-for-disassembly and design-for-repair strategies, helping firms create products that are easier to maintain, upgrade, or recycle. These approaches not only improve environmental outcomes but also enhance customer satisfaction and loyalty by providing more durable and functional products. Despite the clear advantages, adopting big data in circular supply chains is not without obstacles. Interoperability issues, data quality challenges, high implementation costs, privacy concerns, and ethical dilemmas all require careful consideration. Companies need to invest in governance structures, standardize data formats, and establish ethical policies to ensure predictive models, monitoring systems, and automated recovery decisions are fair and reliable. Addressing these challenges is essential not only to realize the full benefits of data-driven circularity but also to maintain trust among stakeholders and end users. Looking ahead, the role of big data in enabling circularity is expected to grow as technologies advance, computing power expands, and data becomes more widely available. Emerging developments in AI, hybrid modeling, real-time simulations, and collaborative platforms are likely to improve predictive accuracy, operational agility, and overall sustainability performance. Small and medium-sized enterprises could particularly benefit from scalable, low-cost digital solutions that allow them to join circular practices without major financial or technical obstacles. By continuously learning from operations, refining predictive models, and integrating feedback into product design and recovery processes, organizations can build supply chains that are more resilient, adaptive, and sustainable. Big data-driven circularity represents a strategic intersection of technology, sustainability, and operational effectiveness. Closed-loop supply chain models, powered by data analytics and digital tools, equip firms to anticipate challenges, optimize resource flows, and turn EOL products into sources of value. Companies adopting these approaches not only reduce environmental impacts and resource waste but also gain a competitive advantage through improved efficiency, compliance, and customer engagement. As global pressures for sustainable operations increase, data-driven circular supply chains are set to become a central component of long-term organizational resilience, profitability, and social responsibility.

REFERENCES

Alhathlaul, N., Lakhouit, A., Abdalla, G. M. T., Alghamdi, A., Shaban, M., Alshahir, A., Alshahr, S., Alali, I., & Mutlaq Alshammari, F. (2025). Assessing Waste Management Using Machine Learning Forecasting for Sustainable Development Goal Driven. *Sustainability*, *17*(19), 8654. DOI: 10.3390/su17198654

Andersen, T. (2022). A comparative study of national variations of the European WEEE directive: Manufacturer's view. *Environmental Science and Pollution Research International*, *29*(14), 19920–19939. DOI: 10.1007/s11356-021-13206-z PMID: 33665699

Awan, U., Sroufe, R., & Shahbaz, M. (2021). Industry 4.0 and the circular economy: A literature review and recommendations for future research. *Business Strategy and the Environment*, *30*(4), 2038–2060. DOI: 10.1002/bse.2731

Baah, C., Afum, E., Agyabeng-Mensah, Y., & Agyeman, D. O. (2022). Stakeholder Influence on Adoption of Circular Economy Principles: Measuring Implications for Satisfaction and Green Legitimacy. *Circular Economy and Sustainability*, *2*(1), 91–111. DOI: 10.1007/s43615-021-00093-2

Bag, S., Luthra, S., Mangla, S. K., & Kazancoglu, Y. (2021). Leveraging big data analytics capabilities in making reverse logistics decisions and improving remanufacturing performance. *International Journal of Logistics Management*, *32*(3), 742–765. DOI: 10.1108/IJLM-06-2020-0237

Berlato, M., Binni, L., Durmus, D., Gatto, C., Giusti, L., Massari, A., Toldo, B. M., Cascone, S., & Mirarchi, C. (2025). Digital Platforms for the Built Environment: A Systematic Review Across Sectors and Scales. *Buildings (Basel, Switzerland)*, *15*(14), 2432. DOI: 10.3390/buildings15142432

Budak, A. (2020). Sustainable reverse logistics optimization with triple bottom line approach: An integration of disassembly line balancing. *Journal of Cleaner Production*, *270*, 122475. DOI: 10.1016/j.jclepro.2020.122475

Burke, H., Zhang, A., & Wang, J. X. (2023). Integrating product design and supply chain management for a circular economy. *Production Planning and Control*, *34*(11), 1097–1113. DOI: 10.1080/09537287.2021.1983063

Cenci, M. P., Scarazzato, T., Munchen, D. D., Dartora, P. C., Veit, H. M., Bernardes, A. M., & Dias, P. R. (2022). Eco-Friendly Electronics—A Comprehensive Review. *Advanced Materials Technologies*, *7*(2). Advance online publication. DOI: 10.1002/admt.202001263

Chang, Y., Iakovou, E., & Shi, W. (2020). Blockchain in global supply chains and cross border trade: A critical synthesis of the state-of-the-art, challenges and opportunities. *International Journal of Production Research*, *58*(7), 2082–2099. DOI: 10.1080/00207543.2019.1651946

Chauhan, S., Singh, R., Gehlot, A., Akram, S. V., Twala, B., & Priyadarshi, N. (2022). Digitalization of Supply Chain Management with Industry 4.0 Enabling Technologies: A Sustainable Perspective. *Processes (Basel, Switzerland)*, *11*(1), 96. DOI: 10.3390/pr11010096

Chen, M., & Ogunseitan, O. A. (2021). Zero E-waste: Regulatory impediments and blockchain imperatives. *Frontiers of Environmental Science & Engineering*, *15*(6), 114. DOI: 10.1007/s11783-021-1402-x

Chen, Z., Hong, S., Ji, X., Shi, R., & Wu, J. (2022). Refurbished products and supply chain incentives. *Annals of Operations Research*, *310*(1), 27–47. DOI: 10.1007/s10479-021-04016-0

David, I., Bork, D., & Kappel, G. (2024). Circular systems engineering. *Software & Systems Modeling*, *23*(2), 269–283. DOI: 10.1007/s10270-024-01154-4

Dumée, L. F. (2022). Circular Materials and Circular Design—Review on Challenges Towards Sustainable Manufacturing and Recycling. *Circular Economy and Sustainability*, *2*(1), 9–23. DOI: 10.1007/s43615-021-00085-2 PMID: 34888565

Emon, M. M. H. (2025a). Circularity Meets AI: Revolutionizing Consumer Engagement Through Green Marketing. In *Transforming Business Practices With AI-Powered Green Marketing* (pp. 169–208). IGI Global Scientific Publishing. https://doi.org/DOI: 10.4018/979-8-3373-3017-4.ch007

Emon, M. M. H. (2025b). Ethical Intelligence in Motion: Leveraging AI for Responsible Sourcing in Supply Chain and Logistics. In *Navigating Responsible Business Practices Through Ethical AI* (pp. 207–240). https://doi.org/DOI: 10.4018/979-8-3373-3104-1.ch008

Emon, M. M. H. (2025c). Purpose-Driven Intelligence in Green Marketing: Leveraging AI for CSR-Centric and Sustainable Brand Positioning. In *Transforming Business Practices With AI-Powered Green Marketing* (pp. 89–122). IGI Global Scientific Publishing. https://doi.org/DOI: 10.4018/979-8-3373-3017-4.ch004

Emon, M. M. H. (2025d). Cybersecurity in the Smart City Era: Overcoming Challenges With Modern Cryptographic Solutions. In *Securing Smart Cities Through Modern Cryptography Technologies* (pp. 43–74). IGI Global Scientific Publishing. https://doi.org/DOI: 10.4018/979-8-3373-3326-7.ch002

Emon, M. M. H., & Chowdhury, M. S. A. (2025). AI and IoT-Powered Smart Logistics: Transforming Supply Chains for Efficiency and Sustainability. In *Emerging Trends in Smart Logistics Technologies* (A. Hlali, pp. 45–72). IGI Global Scientific Publishing. https://doi.org/DOI: 10.4018/979-8-3373-2434-0.ch002

Emon, M. M. H., & Khan, T. (2025a). The Role of Traditional Media in Crisis Amplification: How Mainstream Media Magnifies Fake News and Ethical Dilemmas in Supply Chain Crises. In *Mass Media and Impact of Fake News on Supply Chains* (pp. 59–90). IGI Global., DOI: 10.4018/979-8-3373-2175-2.ch003

Emon, M. M. H., & Khan, T. (2025b). Strengthening Bonds: The Strategic Role of Customer Relationship Management in Loyalty and Retention. In Ananthan, S., Kohli, A., Manickam, T., & Dhanabalan, T. (Eds.), *Strategic Innovation and Sustainable Customer-Centric Growth* (pp. 27–56). IGI Global Scientific Publishing., DOI: 10.4018/979-8-3373-6955-6.ch002

Emon, M. M. H., & Khan, T. (2025c). Exploring the mediating role of green logistics in enhancing green supply chain performance: Evidence from Bangladesh. *Journal of Engineering Research.* Advance online publication. DOI: 10.1016/j.jer.2025.10.003

Emon, M. M. H., Nath, A., & Nipa, M. N. (2025). *AI for a Greener Tomorrow: Harnessing Artificial Intelligence for Environmental Sustainability.* IGI Global Scientific Publishing., DOI: 10.4018/979-8-3373-2387-9.ch010

Emon, M. M. H., Nath, A., Rahman, K. M., Kutub, J., Rifat, H. H., & Mahsin-Ul-Islam, M. (2025). Evaluating Artificial Intelligence Integration for Improving Supply Chain Efficiency in the Context of Bangladesh's E-Commerce Sector. *2025 IEEE 7th International Conference on Sustainable Technologies For Industry 5.0 (STI)*, 1–6. https://doi.org/DOI: 10.1109/STI69347.2025.11367608

Emon, M. M. H., Rahman, K. M., Islam, M. S., Nath, A., Kutub, J., & Santa, N. A. (2025). Determinants of Explainable AI Adoption in Customer Service Chatbots: Insights from the Telecom Sector of Bangladesh. *2025 IEEE 7th International Conference on Sustainable Technologies For Industry 5.0 (STI)*, 1–6. https://doi.org/DOI: 10.1109/STI69347.2025.11367590

Emon, M. M. H., Rahman, K. M., Nath, A., Mahsin-Ul-Islam, M., Rifat, H. H., & Kutub, J. (2025). Exploring Drivers of Sustainable E-Commerce Adoption among SMEs in Bangladesh: A TOE Framework Approach for Industry 5.0 Transformation. *2025 IEEE 7th International Conference on Sustainable Technologies For Industry 5.0 (STI)*, 1–6. https://doi.org/DOI: 10.1109/STI69347.2025.11367600

Farhana, K., Kadirgama, K., Mahamude, A. S. F., & Mica, M. T. (2022). Energy consumption, environmental impact, and implementation of renewable energy resources in global textile industries: An overview towards circularity and sustainability. *Materials Circular Economy*, *4*(1), 15. DOI: 10.1007/s42824-022-00059-1

Farshadfar, Z., Khajavi, S. H., Mucha, T., & Tanskanen, K. (2025). Machine learning-based automated waste sorting in the construction industry: A comparative competitiveness case study. *Waste Management (New York, N.Y.)*, *194*, 77–87. DOI: 10.1016/j.wasman.2025.01.008 PMID: 39787669

Fu, X., Alevizou, P. J., Cheng, R., & Ma, K. (2025). Explore the meanings beyond motives behind second-hand clothing consumption practice: From the theory of practice perspective. *Journal of Fashion Marketing and Management*, *29*(7), 1320–1342. DOI: 10.1108/JFMM-05-2024-0196

García, Á., Bregon, A., & Martínez-Prieto, M. A. (2022). A non-intrusive Industry 4.0 retrofitting approach for collaborative maintenance in traditional manufacturing. *Computers & Industrial Engineering*, *164*, 107896. DOI: 10.1016/j.cie.2021.107896 PMID: 36569781

Hussain, Z. (2022). Environmental and Economic-oriented Transport Efficiency: The Role of Climate Change Mitigation Technology. *Environmental Science and Pollution Research International*, *29*(19), 29165–29182. DOI: 10.1007/s11356-021-18392-4 PMID: 34993827

Jensen, H. H. (2025). Internal IT: The Backbone System of Circular Business Models. In *Circular Economy Opportunities and Pathways for Manufacturers* (pp. 291–321). https://doi.org/DOI: 10.1007/978-3-031-75279-7_11

Kandpal, V., Jaswal, A., Santibanez Gonzalez, E. D. R., & Agarwal, N. (2024). *Circular Economy Principles: Shifting Towards Sustainable Prosperity* (pp. 125–165). https://doi.org/DOI: 10.1007/978-3-031-52943-6_4

Kennedy, S., & Linnenluecke, M. K. (2022). Circular economy and resilience: A research agenda. *Business Strategy and the Environment*, *31*(6), 2754–2765. DOI: 10.1002/bse.3004

Khahro, S. H., Kumar, D., Siddiqui, F. H., Ali, T. H., Raza, M. S., & Khoso, A. R. (2021). Optimizing Energy Use, Cost and Carbon Emission through Building Information Modelling and a Sustainability Approach: A Case-Study of a Hospital Building. *Sustainability*, *13*(7), 3675. DOI: 10.3390/su13073675

Khan, T., & Emon, M. M. H. (2025a). Preparing for the Next Disruption: Lessons Learned From Past Crises and Building a Playbook for Future Supply Chain Shocks. In *Supply Chain Disruptions and Impact on Global Inflation* (pp. 253–286). IGI Global Scientific Publishing. https://doi.org/DOI: 10.4018/979-8-3373-1982-7.ch010

Khan, T., & Emon, M. M. H. (2025b). Resilient Supply Chains: Lessons From Past Crisis Strategies Companies Can Adopt to Create More Resilient Supply Chains. In *Mass Media and Impact of Fake News on Supply Chains* (pp. 285–318). IGI Global. https://doi.org/DOI: 10.4018/979-8-3373-2175-2.ch011

Khan, T., & Emon, M. M. H. (2025c). The role of digital supply chain practices in enhancing firm performance: Insights from the manufacturing sector of Bangladesh. *Brazilian Journal of Operations & Production Management*, *22*(2), 2493. DOI: 10.14488/BJOPM.2493.2025

Khan, T., Emon, M. M. H., Rahman, K. M., Nipa, M. N., & Fuad, M. N. (2025). The Role of AI in Driving Customer Engagement Through Technological, Organizational and Environmental Enablers in E-Commerce. *2025 International Conference on Quantum Photonics, Artificial Intelligence, and Networking (QPAIN)*, 1–6. https://doi.org/DOI: 10.1109/QPAIN66474.2025.11171949

Khan, T., Emon, M. M. H., & Rahman, S. (2024). Marketing Strategy Innovation via AI Adoption: A Study on Bangladeshi SMEs in the Context of Industry 5.0. *2024 6th International Conference on Sustainable Technologies for Industry 5.0 (STI)*, 1–6. https://doi.org/DOI: 10.1109/STI64222.2024.10951050

Khan, T., & Hasan Emon, M. M. (2024). Determinants of AI Image Generator Adoption Among Marketing Agencies: The Mediating Effects of Perceived Usefulness. *2024 IEEE 3rd International Conference on Robotics, Automation, Artificial-Intelligence and Internet-of-Things (RAAICON)*, 177–182. https://doi.org/DOI: 10.1109/RAAICON64172.2024.10928548

Kumar, G., Basri, S., Imam, A. A., Khowaja, S. A., Capretz, L. F., & Balogun, A. O. (2021). Data Harmonization for Heterogeneous Datasets: A Systematic Literature Review. *Applied Sciences (Basel, Switzerland)*, *11*(17), 8275. DOI: 10.3390/app11178275

Kumar, S., Verma, A. K., & Mirza, A. (2024). *Opportunities and Challenges for Data-Driven and Circular Economy.*, DOI: 10.1007/978-981-97-5656-8_7

Lanzalonga, F., Marseglia, R., Irace, A., & Biancone, P. Pietro. (2024). The application of artificial intelligence in waste management: Understanding the potential of data-driven approaches for the circular economy paradigm. *Management Decision*. Advance online publication. DOI: 10.1108/MD-10-2023-1733

Lin, H., Lin, J., & Wang, F. (2022). An innovative machine learning model for supply chain management. *Journal of Innovation & Knowledge*, *7*(4), 100276. DOI: 10.1016/j.jik.2022.100276

Loock, M. (2020). Unlocking the value of digitalization for the European energy transition: A typology of innovative business models. *Energy Research & Social Science*, *69*, 101740. DOI: 10.1016/j.erss.2020.101740

Mansouri, N., Nasri, S., Mnassri, A., Lashab, A., Vasquez, J. C., Cherif, A., & Rezk, H. (2025). Electric Vehicle Charging Infrastructure: Impacts and Future Challenges of Photovoltaic Integration with Examples from a Tunisian Case. *World Electric Vehicle Journal*, *16*(7), 349. DOI: 10.3390/wevj16070349

Michalski, D. (2024). Operationalization of ESG-Integrated Strategy Through the Balanced Scorecard in FMCG Companies. *Sustainability*, *16*(21), 9174. DOI: 10.3390/su16219174

Mohanraj, E., N, E., S, S., & S, S. (2024). Digital Twins for Automotive Predictive Maintenance. *2024 International Conference on Inventive Computation Technologies (ICICT)*, 1579–1584. https://doi.org/DOI: 10.1109/ICICT60155.2024.10544392

Mohanraj, R., & Balaji, S. N. (2025). Digital Twin Technology: A Comprehensive Review of Modeling, Applications, Challenges and Future Directions in Complex System Integration. *Archives of Computational Methods in Engineering*. Advance online publication. DOI: 10.1007/s11831-025-10397-3

Mostaghel, R., & Chirumalla, K. (2021). Role of customers in circular business models. *Journal of Business Research*, *127*, 35–44. DOI: 10.1016/j.jbusres.2020.12.053

Nandi, S., Sarkis, J., Hervani, A. A., & Helms, M. M. (2021). Redesigning Supply Chains using Blockchain-Enabled Circular Economy and COVID-19 Experiences. *Sustainable Production and Consumption*, *27*, 10–22. DOI: 10.1016/j.spc.2020.10.019 PMID: 33102671

Nilashi, M., Baabdullah, A. M., Abumalloh, R. A., Ooi, K.-B., Tan, G. W.-H., Giannakis, M., & Dwivedi, Y. K. (2025). How can big data and predictive analytics impact the performance and competitive advantage of the food waste and recycling industry? *Annals of Operations Research*, *348*(3), 1649–1690. DOI: 10.1007/s10479-023-05272-y

Niu, N., Zhang, H., Wang, M., Lu, Y., Ma, J., & Zhang, B. (2025). Circular economy efficiency improvements contribute to achieving Net-Zero: Empirical evidence from China. *Computers & Industrial Engineering*, *201*, 110700. DOI: 10.1016/j.cie.2024.110700

Ogwu, M. C., & Kosoe, E. A. (2025). Innovative Approaches to Recycling, Upcycling, and Downcycling for Sustainable Waste Management. *CleanMat*, *2*(3), 242–261. DOI: 10.1002/clem.70013

Olivares-Aguila, J., & ElMaraghy, W. (2021). System dynamics modelling for supply chain disruptions. *International Journal of Production Research*, *59*(6), 1757–1775. DOI: 10.1080/00207543.2020.1725171

Pasupuleti, V., Thuraka, B., Kodete, C. S., & Malisetty, S. (2024). Enhancing Supply Chain Agility and Sustainability through Machine Learning: Optimization Techniques for Logistics and Inventory Management. *Logistics (Basel)*, *8*(3), 73. DOI: 10.3390/logistics8030073

Psarommatis, F., May, G., & Azamfirei, V. (2025). Product reuse and repurpose in circular manufacturing: A critical review of key challenges, shortcomings and future directions. *Journal of Remanufacturing*, *15*(2–3), 273–310. DOI: 10.1007/s13243-025-00153-y

Ramanathan, U., He, Q., Subramanian, N., Gunasekaran, A., & Sarpong, D. (2023). Collaborative closed-loop supply chain framework for sustainable manufacturing: Evidence from the Indian packaging industry. *Technological Forecasting and Social Change*, *191*, 122489. DOI: 10.1016/j.techfore.2023.122489

Sahoo, S., Upadhyay, A., & Kumar, A. (2023). Circular economy practices and environmental performance: Analysing the role of big data analytics capability and responsible research and innovation. *Business Strategy and the Environment*, *32*(8), 6029–6046. DOI: 10.1002/bse.3471

Shah, H. H., Amin, M., & Pepe, F. (2023). Maximizing resource efficiency: Opportunities for energy recovery from municipal solid waste in Europe. *Journal of Material Cycles and Waste Management*, *25*(5), 2766–2782. DOI: 10.1007/s10163-023-01733-5

Shamsuddoha, M., Khan, E. A., Chowdhury, M. M. H., & Nasir, T. (2025). Revolutionizing Supply Chains: Unleashing the Power of AI-Driven Intelligent Automation and Real-Time Information Flow. *Information (Basel)*, *16*(1), 26. DOI: 10.3390/info16010026

Sijariya, R., Garg, V., & Tiwari, P. (2025). SDGs for Organizational Sustainability: Integrating Digital Technologies for a Digital Circular Economy. In *Sustainable Innovations and Digital Circular Economy* (pp. 307–327). Springer Nature Singapore., DOI: 10.1007/978-981-96-1064-8_16

Simaei, E., & Rahimifard, S. (2024). AI-based decision support system for enhancing end-of-life value recovery from e-wastes. *International Journal of Sustainable Engineering*, *17*(1), 80–96. DOI: 10.1080/19397038.2024.2306293

Sun, L., Dong, H., Dai, Y., Dong, J., Fujii, M., Geng, Y., Lou, Z., & Liu, X. (2024). Environmental benefit of recycling plastics from waste electrical & electronic equipment. *Resources, Conservation and Recycling*, *211*, 107855. DOI: 10.1016/j.resconrec.2024.107855

Tian, H., Yan, M., Zhou, J., Wu, Q., Tiong, Y. W., Lam, H. T., Zhang, J., & Tong, Y. W. (2023). A closed loop case study of decentralized food waste management: System performance and life cycle carbon emission assessment. *The Science of the Total Environment*, *899*, 165783. DOI: 10.1016/j.scitotenv.2023.165783 PMID: 37495140

Tombido, L. (2025). Resilient and sustainable closed-loop supply chains (CLSCs): A research agenda. *Journal of Responsible Production and Consumption*, *2*(1), 256–289. DOI: 10.1108/JRPC-03-2024-0012

KEY TERMS AND DEFINITIONS

Big Data: Large, complex datasets generated from multiple sources that can be analyzed to reveal patterns, trends, and insights, enabling informed decision-making across supply chains.

Circular Economy (CE): An economic model aimed at minimizing waste and resource consumption by promoting reuse, refurbishment, recycling, and closed-loop production processes.

Closed-Loop Supply Chain (CLSC): A supply chain system that integrates forward and reverse logistics to recover, remanufacture, or recycle products at the end of their lifecycle.

Digital Twin: A virtual replica of a physical product, process, or system that enables simulation, monitoring, and optimization without direct physical intervention.

Internet of Things (IoT): A network of interconnected devices and sensors that collect and transmit real-time data to monitor product usage, condition, and lifecycle performance.

Predictive Analytics: The use of statistical models, ML, and data analysis to forecast future events, such as product returns, failures, or material recovery potential.

Resource Recovery: The process of reclaiming valuable materials or components from returned, used, or discarded products to reduce waste and support circular economic goals.

Reverse Logistics: The process of managing the return, recovery, recycling, or disposal of products from the end consumer through the supply chain.

Chapter 8
From Transparency to Circularity: Enhancing Supply Chain Sustainability Through Big Data

Shakerod Munuhwa
http://orcid.org/0000-0002-0952-6514
Glasgow Caledonian University, UK

ABSTRACT

Global supply chains are under increasing scrutiny to address environmental, social, and governance (ESG) challenges while maintaining competitiveness and resilience. Big data has emerged as a transformative tool that not only improves transparency but also enables the transition towards circular economy models. This chapter investigates how big data analytics can support the shift from linear practices to circular supply chains that prioritise resource efficiency, waste reduction, and product life-cycle optimisation. It examines the role of big data in enhancing supply chain visibility, enabling predictive decision-making, and fostering collaboration across stakeholders. Case examples will demonstrate how industries such as food, apparel, and manufacturing are using big data to achieve traceability, reduce carbon footprints, and enable closed-loop systems. The chapter will also critically discuss barriers, including governance, interoperability, and ethical concerns, while offering a practical framework for integrating big data into circular supply chain strategies.

OVERVIEW

Global supply chains are increasingly confronted with complex sustainability challenges arising from climate change, resource scarcity, regulatory pressures, and

DOI: 10.4018/979-8-3373-6896-2.ch008

heightened stakeholder expectations. Traditional linear models based on extraction, production, consumption, and disposal exacerbate environmental degradation and social inequalities across the supply chain network (Geissdoerfer et al., 2017). Key issues include excessive carbon emissions, poor labour practices, waste generation, and inefficiencies in resource utilisation. These challenges highlight the urgent need for innovative approaches that can balance economic growth with environmental and social responsibility (Seuring & Müller, 2008).

To address these challenges, there is a growing call to move beyond mere transparency in supply chains, which focuses on visibility, traceability, and disclosure of practices, towards circularity, which seeks to redesign systems to eliminate waste and enable closed-loop processes (Ellen MacArthur Foundation, 2019). Transparency is a necessary first step, as it provides visibility into supplier practices and product lifecycles, yet it does not by itself drive systemic change. Circular supply chains, by contrast, embed sustainability into the entire value network by promoting reuse, remanufacturing, recycling, and resource efficiency, thereby reducing dependency on finite resources (Sibanda et al., 2025).

Big data emerges as a powerful enabler in this transition from transparency to circularity. The proliferation of digital technologies such as the Internet of Things (IoT), blockchain, and predictive analytics allows firms to collect, integrate, and analyse vast datasets across their global networks. These data-driven insights improve visibility, support real-time decision-making, and enable proactive management of sustainability risks and opportunities (Wamba et al., 2017). For instance, big data applications can track material flows, optimise logistics to reduce emissions, and forecast demand to minimise overproduction and waste. In this way, big data analytics not only enhances supply chain transparency but also provides the foundation for implementing circular economy principles at scale.

The chapter builds on these arguments by exploring how big data can be harnessed to address sustainability challenges in global supply chains, facilitate the transition from transparency to circularity, and provide actionable frameworks for both academics and practitioners. The next section focuses on the conceptual framework.

CONCEPTUAL FRAMEWORK

The proposed conceptual framework, Transparency to Circularity Through Big Data, delineates the mechanisms through which Big Data technologies enable the evolution of supply chains from transparency-oriented operations to fully circular systems. In the context of sustainable supply chain management, transparency defined by the extent to which firms can trace, monitor, and disclose material and information flows is a foundational prerequisite for circularity. By leveraging Big Data tools such as the Internet of Things (IoT), blockchain, and predictive analytics, organisations can achieve end-to-end visibility, improve data accuracy, and enhance stakeholder accountability (Beske & Seuring, 2014; Kumar et al., 2021). This transparency forms the basis for informed decision-making related to product design, resource recovery, and reverse logistics, ultimately enabling the implementation of circular practices such as reuse, remanufacturing, and recycling. The framework therefore conceptualises Big Data as both a technological and strategic enabler that bridges the gap between supply chain transparency and circularity, fostering resilience, efficiency, and sustainability across global production networks.

Transparency to Circularity Through Big Data

Figure 1. Transparency to Circularity Through Big Data

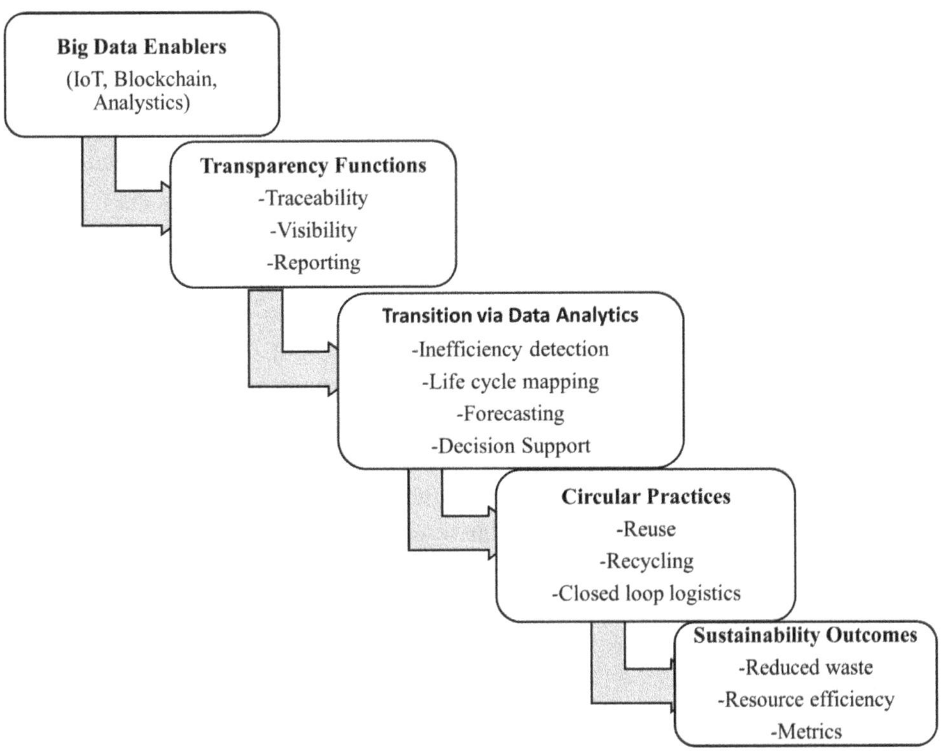

The proposed conceptual framework illustrates how Big Data technologies can facilitate the transition from supply chain transparency to circularity, thereby strengthening sustainability outcomes. At its core, the framework recognises that transparency characterised by traceability, visibility, and reporting is an essential precursor to circular supply chain practices. Without the ability to capture and share accurate data across multiple tiers, it becomes difficult for firms to identify inefficiencies, monitor resource flows, or design closed-loop systems (Beske & Seuring, 2014; Kumar et al., 2021).

Big Data acts as the central enabler in this transition. Tools such as the Internet of Things (IoT), blockchain, and advanced data analytics generate and process vast amounts of information in real time. IoT sensors capture product lifecycle data (Atzori et al., 2010), blockchain ensures immutability and trust in transactions (Saberi et al., 2019), while analytics convert raw data into actionable insights (Wamba et al., 2017). These enablers transform transparency into a dynamic capability rather than a static reporting function. By integrating such technologies, organisations can identify opportunities for material recovery, predict maintenance needs, and track environmental performance indicators more effectively (Bag et al., 2021).

The framework further highlights how enhanced transparency provides the foundation for circular practices. Once firms achieve visibility of product flows and resource use, they can embed strategies such as reuse, recycling, remanufacturing, and closed-loop logistics (Genovese et al., 2017). For example, traceability data enables reverse logistics systems to function efficiently, ensuring that end-of-life products are collected and reintegrated into the supply chain (Batista et al., 2018). Similarly, predictive analytics supports demand forecasting and inventory optimisation, reducing both overproduction and waste (Papadopoulos et al., 2017).

Finally, the framework positions sustainability outcomes reduced waste generation, improved resource efficiency, and measurable sustainability metrics as the ultimate results of the transition. These outcomes not only align with global environmental targets but also contribute to long-term business competitiveness by lowering costs and enhancing brand reputation (Ellen MacArthur Foundation, 2019; Rajesh, 2020). The conceptual model therefore underscores the pivotal role of Big Data in bridging the gap between transparency and circularity, enabling supply chains to evolve into more resilient and sustainable systems.

BIG DATA AND SUSTAINABLE SUPPLY CHAINS

Big data in supply chain management refers to the collection, integration, and analysis of vast amounts of structured and unstructured data generated across supply chain activities, from procurement to distribution (Waller & Fawcett, 2013). Its use extends beyond operational efficiency to advancing sustainability objectives. By leveraging advanced analytics, machine learning, and predictive modelling, firms can monitor supplier practices, optimise transportation routes, reduce waste, and improve energy efficiency (Dubey et al., 2019). Big data also plays a critical role in aligning supply chain practices with Environmental, Social, and Governance (ESG) frameworks by enabling accurate reporting, stakeholder accountability, and performance benchmarking (Marques & Cunha, 2020). Moreover, it strengthens the implementation of circular economy principles by providing insights into product life cycles, enabling resource recovery, and supporting closed-loop supply chains (Centobelli et al., 2020). Thus, big data is increasingly recognised as a strategic enabler of sustainable and circular supply chain models.

Figure 2. Big data in supply chain management

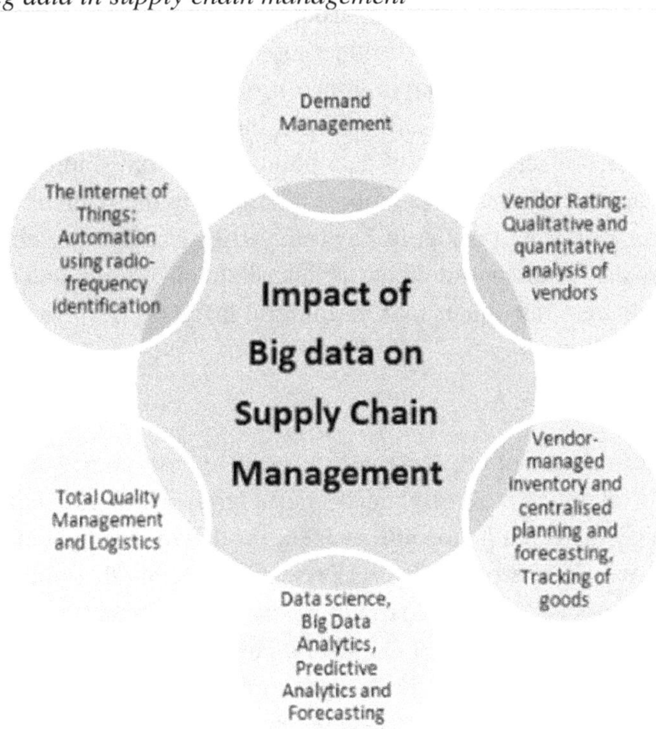

Adapted from https://www.setlog.com/en/driving-supply-chain-success-with-big-data-and-analytics

THE FIVE V'S OF BIG DATA IN SUPPLY CHAIN MANAGEMENT

The adoption of big data analytics has become increasingly critical in modern supply chains, where complex, globalised networks generate, transmit, and utilise unprecedented amounts of information. The conceptual framework of the "Five

V's" Volume, Velocity, Variety, Veracity, and Value offers a structured lens through which to understand the challenges and opportunities associated with big data in supply chain contexts (Laney, 2001; Wamba et al., 2015). Each dimension presents distinct implications for decision-making, operational efficiency, and strategic competitiveness.

Volume

In modern supply chains, the deployment of technologies such as sensors, barcodes, enterprise resource planning (ERP) systems, and advanced databases results in the generation of enormous quantities of data every second. These datasets capture transactions, product movements, customer interactions, and environmental conditions, creating a continuous stream of information that organisations must process and manage (Chen et al., 2012). For example, global logistics companies such as DHL and Maersk collect millions of data points daily from shipping routes, fleet performance, and warehousing operations, highlighting the scale of data involved in operational monitoring (Waller & Fawcett, 2013). Managing such vast quantities requires scalable storage solutions, advanced cloud systems, and sophisticated algorithms to process raw inputs into meaningful insights.

Velocity

The speed dimension of big data refers not only to how quickly data is collected but also to how reliably it is transmitted, how efficiently it is stored, and how rapidly it can be transformed into actionable insights. In dynamic supply chain environments, where real-time responsiveness is essential, velocity determines the ability of organisations to act quickly on disruptions, such as port delays or sudden changes in consumer demand (Sivarajah et al., 2017). Furthermore, velocity encompasses the responsiveness of analytical tools, algorithms, and decision-making models, which must operate at high speed to enable proactive interventions and mitigate risks before they escalate (Wamba et al., 2020).

Variety

Supply chain data is characterised by its diversity in both form and source. Information originates from industrial sensors, logistics networks, retail stores, transportation systems, and household-level devices, all producing data in different formats (Akter & Wamba, 2016). This heterogeneity makes data management highly complex, as structured records such as inventory databases must be integrated with unstructured inputs, including video surveillance, GPS signals, and social media feeds. When successfully harnessed, variety provides a holistic perspective of supply chain performance, allowing firms to capture consumer sentiment, track real-time logistics, and monitor production lines simultaneously (Chae, 2015).

Veracity

A critical challenge in big data is ensuring the accuracy, trustworthiness, and compliance of information. Supply chains often face issues of incomplete, inconsistent, or ambiguous data, which complicates validation and quality verification processes (Zhong et al., 2016). Data uncertainty may arise from technical errors, human input mistakes, or external disruptions such as cyberattacks. To address these concerns, organisations must implement robust mechanisms for error detection, advanced security systems, and standardised reporting protocols to ensure reliability. Veracity is particularly significant in highly regulated industries, such as pharmaceuticals and food supply chains, where compliance and safety are directly dependent on accurate information (Wamba et al., 2015).

Value

The ultimate aim of big data is to generate value by improving business insights, enhancing decision-making, and optimising processes across industries. However, extracting value is not straightforward; it requires aligning analytical outcomes with organisational goals, assessing the cost-effectiveness of insights, and ensuring that findings translate into measurable performance improvements (Mikalef et al., 2020). In supply chain contexts, value may manifest as reduced operational costs, enhanced forecasting accuracy, improved sustainability practices, or greater resilience against disruptions. For example, predictive analytics based on big data has enabled firms like Amazon to refine inventory planning and last-mile delivery, resulting in higher efficiency and customer satisfaction (Hazen et al., 2016). Thus, value represents the culmination of the other four V's, translating raw data into competitive advantage.

FROM TRANSPARENCY TO CIRCULARITY

Transparency is a foundational element of sustainable supply chains, as it enables traceability, monitoring, and compliance across the value chain. Through big data analytics, organisations can track raw materials from origin to end-use, ensuring ethical sourcing and adherence to environmental standards (Beske-Janssen et al., 2015). Transparency also fosters consumer trust and regulatory compliance by making supply chain activities visible and verifiable in real time. Circularity builds on this by focusing on optimising resources, implementing reverse logistics, and creating closed-loop systems that minimise waste and extend product life cycles (Geissdoerfer et al., 2017). Big data bridges transparency and circularity by integrating traceability with actionable insights. For example, sensor-generated data from Internet of Things (IoT) devices can inform predictive maintenance, while advanced analytics can identify opportunities for remanufacturing or recycling (Bag et al., 2020). In this way, big data transforms transparency into a driver of circular practices, making sustainability not only measurable but also operationally achievable. Figure 3 below exhibits benefits of transparency in a circular economy.

Figure 3. Benefits of Transparency in the Circular Economy

Benefits Of Transparency In The Circular Economy

Transparency plays a pivotal role in advancing the circular economy by fostering accountability, strengthening stakeholder trust, and enabling efficient resource flows. Without transparent systems of reporting and disclosure, it becomes difficult to track the movement of materials, assess environmental impacts, or ensure that circular practices are genuinely implemented. As highlighted in the accompanying infographic, four central benefits emerge from embedding transparency into circular models: reduced waste, improved resource efficiency, enhanced trust, and economic savings. These benefits collectively demonstrate how openness in information sharing can accelerate the transition from linear to circular systems.

Firstly, reduced waste is one of the most immediate outcomes of transparency. By implementing traceability mechanisms, organisations can closely monitor material flows and detect points of loss or inefficiency across the supply chain (Ellen MacArthur Foundation, 2019). Such visibility supports the redesign of production systems to maximise reuse, repair, and recycling. For instance, digital product passports and blockchain technologies provide real-time insights into a product's lifecycle, enabling companies to prevent waste generation at source (Geissdoerfer et al., 2017). Transparent reporting therefore ensures that inefficiencies are identified early, and materials can be redirected into productive use rather than discarded (Chikwere et al, 2023).

Secondly, improved resource efficiency is achieved when organisations openly disclose data on their inputs, outputs, and operational processes. Transparency allows for benchmarking across industries, encouraging firms to optimise production systems and reduce unnecessary consumption of energy, water, and raw materials (Korhonen et al., 2018). Importantly, transparent practices enable the development of closed-loop systems in which resources are retained within value chains for longer, minimising reliance on virgin raw materials and alleviating pressure on natural ecosystems. This approach aligns with the broader sustainability agenda, as efficient resource use directly reduces greenhouse gas emissions and other environmental burdens.

Thirdly, enhanced trust is a crucial social dimension of transparency. Stakeholders—including consumers, regulators, and supply chain partners—are increasingly demanding verifiable evidence of sustainable practices. Open communication of sustainability performance mitigates the risk of "greenwashing," where organisations exaggerate or misrepresent their environmental achievements (Bocken et al., 2021). By making sustainability claims verifiable, transparency legitimises circular practices and strengthens the social licence to operate. This trust, in turn, encourages greater collaboration across supply chains, creating ecosystems where actors are willing to share knowledge, co-invest in innovations, and collectively pursue circular solutions.

Finally, economic savings arise as a tangible outcome of transparent practices. When firms disclose material flows and lifecycle data, they are better positioned to make informed decisions that reduce costs and unlock new revenue streams. For example, identifying by-products that can be repurposed for secondary markets not only prevents waste but also generates financial value (Lewandowski, 2016). Transparency can also reduce regulatory risks, as organisations that disclose and address inefficiencies proactively may face fewer penalties and compliance costs. Furthermore, by lowering waste disposal expenses and extending product lifecycles, transparency enhances long-term profitability while simultaneously supporting sustainability goals.

APPLICATIONS OF BIG DATA IN CIRCULAR SUPPLY CHAINS

Big data technologies offer multiple applications that enhance circular supply chain management. Predictive analytics enables firms to anticipate demand more accurately, thereby reducing overproduction and minimising waste (Choi et al., 2018). By forecasting demand patterns and product returns, organisations can optimise inventory levels and align production schedules with real market needs, supporting both cost efficiency and sustainability. In addition, Internet of Things (IoT) and sensor technologies allow real-time lifecycle monitoring of products, enabling organisations to track material usage, wear and tear, and end-of-life recovery potential (Manavalan & Jayakrishna, 2019). This continuous flow of information facilitates timely interventions, such as repair, reuse, or remanufacturing, which are central to circular economy practices.

Blockchain further strengthens circular supply chains by ensuring traceability and trust across the network. Through immutable records, blockchain technology guarantees authenticity in ethical sourcing, fair labour practices, and environmentally friendly processes (Saberi et al., 2019). Data sharing also fosters stronger collaboration with suppliers and consumers, allowing stakeholders to co-create sustainable solutions. For instance, big data platforms can provide insights on consumer usage patterns, encouraging behaviours such as product returns for recycling or participation in sharing models (Bag et al., 2020). Collectively, these technologies integrate to drive circularity by closing loops, improving transparency, and reducing environmental impact.

Figure 4. Applications of big data in circular supply chains

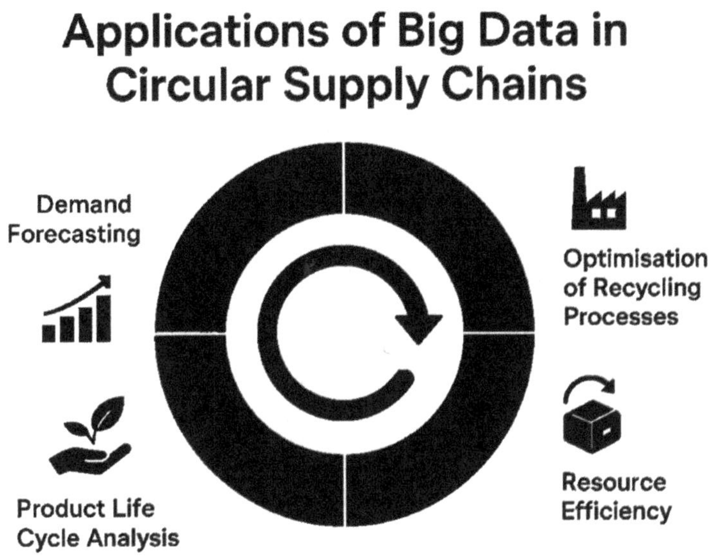

The integration of big data analytics into circular supply chains provides firms with unprecedented capabilities to enhance efficiency, minimise waste, and support sustainability-driven decision-making. Four central applications are particularly prominent: demand forecasting, optimisation of recycling processes, product life cycle analysis, and resource efficiency. These applications collectively strengthen the operationalisation of circular economy principles.

Demand Forecasting

Accurate demand forecasting is critical in ensuring that supply chains remain responsive yet sustainable. Traditional forecasting methods often relied on historical sales data, which can be insufficient in dynamic markets characterised by shifting consumer preferences and volatile environmental conditions. Big data enables the application of predictive modelling techniques that draw upon diverse and real-time data sources, such as consumer purchasing behaviour, weather conditions, social media trends, and macroeconomic indicators (Choi et al., 2018). In the context of circular supply chains, improved forecasting reduces the risks of overproduction, which is a primary driver of inventory waste, resource depletion, and unnecessary emissions. By aligning production more closely with actual demand, firms are able to reduce surplus stock, optimise resource allocation, and ensure that reverse logistics systems are not burdened with excess returns or unsold products. Furthermore, demand forecasting contributes to closing material loops by predicting demand for refurbished, recycled, or remanufactured goods, thereby enhancing the economic viability of circular initiatives (Chikwere et al, 2023).

Optimisation of Recycling Processes

Recycling processes form a central component of circular supply chains, as they enable the recovery of valuable resources and reduce reliance on virgin raw materials. Big data analytics supports the optimisation of recycling by monitoring and tracking material flows at multiple stages of the supply chain. Sensor-generated data, radio frequency identification (RFID) technologies, and advanced image recognition algorithms facilitate the identification of material types, improving sorting accuracy and recovery efficiency (Zhang et al., 2021). These technologies can significantly reduce contamination levels in recycling streams, thereby increasing the quality and quantity of recovered resources. For example, machine learning algorithms applied to recycling facilities can dynamically adjust sorting mechanisms in real time, responding to variations in material composition. This not only minimises landfill dependency but also creates opportunities to reintegrate secondary raw materials into production loops, thereby advancing circularity. Additionally, big data enables the evaluation of recycling system performance across geographies, allowing firms and policymakers to identify inefficiencies and improve the design of waste management infrastructure (Dubey et al., 2019).

Product Life Cycle Analysis (PLCA)

Big data significantly enhances the capacity of firms to conduct comprehensive product life cycle analysis (PLCA). Traditional life cycle assessments often relied on sample data and static assumptions, which limited their precision and scalability. With big data, information can be collected across all stages of a product's life from design and manufacturing to usage and end-of-life disposal providing high-resolution insights into environmental and economic impacts (Gupta et al., 2019). Integrating sensor data, usage analytics, and feedback from reverse logistics enables companies to identify critical "hotspots" where resource consumption, emissions, or waste are concentrated. These insights support evidence-based product redesign, making it easier to develop goods that are more durable, repairable, and recyclable. Moreover, big data-driven PLCA facilitates scenario modelling, where firms can assess the long-term implications of design changes, material substitutions, or new business models such as product-as-a-service. As a result, PLCA not only informs sustainable product design but also strengthens accountability by enabling transparent reporting to stakeholders (Pereira et al., 2020).

Resource Efficiency

Achieving resource efficiency is central to the sustainability objectives of circular supply chains. Big data supports this goal by enabling real-time monitoring and optimisation of energy, water, and raw material consumption across supply chain operations (Wamba et al., 2018). By integrating data streams from production facilities, logistics networks, and distribution centres, firms can identify inefficiencies and implement corrective actions more rapidly. For example, predictive analytics can anticipate machinery failures or process bottlenecks, reducing downtime and preventing resource-intensive disruptions. Benchmarking capabilities also allow firms to compare resource use across sites or suppliers, driving continuous improvement and fostering collaboration around sustainability goals. Importantly, resource efficiency improvements generate both economic and environmental benefits: firms reduce operational costs while simultaneously lowering carbon emissions, water use, and waste. This dual impact strengthens the competitiveness of firms while aligning supply chain operations with global sustainability agendas such as the United Nations' Sustainable Development Goals (SDGs) (Chibaro et al, 2025).

CASE ILLUSTRATIONS

Big data technologies have become a cornerstone of sustainable supply chain transformation across multiple industries. By leveraging advanced analytics, Internet of Things (IoT) devices, and blockchain systems, organisations can enhance transparency, efficiency, and environmental responsibility in their operations. The following case studies illustrate how different sectors—specifically the food and fashion industries apply big data to achieve sustainability goals. In the food sector, predictive analytics and IoT-enabled monitoring reduce food loss and waste by improving cold chain management and demand forecasting. In contrast, the fashion and apparel industry harnesses data analytics and blockchain to promote ethical sourcing, enhance material traceability, and support circular economy initiatives. Together, these examples demonstrate how data-driven innovation translates sustainability objectives into tangible operational and environmental outcomes.

Case 1: Food Industry – Reducing Food Loss through IoT and Predictive Analytics

In the food industry, big data technologies have revolutionised how companies manage perishables and minimise waste. For instance, multinational retailer Tesco has integrated IoT-enabled cold chain monitoring systems across its distribution centres and delivery fleets. These systems continuously collect real-time data on temperature, humidity, and product movement, ensuring that perishable goods such as dairy, fruits, and vegetables remain within optimal storage conditions (Banaeian et al., 2019).

If sensors detect deviations such as rising temperatures in a refrigerated truck—the system instantly triggers alerts for corrective action, reducing spoilage and ensuring food safety. Moreover, predictive analytics helps Tesco forecast demand more accurately by analysing consumer purchasing patterns, seasonal trends, and promotional effects. This data-driven approach aligns inventory levels with expected sales, minimising overstocking and preventing unsold products from becoming waste.

Through these innovations, Tesco and similar retailers not only reduce food loss but also lower carbon emissions and enhance supply chain transparency, aligning operations with UN Sustainable Development Goal 12 (Responsible Consumption and Production). Table 1 below depicts how Tesco UK managed sustainability using big data technology.

Table 1. Tesco UK Sustainability through big data

Aspect	Description
Industry	Food and Retail Sector
Organisation Example	Tesco (UK-based multinational retailer)
Sustainability Focus	Reduction of food loss and waste; improved resource efficiency
Technologies Applied	Internet of Things (IoT), Predictive Analytics, Data Integration Systems
Application	IoT-enabled cold chain monitoring systems collect real-time temperature and humidity data during storage and transport of perishable goods. Predictive analytics aligns stock levels with consumer demand to reduce overproduction and spoilage.
Key Activities	- Installation of sensors in cold storage and transport vehicles - Real-time data transmission and alert systems for deviations - Data analysis to forecast demand and optimise inventory

continued on following page

Table 1. Continued

Aspect	Description
Benefits Achieved	- Reduced food spoilage through proactive monitoring - Enhanced product quality and food safety - Lowered carbon footprint from waste reduction - Cost savings from efficient inventory management
Challenges Encountered	- High initial investment in IoT infrastructure - Integration of data across suppliers and logistics partners - Need for staff training in data analytics
Sustainability Outcomes	- Decreased volume of unsold goods discarded - Improved supply chain transparency - Contribution to SDG 12: Responsible Consumption and Production
Key Reference	Banaeian et al. (2019) – Big data applications in food supply chains

Case 2: Fashion and Apparel Industry – Promoting Ethical Sourcing and Circularity

In the fashion and apparel sector, big data has emerged as a key enabler of both ethical sourcing and sustainable production throughout the supply chain. A leading example is H&M, which has adopted blockchain-based traceability systems in combination with big data analytics to promote responsible sourcing and advance its circular fashion initiatives (Pedersen et al., 2019). Through these technologies, H&M can trace the origin of raw materials such as organic cotton, recycled polyester, or sustainably produced wool back to certified suppliers and production facilities. This transparency helps the company verify compliance with ethical labour standards, environmental regulations, and fair-trade principles, thereby strengthening consumer trust and accountability across the supply chain.

Beyond sourcing, data analytics plays a central role in supporting H&M's circular economy strategy. The company collects and analyses large volumes of consumer, sales, and product lifecycle data to better understand clothing usage patterns, disposal behaviour, and material recovery potential. Insights from this data inform the design of take-back and recycling initiatives such as the "Garment Collecting" programme, which operates in thousands of H&M stores worldwide. By analysing purchase histories, return patterns, and geographic data, H&M optimises the location and capacity of collection points, ensuring efficient logistics and higher participation rates.

Furthermore, advanced sorting technologies powered by big data and AI-driven image recognition allow collected garments to be categorised by fabric type, condition, and recyclability. These materials are then either reused, upcycled into new products, or processed into textile fibres for future collections. This data-driven circular model significantly reduces textile waste sent to landfills, conserves natural resources, and minimises the environmental footprint of apparel production. It also promotes consumer engagement by encouraging responsible consumption and participation in sustainable fashion practices (Chikwere et al, 2025).

Ultimately, H&M's approach illustrates how the integration of big data, blockchain, and analytics can operationalise sustainability principles in a highly resource-intensive industry. By leveraging these technologies, the company not only enhances supply chain transparency but also transforms linear production systems into circular, regenerative models that align with broader sustainable development goals (SDGs), particularly SDG 12 – Responsible Consumption and Production and SDG 13 – Climate Action.

BARRIERS AND CHALLENGES

While big data holds transformative potential for advancing circular economy goals, its effective implementation is constrained by several interconnected barriers. These challenges can be broadly categorised into technological, ethical and legal, organisational, and governance-related barriers.

Technological Barriers

One of the most significant obstacles is the persistence of data silos and the lack of interoperability among supply chain partners. Many organisations use isolated or incompatible information systems that prevent seamless data integration across suppliers, manufacturers, distributors, and consumers (Wamba et al., 2018). This fragmentation leads to incomplete visibility of material flows, reducing the capacity to generate meaningful insights for circular activities such as product recovery, remanufacturing, and waste reduction.

In addition, the absence of standardised data formats and communication protocols further complicates collaboration between stakeholders. Without harmonised data structures, it becomes difficult to merge environmental, social, and operational information into a coherent analytical framework. Addressing these issues requires the development of interoperable digital platforms, investment in data integration tools, and the adoption of industry-wide standards to enable secure and efficient data exchange.

Ethical and Legal Barriers

The use of big data in supply chains raises serious ethical, privacy, and legal concerns. Data collection often involves tracking and analysing sensitive information from suppliers, consumers, and employees, which may lead to concerns about data misuse, unauthorised surveillance, or breaches of confidentiality (Martin, 2015). For instance, monitoring workers' productivity or tracking raw materials through digital tags could unintentionally expose private or commercially sensitive information.

To mitigate these risks, organisations must ensure compliance with data protection regulations such as the General Data Protection Regulation (GDPR). Implementing ethical data governance frameworks, establishing clear consent mechanisms, and maintaining transparency in data-sharing practices are essential steps to uphold trust and accountability in big data ecosystems.

Organisational and Resource Barriers

Implementing big data analytics demands substantial financial investment and technical expertise, both of which can be challenging for small and medium-sized enterprises (SMEs). Many firms struggle to acquire the necessary skills in data science, machine learning, and advanced analytics, leading to underutilisation of available technologies (Mikalef et al., 2019). Furthermore, the costs associated with infrastructure such as sensors, cloud storage, and data processing platforms can be prohibitive for resource-constrained organisations.

Cultural resistance to digital transformation also poses a challenge. Traditional supply chain managers may be reluctant to rely on data-driven decision-making, particularly when short-term financial pressures conflict with longer-term sustainability goals. Overcoming these barriers requires targeted capacity-building initiatives, public-private partnerships, and investment incentives to encourage technology adoption among smaller firms.

Governance and Strategic Barriers

Even when technology and resources are available, the absence of effective governance structures can hinder the integration of big data into circular supply chain strategies. Aligning big data initiatives with sustainability objectives requires cross-departmental coordination and clear leadership commitment. In many cases, firms lack the strategic frameworks to balance economic performance with environmental and social impact (Wamba et al., 2018).

Governance challenges also emerge from unclear data ownership and accountability within multi-stakeholder supply chains. Establishing shared governance mechanisms such as data stewardship models and joint sustainability metrics can promote collaboration and ensure that big data initiatives support the collective transition towards circularity.

FRAMEWORK FOR IMPLEMENTING BIG DATA IN CIRCULAR SUPPLY CHAINS

Developing a structured framework for implementing big data in circular supply chains is essential for transforming sustainability ambitions into practical outcomes. A strategic roadmap for organisations should begin with an assessment of current data maturity, followed by the identification of priority areas such as demand forecasting, waste reduction, or reverse logistics (Mikalef et al., 2019). From there, organisations can progressively adopt advanced analytics, Internet of Things (IoT), and blockchain to build an integrated system that supports closed-loop supply chains. Critical to this roadmap is ensuring interoperability across platforms and fostering collaboration among stakeholders, including suppliers, distributors, and consumers (Wamba et al., 2020).

Equally important is the alignment of data-driven initiatives with sustainability goals. Rather than treating big data adoption as a purely technological upgrade, firms must integrate it into Environmental, Social, and Governance (ESG) strategies and circular economy principles. For instance, analytics should be leveraged to reduce carbon emissions, promote ethical sourcing, and maximise product life cycles (Munuhwa et al., 2025; Dubey et al., 2019). This alignment requires not only technological capability but also a cultural shift within organisations, encouraging managers to view data as a driver of long-term value rather than short-term efficiency. From a policy perspective, governments and industry bodies play a key role in creating supportive regulatory environments, offering incentives for sustainable practices, and setting standards for data sharing. Managerially, firms must invest in workforce training, governance frameworks, and ethical data management to ensure responsible use of big data in supply chain contexts (Saberi et al., 2019). Table 2 illustrates a framework that can be used to implement big data in supply chains with some example of activities.

Table 2. Framework for Implementing Big Data in Circular Supply Chains (BD-CSCF)

Stage	Key Focus	Big Data Tools & Technologies	Example Activities	Expected Outcomes
1. Data Acquisition	Collect real-time and historical data across the supply chain.	IoT sensors, RFID tags, barcode systems, GPS trackers, smart meters.	Tracking material flow, monitoring temperature/ humidity, collecting usage and return data from customers.	Creation of reliable, continuous data streams for supply chain visibility.
2. Data Integration & Storage	Consolidate data from multiple internal and external sources.	Cloud storage, data lakes, ERP integration, blockchain platforms.	Merging supplier, logistics, and consumer data into a single interoperable platform.	Enhanced transparency and traceability of materials and products.
3. Data Processing & Analytics	Transform raw data into actionable insights.	Machine learning, predictive analytics, big data analytics platforms (e.g., Hadoop, Spark).	Predicting demand, optimising inventory, forecasting maintenance needs, identifying recycling potential.	Improved decision-making for resource efficiency and waste reduction.
4. Circular Decision-Making	Use analytics to support circular strategies (reuse, remanufacture, recycle).	Decision-support systems (DSS), AI-driven optimisation models.	Designing take-back schemes, selecting materials for reuse, scheduling remanufacturing operations.	Operationalisation of circular economy principles through data insights.
5. Performance Monitoring & Feedback	Evaluate outcomes and continuously improve circular practices.	Dashboards, KPI tracking, sustainability analytics.	Measuring waste reduction, carbon savings, and material recovery rates.	Continuous improvement and long-term sustainability performance.

CONCLUSION AND FUTURE RESEARCH DIRECTIONS

This discussion highlights that big data has significant potential to enable circular supply chains by fostering transparency, predictive efficiency, and collaboration. Applications such as predictive analytics, IoT-enabled monitoring, and blockchain-driven traceability demonstrate how digital tools can operationalise sustainability and circularity. At the same time, barriers such as data silos, ethical concerns, and investment challenges underline the importance of holistic frameworks that integrate technological, organisational, and policy dimensions.

Future research should expand on several key opportunities. First, empirical studies across diverse industries are needed to examine the effectiveness of big data applications in real-world circular supply chain models. Second, there is a need for longitudinal research on how big data adoption evolves within organisations and how it impacts long-term sustainability outcomes. Third, further exploration of the intersection between artificial intelligence, big data, and circularity could yield innovative pathways for designing intelligent, adaptive supply chains. Finally, research should address the governance and ethical implications of big data in global supply chains, especially in contexts where regulatory oversight is limited. By advancing these areas, scholars and practitioners alike can help ensure that big data becomes not only a technological enabler but also a strategic driver of sustainable and resilient supply chains.

CONTRIBUTION TO THE BOOK

This chapter will provide a unique perspective by framing big data not only as a tool for transparency but as a critical enabler of circularity in supply chains. It will contribute to both theory and practice by presenting a conceptual framework supported by industry examples, helping managers, policymakers, and academics understand how to integrate big data into sustainable and circular supply chain strategies.

REFERENCES

Akter, S., & Wamba, S. F. (2016). Big data analytics in E-commerce: A systematic review and agenda for future research. *Electronic Markets*, *26*(2), 173–194. DOI: 10.1007/s12525-016-0219-0

Atzori, L., Iera, A., & Morabito, G. (2010). The Internet of Things: A survey. *Computer Networks*, *54*(15), 2787–2805. DOI: 10.1016/j.comnet.2010.05.010

Bag, S., Gupta, S., & Kumar, S. (2021). Industry 4.0 adoption and supply chain sustainability: Empirical evidence from emerging economies. *International Journal of Production Economics*, *231*, 107831. DOI: 10.1016/j.ijpe.2020.107831

Bag, S., Gupta, S., Kumar, S., & Sivarajah, U. (2020). Role of big data and predictive analytics for supply chain sustainability. *International Journal of Production Research*, *58*(17), 5558–5582. DOI: 10.1080/00207543.2020.1735667

Banaeian, N., Mobli, H., Fahimnia, B., Nielsen, I. E., & Omid, M. (2019). Green supplier selection using fuzzy group decision making methods: A case study from the agri-food industry. *Computers & Operations Research*, *89*, 337–347. DOI: 10.1016/j.cor.2016.02.015

Batista, L., Bourlakis, M., Smart, P., & Maull, R. (2018). In search of a circular supply chain archetype – A content-analysis-based literature review. *Production Planning and Control*, *29*(6), 438–451. DOI: 10.1080/09537287.2017.1343502

Beske, P., & Seuring, S. (2014). Putting sustainability into supply chain management. *Supply Chain Management*, *19*(3), 322–331. DOI: 10.1108/SCM-12-2013-0432

Beske-Janssen, P., Johnson, M., & Schaltegger, S. (2015). 20 years of performance measurement in sustainable supply chain management – What has been achieved? *Supply Chain Management*, *20*(6), 664–680. DOI: 10.1108/SCM-06-2015-0216

Bocken, N. M. P., Boons, F., & Baldassarre, B. (2021). Sustainable business model experimentation by understanding ecologies of business models. *Journal of Cleaner Production, 295*, 126361. DOI: 10.1016/j.jclepro.2021.126361

Centobelli, P., Cerchione, R., & Esposito, E., & Shashi. (2020). Pursuing supply chain sustainability through Big Data Analytics: A systematic literature review. *Journal of Cleaner Production, 259*, 120705. DOI: 10.1016/j.jclepro.2020.120705

Chae, B. (2015). Insights from hashtag #supplychain and Twitter analytics: Considering Twitter and Twitter data for supply chain practice and research. *International Journal of Production Economics, 165*, 247–259. DOI: 10.1016/j.ijpe.2014.12.037

Chen, H., Chiang, R. H. L., & Storey, V. C. (2012). Business intelligence and analytics: From big data to big impact. *Management Information Systems Quarterly, 36*(4), 1165–1188. DOI: 10.2307/41703503

Chibaro, M., Mupfiga, C., Mahwine, M. L., Chikwere, D., Mbudaya, J., & Kanyepe, J. (2025). Green supply chain management and agricultural performance: Towards ecological supply chain management from sustainable supply systems. In *Integrating Agriculture, Green Marketing Strategies, and Artificial Intelligence* (pp. 285–316). IGI Global Scientific Publishing.

Chikwere, D., Mbudaya, J., Chihwayi, H., & Chikwere, D. (2023). Food supply chain decarbonisation: Towards zero emissions in the beverages value chain – A case of Delta, Zimbabwe. *Journal of Tianjin University Science and Technology, 10*, 1–15.

Chikwere, D., Munuhwa, S., & Chibaro, M. (2025). Advancing sustainable green marketing agenda in Africa through green supply chain management. In *Sustainable Green Marketing Strategies for a Circular Economy: African Realities and Imperatives* (pp. 161–182). Springer Nature Switzerland.

Choi, T. M., Wallace, S. W., & Wang, Y. (2018). Big data analytics in operations management. *Production and Operations Management, 27*(10), 1868–1888. DOI: 10.1111/poms.12838

Dubey, R., Gunasekaran, A., Childe, S. J., Papadopoulos, T., Luo, Z., Wamba, S. F., & Roubaud, D. (2019). Can big data and predictive analytics improve social and environmental sustainability? *Technological Forecasting and Social Change, 144*, 534–545. DOI: 10.1016/j.techfore.2017.06.020

Ellen MacArthur Foundation. (2019). *Completing the picture: How the circular economy tackles climate change*. Ellen MacArthur Foundation.

Geissdoerfer, M., Savaget, P., Bocken, N. M. P., & Hultink, E. J. (2017). The circular economy – A new sustainability paradigm? *Journal of Cleaner Production, 143*, 757–768. DOI: 10.1016/j.jclepro.2016.12.048

Genovese, A., Acquaye, A. A., Figueroa, A., & Koh, S. C. L. (2017). Sustainable supply chain management and the transition towards a circular economy: Evidence and some applications. *Omega, 66*, 344–357. DOI: 10.1016/j.omega.2015.05.015

Gupta, H., Kusi-Sarpong, S., & Rezaei, J. (2019). Barriers and overcoming strategies to supply chain sustainability innovation. *Resources, Conservation and Recycling, 146*, 307–316. DOI: 10.1016/j.resconrec.2019.03.015

Hazen, B. T., Boone, C. A., Ezell, J. D., & Jones-Farmer, L. A. (2016). Data quality for data science, predictive analytics, and big data in supply chain management: An introduction to the problem and suggestions for research and applications. *International Journal of Production Economics, 154*, 72–80. DOI: 10.1016/j.ijpe.2014.04.018

Korhonen, J., Honkasalo, A., & Seppälä, J. (2018). Circular economy: The concept and its limitations. *Ecological Economics, 143*, 37–46. DOI: 10.1016/j.ecolecon.2017.06.041

Kumar, S., Mangla, S. K., Luthra, S., & Rana, N. P. (2021). Big data analytics and sustainability of supply chains: A bibliometric and framework-based review. *Technological Forecasting and Social Change, 163*, 120464. DOI: 10.1016/j.techfore.2020.120464

Laney, D. (2001). 3D data management: Controlling data volume, velocity, and variety. *META Group Research Note, 6*, 1–4.

Lewandowski, M. (2016). Designing the business models for circular economy—Towards the conceptual framework. *Sustainability, 8*(1), 43. DOI: 10.3390/su8010043

Manavalan, E., & Jayakrishna, K. (2019). A review of Internet of Things (IoT) embedded sustainable supply chain for industry 4.0 requirements. *Computers & Industrial Engineering, 127*, 925–953. DOI: 10.1016/j.cie.2018.11.030

Marques, L., & Cunha, J. (2020). Big data and supply chain management: A review and bibliometric analysis. *Production, 30*, e20200020. DOI: 10.1590/0103-6513.20200020

Martin, K. (2015). Ethical issues in the big data industry. *MIS Quarterly Executive, 14*(2), 67–85.

Mikalef, P., Boura, M., Lekakos, G., & Krogstie, J. (2020). Big data analytics capabilities and innovation: The mediating role of dynamic capabilities and moderating effect of the environment. *British Journal of Management, 31*(2), 402–428. DOI: 10.1111/1467-8551.12324

Mikalef, P., Pappas, I. O., Krogstie, J., & Giannakos, M. (2019). Big data analytics capabilities: A systematic literature review and research agenda. *Information Systems and e-Business Management, 17*, 547–578. DOI: 10.1007/s10257-018-0377-y

Munuhwa, S., Mawonde, D., Mandere, T. S., & Nyemba, P. M. (2025). The role of robotics in enhancing green procurement practices: a systematic literature review. *Green Supply Chain Management in the Constrained Economy: Artificial Intelligence and Machine Learning*, 75-102.

Papadopoulos, T., Gunasekaran, A., Dubey, R., Altay, N., Childe, S. J., & Fosso-Wamba, S. (2017). The role of big data in explaining disaster resilience in supply chains for sustainability. *Journal of Cleaner Production, 142*, 1108–1118. DOI: 10.1016/j.jclepro.2016.03.059

Pedersen, E. R. G., Gwozdz, W., & Hvass, K. K. (2019). Exploring the relationship between business model innovation, corporate sustainability, and organisational values within the fashion industry. *Journal of Business Ethics, 155*, 623–641. DOI: 10.1007/s10551-017-3562-0

Rajesh, R. (2020). Exploring the sustainability performances of firms using big data analytics and circular economy strategy. *Journal of Cleaner Production, 277*, 123632. DOI: 10.1016/j.jclepro.2020.123632

Saberi, S., Kouhizadeh, M., Sarkis, J., & Shen, L. (2019). Blockchain technology and its relationships to sustainable supply chain management. *International Journal of Production Research, 57*(7), 2117–2135. DOI: 10.1080/00207543.2018.1533261

Seuring, S., & Müller, M. (2008). From a literature review to a conceptual framework for sustainable supply chain management. *Journal of Cleaner Production, 16*(15), 1699–1710. DOI: 10.1016/j.jclepro.2008.04.020

Sibanda, V., Mhlanga, J., & Munuhwa, S. (2025). Circular Economy Practices in Supply Chain Management. In *Eco-Logistics and Sustainable Supply Chain Innovations* (pp. 13–38). IGI Global Scientific Publishing.

Sivarajah, U., Kamal, M. M., Irani, Z., & Weerakkody, V. (2017). Critical analysis of big data challenges and analytical methods. *Journal of Business Research, 70*, 263–286. DOI: 10.1016/j.jbusres.2016.08.001

Waller, M. A., & Fawcett, S. E. (2013). Data science, predictive analytics, and big data: A revolution that will transform supply chain design and management. *Journal of Business Logistics, 34*(2), 77–84. DOI: 10.1111/jbl.12010

Wamba, S. F., Akter, S., Edwards, A., Chopin, G., & Gnanzou, D. (2017). How "big data" can make big impact: Findings from a systematic review and a longitudinal case study. *International Journal of Production Economics, 165*, 234–246. DOI: 10.1016/j.ijpe.2014.12.035

Wamba, S. F., Gunasekaran, A., Dubey, R., & Childe, S. J. (2020). Big data analytics in operations and supply chain management: State of the art and research opportunities. *Annals of Operations Research, 270*, 313–336. DOI: 10.1007/s10479-016-2235-0

Wamba, S. F., Gunasekaran, A., Dubey, R., & Ngai, E. W. T. (2018). Big data analytics in operations and supply chain management: A systematic review and future research agenda. *International Journal of Production Economics, 194*, 828–844. DOI: 10.1016/j.ijpe.2017.11.020

Wamba, S. F., Queiroz, M., Trinchera, L., & Kamdjoug, J. R. K. (2020). Dynamics between big data analytics capabilities and firm's performance: Insights from a resource-based view and dynamic capabilities perspective. *Information & Management, 57*(2), 103207. DOI: 10.1016/j.im.2019.103207

Zhang, A., Venkatesh, V. G., Liu, Y., Wan, M., & Qu, T. (2021). A digital twin-enabled approach for improving circular supply chain performance. *Resources, Conservation and Recycling, 164*, 105119. DOI: 10.1016/j.resconrec.2020.105119

Zhong, R. Y., Newman, S. T., Huang, G. Q., & Lan, S. (2016). Big data for supply chain management in the service and manufacturing sectors: Challenges, opportunities, and future perspectives. *Computers & Industrial Engineering, 101*, 572–591. DOI: 10.1016/j.cie.2016.08.016

Chapter 9
Quantum-Inspired Big Data Analytics for Sustainable and Resilient Global Supply Chains

M. Jomon Jose
http://orcid.org/0009-0003-4341-9936
Sahrdaya Institute of Management Studies, Kodakara, India

Jyothis Rachel Mathews
http://orcid.org/0009-0003-8279-6080
Ahalia School of Management, Palakkad, India

ABSTRACT

The escalating complexity of global supply chains requires analytical capacity beyond that traditionally offered by big data systems. With such disturbances as pandemics, climate shocks and geopolitical tensions growing in scale and intensity, the simultaneous pursuit of sustainability and resilience has emerged as a key strategic challenge. In this chapter, the authors study how quantum-inspired big data analytics can be leveraged to facilitate sustainable and resilient global supply chain systems. Based on the synthesis of Resilience Theory, Complex Systems Theory and Sustainability Frameworks, the research propose a conceptual framework that demonstrates how quantum-inspired algorithms contribute to predictive modelling, decision optimisation and risk intelligence.

DOI: 10.4018/979-8-3373-6896-2.ch009

INTRODUCTION

Fueled by rapid globalization, increasing regulatory burdens, technological disruption, and an evolving set of sustainability requirements from end consumers, governments, and investors, global supply chains have been undergoing a steady expansion of complexity and fragility in recent years. The need for sustainability has become a challenge for supply chains to not only efficiently provide products and services but also have minimal impact on the environment, be socially responsible, and have economic sustainability. Meanwhile, resilience—the capability of a supply chain to foresee, adjust to, bounce back from, and grow from disruptive events—has gained prominence as a high-priority strategic consideration in light of ongoing challenges to global logistics networks posed by the likes of the COVID-19 pandemic, natural disasters, geopolitical instability, and supply constraints (Iftikhar et al., 2024).

Conventional BDA has already made great strides in supply chain management, providing mechanisms for visibility in real-time, demand prediction, inventory management, logistics optimization, and supplier risk analysis (Salwa, 2024; Bag et al., 2020). These functions have been at the heart of firms' ability to track performance, uncover patterns, and make informed decisions. Yet for all these achievements, the challenges facing traditional analytics are now plain in the scale and complexity of today's global networks. Big data methods tend to face challenges for high-dimensional, interrelated, and dynamic systems like multi-tier supply chains, where local disruptions (supply shortages, environmental disasters, economic downturns, etc.) might cascade and be magnified across geographies and time. For instance, although BDA improves forecasting and visibility, systematic reviews report that the exploitation of BDA to foster supply chain resilience is fragmented and in its infancy (Zamani et al., 2023; Dubey et al., 2022). Moreover, with sustainability goals, analytics must go beyond operational efficiency to include multi-objective optimization (economic, environmental, social) and the management of the inevitable trade-offs between performance and responsibility. However, many of the existing BDA techniques continue to be reactive as opposed to adaptive, concentrating on detection and reaction rather than proactive scenario-planning, optimization under uncertainty, or system redesign for resilience and sustainability (Jiang et al., 2025).

Quantum-inspired analytics have started gaining attention as a computational flow suitable for the next generation of computing approaches to overcome some of these challenges. Although large-scale quantum computing is still in its infancy, quantum-inspired methods are based on some fundamental aspects of quantum mechanics—e.g., superposition, entanglement and parallelism— but are executed on classical computing platforms (Munim et al., 2024; Vudugula et al., 2025). These techniques allow for the investigation of extremely large solution spaces, the parallel processing of several scenarios, and the accelerated resolution of intricate combinatorial problems. In the context of supply chains, quantum-inspired analytics may also be able to address multi-objective optimisation in a multi-dimensional sense [e.g.], cost, carbon emissions, and service level), dynamic routing in the face of uncertain, evolving environments, supplier network design under risk and sustainability constraints, and proactive real-time decision-making. For example, recent surveys claim that quantum computing applications in supply chain optimization can enhance resilience and environmental impacts by tackling optimization problems that are not tractable by classical computing (Jiang et al., 2023; Ajagekar & You, 2024).

While quantum-inspired approaches are intriguing, there is still a big gap in the research relating to the combination of quantum-inspired analytics with big data, sustainability, and resilience in the context of global supply chains. Like big data and supply chain sustainability, the extant literature considers data-driven capacity (Santos-de León, 2020; Bag et al., 2021), while the literature that investigates supply chain resilience through data analysis is emerging (Zamani et al., 2023; Iftikhar et al., 2024). Nevertheless, the quantum-inspired analytics within sustainable and resilient supply chains are less integrated, thus creating a potential for more adaptive, multi-objective, and next-generation analytic methods (Munim et al., 2024; Al-Banna et al., 2024) which are still under-researched. As one systematic review observed, "there remains a scarcity of closed-loop supply chain design or circular economy application even in the data analytics arena of resilience research" (Munim et al., 2024). In addition, the application of quantum-inspired analytics in supply chains as a practical matter is still in its infancy, affording the fertile ground of theoretical development, empirical substantiation, and industry–academic partnership. This is of particular significance for global supply chains involving multiple tiers, geographies, and varying levels of technology readiness, as it is at this intersection that the driving forces of sustainability and resilience are most prominently represented.

Hence, the objective of this chapter is to conceptualise and offer a single framework for exploiting quantum-inspired big data analytics for the development of sustainable and resilient global supply chains. Specific objectives of this chapter are to: (a) describe the background and need for the twin requirements of sustainability and resilience; (b) examine the inadequacies of conventional big data analytics in dealing with evolutionary, multi-objective supply chain systems; (c) consider the rise and potential of quantum inspired analytics as a paradigm changing tool; (d) delineate and clarify the research challenge at the confluence of sustainability, resilience and next generation analytics; and (e) present the conceptual model, practical implication and future research directions.

IDENTIFIED GAPS AND CHAPTER CONTRIBUTION

Gap 1 — Theoretical grounding: Existing literature discusses quantum-inspired methods and classical BDA largely separately; few works explicitly ground QIBDA within supply-chain theories (Resilience, Complex Systems, TBL/CE), limiting the mechanistic explanation of how QIBDA yields resilience and sustainability outcomes.

Gap 2 — Integrative framework: There is no widely accepted conceptual model that links QIBDA (IV) to resilience and sustainability (DVs) through clear mediators (predictive modeling, decision optimization, risk intelligence) across multi-tier networks.

Gap 3 — Applied mapping and feasibility: Empirical and practical guidance is limited on how to operationalize QIBDA in real supply-chain settings (data interoperability, governance, scalability, and boundary conditions).

This chapter addresses these gaps by (a) explicitly grounding QIBDA in Resilience Theory, Complex Systems Theory and Sustainability frameworks; (b) proposing a mediator-based conceptual model that explains mechanisms; and (c) mapping five practical application domains with illustrative examples and governance considerations.

LITERATURE REVIEW

Big Data Analytics in Supply Chain Management

Big data analytics (BDA) has advanced from traditional reporting and descriptive analysis to more sophisticated predictive and prescriptive analysis, combined with machine learning, real-time analytics, and complex event processing to facilitate decision making in the supply chain (Lee & Mangalaraj, 2022). Initially, applications focused on visibility—monitoring shipments, inventory levels, and supplier performance—whereas current efforts deal with demand forecasting, dynamic inventory optimization, route planning, and procurement intelligence that combine structured ERP data with unstructured data such as social media, weather feeds, and news (Xu et al., 2023; Lee & Mangalaraj, 2022; Talwar et al., 2021). Methods such as time-series models, ensemble machine learning techniques, reinforcement learning for dynamic decisions, and solvers for routing and scheduling are becoming more widely integrated into commercial supply-chain management systems (Xu et al., 2023; Runtuk et al., 2022).

Sustainability and Resilience in Global Supply Chains

Resilience and sustainability have emerged as two separate but closely related streams of research in supply chain management. The concept of sustainability is usually considered through the lens of the Triple Bottom Line (TBL) that considers economic, environmental, and social performance as mutual goals (Tundys, 2023). Sustainable supply chain literature also extended to circular economy strategies—such as product life-extension, remanufacturing, reverse logistics—that save resources and minimize waste while creating value (Setyadi et al., 2025). Simultaneously, the supply chain resilience literature focuses on processes and capabilities that facilitate anticipation, absorption, recovery, and adaptation to disruptions (Zamani et al., 2023). Traditional resilience views promote redundancy, flexibility, visibility, and cooperation, whereas recent research highlights dynamic capabilities and adaptive governance as mechanisms leading to resilient systems that are able to evolve in the presence of chronic stressors (Zamani et al., 2023; Li et al., 2025; Kaneberg et al., 2025).

Emergence of Quantum-Inspired Computing

Quantum computing has been touted for its potential to offer speed-ups for certain types of problems, especially for large-scale combinatorial optimization and sampling problems, relative to classical algorithms. Meanwhile, quantum-inspired computing has developed, namely algorithmic methods that draw from principles of quantum mechanics (e.g., parallel state exploration, annealing metaphors, probabilistic sampling) but can be run on classical hardware or on hybrid classical–quantum infrastructures (Núñez-Merino et al., 2024). Quantum-inspired algorithms span quantum annealing emulations, tensor network methods as well as probabilistic amplitude amplification analogues that are suitably modified for execution on classical GPU/CPU architectures. These methods can be used to speed up the exploration of large solution spaces and deliver new heuristics for optimization problems related to supply chain design (Núñez-Merino et al., 2024; Shamsuddoha et al., 2025).

Table 1 presents a comparative overview of traditional big data analytics and quantum-inspired big data analytics, highlighting their relative strengths in addressing complexity, uncertainty, and sustainability challenges in global supply chains.

Table 1. Comparison of Traditional Big Data Analytics and Quantum-Inspired Big Data Analytics in Supply Chains

Dimension	Traditional Big Data Analytics	Quantum-Inspired Big Data Analytics
Computational approach	Classical, sequential processing	Parallel probabilistic exploration
Optimization capability	Local or heuristic-based	Global and multi-objective optimization
Handling uncertainty	Reactive, limited scenario analysis	Proactive, large-scale scenario simulation
Sustainability focus	Cost and efficiency dominant	Integrated economic, environmental, social objectives
Suitability for complex systems	Limited for nonlinear interactions	High suitability for complex adaptive systems

Source: Secondary Data

THEORETICAL FRAMEWORK

Sustainable and resilient global supply chains are conceptualized as complex adaptive systems, evolving in response to internal and external disruptions (Surucu-Balci & Balci, 2022). The theoretical background of this chapter is based on Resilience Theory, Complex Systems Theory, and Sustainability Frameworks (with a focus on the Triple Bottom Line (TBL) and Circular Economy (CE) models). These perspectives combined give a theoretical base for discussing how Quantum-Inspired Big Data Analytics (QIBDA) could contribute to increasing adaptiveness, smartness, and system-sustainability in Supply Chains of today. Resilience Theory, Complex Systems Theory (CST), the Triple Bottom Line (TBL), and Circular Economy (CE) each illuminate different dimensions of sustainable and adaptive supply chains, but together they provide a unified conceptual foundation for quantum-inspired analytics. Resilience Theory highlights anticipation, absorption, and recovery capacities, which require continuous sensing, predictive capabilities, and adaptive decision-making. CST emphasizes nonlinearity, emergence, and interconnectedness within supply networks, underscoring the need for high-dimensional modeling and optimization capable of handling cascading effects. TBL and CE frameworks introduce the sustainability mandate—requiring environmental efficiency, social responsibility, and closed-loop resource flows—which aligns with multi-objective optimization challenges. When interwoven, these theories jointly justify the need for an analytics paradigm that can simultaneously manage uncertainty, complexity, and sustainability trade-offs—precisely the strengths offered by quantum-inspired big data analytics.

Theoretical Integration: Resilience, Complexity, and Sustainability

Resilience Theory has its roots in ecology and systems science, which considers resilience as the ability of a system to absorb disturbance, to undergo change and still maintain its core function and structure (Holling 1973; Folke 2016). Complex Systems Theory (CST) CST adds to this perspective by conceptualizing supply chains as nonlinear, coevolving, and self-organising networks with emergent properties, feedback mechanisms, and learning processes (Choi et al., 2001; Pires et al., 2025). In these types of systems, disturbances at local scales can nonlinearly propagate to generate ripple effects across multiple tiers and even different regions. The self-organizing and adaptive intelligence—capable of sensing, interpreting, and responding to dynamic environments—of such systems determines their resilience (Ghorbani et al., 2023). Traditional analytics is broken when it comes to trying to incorporate this nonlinearity and emergence, because all the traditional models seem to be predicated on stability, linear relationships, and centralized control. Yet, quantum-inspired analytics offers computational methods that are more suitable for searching high-dimensional, interdependent solution spaces and adaptive optimization, and seem closer to CST tenets of distributed intelligence and feedback adaptation (Bag et al., 2024).

The Sustainability Context – such as the TBL – adds the normative/performance lens and highlights that supply chains need to strive for not only economic squeeze but also environmental stewardship and social responsibility (Elkington, 1998; Prajapati et al., 2025). The Circular Economy (CE) is an emerging concept that promotes sustainability through the design of closed-loop systems that minimise waste, recover resources, and regenerate value (Geissdoerfer et al., 2017; Khanna et al., 2025). When these views of sustainability are combined with resilience and complexity, a systems-level understanding results: sustainable–resilient supply chains are those that preserve ecological and social equilibrium and are dynamically responsive to interruption (Zia et al., 2024). Together, these frameworks support the case for the development of an emerging generation of analytics equipped to address multiple (economic, environmental, social) objectives and nonlinear, uncertain, interdependent dynamics. In this theoretical framework, Quantum-Inspired Big Data Analytics is situated as a facilitator of system intelligence and adaptive capacity.

Quantum-Inspired Analytics as a Driver of Adaptive Capacity

The integration of quantum-inspired analytics into supply chain technologies introduces a shift in the paradigm from traditional data-driven optimization to cognitive adaptation. Quantum-inspired algorithms, including simulated quantum annealing, tensor network optimization, and parallel probabilistic inference, exhibit properties of superposition and entanglement in classical computing frameworks (Núñez-Merino et al., 2024; Shamsuddoha et al., 2025). These features make it possible to investigate several candidate solutions at once and to find a good solution in enormous decision spaces.

Such capacity-building in resilience terms increases adaptive capacity - the capacity of the system to predict, prepare for, and manage disturbances. Classical big data analytics focuses on maximizing efficiency in known conditions, while QIBDA fosters exploratory intelligence to enable supply chains to simulate multiple "what-if" analyses, identify systemic vulnerabilities, and develop adaptable contingency plans (Zamani et al., 2023; Giannakis et al., 2025). With machine learning and optimization embedded in quantum-inspired frameworks, decision-makers can find more robust policies that are valid under both uncertainty and nonlinearity.

From the point of view of the theory of Complex Systems, quantum-inspired analytics facilitates distributed sensing and decentralized decision making. Instead of a single central optimizer, individual nodes (suppliers, warehouses, distribution hubs) are enabled to process local data, coordinate through shared probabilistic models, and cooperate in performing a collective optimization—mirroring the self-organizing nature of complex adaptive systems (Choi et al., 2001; Pires et al., 2025; Ghorbani et al., 2023). This distributed intelligence enhances both the responsiveness to the environment and the robustness of the system.

In terms of Sustainability, QIBDA affords the computational capabilities to address the competing goals – profit, planet, and people - as a multi-objective problem. For instance, it can determine supply chain arrangements that reduce carbon footprint and cost, and enhance social impact indices. Such trade-offs were often computationally intractable with classical solution methods but become tractable with quantum-inspired optimization (Lee & Mangalaraj, 2022; Chen et al., 2025). As such, QIBDA enables the transition to circular, adaptive, and learning-based supply chains—those that not only survive but responsibly advance in turbulent global landscapes (Khanna et al., 2025).

Conceptual Model Development

The conceptual model proposed in this study (Figure 1) associates Quantum-Inspired Big Data Analytics (QIBDA) as the Independent Variable (IV) with two principal Dependent Variables (DVs)-Supply Chain Resilience and Sustainability Outcomes mediated by three inter-dependent Mediating Variables-Predictive Modeling, Decision Optimization, and Risk Intelligence. Independent Variable – Quantum-Inspired Big Data Analytics (QIBDA): QIBDA refers to a synergy of quantum-inspired optimization algorithms with big data architecture, providing enhanced computational power that enables exploration of more scenarios and performing adaptive learning. It includes both technology (hardware/software) and cognitive (learning and adapting) capabilities (Núñez-Merino et al., 2024; Shamsuddoha et al., 2025). The mediating variables—predictive modeling, decision optimization, and risk intelligence—derive directly from the combined insights of the theoretical lenses. Predictive modeling aligns with Resilience Theory's emphasis on early warning and anticipation, as well as CST's requirement for sensing nonlinear interactions across multi-tier systems. Decision optimization corresponds to CE and TBL demands for balancing environmental, social, and economic objectives while redesigning processes toward circularity. Risk intelligence connects CST's understanding of systemic propagation with Resilience Theory's adaptive capacity, enabling firms to understand how disruptions evolve and how responses can be optimized. Together, these mediators explain how quantum-inspired analytics (IV), through enhanced computational power and scenario exploration, influence the dependent variables—supply chain resilience and sustainability outcomes (DV). The directionality is thus theoretically anchored: QIBDA enhances the mediators, and the mediators drive improvements in resilience and sustainability.

- Mediating Variable 1 – Predictive Modeling: Predictive modeling embodies the ability of the system to forecast future states through the recognition of patterns in massive amounts of data. QIBDA improves predictive performance through parallel processing of several probable results and taking into account of nonlinear correlations that lie beyond the limits of classical regression or machine learning (Lee & Mangalaraj, 2022). Improved prediction under uncertainty enhances in turn proactive decision-making and utilization of resources.
- Mediating Variable 2 - Decision Optimization: Decision optimization is the process of seeking optimal or near-optimal solutions in the presence of multiple and heterogeneous constraints. Taking into consideration the trade-offs involved with sustainable and resilient supply chains (Tundys, 2023; Zia et al., 2024), QIBDA facilitates the joint optimization of economic, environmental and social goals. This mediation connects computational power with strategic sustainability outcomes.
- Mediating Variable 3 – Risk Intelligence: Risk intelligence refers to the ability to detect, evaluate, and respond to potential disturbances in the supply system. QIBDA also enables real-time anomaly detection and scenario stress testing to assist the industry in evolving from reactive to anticipatory resilience (Zamani et al., 2023; Mondragon et al., 2025). Systems develop adaptive intelligence consistent with Resilience Theory's emphasis on renewal and transformation by continuously learning from disruptions.

- Dependent Variables – Supply Chain Resilience and Sustainability Outcomes: The end results are exhibited in two correlated performance domains. Resilience outcomes include responsiveness (buffering), redundancy, agility (Ponomarov & Holcomb, 2009), as well as (Giannakis et al., 2025) recovery speed. Sustainability results include lowered emissions, increased resource efficiency and validation of social responsibility indices (Elkington, 1998; Geissdoerfer et al., 2017; Prajapati et al., 2025). Through its mediating factors, QIBDA is responsible for both, resulting in supply chains that are effective more Share Page but also ethical, circular, and resilient. In conceptual terms, QIBDA influences predictive capability (anticipating change), optimization capability (balancing multi-objective trade-offs), and risk intelligence (adapting to uncertainty). These mechanisms collectively enhance resilience and sustainability performance. This multi-layered linkage embodies the synthesis of Resilience Theory (adaptation and learning), Complex Systems Theory (self-organization and nonlinearity), and Sustainability Frameworks (triple bottom line balance).

Figure 1. Conceptual Framework Diagram

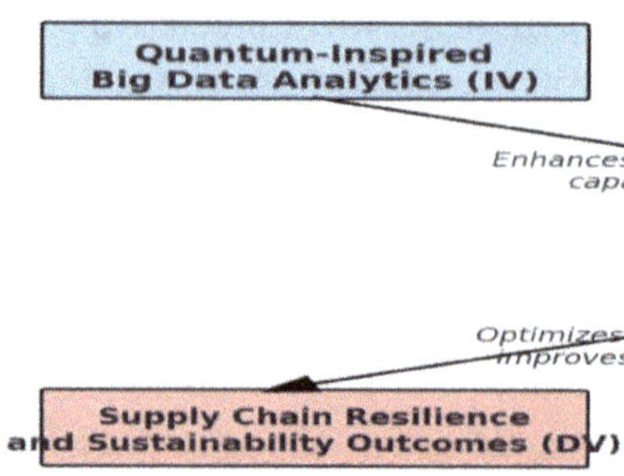

Source: Secondary Data

Figure 1 illustrates the proposed conceptual model linking Quantum-Inspired Big Data Analytics (QIBDA) with supply chain resilience and sustainability outcomes through the mediating mechanisms of predictive modeling, decision optimization, and risk intelligence. Based on the integration of Resilience Theory, Complex Systems Theory, and Sustainability Frameworks, the theoretical framework claims that Quantum-Inspired Big Data Analytics, as a generative mechanism, provides predictive foresight, multi-objective optimization, and adaptive risk intelligence. These mediation processes convert technological capability into organizational resilience and sustainability results. The model suggests that the use of QIBDA enables supply chains to evolve from reactive, efficiency-based constructs into adaptive, intelligent, and sustainable networks that can learn, evolve, and prosper in the face of volatility.

METHODOLOGICAL ORIENTATION

Adopted within this chapter is a conceptual and realiza-bilistic research methodology, that investigates to what extent quantum-inspired big data analytics can enable global supply chain sustainability and resilience. In contrast to empirical research, which draws on statistical hypothesis testing, conceptual research is concerned with the integration of interdisciplinary knowledge in the development of theory and a forward-looking view (Meredith, 1993; Ketokivi & Choi, 2022). This research is intended to begin to close the divide between emergent computational paradigms in the form of quantum-inspired analytics and the real-world implications of sustainable supply chain management. Since this is a new topic and this paper is based on theory, the conceptual methodology to synthesise different perspectives and generate a coherent model to subsequently guide empirical testing is suitable. To strengthen methodological transparency and replicability, an integrative review procedure was followed using a systematic but flexible screening strategy consistent with conceptual chapter development. Literature was collected from Scopus, Web of Science, IEEE Xplore, ScienceDirect, and Google Scholar, covering the period 2010–2025 to capture advances in big data analytics, sustainability, resilience, and quantum-inspired methods. Inclusion criteria focused on peer-reviewed journal articles, high-quality conference papers, industry whitepapers, and systematic reviews relevant to supply chain analytics, sustainability frameworks, resilience theory, and quantum-inspired optimization. Exclusion criteria removed sources lacking methodological clarity, purely technical quantum-computing papers without managerial relevance, and publications unrelated to supply-chain sustainability or resilience. Screening followed a two-stage process: (1) title and abstract review to assess relevance and conceptual alignment; and (2) full-text assessment to determine theoretical contribution and fit with the chapter's integrative objective. This approach ensured that the selected literature supports theory building, conceptual modeling, and forward-looking analysis aligned with the chapter's purpose.

The focus of the study is on building theory through the integration of extant literature, secondary data, and conceptual thought. This is compatible with the theory-building approach traditionally adopted in management and systems science, in which constructs and relationships are 'imported and adopted' from a variety of heterogeneous bases to construct new integrative models (Wacker, 1998; Ketchen et al., 2022). The chapter, then, serves as a first-step inquiry and attempts to detect causal mechanisms or mediating routes through which quantum-inspired analytics could potentially improve predictive modeling, decision optimization, and risk intelligence—core mediators that shape sustainable and resilient outcomes.

This is a cross-disciplinary study utilizing the synthesis approach, combining the knowledge from operations management, computer science, and sustainability. Each of these fields offers a different perspective on the relationship between data analytics and supply chain performance. The research uses process advantages from operations management theory, dynamic capabilities and engineering resilience (Ivanov, 2021; Ivanov, 2024). It is also informed by nascent ideas from computer science related to quantum-inspired algorithms, hybrid computing, and probabilistic modeling (Phillipson, 2024; Shamsuddoha et al., 2025). From sustainability studies, the TBL and Circular Economy are brought in, which effectively situate both the environment and society as aspects that should be considered in thinking materially and in operation (Geissdoerfer et al., 2017; Centobelli et al., 2021).

In order to develop a strong conceptual approach, this chapter adopts a path in the literature synthesis which is guided by the integrative review method (cf. Torraco, 2016; Snyder, 2019). This is the process of discovering, appraising, and synthesizing research from multiple domains to generate new frameworks or perspectives on a topic, as opposed to synthesizing within a domain, essentially performing meta-analyses. The review includes peer-reviewed journal articles, conference papers, and reputable institutional reports from 2010–2025. The present paper selects the above-mentioned sources from prominent databases like Scopus, Web of Science, and IEEE Xplore based on keywords related to quantum-inspired algorithms, big data analytics applications in logistics, digital sustainability, and resilience engineering.

The chapter builds on scientific literature and includes secondary data sources, such as industry whitepapers, benchmarking reports, and case reports of technology providers (e.g., IBM, Google, D-Wave Systems) and global supply chain network providers (e.g., DHL, Maersk, Siemens). These reports deliver real-life perspectives on the state of readiness and roadblocks faced in applying big data analytics to sustainability and resilience objectives. Benchmarking reports on digital supply chain transformation and quantum computing readiness provide some empirical evidence on technological maturity and adoption trends among conceptual assumptions (OECD, 2022; Ajagekar & You, 2024). The inclusion of these types of sources also helps to anchor theoretical propositions in practice and therefore connects academic theory and managerial relevance.

The development of an analytical tool emancipates us as we look to the future, shifting our focus more towards theoretical construction and interpretation in this chapter, rather than empirical analysis. The positivist informational view, combined with an interpretive paradigm, acknowledges that sustainability, resilience, and status are multifaceted, emerging from socio-technical and organisational contexts

(Carter et al., 2020; Centobelli et al., 2021). Hence, instead of trying to find general laws that apply universally, this chapter aims to enhance conceptual clarity on how emerging computational technologies impact supply chain dynamics. This perspective highlights the investigation of the "how" and "why" applying quantum-inspired analytics might enhance systemic adaptability, decision intelligence, and sustainable outcomes. The interpretative perspective is consistent with complexity theory, which suggests a centrality of feedback, interdependencies, and nonlinearity in global supply chains Choi et al, 2001; Surucu-Balci & Balci, 2022)

The theory construction aspect of the method consists in the emergence of constructs and their relationships on the basis of patterns formed in both the reviewed literature as well as the actual trends in practice. 4 Discussion of research results The previously developed conceptual model for this chapter presumes Quantum-Inspired Big Data Analytics as the explanatory variable whose impact on Supply Chain Resilience and Sustainability Outcomes is mediated by Predictive Modeling, Decision Optimization, and Risk Intelligence. Each of these intermediaries is a realm in which quantum-inspired computation has the potential to add a considerable degree of analytical power and strategic flexibility. For instance, predictive modeling can take advantage of the capability of quantum-inspired systems to search large solution spaces, while decision optimization can use classical–quantum hybrids to tackle nonlinear logistics and inventory problems (Núñez-Merino et al., 2024; Chen et al., 2025).

This methodological stance also focuses on prospective conceptualization – anticipating future trajectories of research and practice as opposed to engaging in analyses of present data sets. Quantum-inspired analytics is a new area, and its adoption in sustainable supply chain management is at an initial phase. Therefore, conceptual modeling offers a guide for researchers and practitioners by highlighting important variables, relationships, and potential causal mechanisms. Prospective empirical research may operationalize these constructs through quantitative or simulation studies to empirically test and further develop the framework (Ivanov & Dolgui, 2021; Phillipson, 2024).

Demands of technology innovation and sustainability are furthermore considered in terms of interdisciplinary convergence within the approach. The chapter, integrating computational science with sustainable operations research, illustrates the sort of interdisciplinary research needed to tackle complex global issues. This integration enhances not only academic insight but also delivers knowledge-based strategic implications for global supply network (GSN) design for policy-makers and business executives who desire to develop adaptive and responsible GSNs (Aldrighetti et al., 2021; Ivanov, 2024).

APPLICATIONS OF QUANTUM-INSPIRED BIG DATA ANALYTICS

Quantum-inspired big data analytics (QIBDA) represents a frontier in supply-chain intelligence that merges advanced optimization with sustainable operations. Drawing from the principles of quantum mechanics—such as superposition, entanglement, and tunneling—but implemented on classical architectures, QIBDA enables organizations to analyze massive, nonlinear datasets at unprecedented speed and scale (Núñez-Merino et al., 2024). The following sections outline five key application areas in which QIBDA transforms predictive modeling, resource optimization, procurement, circular logistics, and decision-making under uncertainty. Together, these domains illustrate how quantum-inspired computation can enhance the sustainability and resilience of global supply networks.

Predictive Modeling for Disruption Management

Global supply chains are extremely susceptible to systemic shocks, including pandemics, port congestion, cyberattacks, and geopolitical wars. Conventional predictive models traditionally tend to employ linear regression or machine-learning approaches, which presuppose data stationarity and can not adequately capture the intricate interdependencies between suppliers, transport routes, and demand patterns (Ivanov, 2021). In contrast, quantum-inspired algorithms, which can handle high-dimensional data more effectively, offer the potential for earlier disruption detection and better risk prediction. A highly promising technique is based on quantum-inspired probabilistic modeling, which exploits Monte-Carlo simulations and Ising-model representations to estimate the propagation of p-disruptions in supply-chain networks (Jahin et al., 2023). For example, they could run simulations of millions of supply-chain states all at once to anticipate bottlenecks before they develop. During the COVID-19 pandemic, these models could have contributed to better matching demand with supply and reduced the cases of either excess inventory or stock-outs.

Furthermore, quantum-inspired neural networks (QiNNs) enable dynamic prediction with data uncertainty through quantum annealing–based optimization of the error function (Yarkoni et al., 2022). Such models are able to process signals from IoT-enabled logistics, social-media sentiment, and weather data to predict potential disruptions within seconds of becoming known. Hence, QIBDA enhances the capability of resilience engineering to sense, respond, and recover (Li, Y., Wang, X., Zhang, L., & Chen, J., 2025) from shocks, which is the cornerstone of adaptive supply-chain management. For example, a global electronics manufacturer used a quantum-inspired Monte Carlo simulation to evaluate 50,000 disruption scenarios involving semiconductor shortages, enabling procurement teams to identify alternative suppliers two weeks earlier than classical forecasting models would permit. This early-warning insight reduced projected downtime by nearly 18%, demonstrating the practical advantage of quantum-inspired predictive capabilities in volatile supply ecosystems.

Optimization for Sustainable Resource Allocation

Optimization is at the core of supply-chain sustainability. This means balancing the work of production, the cost, the energy consumption, and the emissions control. Traditional linear programming and heuristic approaches are usually not successful in the presence of many local minima or nonconvex constraints in the optimization landscape. Quantum-inspired optimization algorithms (e.g., QAOA and SQA) are particularly successful in this type of problem as they explore global solution spaces more efficiently (Shamsuddoha et al., 2025). In production scheduling, quantum-inspired solvers solve a multi-objective optimization problem in which a company tries to minimize the makespan and the energy consumption. Similarly, this can be extended to, for instance, transport and logistics, where the route planning can be optimized with cost and carbon emissions as parameters. DHL and Toyota have, for example, trialed hybrid quantum optimization to cut fuel use and idle time in fleet management (Núñez-Merino et al., 2024).

In addition to operational efficiency, QIBDA promotes a sustainable allocation of resources by embedding environmental variables directly in the objective function. Thus, resource allocation decisions are influenced by energy intensity, waste generation, and social-impact scores in addition to the more traditional cost-based indicators. When sustainability is expressed as a quantifiable constraint, trade-offs become transparent, and decision-making can be aligned with the Triple Bottom Line of people, planet, and profit (Prajapati et al., 2025). As a practical illustration, a European logistics firm piloted a quantum-inspired multi-objective optimizer for fleet routing under carbon-emission constraints. The algorithm evaluated millions of route combinations in seconds, identifying paths that lowered fuel consumption by 9% while maintaining delivery lead times. Such results highlight how quantum-inspired optimization can simultaneously improve cost efficiency and environmental sustainability. Thus, quantum-inspired optimization allows a transition from reactive sustainability – fulfilling compliance requirements after decisions are made – to proactive sustainability, where environmental and moral considerations shape operational decisions on-the-fly.

Intelligent Procurement and Selection of Suppliers

Procurement is a key leverage point for including sustainability and resilience in supply chains. While factors such as price, quality , and lead-time form the basis for supplier selection, modern-day purchasing has to take account of social responsibility, ethical sourcing, and carbon-footprint issues (Carter et al., 2020). Quantum-inspired analytics enables this transition by analysing large multidimensional supplier data and executing multi-criteria decision analysis (MCDA) with enhanced computational efficiency.

Quantum-boosted decision trees or variational quantum classifiers can be used to find suppliers that comply with quality and cost requirements and also with environmental and social regulations (Whig et al., 2024). As an example, a buying manager might run optimization scenarios that trade off supplier diversity with compliance risk and sustainability performance. Including real-time information, such as deforestation measures verified by satellite, or labor audits, QIBDA enables ethical sourcing decisions that enhance a company's social responsibility and brand integrity.

In addition, supplier networks tend to have a complicated web of interdependencies that means disruptions at one node ripple through others. Quantum-inspired graph analytics can also be used to represent and analyze the relationships among suppliers to detect system-wide little failures and areas of resilience. The outcome is a procurement process that is smarter, faster, and more transparent that can deliver on both sustainability and resilience goals (Dhaliwal et al., 2024).

Circular Economy and Reverse Logistics

The circular-economy model promotes closed-loop supply chains that enable the recirculation of products, materials , and resources through reuse, remanufacturing, and recycling to form a waste-minimizing system (Geissdoerfer et al., 2017). Such networks are difficult to manage because of the underlying complex routing and resource-recovery problems that need to be solved. Quantum-inspired optimization provides a novel solution for the design of effective reverse-logistics systems and closed-loop production lines.

By using quantum-inspired algorithms, it is possible to calculate optimized routes for the collection of post-consumer products with the lowest-energy expenditure and the highest recovery rates (Vaddy et al., 2024). Also, hybrid solvers such as quantum-inspired and classical computing, calculate the best disassembly and recycling schedules by analyzing millions of potential configurations. These are the kind of sustainability targets that companies can start to embed in operations with the help of these tools, whether that is zero waste or net-zero carbon emissions.

Circular-economy solutions also leverage quantum-inspired material-flow modeling, which tracks resource cycles and multi-generation life- cycle effects. For instance, QIBDA can be used to estimate returns, evaluate remanufacturing feasibility, and develop consumer participation incentive schemes to the effect of success in the participation in recycling programs in electronics manufacturing (Thiyagarajan & Rajendran, 2024).

By bringing visibility and efficiency in reverse flow, quantum-inspired analytics bridges the disconnect of the linear value chain, which finishes with disposal and circular ecosystems where waste is a resource. This shift serves not only to sustainability, but to more sustainable, resilient outcomes, as it decreases reliance on virgin material supply and unstable commodity markets.

Decision-Making under Uncertainty

Making decisions in uncertain environments is still a key challenge for global supply chains subject to volatile demand, prices, and disruptions that are difficult to predict. Traditional optimization models often make deterministic assumptions or utilize small probabilistic samples, which may underestimate the risk exposure. Quantum-inspired algorithms allow enterprises to conduct scenario planning and resilience modeling at much deeper computational levels.

Like hybrid quantum-machine-learning (QML) methods that analyze a pool of stochastic scenarios at once and find robust strategies that work well over a multitude of possible futures (Khan et al., 2025). In inventory control, these methods enable the firm to compute optimal safety-stock levels for probabilistic demand distributions rather than deterministic forecasts. In strategic planning, QIBDA can analyze trade-offs in cost, service, and sustainability under uncertain geopolitical or climate conditions.

One of the key benefits of QIBDA in managing uncertainty is that it can take into account nonlinear effects, such as how a delay in the production of semiconductors can affect the automotive and consumer-electronics industries. Such complicated network effects are usually outside the range of classical models but are representable by quantum-inspired tensor-network frameworks capturing multi-node correlations (Gutta et al., 2024). In the end, the convergence of quantum-inspired computing and big-data infrastructures allows decision-makers to break out of a reactive crisis-response posture and progress toward anticipatory resilience. Instead of focusing on what happened, organizations can focus on what will happen next and what the best course of action is under uncertainty.

Table 2 summarizes key application domains of quantum-inspired big data analytics and their corresponding sustainability and resilience outcomes.

Table 2. Application Areas of Quantum-Inspired Big Data Analytics in Sustainable and Resilient Supply Chains

Application Area	Key Function	Sustainability / Resilience Outcome
Disruption prediction	Scenario simulation	Early warning and reduced downtime
Resource optimization	Multi-objective optimization	Reduced emissions and energy use
Supplier selection	Multi-criteria decision analysis	Ethical sourcing and risk reduction
Reverse logistics	Route and recovery optimization	Circular economy enablement
Uncertainty planning	Probabilistic scenario evaluation	Robust and adaptive decision-making

Source: Secondary Data

MANAGERIAL AND POLICY IMPLICATIONS

Embedding quantum-inspired big data analytics (QIBDA) in the global supply chains is a transformational opportunity for managers and policymakers to hold the tension between technological innovation and sustainability imperatives. As organizations contend with growing supply chain complexity, environmental responsibility, and geopolitical interruptions, the capacity to utilize quantum-inspired algorithms to improve prediction accuracy, decision making, and resilience is not merely a strategic advantage but also a necessity. This section addresses the managerial decisions and policy options for the responsible and effective uptake of quantum-inspired analytics with a focus on sustainability, ethical governance, and organizational capability building.

From a managerial standpoint, the implementation of QIBDA on make span minimization of the supply chain demands a rethinking of the decision-making processes in supply chain management. The traditional analytics systems are based on historical data and hence are mostly reactive in nature, which are used to predict the future and help in making decisions in the present (Ivanov & Dolgui, 2021). On the other hand, the quantum-inspired approaches allow for a more proactive, forward-thinking modeling perspective based on probability theory, integrating uncertainty, dynamic dependencies, and nonlinear interactions among supply chain variables (Núñez-Merino et al., 2024). Managers thus need to move from deterministic decision models to probabilistic and adaptive decision models. This requires a new investment of resources in people: data scientists, supply chain analysts, and sustainability officers who can work together to understand and act on insights enhanced by quantum. In addition, the management should develop a data culture in which strategic decisions could be dynamically adjusted along with feedback loops between digital simulations and empirical results (Bag et al., 2021).

A key managerial implication relates to the configuration of hybrid decision-making systems, which combine classical computing-based decision support with quantum-inspired optimization algorithms. Although full-scale quantum computing is still mostly in the research stage, hybrid solutions are increasingly offering concrete advantages in areas such as logistics optimization, demand forecasting, and sustainability analytics (Shamsuddoha et al., 2025). For example, quantum-inspired algorithms are being tested by such corporations as Volkswagen and DHL to optimize routes and carbon-constrained inventory (Phillipson, 2024). As a result, executives will have to strive for a hybrid approach to adoption -- starting with hybrid systems that enable seamless integration with current big data environments while simultaneously seeding capabilities for quantum-native systems. This staggered approach mitigates technological risk while allowing for early benefits in performance and sustainability.

The inclusion of quantum-inspired analytics further enables the management to focus on the operational goals of the Triple Bottom Line, i.e., economic, environmental, and social sustainability (Elkington, 1998). Quantum-based predictive models can predict bottlenecks in resources, patterns of optimal energy usage, and waste reduction in the entire supply chain network. For instance, predictive optimization models adjust trade-offs between transportation efficiency and carbon emissions in real time and hence enable companies to identify logistics routes that reduce the overall environmental impact while ensuring service quality (Dubey et al., 2020). When such algorithms are integrated into enterprise resource planning (ERP) and supplier management systems, businesses can begin pursuing real-time sustainability management — a significant leap beyond traditional periodic audits or static dashboards."

From a governance perspective, the responsible use of quantum-inspired analytics will require strong data ethics, transparency, and accountability. As supply chains become digitized, they are producing huge data sets with sensitive operational and environmental details. Thus, governance frameworks need to be able to guarantee that the use of data respects the (rights-based) principles of justice, privacy, and environmental soundness (Floridi, 2021). Policies should mandate algorithmic transparency so stakeholders—including regulators, partners, and consumers—can see how decisions related to sustainability are scripted and optimized. Furthermore, they advocate that managers institutionalize ethical review committees or "digital sustainability boards" to track potential biases and to keep them aligned with the United Nations Sustainable Development Goals (SDGs) (Chen et al., 2025).

Another important policy implication is in the field of national and international regulation of technology for sustainability. Policymakers need to understand that QIBDA is a dual-use technology—one that can tip the scales toward sustainable innovation but also potentially having adverse effects such as energy-intensive computation or algorithmic opacity. So, governments should also promote creation and delivery of energy-saving quantum-inspired algorithms via e.g., tax breaks, R&D funding, and PPPs. Additionally, the adoption of QIBDA in the systems of carbon accounting and emissions reporting might increase global traceability standards, helping firms to better align with frameworks as the Paris Agreement or the Carbon Border Adjustment Mechanism of the European Union (European Commission, 2023).

Readiness and ability building at the level of an organization is what shapes the likelihood of successful uptake of QIBDA methods. Before adopting quantum-inspired systems, organizations need to evaluate their digital readiness, data infrastructure, and human capabilities. Jeble et al. (2023) argue that digital transformation initiatives implode due to firms ignoring the socio-technical fusion needed to bring advanced analytics to life. Hence, training, pilot projects and cross functional innovation labs need to be prioritized to link technical know-how with managerial intuition. Managers should also adopt a modular technology architecture – which allows them to experiment flexibly with quantum-inspired modules and to maintain backward compatibility with legacy systems.

Part of the QIBDA adoption is also agreeing to a shift in thinking — realizing that the supply chain is an adaptive, connected, and dynamic system rather than a linear sequence of events in manufacturing. This view is consistent with the PhD-level thinking underpinning Complex Systems Theory, which holds that minor modifications at one node in the network can result in unpredictable ripple effects throughout the network (Holland, 2014). Quantum-inspired analytics, by capturing complex interdependencies in its probabilistic models, provides managers with new instruments for scenario analysis and testing resilience. This leads to improved anticipation of perturbations (e.g., natural disasters, trade wars, cyberattacks) and aids in tailoring adaptive strategies that foster the continuity of supply in the face of disturbance [Ivanov, 2024].

Lastly, the coordination of corporate strategies and policies support is essential. The implementation of QIBDA can only succeed with a multi-tier ecosystem, in which the private sector innovation is steered by clear ethical principles, regulatory incentives and common sustainability objectives. Encourage policy makers to facilitate the formation of cooperative research clusters, standards organizations, and cross-industry data sharing platforms to promote learning and interoperability (Ajagekar & You, 2024).Managers, for their part, must lead the way in turning policy frameworks into clear, actionable sustainability strategies and ensure that technology serves the well-being of people and the planet—not short-term profits.

FUTURE RESEARCH DIRECTIONS

The rise of quantum inspired big data analytics (QIBDA) provides an interesting but largely unexplored research avenue in green and resilient supply chain management. While advancements in conceptual and theoretical research have demonstrated their potential, largely unvalidated. Subsequent research is encouraged to investigate how quantum-inspired models can be realized on practical environments, evaluated, and optimized in various industries. The integration of QIBDA with other digital technologies, for example, artificial intelligence (AI), the Internet of Things (IoT), and blockchain, offers impactful potential opportunities for multi-dimensional resilience and transparency as well as adaptive intelligence in global operations. In addition, cross-sectoral investigations, simulation-based modelling, and mixed-method strategies might enhance the empirical rigor and contextual insight needed to advance from theory to practice.

One of the future research urgencies is on the empirical verification of quantum-inspired SC paradigms. Until now, the majority of debate has been at the theoretical stage, based on theoretical efficiency and sustainability gains of such schemes (Phillipson, 2024). Nevertheless, studies on practical application are necessary to assess whether QIBDA can surpass traditional big data analytics in predictive accuracy, computation efficiency, and environmental effects. Researchers need to conceive of pilot projects with logistics companies, manufacturers, and policy agencies to actually measure gains in resilience and sustainability. Such case-based empirical research may, for example, investigate the role of quantum-inspired optimization in during-disruption lead time management or in production scheduling waste minimization. This would provide tangible proof of the transformative power of these technologies, thereby closing the current gap between theory and practice (Ivanov & Dolgui, 2021).

Future research could investigate the merging of QIBDA with AI, IoT, and blockchain services for the fruition of an integrative digital ecosystem. Artificial intelligence, as a data-driven approach to learn and adapt, can also be utilized to complement quantum-inspired methods in dynamic optimization and anomaly detection (Shamsuddoha et al., 2025). IoT InS Prior to our work, IoT InS, which is based on the feature of real-time sensory and operational data of IoT systems as a series of continuous data streams, serves as a widely adopted input form to quantum-inspired models to analyze and interpret under uncertainty. In parallel, blockchain can bring transparency and trust to the data sharing process, establishing a tamper-proof ledger of sustainable actions and supplier engagement (Ethirajan & Kandasamy, 2025). Interactions among these technologies may eventually yield "cognitive supply chains" that are not only resilient but self-correcting—capable of predicting disruptions, reassigning resources, and reducing environmental impacts on their own. Examining this triadic synthesis is widely considered to be one of the most promising areas for cross-disciplinary study.

Cross-cutting utilization forms another promising avenue. Although the majority of discussion has so far centered around manufacturing and logistics, the quantum-inspired analytics paradigm can also be applied to health care, energy, and agriculture, where resiliency and sustainability are just as important. US healthcare supply chains could also benefit from QIBDA by improving the distribution of medical supplies during pandemics to make the allocation more equitable and efficient in the face of severe uncertainty (Chen et al., 2025). In oil and gas, it could be used for grid optimization, renewable energy prediction, and carbon emission mitigation via capturing intricate relationships among supply routes and demand nodes (Faraji et al., 2024). In agriculture, quantum-inspired predictive analytics could improve crop-yield prediction, irrigation management, and food logistics, with a direct impact on the United Nations' Sustainable Development Goals (SDGs) on zero hunger and responsible production. For these reasons, future research should extend the empirical base beyond manufacturing into these socially and ecologically vital fields.

A further direction for future research pertains to simulation-based and mixed-method studies designs. Simulation modeling offers a laboratory in which to evaluate the performance of quantum-inspired algorithms in the presence of a variety of disruption events, e.g., trade wars, climate shocks, or cyberattacks, without the potential for catastrophic fallout. For example, the agent-based modeling (ABM) and system dynamics (SD) approaches can be integrated with quantum-inspired optimization to model adaptive decision-making within global value chains (Lv, 2025). Mixed-method designs that couple quantitative simulations with qualitative interviews or case studies can provide additional insight into how organizations adopt and make sense of QIBDA. This approach would allow researchers to observe both the quantifiable effects and the human, organizational and cultural elements associated with technological transformation. There is also a need for further study of the ethical and ESG consequences of the QIBDA. As computational power grows, so do challenges—energy consumption, data sovereignty and algorithmic bias (Floridi, 2021). Subsequent research should evaluate the overall sustainability impact of QIBDA to confirm that its introduction is consistent with the tenets of responsible innovation and digital ethics.

Ultimately, research capacity building and education system with a labor force for quantum-inspired decision making needs to be analyzed by scholars. As these technologies become more popular, supply chain professionals, data scientists and policy makers all need to develop a common language around quantum-inspired analytics and sustainability concepts. Research on pedagogical models, including interdisciplinary graduate programs, online learning modules, and professional certifications, can promote widespread and equitable adoption. This line of work is critical for broadening the availability of QIBDA and avoiding the formation of a digital divide between high-tech and developing nations (World Economic Forum, 2022).

CONCLUSION

The integration of sustainability, resilience, and big data has tipped the future direction of global supply chain management. This chapter has shown that quantum-inspired big data analytics (QIBDA) can be considered as an enabler of a new paradigm, which can deal with the increasing complexity, volatility and environmental concerns in current supply networks. Integrating theoretical views from Resilience Theory, Complex Systems Theory and Sustainability Frameworks, it has presented a conceptual model with quantum-inspired computation as a strategic enabler of adaptive intelligence, real-time optimization, and sustainable performance. The commentaries on the previous sections highlight that the road to sustainable and resilient supply chains is no longer about improving process efficiency—it involves intelligent systems that learn, predict, and adapt in the face of uncertainty.

Fundamentally, QIBDA abandons the classical deterministic analytics in favor of probabilistic and non-linear models inspired by quantum mechanics. Traditional big data solutions, even when effective, find it challenging to handle the explosive growth of diverse data streams, and to model complex dependencies on actors of global supply chains (Ivanov & Dolgui, 2021). Quantum-inspired analytics, on the other hand, applies principles such as superposition, entanglement and tunneling (transposed to classical computation) to solve complex decision-making problems more efficiently. This leads to exponentially faster analysis, higher predictive accuracy, and simultaneous exploration of multiple solution pathways (Phillipson, 2024). To our knowledge, the conceptual innovative value of this chapter is centered in illustrating how such computing advancements can be applied, not just for operational benefits, but to unframe the value of sustainability and resilience as primary strategic outcomes of supply chain systems.

REFERENCES

Ajagekar, A., & You, F. (2024). Quantum-inspired optimization for sustainable supply chain management: A review. *Computers & Chemical Engineering, 180*, 108125. Advance online publication. DOI: 10.1016/j.compchemeng.2023.108125

Al-Banna, A., Yaqot, M., & Menezes, B. C. (2024). Investment strategies in Industry 4.0 for enhanced supply chain resilience: An empirical analysis. *Cogent Business & Management, 11*(1), 2298187. Advance online publication. DOI: 10.1080/23311975.2024.2298187

Aldrighetti, R., Zennaro, I., Finco, S., & Battini, D. (2021). Healthcare supply chain simulation with disruption considerations: A systematic literature review and bibliometric analysis. *Sustainability, 13*(13), 7104. Advance online publication. DOI: 10.3390/su13137104

Bag, S., Rahman, M. S., Srivastava, G., Kilbourn, P., & Wood, L. C. (2024). System thinking skills and their effect upon supply chain resilience. *Systems Research and Behavioral Science, 41*(6), 837–853. DOI: 10.1002/sres.3072

Bag, S., Wood, L. C., Mangla, S. K., & Luthra, S. (2020). Procurement 4.0 and its implications on business process performance in a circular economy. *Resources, Conservation and Recycling, 152*, 104502. Advance online publication. DOI: 10.1016/j.resconrec.2019.104502

Bag, S., Wood, L. C., Xu, L., Dhamija, P., & Kayikci, Y. (2021). Big data analytics in sustainable supply chain management: A focus on manufacturing supply chains. *Sustainability, 13*(13), 7101. Advance online publication. DOI: 10.3390/su13137104

Carter, C. R., Rogers, D. S., & Choi, T. Y. (2020). Toward the theory of the supply chain. *The Journal of Supply Chain Management, 56*(2), 18–28. DOI: 10.1111/jscm.12237

Centobelli, P., Cerchione, R., Esposito, E., & Oropallo, E. (2021). Surfing blockchain wave, or drowning? Shaping the future of distributed ledgers and the role of business models. *Technological Forecasting and Social Change, 165*, 120463. Advance online publication. DOI: 10.1016/j.techfore.2020.120463

Chen, Z.-S., Tan, Y., Ma, Z., Zhu, Z., & Skibniewski, M. J. (2025). Unlocking the potential of quantum computing in prefabricated construction supply chains: Current trends, challenges, and future directions. *Information Fusion, 120*, 103043. Advance online publication. DOI: 10.1016/j.inffus.2025.103043

Choi, T. Y., Dooley, K. J., & Rungtusanatham, M. (2001). Supply networks and complex adaptive systems: Control versus emergence. *Journal of Operations Management, 19*(3), 351–366. DOI: 10.1016/S0272-6963(00)00068-1

Dhaliwal, N., Aghera, S., Whig, P., & Remala, R. (2024). Advanced analytics and quantum computing for revolutionizing procurement strategies. In *Quantum computing and supply chain management: A new era of optimization* (pp. 304–330). IGI Global., DOI: 10.4018/979-8-3693-4107-0.ch016

Dubey, R., Gunasekaran, A., Bryde, D. J., Dwivedi, Y. K., & Papadopoulos, T. (2022). Blockchain technology for enhancing swift-trust, collaboration and resilience within a humanitarian supply chain setting. *International Journal of Production Research, 60*(11), 3381–3398. DOI: 10.1080/00207543.2020.1722860

Dubey, R., Gunasekaran, A., Childe, S. J., & Papadopoulos, T. (2020). Big data analytics and artificial intelligence for sustainable global supply chains. *Journal of Cleaner Production, 262*, 121313. Advance online publication. DOI: 10.1016/j.jclepro.2020.121313

Elkington, J. (1998). *Cannibals with forks: The triple bottom line of 21st-century business.* Capstone.

Ethirajan, M., & Kandasamy, J. (2025). Quantum computing as an enabler for sustainable circular economy: Emerging trends and future directions. *Sustainable Operations and Computers, 6*, 136–148. DOI: 10.1016/j.susoc.2024.12.001

European Commission. (2023). Regulation (EU) 2023/956 of the European Parliament and of the Council of 10 May 2023 establishing a carbon border adjustment mechanism. *Official Journal of the European Union, L, 130*(52).

Faraji, F., Hajipour, V., & Rahimnia, F. (2024). Quantum computing for climate resilience and sustainability challenges. *arXiv*. https://arxiv.org/abs/2409.10029

Folke, C. (2016). Resilience (republished). *Ecology and Society, 21*(4), 44. Advance online publication. DOI: 10.5751/ES-09088-210444

Geissdoerfer, M., Savaget, P., Bocken, N. M. P., & Hultink, E. J. (2017). The circular economy – A new sustainability paradigm? *Journal of Cleaner Production, 143*, 757–768. DOI: 10.1016/j.jclepro.2016.12.048

Ghorbani, M., Yazdani, M., Govindan, K., & Basagni, S. (2023). Circular supply chains as complex adaptive systems: A simulation-based study. *IFAC-PapersOnLine, 56*(2), 318–323. DOI: 10.1016/j.ifacol.2023.10.1596

Giannakis, M., Papadopoulos, T., Dubey, R., Yan, Z., & Spanaki, K. (2025). Are we truly ready for what is coming? A reflection on supply chain resilience challenges in the face of megatrends. *International Journal of Production Economics*, *272*, 109238. Advance online publication. DOI: 10.1016/j.ijpe.2025.109238

Gutta, L. M., Dhamodharan, B., Dutta, P. K., & Remala, R. (2024). AI-infused quantum machine learning for enhanced supply chain forecasting. In *Quantum computing and supply chain management: A new era of optimization* (pp. 16–44). IGI Global., DOI: 10.4018/979-8-3693-4107-0.ch002

Holland, J. H. (2014). *Complexity: A very short introduction*. Oxford University Press.

Holling, C. S. (1973). Resilience and stability of ecological systems. *Annual Review of Ecology and Systematics*, *4*, 1–23. DOI: 10.1146/annurev.es.04.110173.000245

Iftikhar, A., Ali, I., Arslan, A., & Tarba, S. (2024). Digital innovation, data analytics, and supply chain resiliency: A bibliometric-based systematic literature review. *Annals of Operations Research*, *333*(2), 825–848. DOI: 10.1007/s10479-022-04765-6 PMID: 35611176

Ivanov, D. (2021). Exiting the COVID-19 pandemic: Aftershock risks and avoidance of disruption tails in supply chains. *Annals of Operations Research*, *319*(1), 149–172. DOI: 10.1007/s10479-021-04092-6 PMID: 33840871

Ivanov, D. (2024). Viable supply chain model: Integrating agility, resilience, and sustainability perspectives—Lessons from and thinking beyond the COVID-19 pandemic. *Annals of Operations Research*, *319*(1), 839–857. DOI: 10.1007/s10479-020-03640-6 PMID: 32836614

Ivanov, D., & Dolgui, A. (2021). A digital supply chain twin for managing the disruption risks and resilience in the era of Industry 4.0. *Production Planning and Control*, *32*(9), 775–788. DOI: 10.1080/09537287.2020.1768450

Jahin, M. A., Shovon, M. S. H., Islam, M. S., Shin, J., Mridha, M. F., & Tanweer, M. R. (2023). QAmplifyNet: Pushing the boundaries of supply chain backorder prediction using interpretable hybrid quantum-classical neural network. *Scientific Reports*, *13*(1), 18225. Advance online publication. DOI: 10.1038/s41598-023-45406-7 PMID: 37880386

Jeble, S., Kumari, S., Venkatesh, V. G., & Singh, M. (2023). Challenges of big data analytics for sustainable supply chains in healthcare – A resource-based view. *Benchmarking*, *30*(9), 3461–3483. DOI: 10.1108/BIJ-07-2022-0433

Kaneberg, E., Herold, D. M., Piotrowicz, W., & Gabellini, G. (2025). Supply chain resilience and critical dynamic capabilities: A balanced scorecard approach. *Logistics Research*, *13*(1), 2523957. Advance online publication. DOI: 10.1080/21693277.2025.2523957

Ketchen, D. J.Jr, Crook, T. R., Craighead, C. W., & Cheng, L. (2022). Toward a theory of supply chain entrepreneurial embeddedness in disrupted and normal states. *The Journal of Supply Chain Management*, *58*(1), 5–26. DOI: 10.1111/jscm.12283

Ketokivi, M., & Choi, T. (2022). Building and testing necessity theories in supply chain management. *The Journal of Supply Chain Management*, *58*(2), 3–22. DOI: 10.1111/jscm.12287

Khan, M., Amin, F., Din, M. U., Abid, M. A., & de la Torre, I. (2025). Enhancing e-commerce logistics efficiency and sustainability via quantum computing and artificial intelligence-based quantum hybrid models. *The Journal of Supercomputing*, *81*(1), 1–32. DOI: 10.1007/s11227-025-07959-4

Khanna, R., Sharma, R. K., Sharma, A., & Mahajan, R. (2025). Circular supply chain management: Bridging business innovation and sustainability through best practices. *Journal of Circular Economy*, *3*(1), 1–15. DOI: 10.1007/s44251-024-00048-1

Lee, I., & Mangalaraj, G. (2022). Big data analytics in supply chain management: A systematic literature review and research directions. *Big Data and Cognitive Computing*, *6*(1), 17. Advance online publication. DOI: 10.3390/bdcc6010017

Li, Y., Wang, X., Zhang, L., & Chen, J. (2025). Supply chain resilience: A literature review based on bibliometric analysis. *International Journal of Logistics Research and Applications*. Advance online publication. https://doi.org/DOI: 10.1080/13675567.2025.2554801

Lv, B. (2025). Supply chain resilience modeling based on dynamic hypergraph and quantum reinforcement learning for low-altitude-ground networks. *Transportation Research Part E, Logistics and Transportation Review*, *183*, 103467. Advance online publication. DOI: 10.1016/j.tre.2024.103467

Meredith, J. (1993). Theory building through conceptual methods. *International Journal of Operations & Production Management*, *13*(5), 3–11. DOI: 10.1108/01443579310028120

Mondragon, A. E. C., Mastrocinque, E., Tsai, J.-F., Flynn, B. B., & Hogg, P. J. (2025). Examining Industry 5.0 and supply chain performance. *Logistics Research*, *18*(1), 2501181. Advance online publication. DOI: 10.1080/21693277.2025.2501181

Munim, Z. H., Vladi, O., & Hossain, N. U. I. (2024). Data analytics applications in supply chain resilience and sustainability management: The state of the art and a way forward. In *IvySCI* (pp. 1–24). Springer., DOI: 10.1007/978-3-031-29823-3_1

Núñez-Merino, M., Maqueira-Marín, J. M., Moyano-Fuentes, J., & Castaño-Moraga, C. A. (2024). Quantum-inspired computing technology in operations and logistics management. *International Journal of Physical Distribution & Logistics Management*, *54*(1), 1–28. DOI: 10.1108/IJPDLM-02-2023-0065

Phillipson, F. (2024). Quantum computing in logistics and supply chain management: An overview. *arXiv*. https://arxiv.org/abs/2402.17520

Pires, A., Oliveira, F. R., Azevedo, S. G., & Neto, J. (2025). Measuring the complexity of supply chains using Shannon entropy. *Applied System Innovation*, *8*(4), 105. Advance online publication. DOI: 10.3390/asi8040105

Ponomarov, S. Y., & Holcomb, M. C. (2009). Understanding the concept of supply chain resilience. *International Journal of Logistics Management*, *20*(1), 124–143. DOI: 10.1108/09574090910954873

Prajapati, M., Kant, R., Tripathi, S. M., & Shankar, R. (2025). Exploring sustainable pathways: A systematic literature review of triple bottom line in supply chain management. *Sustainable Operations and Computers*, *6*, 223–241. DOI: 10.1016/j.susoc.2025.03.002

Runtuk, J. K., & Sidjabat, F., Jsslynn, & Jordan, F. (2022). Big data in supply chain management: A systematic literature review. *Green Intelligent Systems and Applications*, *2*(2), 108–117. DOI: 10.53623/gisa.v2i2.115

Salwa, N. (2024). Real-time analytics and supply chain transformation in the digital era. *Sinergi International Journal of Logistics*, *1*(3). Advance online publication. DOI: 10.61194/sijl.v1i3.613

Santos-de León, N. J. (2020). Sustainable supply chain in the era of Industry 4.0 and big data: A systematic analysis of literature and research. *Sustainability*, *12*(10), 4108. Advance online publication. DOI: 10.3390/su12104108

Setyadi, A., Pawirosumarto, S., & Damaris, A. (2025). Toward a resilient and sustainable supply chain: Operational responses to global disruptions in the post-COVID-19 era. *Sustainability*, *17*(13), 6167. Advance online publication. DOI: 10.3390/su17136167

Shamsuddoha, M., Kashem, M. A., Nasir, T., Hossain, A. I., & Ahmed, M. F. (2025). Quantum computing applications in supply chain information and optimization: Future scenarios and opportunities. *Information (Basel)*, *16*(8), 693. Advance online publication. DOI: 10.3390/info16080693

Snyder, H. (2019). Literature review as a research methodology: An overview and guidelines. *Journal of Business Research*, *104*, 333–339. DOI: 10.1016/j.jbusres.2019.07.039

Surucu-Balci, E., & Balci, G. (2022). Steering supply chains from a complex systems perspective. *European Journal of Management Studies*, *27*(1), 5–35. DOI: 10.1108/EJMS-04-2021-0030

Talwar, S., Kaur, P., Fosso Wamba, S., & Dhir, A. (2021). Big data in operations and supply chain management: A systematic literature review and future research agenda. *International Journal of Production Research*, *59*(11), 3509–3534. DOI: 10.1080/00207543.2020.1868599

Thiyagarajan, S., & Rajendran, R. K. (2024). Quantum approaches to sustainable resource management in supply chains. In *Quantum computing and supply chain management: A new era of optimization* (pp. 208–230). IGI Global., DOI: 10.4018/979-8-3693-4107-0.ch011

Torraco, R. J. (2016). Writing integrative literature reviews: Using the past and present to explore the future. *Human Resource Development Review*, *15*(4), 404–428. DOI: 10.1177/1534484316671606

Tundys, B. (2023). Triple bottom line aspects and sustainable supply chain resilience. *Frontiers in Environmental Science*, *11*, 1161437. Advance online publication. DOI: 10.3389/fenvs.2023.1161437

Vaddy, R. K., Dhamodharan, B., & Jain, A. (2024). Quantum computing applications in real-time route optimization for supply chains. In *Quantum computing and supply chain management: A new era of optimization* (pp. 102–126). IGI Global., DOI: 10.4018/979-8-3693-4107-0.ch006

Wacker, J. G. (1998). A definition of theory: Research guidelines for different theory-building research methods in operations management. *Journal of Operations Management*, *16*(4), 361–385. DOI: 10.1016/S0272-6963(98)00019-9

Whig, P., Mudunuru, K. R., & Remala, R. (2024). Quantum-inspired data-driven decision making for supply chain logistics. In *Quantum computing and supply chain management: A new era of optimization* (pp. 62–88). IGI Global., DOI: 10.4018/979-8-3693-4107-0.ch004

Xu, J., Pero, M., & Fabbri, M. (2023). Unfolding the link between big data analytics and supply chain planning. *Technological Forecasting and Social Change*, *196*, 122805. Advance online publication. DOI: 10.1016/j.techfore.2023.122805

Yarkoni, S., Plaat, A., & Aarts, E. H. L. (2022). Quantum-inspired algorithms for combinatorial optimization: A review. *ACM Computing Surveys*, *54*(8), 1–36. DOI: 10.1145/3477141

Zamani, E. D., Smyth, C., Gupta, S., & Dennehy, D. (2023). Artificial intelligence and big data analytics for supply chain resilience: A systematic literature review. *Annals of Operations Research*, *327*(2), 605–632. DOI: 10.1007/s10479-022-04765-6 PMID: 36212520

Zia, M., Mumtaz, S., & Raza, A. (2024). Green supply chain management practices and triple bottom line performance: Moderating role of total quality management and Industry 4.0 technologies. *Journal of Environmental Management*, *360*, 121082. Advance online publication. DOI: 10.1016/j.jenvman.2024.121082

KEY TERMS AND DEFINITIONS

Circular Economy: An economic model focused on minimizing waste and maximizing resource reuse through closed-loop production and consumption systems.

Complex Adaptive Systems: Systems composed of interconnected agents whose interactions result in nonlinear behaviour, emergence, and self-organization.

Decision Optimization: The process of identifying optimal or near-optimal decisions under multiple constraints and objectives, including cost, service level, and sustainability criteria.

Predictive Modelling: Analytical techniques used to forecast future events or system states based on historical and real-time data patterns.

Quantum-Inspired Big Data Analytics (QIBDA): Computational approaches inspired by principles of quantum mechanics—such as superposition and probabilistic exploration—implemented on classical computing platforms to solve complex, large-scale data analytics problems.

Risk Intelligence: An organization's ability to identify, assess, and respond to potential risks using data-driven insights and adaptive learning mechanisms.

Supply Chain Resilience: The capability of a supply chain to anticipate, absorb, recover from, and adapt to disruptive events while maintaining continuity of operations.

Sustainable Supply Chain: A supply chain that integrates economic viability, environmental stewardship, and social responsibility across its operations and network partners.

Chapter 10

Policy, Governance, and Global Collaboration for Data-Driven Sustainable Supply Chains: A Study on the Least Developed Countries

Mostofa Tanjil Ahmed
http://orcid.org/0009-0006-1535-5340
Army Institute of Business Administration, Bangladesh University of Professionals, Bangladesh

Nafisa Tasnuva
http://orcid.org/0009-0001-0602-595X
Army Institute of Business Administration, Bangladesh University of Professionals, Bangladesh

Md. Rahat Khan
http://orcid.org/0000-0002-9197-0365
Army Institute of Business Administration, Bangladesh University of Professionals, Bangladesh

ABSTRACT

The study aimed to review and develop a policy framework for data-driven, sustainable supply chain governance and global collaboration in LDCs. The study was based on secondary data and an exploratory design based on general case studies of Bangladesh, Rwanda, Uganda, Nepal, Ghana, Cambodia, and Bhutan. The findings reveal that infrastructure deficits, institutional failure, technical power

DOI: 10.4018/979-8-3373-6896-2.ch010

shortfalls, and political and administrative gaps hinder transformation despite hopeful changes. The study adopts a seven-step integrated policy approach to create digital infrastructure, data governance frameworks, analytics functionality, traceability frameworks, adaptive governance functions, multi-stakeholder cooperation, and inclusive socio-economic outcomes. The study provides a theoretical framework for sustainable supply chain digitization in a resource-scarce context and offers practical guidance for policymakers, practitioners, and international development organizations.

INTRODUCTION

The introduction of a global trend in using data as a means of designing sustainable supply chains has fundamentally changed the way business is now conducted, how it competes, and how businesses generate value in the new international business environment (World Bank, 2024). The use of the assisted technologies of artificial intelligence, blockchain, Internet of Things (IoT), and big data analytics allowed supply chain participants to increase transparency, resource distribution, and environmental and social performance on multilateral networks (UNCTAD, 2023). The adoption of data-driven technologies into the supply chain management systems is a strategic necessity in developed economies, which has allowed real-time monitoring, predictive analytics, and evidence-based decision-making that simultaneously help to achieve the goals of operational efficiency and sustainability (OECD, 2024). Nevertheless, the process of implementing and using data-driven sustainable supply chains in least developed countries (LDCs) is quite limited by the complex issues associated with the policy frameworks, the system of governance, technical infrastructure, and the multilateral collaboration schemes (Khan & Pervin, 2024). Supply chain sustainability in LDCs is not just a business issue but is a key factor that defines economic growth, social inclusion, and environmental sustainability. These nations are exposed to unique threats such as poor digital infrastructure (low levels of broadband connectivity, unreliable power supply), low institutional capacity to regulate data, thousands of regulatory infrastructures on data protection and privacy, low availability of advanced technologies, and limited budget to invest in digital transformation (World Bank, 2023). In addition, the available literature shows that the success of data-driven supply chain projects in developing countries also depends largely on the standard of governance institutions, policy environment consistency, and the level of international cooperation and knowledge transfer mechanisms (Hendricks & Mwapwele, 2024).

Nevertheless, there is an increasing body of evidence that data-driven methods of supply chain management bring significant prospects of value addition and sustainable growth in LDCs. They can improve the visibility of the supply chain (especially of agricultural and extractive products), they can decrease the information asymmetries between the international purchasers and local producers, they can enhance the adherence to international sustainability regulations, they can provide entry into international markets, and they can make it easier to monitor environmental and social effects all the way up the value chain. However, to implement successfully, context-sensitive methods must be adopted wherein local institutional realities, cultural concerns, capacity limitations, and a sense of responsible inclusion into digital transformation, which does not build up the already existing inequalities, are taken into consideration (UNCTAD, 2024). Policy frameworks and governance systems have a significant role to play in facilitating or limiting the implementation of data-driven sustainable supply chains in LDCs. Good policies should cover various aspects such as building digital infrastructure, data sovereignty and protection, building technical capacity, incentives to invest, and also harmonization of regulations to international standards. Moreover, global supply chains are also transnational, which requires a well-developed international collaboration system that will facilitate the transfer of technology, knowledge, financial assistance, and harmonization of sustainability standards between various regulatory jurisdictions (International Trade Centre, 2023). Global cooperation is especially important in the case of LDCs because such nations frequently do not have the resources, experience, and institutional capabilities to develop and deploy complex data-based supply chain systems on their own.

The policy, government, or international partnering of the data-driven sustainable supply chain has little academic attention, especially in LDCs, where institutional settings are significantly distinct than developed economies. Although much has been done to study either the adoption of technologies in supply chains or the sustainability efforts in the developing nations, there is still a noteworthy gap in the knowledge on how the policy frameworks, governance, and international collaboration interact to facilitate or hinder the deployment of data-driven sustainable supply chains in resource-capacitated settings. The above knowledge gap is especially problematic due to the mounting pressure on LDCs to engage in sustainable global value chains and, at the same time, seek their own development goals. Thus, one can develop the following research questions:

> **RQ1.** Which sorts of policy, governance, and global collaboration for data-driven sustainable supply chains are practiced in the least developed countries (LDCs)?
>
> **RQ2.** How do policy, governance, and global collaboration help LDCs to build and embed data-driven sustainable supply chains, and what are the best mechanisms of international cooperation?

RQ3. Which types of integrated framework can be applicable to get an edge in policymakers, international bodies, and practitioners working in supply chains in LDCs to harness data-driven solutions to sustainable supply chain development?

To Address all the above research questions, the research will identify and examine the policy frameworks, governance, and institutional constraints that limit the sustainability of the supply chain in the LDCs, to explore how emerging technologies (big data analytics, blockchain, IoT, and AI) can improve the sustainability of supply chains, to learn the differences between LDC practices and international standards through comparative country analysis, and to come up with an integrated policy process model linking digital transformation to governance frameworks and international cooperation that is appropriate under resource-constrained LDC settings. The following sections will deal with the associated theories and literature on data-based supply chain management and policy governance models in the LDCs. The third part will state the research methodology in detail. The fourth and fifth sections then follow, which report the data analysis, findings and result discussion respectively. Lastly, a conclusion of the research will be presented, in terms of its theoretical contribution, its practical implications to policy makers and practitioners, research limitations, and a research direction as well

RELATED THEORIES AND LITERATURES

Data-Driven Supply Chain Theories

Modern sustainable operations rely on the data-driven supply chain to make smart, real-time decisions using analytics, AI, and digital integration. Data analytics integration has transformed supply chain management by making global networks more visible, efficient, and robust. Big data analytics is particularly disruptive since it helps organisations monitor environmental and social developments, improve coordination, and improve value chain sustainability (Bag et al., 2023). Meanwhile, research shows that information-based sustainability projects work best when suppliers and international partners collaborate. International cooperation and lead company engagement are crucial to cascading responsible practices across supply chains, especially to smaller or local suppliers (Bai et al., 2021). The interventions encourage enterprises to follow environmental standards and promote industry-government cooperation. Research shows that blockchain and digital supply chain twins can promote global openness and responsibility (Kamble et al., 2020). The rapid development of analytical tools has made the digital supply chain predictive and prescriptive. Data-driven supply chains use AI and ML models to predict demand, optimise inventories, and reduce carbon emissions through transportation planning (Bagherpasandi et al., 2025). Big data analytics can assist manufacturing organisations in developing eco-efficient production processes, improving environmental performance and resource utilisation without affecting profitability (Mageto, 2021). In emerging economies, organisations are leveraging analytics and IoT to become more competitive and sustainable with limited resources (Munir et al., 2023).

Meanwhile, big data analytics has been shown to boost organisations' dynamic capability—their ability to adapt to environmental change, technology changes, and operational processes to maintain competitive advantage. According to Shamout (2019), data-driven organisations are more adaptive and innovative, making them more resilient to supply interruptions and external shocks. The Global Competitiveness Index (GCI) improves six logistical performance factors, including customs efficiency, infrastructure, and service quality. Better governance, policy execution, and global competitiveness can enable data-driven supply chain development (Chen & Hasan, 2020). Liner Shipping Connector (LSC) and Global Competitiveness Index (GCI) predict Logistics Performance (LP) improvement through port quality and infrastructure. These findings emphasise the need for policies, governance, and international cooperation for logistics efficiency (Chen & Hasan, 2023). Research shows that demand management, the information system, and technology innovation are key to improving logistics performance (Hasan et al., 2024). Digital infrastructures built on high-level analytics tools can help organisations predict market shifts, manage supply and demand, and gain network awareness. Data-driven decision systems discover energy inefficiencies, cut emissions, and innovate production and distribution cycles.

Policy Governance and Collaboration Theories

According to technology governance philosophies, regulatory structures should evolve with digital technologies. Governments should adopt adaptable rules that enable blockchain, big data analytics, and AI without ensuring ethical and responsible data use. Digital governance and regulatory monitoring balance innovation, freedom, and sustainability compliance. Global linkages allow enterprises in the least developed nations to use shared knowledge, technology, and capacity building, which will improve supply chain resilience and sustainability. Digital data-sharing platforms have helped these partnerships promote innovation and address structural shortcomings (Dutil & Williams, 2017). Digitalisation without strong governance and institutional capabilities does not produce sustainable supply chain results. The least developed countries' lack of technology infrastructure, policy execution, and institutional capacity often prevents digital solution adoption (Hendricks &

Mwapwele, 2024) Since policy and governance combine digital tools and regulatory procedures, they help sustain the environment and society. Research shows that a country with a robust digital governance framework may better assess sustainability metrics, improve supply chain traceability, and strengthen long-term resiliency to global disruptions.

Online data-sharing practices increase transparency of supplier actions and social indicators throughout multi-tier supply chains and can reveal the tension between short-term business interests and long-term social sustainability, but smaller suppliers in the least-developed countries need a governance system that actively involves and defends against marginalization (Govindan, et al., 2021).

The absorption capacity of firms and organisational learning will determine whether digital instruments (IoT, analytics) can be turned into quantifiable sustainability benefits, as the lack of internal abilities and stakeholder interaction prevents data from being turned into environmental or social benefits (Ngo et al., 2023). Data-driven sustainable supply chain management in other sectors, such as the textile industry, will require standardised, interoperable indicators and consistent stakeholder practices. In LDCs, where ethical-buyer demands may be even more stringent, data-driven sustainable supply chain management will continue to be a problem. Various stakeholder groups pressurise, enable resources, or transfer knowledge to increase digital tool adoption, and multi-actor collaboration (public/private partnership, donor/firm initiative, industry alliance) mediates this process. However, heterogeneous motivations and power discrepancies suggest that collaborative governance is not passive. (Siems et al., 2023). When combined with network and collaboration approaches, stakeholder theory shows that stakeholders are nodes in an interdependent system and that digital platforms change salience and influence games between stakeholders. Governance design should prevent stronger players in LDC supply networks from taking information advantages from weaker counterparts (Mahajan et al., 2023).

Due to the institutionalisation of collaborative processes and trust, formal collaboration mechanisms, joint planning, shared KPIs, and data-sharing agreements improve environmental and social performance by making shared information the driving force behind coordinated decisions and joint investment, which is valuable for LDC supply chains with trust shortages and poor contracting. The emerging economy's supply chains are still being digitalised, and companies are not fully adopting Industry 4.0 technologies like IoT, big data analytics, and drones, which can improve information-sharing, traceability, waste minimisation, and partner collaboration, resulting in more sustainable supply chains (Akbari & Hopkins, 2022). Blockchain technology in developing country supply chains increases trust, transparency, and accountability by ensuring data authenticity and reducing information asymmetry by tethering collaborative networks to cryptographically verifiable data exchange and facilitating stakeholder alignment and cooperation in collaborative governance.

Further implementation of Industry 4.0 technologies (IoT, AI, remote sensing) leads to more precise sustainability indicators throughout supply chains, making interventions timely and improving traceability, but measurement alone is not an action, and institutional structures should turn data into enforceable sustainability practices (Zhao et al., 2023). Digital transformation and information systems enable lifecycle assessment, predictive analytics in waste minimisation, and automated compliance tracking, but only with interoperability standards and institutional data sharing (Stroumpoulis et al., 2024). Blockchain, Internet of Things, and machine-vision measurement tools can connect sensor-made measurements to unalterable records to improve sustainability reports and allow buyers and regulators to check sustainability across the international chain of supply, where auditing is expensive (Kshetri, 2021). Another study predicts port infrastructure quality shows Asian economy variations. This data-driven projection would help policymakers identify underperforming regions and create particular policies (Hasan et al., 2022).

Policy and Practice of Data-Driven SCM in Least Developed Countries (LDCs)

The volume of data from end-to-end supply chain management (SCM) procedures is rapidly escalating, intensifying the necessity for big data analysis. Consequently, researchers and organisations are endeavouring to cultivate big data analytics (BDA) competencies. Nonetheless, despite the increase in scholarly articles on Big Data Analytics in Supply Chain Management, some firms, particularly in Least Developed Countries, are encountering difficulties with the adoption of Big Data Analytics (Bahangulu & Owusu-Berko, 2025). Key challenges to the success of data-driven supply chain management in least developed countries include algorithmic bias, privacy and ethical concerns, and the intent to engage in digital transformation. A handful of numbers have succeeded, while others have failed to make prudent decisions (Nguyen et al., 2022). This necessitates further investigation into the pertinent themes in LDCs. Bangladesh is often used in research on manufacturing and supply chain big data analytics adoption challenges. Even though companies know analytics can improve forecasting, inventory management, and production, limited digital infrastructure, lack of technical expertise, high perceived cost, and organisational resistance slow BDA implementation in Bangladeshi supply chains. These articles recommend bridging the competencies gap, investing in data infrastructure, and encouraging industry-academic cooperation to turn analytics investments into quantifiable sustainability and performance outcomes (Moktadir et al., 2019). Uganda uses digital reporting, central dashboards, and data-use methods to improve forecasting, distribution planning, and accountability in its health system and essential-goods supply chain. Health-supply programs in Uganda show that using routine information in decision-making reduces lead-time and improves in-country logistics, but these changes require continued investment in data governance, interoperability, and human capacity development. Practitioners agree that data systems should be included in institutional fortification efforts to sustain supply-chain improvements (Lugada et al., 2022).

Logistics competence, infrastructure quality, and tracking systems are most important to efficiency, and LDCs need better policy, digital governance, and international cooperation to create sustainable and data-driven supply chains (Hasan et al., 2025). Recent Nepalese food and agricultural supply chain research shows how restricted rural logistics, fragmented data gathering, and weak cold-chain infrastructure hurt data tools. According to mid-hill food system research, digital collection (mobile reporting), local aggregating centres, and the cooperation platform can improve food flow during seasonal shocks, but policy and investment are needed to use the data systems locally and cost-effectively (Poudel & Shaw, 2024). Piloan experiments and case studies in Rwanda demonstrate how IoT and simple digital monitoring systems may improve health and agricultural logistics supply-chain visibility with training and governance. Smaller-scale IoT applications show fewer stockouts and improved commodity distribution, but success depends on a stable connection, local technical resources, and long-term institutional support to expand pilots to national levels.

Ghana's agricultural value chains research suggests blockchain and big data pilot projects could improve traceability, access to small-holder finance, and export compliance, but field research has found cost, interoperability, and governance issues to scale. Blended interventions (technical pilots, regulatory guidelines, cooperative capacity building) are proposed to give small producers traceability and finance innovations without the complexity or cost (Mohammed et al, 2024). Research shows that hyperautomation will build data-driven governance and sustainability in supply chains beyond efficiency. Due to infrastructural, policy, and capacity restrictions, LDCs rarely apply it. Thus, regulatory intervention, governance norms, and international cooperation are needed to turn hyperautomation into inclusive and sustainable industry growth in LDCs (Hasan et al., 2026) Big data analytics and green supply-chain efforts in Bangladeshi manufacturing cannot achieve sustainability benefits alone. Clear green SCM practices and organisational willingness to convert data insights into less waste, improved resource allocation, and quantifiable environmental performance are needed.

Recent case studies in Bangladesh's ready-made garments (RMG) industry show that ERP, IoT, and other digital tools can reduce lead times, inventory accuracy, and supplier coordination when used with process re-engineering and employee training. E-commerce and online entrepreneurship in Bhutan show that SMEs and cottage industries can export more if logistical and payment-gateway barriers are removed (Shrivastava et al., 2024). Policy and practitioner reports on digital supply-chain pilots in Bangladesh recommend blended interventions like technical pilots, capacity building, and fintech-integration to make payments and finance data to small producers and micro-enterprises, regardless of cost or complexity (Emon & Khan, 2025). Recent studies on integrating blockchain and machine-learning into Rwanda's supply chain have found that permanent records, prediction, traceability, lendability to small suppliers, and logistics efficiency can improve. However, field research has cautioned that cost, lack of competency, and regulatory uncertainty prevent rapid adoption (Ndemo, 2025)

Stakeholder and collaborative governance studies in Rwandan health supply chains indicated that data-driven systems require coordinated government, donor, technology, and local health actor relationships. These studies show that robust multi-stakeholder frameworks help embed data use in corporate practises, ease capacity transfer, and provide institutional support for long-term performance advantages (Tuyishime & Adewusi, 2025). Green public procurement (GPP) evaluation in Bhutan shows that limited supply-chain openness, data systems, and institutional coordination hinder sustainable purchasing practices. Bhutan may achieve its sustainable-procurement goals through operational supply-chain reforms by building integrated digital procurement systems, data interoperability, and regulatory frameworks (Suberi, 2022). Research on Ugandan health supply chains reveals how digital inventory and logistics information has improved responsiveness and decision-making. An examination of emergency logistics in Uganda during the COVID-19 pandemic found that web-based electronic logistics management information systems (eLMIS) enabled real-time monitoring of the flow of commodities from national warehouses to district premises, which sped up order processing and improved resource allocation, despite implementation challenges.

A study that ranked Nepal's industrial readiness for Industry 4.0 found that while interest in cyber-physical systems, IoT, and big-data analytics in manufacturing is growing, firms lack skilled workforce, weak leadership, inappropriate governance mechanisms, and poor technology infrastructure (Rajbhandari et al., 2022). A study of small and medium-sized businesses in Ghana found that supply chain intelligence—the ability to gather and use supply-chain data to make a decision—can positively impact operational performance, but only if supply chains collaborate well. Without networked partnerships and information sharing, data capabilities are insufficient. Digital technologies improve supply chain capabilities and performance in Bangladesh's manufacturing sector. For example, a study on the ready-made garments industry found that companies that have adopted digital supply-chain systems have improved visibility, coordination, and transparency (Hosain, 2025).

METHODOLOGY

The study is qualitative research, which is based on the theoretical notions and supported by the detailed secondary data analysis (published journal articles, reports, official websites, newspapers, blogs, etc.) (Khan & Sarkar, 2024; Khan et al., 2025).

Study Design

The paper aimed to examine the extent to which policy frameworks, governance systems, and mechanisms of global collaboration determine the adoption of data-driven sustainable supply chains by the least developed countries (LDCs). The study is designed as exploratory in nature, with the administration of secondary data sources. The overall summary of the study design is presented in Figure 1.

Data Collection Procedure

Data collection was conducted judgmentally with the help of secondary sources such as peer-reviewed academic articles, institutional reports (UNCTAD, 2023; OECD, 2024; World Bank, 2024; ITC, 2023), policy-making documents, and country-specific cases. The sources are chosen in such a way that they capture both the theoretical approach and the real-world experience, which informs data-driven sustainable development of the supply chains in LDCs. Table 1 discusses the information concerning the sources of data.

Table 1. Data Sources

Source Type	Countries/Regions Covered	Number of Documents	Sources
Institutional Reports	LDCs (general, cross-country focus)	12	UNCTAD (2022-2023); OECD (2024); World Bank (2023-2025); and others
Academic Journal Articles	Bangladesh, Indonesia, Ghana, Rwanda, Uganda, Nepal,	40+	Available in Reference List
Country Case Examples	Bangladesh, Rwanda, Uganda, Nepal, Ghana, Bhutan, Latvia	16	Moktadir et al. (2019); Lugada et al. (2022); Poudel (2024); Nkezabera & Dinesh, (2025); Mohammed et al. (2024); and others
Policy & Development Documents	General LDCs, Sub-Saharan Africa, South Asia	20	UNCTAD (2023-2024); OECD (2024); World Bank (2023-2024); ITC (2023); and others

Source: Created by Authors

Data Analyzing Techniques

The collected data was refined and filtered manually based on the aim of the research. The content analysis revealed themes that were shared by several reports (e.g., barriers such as infrastructure deficits, governance weaknesses, capacity constraints), opportunities (e.g., mobile-first strategies, blockchain traceability, IoT integration), strategic lever (e.g., policy coherence, multi-stakeholder collaboration, adaptive governance). Besides, framework mapping has been used to structure these insights into a logical process model that is both conceptually easy to understand as well as to be applied practically.

Figure 1. Research Design Flowchart

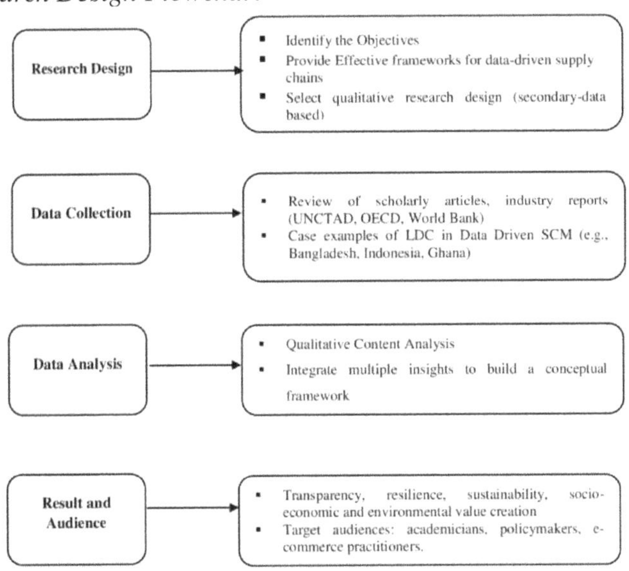

Source: Created by Authors

DATA ANALYSIS AND FINDINGS

The current section provides the key findings on the data-driven sustainable supply chain in Least Developed Countries (LDCs) in terms of a thorough analysis of secondary data gathered in the form of institutional reports, academic journal articles, policy documents, and country-specific case studies. The discussion demonstrates a series of interacting issues that determine the adoption, implementation, and efficacy of data-driven technologies in attaining the sustainability of supply chains in LDCs.

Content Analysis and Generating Themes

Instead of depending on "sense" and "impressions," as some qualitative methods propose, researchers may employ a comprehensive evaluation of the logical prerequisites of analogous characteristics. The word cloud (see Figure 2) emerged as the most advantageous feature for illustrating the relative importance of various elements in Policy, Governance, and Global Collaboration for Data-Driven Sustainable Supply Chains for LDCs (Khan & Arif, 2025).

Figure 2. Word Cloud Analysis

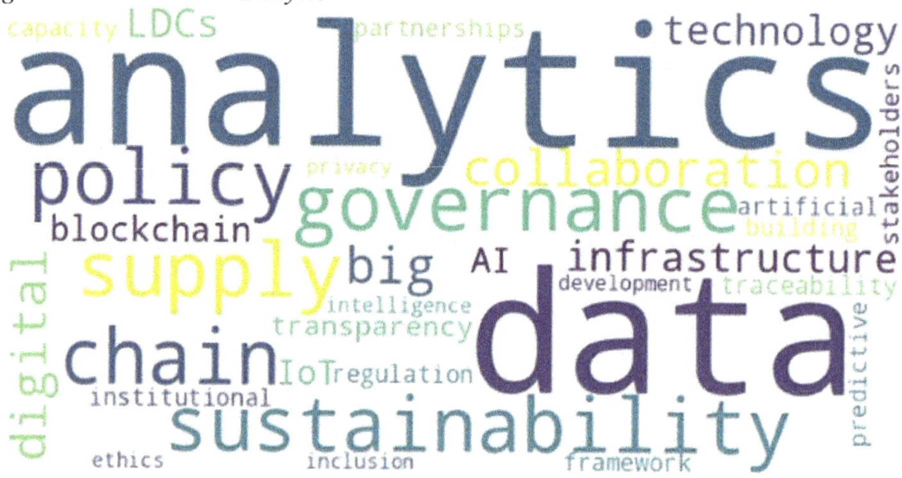

Source: Created by Authors

The altered and recorded data are integrated into a Word file. This will facilitate the manual analysis of word frequency and codification, along with the data arrangement. The findings are presented in Figure 3.

Figure 3. Word Frequency Analysis with Consolidated Themes

Consolidated Themes	Word Counts	% of Total Words
• Digital Infrastructure & Connectivity	280	9%
• Big Data Analytics Adoption & Capabilities	290	9%
• IoT & Sensor Technologies	150	5%
• Blockchain & Traceability	160	5%
• Predictive Analytics & AI	180	6%
• Data Governance & Institutional Frameworks	220	7%
• Stakeholder Cooperation & Multi-Actor Partnerships	210	7%
• Sector-Specific Applications & Case Studies	250	8%
• Regulatory Support & Policy Interventions	220	7%
• Economic & Social Value Creation	180	6%
• Barriers & Challenges Synthesis	280	9%
• Enabling Factors & Success Conditions	260	8%

Source: Created by Authors

Table 2. Summary of the Consolidated Themes and their Outcomes

Analytical Dimension	Key Technologies / Mechanisms	Core Insights from LDC Context	Policy & Governance Implications	Sustainability Outcomes
Digital Infrastructure & Connectivity	■ Broadband ■ Mobile networks ■ Electricity ■ Cloud platforms	Low internet penetration and unstable power remain foundational constraints; mobile-first models partially bridge access gaps.	Public investment in digital infrastructure; incentives for affordable data and energy access	Enables baseline digital participation and inclusion
Big Data Analytics Adoption & Capabilities	■ ERP Software ■ Predictive analytics ■ Dashboards	Analytics adoption is limited by skills gaps, ROI uncertainty, and organizational resistance.	Capacity-building policies and industry–academic partnerships are required	Improves forecasting, inventory control, and resource efficiency
IoT & Sensor Technologies	■ Sensors ■ RFID ■ Real-time tracking	Infrastructure instability and high costs limit large-scale deployment; targeted use cases show high value.	Subsidized pilots and standards for interoperability	Enhances emissions tracking, waste reduction, and transparency

continued on following page

Table 2. Continued

Analytical Dimension	Key Technologies / Mechanisms	Core Insights from LDC Context	Policy & Governance Implications	Sustainability Outcomes
Blockchain & Traceability	■ Distributed ledgers ■ Smart contracts	Improves trust and compliance but faces cost, scalability, and governance challenges	Regulatory sandboxes and cross-border data standards are needed	Strengthens ethical sourcing and market access
Predictive Analytics & AI	■ Machine learning ■ Demand forecasting ■ Optimization models	Data quality and a lack of skilled personnel constrain advanced AI use	Investment in data governance and technical education	Reduces emissions, improves resilience, and operational efficiency
Data Governance & Institutional Frameworks	■ Data standards ■ Privacy laws ■ Interoperability frameworks	Weak enforcement and fragmented governance reduce analytics effectiveness	Adaptive regulatory frameworks and multi-agency coordination	Ensures ethical, reliable, and scalable data use
Stakeholder Cooperation & Multi-Actor Partnerships	■ Data-sharing platforms ■ Public–Private Partnerships	Trust deficits and power asymmetries limit collaboration effectiveness	Inclusive governance mechanisms and fair data-sharing rules	Promotes equitable value distribution
Sector-Specific Applications & Case Studies	■ ERP in business ■ E-health systems ■ Agri-tech platforms	Sectoral outcomes depend on local infrastructure and institutional readiness.	Context-sensitive policy support and pilot scaling	Improves sector resilience and sustainability
Regulatory Support & Policy Interventions	■ Digital Act ■ Procurement policies and sustainability policies	Policy impact depends on implementation capacity and stakeholder engagement.	Iterative, participatory policy-making approaches	Accelerates sustainable digital transformation
Economic & Social Value Creation	■ E-commerce ■ Mobile payments ■ Apps digital platforms	Risk of digital divide if inclusion is not prioritized	Pro-poor digital policies and SME support programs	Job creation, financial inclusion, social equity

**Note: ERP = Enterprise Resource Planning; RFID = Radio-frequency identification; AI = Artificial intelligence; ROI = Return on Investment

Source: Created by Authors

Thematic Analysis from the Generalized Consolidated Themes

- **Digital Infrastructure and Connectivity**: Analysis shows that LDCs' digital infrastructure is one of the biggest barriers to data-driven sustainable supply chains. LDCs have 36 percent internet penetration, compared to 80 percent or greater in wealthier nations (UNCTAD, 2023). Big data analytics, IoT sensors, and blockchain-based traceability solutions are hindered by this digital divide. In Bangladesh, manufacturing companies see big data analytics as an opportunity to improve forecasting, inventory control, and manufacturing efficiency, but current barriers, such as limited digital penetration, technical expertise, cost perceptions, and organizational resistance, slow implementation (Moktadir et al., 2019). Developing capability disjunctures, investing in data infrastructure, and forming industry-academic relationships are crucial to turning analytics efforts into verifiable sustainability benefits. Some LDCs are more digitally prepared than others. Rwanda has used its high smartphone penetration to develop mobile commerce and digital supply chain resolutions, but ineffective infrastructure, bandwidth constraints, and inefficient dispute resolution mechanisms continue to limit expansion (UNCTAD, 2024). The data-driven solutions implemented in Uganda's national health system show that the digital environment can complement forecasting, distribution planning, and accountability, but long-term results require further investment in data governance, interoperability, and human capacity (Lugada et al., 2022). Technology preparedness involves an entire ecosystem of skills, governance structures, and support systems, not just hardware and connections. Mobile-first is a promising way to overcome LDC infrastructure limitations. Mobile money services like bKash in Bangladesh and M-Pesa in East Africa have helped more people become financially included and enabled digital business in places where formal bank adoption has not yet been beneficial (World Bank, 2023). Mobile solutions also lower entrance barriers for unbanked people to digital marketplaces and supply chain systems (OECD, 2024). However, cellphone connection is not enough; steady electricity, a low-cost data plan, and digital literacy are also needed.

- **Big Data Analytics Adoption and Capabilities:** Big data analytics gives LDCs a revolutionary possibility to increase supply chain transparency, efficiency, and sustainability. Researchers found that big data analytics helps organizations track environmental and social transformation, improve coordination, and sustainable value chains (Bag et al., 2023). Analytics enable end-to-end supply chain insight, predictive decision-making, and resource efficiency for environmental and economic sustainability. Despite limited resources, data-driven supply chains are more accommodating and resilient and can easily reorganize structure in response to environmental or market changes, resulting in better sustainability performance (Dubey et al., 2019). However, there are some problems in substantial LDC implementation. For example, the Bangladeshi ready-made garments business recognizes the value of analytics, but lack of technical skills, ROI anxiety, and organisational reluctance limit implementation (Moktadir et al., 2019). The observed documents emphasize that analytics potential alone cannot bring sustainability to operations unless it is supported by organizational commitment to green supply chain management and green supply chain initiatives. In addition to technology infrastructure, data capability depends on organizational learning, absorptive capacity, and strategy alignment to sustainability goals.

- **IoT and Sensor Technologies:** To get operational efficiency, IoT has sustainability benefits. IoT sensors continuously scan the environment to quantify carbon emissions, water, energy, and waste creation at each supply chain stage, providing granular data for sustainability reporting and improvement (Kamble et al., 2020). Web-based electronic logistics management information systems in Uganda's health supply chains allowed real-time monitoring of commodity flow between country warehouses and district facilities, speeding up order processing and resource distribution during the COVID-19 pandemic, but rural areas were difficult to implement (Wasswa et al., 2023). LDCs face distinct infrastructural stability, technical capacity, and economic concerns while implementing IoT. Many rural and remote areas lack reliable electricity and internet, making IoT installation difficult. Another challenge for resource-limited organisations is the initial cost of sensors, data transmission systems, and analytic platforms (Rajbhandari et al., 2022). However, limited deployment of ultra-high priority IoT applications, such as a cold-chain tracker for perishable goods or extreme medical stores, can provide value when built for local limits.
- **Blockchain and Traceability:** The generalized theme establish that blockchain-based applications enhance the quality of real-time data capturing, validation, and product integrity, and prevent unethical practices in global sourcing (Kshetri, 2021). Blockchain enables stakeholder alignment and cooperation by building collaborative governance structures, especially in situations where institutional capacity is insufficient, through the generation of cryptographically verifiable data exchanges. Such an initiative will not only contribute to the improvement in transparency and the maintenance of a fair pricing system but also strengthen the system of governance in the form of joint engagement of governmental bodies, representatives of the business sector, non-governmental organizations, and the local population. On the same note, for instance agricultural value chain in Ghana suggests that blockchain and big data pilot projects have the potential to enhance traceability, enhancing access to finance among small-holders, and expediency export compliance, but the formidable cost, interoperability, and governance issues to scale these interventions (Mohammed et al, 2024). The sustainability advantages of blockchain can be not only traceability but also a larger ethical

and environmental aspect. Blockchain can be used to enable LDC producers to prove compliance with the global sustainability standards, in terms of sourcing, labor, and environment, which could subsequently enhance their market access and price premiums (Zhao et al., 2023). The model of using blockchain in combination with other technologies, including IoT sensors and machine vision measurement tools, can lead to an increase in the integrity of the sustainability report since sensor-generated measurements can be linked to immutable records to allow buyers and regulators to monitor their sustainability compliance in international supply chains where traditional auditing can be costly or impractical (Kshetri, 2021).

- **Predictive Analytics and AI:** The development of artificial intelligence and machine learning applications has moved the field of data-driven supply chain management to predictive and prescriptive applications. Artificial intelligence applications can help companies predict demand, optimize stock levels, and lower the amount of carbon dioxide due to better transportation planning (Chalmeta & Santos-deLeón, 2020). In the manufacturing setting, AI enhanced by the use of big data can organize eco-friendly manufacturing, which would lead to an improvement in environmental outcomes and a reduction in resource use without reducing profitability (Mageto, 2021). The utilization of digital innovations is growing in the economies of the third world as entities are resorting to analytics and AI to achieve competitive advantage and benefits in sustainability despite the lack of resources (Munir et al., 2023). However, there are also certain peculiar barriers to the implementation of AI on LDCs related to the quality, availability, and technical expertise of data. Effective machine learning models require a large amount of historical data to train and this may not be consistently available or consistent throughout most LDC supply chains. There is no access to AI specialists and data scientists, which restricts the ability of firms to develop, deploy, and maintain sophisticated systems of analysis (Rajbhandari et al., 2022). Despite the obstacles, the analysis implies that even comparatively straightforward AI applications, demand forecasting tools, automated anomaly detection systems, etc., could be used to create an impressive amount of value when designed in accordance with the local contexts and limitations.
- **Data Governance and Institutional Frameworks:** Data governance helps LDCs build data-driven supply chains. The study repeatedly states that digitalizing supply chains without a viable governance framework and institutional capacity cannot achieve lasting results (Sodhi & Tang, 2024). In least developed nations, insufficient technology infrastructure, policy execution, and institutional potential hinder digital solution adoption (Hendricks & Mwapwele, 2024). Digital preparation, governance frameworks, and human

resource capability for data-enabled sustainability practices require institutional support and policy frameworks (Mousavi et al., 2008). By researching e-government and public procurement policies, researchers found that such procedures improve LDC supply chain sustainability. Accountability, transparency, and ethical shopping increase third-world environmental and social performance (Adjei-Bamfo et al., 2021). In Uganda, multi-stakeholder arrangements have helped institutionalize data use, transfer capacity, and drive lasting performance gains through coordinated partnerships of government agencies, donors, technology providers, and other local health actors (Tuyishime & Adewusi, 2025). Technological governance theories focus on regulatory frameworks that evolve alongside digital technology. States must create dynamic blockchain, big data analytics, and artificial intelligence rules to enable ethical and responsible data use (Chauhan et al., 2023). Control systems that balance digital innovation and government control balance innovation and sustainability. These governance models strengthen supply chains, which help states achieve sustainable development goals through strategic technology and intersectoral policies. LDCs' data governance issues include data quality, standards, and interoperability, not only regulation. Lack of common information among supply chain partners hinders integration and in-depth analytics (Govindan et al., 2021).

- **Stakeholder Cooperation and Multi-Actor Partnerships:** Formal collaboration systems, such as joint planning, shared key performance indicators, and data-sharing agreements, are associated with better environmental and social performance based on institutionalized collaborative processes and trust-building (Chauhan et al., 2022). In the case of coordinated decisions and joint investments made through the information shared, particularly valuable results can be observed in LDC supply chains with a lack of trust and weak contracting institutions. In the field of SME businesses in Ghana found that supply chain intelligence the aptitude to accumulate and use supply chain data to make business choices gives robust beneficial effects on the operational performance with impacts intensified in the case of a strong collaboration strength of the supply chain, which implies that data capabilities absent a networked connection and information exchange are inadequate (Dza & Atsu, 2024). The collaboration between the stakeholders in LDCs is marked by unique issues of power inequality, opposing interests, and trust deficiencies. Such online data-sharing practices may contribute to transparency in multi-tier supply chains on supplier activity and social indicators, which may result in tensions between short-term business interests and long-term social sustainability (Govindan, et al., 2021). Nonetheless, to allow the smaller suppliers in the least developed countries to occupy equal status, there should be governance mechanisms that actively incorporate the various stakeholders and guard against marginalization. The complementary roles of different groups of stakeholders, such as coercion to change, facilitation of resources, and transfer of knowledge, imply that the multi-actor collaboration based on public-private partnerships, donor-firm, and industry alliance mediates the successful digital tool adoption, whereas the heterogeneous motivations and unequal power distribution imply that collaborative governance should proactively address tradeoffs to realize the beneficial impact of inclusive sustainability (Siems et al., 2023).

- **Applications and Case Studies Sector-Specific:** The comparison highlights data-driven sustainability trends in different sectors and countries, revealing context-specific facilitators and barriers. Based on Bangladeshi ready-made garments case studies, ERP systems, IoT sensors, and other digital tools can reduce lead times, improve inventory accuracy, and improve supplier coordination when combined with process re-engineering and employee training. Digital technologies have improved supply chain capabilities and performance, and companies with digital supply chain systems have higher visibility, coordination, and transparency (Hosain, 2025). For example, Nepal's food and agricultural supply chains demonstrate that rural logistics, fragmented data capture, and poor cold-chain infrastructure limit data tools' effectiveness. Middle-hill food systems show that mobile reporting, local aggregating centres, and cooperation platforms can help food flow resiliency during seasonal shocks, but policy support and investment are needed to make the data systems cost-effective and locally relevant (Poudel & Shaw, 2024). In Ghanaian agricultural value chain research for another instance, using local languages and culture in digital platforms improved customer engagement and value creation, leading to satisfaction. Health supply chains can provide fascinating data-driven solutions in LDCs. In the case of Uganda's inventory and logistics management has improved reactiveness and decision-making with digital information systems. Electronic logistics management information systems offer real-time commodity flow monitoring, which speeds up order processing and improves resource distribution, but rural implementation is difficult (Wasswa et al., 2023). Rwanda's health supply chains explain that coordinated relationships between government, donors, technology providers, and local health actors maintain data-driven systems, and multi-stakeholder arrangements embed data use into routine operations and provide institutional support (Tuyishime & Adewusi, 2025). Data-driven strategies may also work in e-commerce and digital entrepreneurship. The study of online entrepreneurship in Bhutan found that digital markets, mobile payment options, and specific training can help SME and cottage industries export their products after logistics and payment gateway issues are resolved (Shrivastava et al., 2024). According to research on SME e-commerce adoption in Bangladesh, digital platforms and tools can simplify the supplier network and reduce transaction frictions, but poor ICT infrastructure, low digital skills, and asymmetric data quality prevent analytics-based improvement (Abtahi et al., 2023).

- **Regulatory Support and Policy Interventions:** LDC data-driven sustainability transition requires policy actions. Technology-based programmes and adaptive governance systems have enabled emerging economy companies survive the COVID-19 pandemic and minimise supply chain interruptions (Nakpodia et al., 2024). Crisis resilience backed by digital technology policy shows how governments may help supply chains become flexible and sustainable. Several policy mechanisms stand out. First, the strategy to stimulate investment in digital infrastructure like internet access, electrical reliability, and mobile network coverage lays the stage for data-driven approaches. Second, information policies that safeguard privacy, security, cybersecurity, and consumers generate confidence needed to use digital technologies and share data. Third, digital literacy and technical education policies build digital transformation-ready human capital. Fourth, procurement and transparency policies that prioritize sustainability and openness require data-driven initiatives to demonstrate environmental and social performance. The study reveals that policy efficacy depends on implementation capacity and stakeholder involvement. When implementation mechanisms are poor, enforcement is uneven, or parties are unable or unaware of compliance, even well-crafted policies cannot achieve their goals. Iterative interventions into the best regulatory structures, bottom-up stakeholder participation, pilot projects, and active learning and evolution through implementation are typical of LDC policy processes. For example, in Bhutan, green public procurement reviews note that sustainable purchasing policies are often difficult to implement due to a lack of transparency in the supply chain, inadequate data systems, and a lack of institutional coordination, and that developing integrated digital procurement systems, which would provide data interoperability, and enhancing regulatory mechanisms could help achieve sustainable procurement.
- **Economic and Social Value Creation**: The operational and environmental benefits reveal that data-driven sustainable supply chains generate a high level of economic and social value in the LDCs. The growth of e-commerce opens up new jobs in the logistics sector, empowers women and rural entrepreneurs, and promotes financial inclusion by adopting mobile money (UNCTAD, 2023). SMEs and platforms in rural areas and local artisans find new markets and generate inclusive value among marginalized groups. Digital supply chain systems make micro-entrepreneurship possible, which

offers income-generating prospects to groups never involved in the formal economic activity. Nevertheless, as it was also evaluated, there are threats that, unless carefully designed and managed, data-driven systems can only worsen the status quo. The more resourceful, technically advanced, and digitally literate an organization is, the higher its likelihood will be to reap disproportionate benefits of digital transformation, and the more powerless resource-constrained actors can be expected to be. The presence of power gaps in the relationships within a supply chain could be accelerated in case dominant buyers could utilize data access and analytical skills to gain more value out of suppliers without mutual value sharing. These risks can only be addressed through deliberate governance strategies that focus on the inclusion of people, capacity building of the disadvantaged groups, and systems that guarantee fair value-sharing among supply chain networks.

Barriers and Opportunities Synthesis

Integrating the foregoing analytical elements, the analysis finds several broad challenges to using data to support sustainable supply chain growth in LDCs. Infrastructure issues, including weak internet connectivity, inconsistent electricity, bad transportation, and poorly designed logistics systems affect all digital technology applications. Money prevents firms from investing in digital systems, and the unpredictability of the investment's effect makes it hard to justify, especially in small businesses with low resources. technological capacity limitation affects workers' digital literacy from organizational analytical capacities to national technological competence. Lack of data scientists, IT experts, and sustainability professionals hinders data-driven system deployment and administration. Institutional and governance deficiencies, include insufficient rule of law, enforcement mechanisms, inter-agency collaboration, and regulatory frameworks make digital transformation difficult. Culture and conduct also create hurdles. The unwillingness to change, lack of trust in digital solutions, predisposition toward old company culture, and lack of digital technology awareness slow progress. Technical constraints arise from data quality and standards, where inconsistent data gathering procedures, incompatible systems, and limited interoperability hinder analytical work and collaboration with other organizations. Last, sustainability knowledge and prioritizing limits mean that digital capabilities may not be used for environmental and social goals even without incentives, pressure, or cultural commitment to sustainability ideals. Enabling factors and success conditions are listed below.

The analysis also found important enabling variables and success requirements for data-based sustainable development of LDC supply chains despite major hurdles. The next generation of mobile technology makes digital platforms accessible even in areas with poor fixed infrastructure and skips traditional technology development patterns. Growing digital skills in younger generations increases digital transformation ability. Growing sustainability consciousness due to global standards, customer demands, and regulatory constraints drives firms toward data-driven environmental and social policies. Global relationships and developmental aid provide resources, skills, and technical help to create capacity and adopt technologies. Industry alliances and collaborative networks promote knowledge sharing, standardization, and collective problem-solving. Sustainable Development Goals and digital transformation policies create enabling structures and resource allocation. Local entrepreneurial companies and social enterprises solve LDC-specific problems with culturally relevant digital solutions. Technological interventions are crucial to data-based sustainability initiatives in LDCs with complementary organizational, institutional, and capacity-building strategies, according to the study. Combinations of technical pilot-based, regulatory-based, stakeholder-focused, and capability-oriented solutions work better than technology ones. Implementation strategies that allow learning, modification, and refining based on experience outperform rigid plans. Participation of affected stakeholders in design and implementation decisions improves intervention relevance, appropriateness, and sustainability.

DISCUSSION

As the analysis shows, Least Developed Countries (LDCs) have understood the transformational potential of data-driven sustainable supply chains; however, structural constraints (both in infrastructure, governance, and collaboration) greatly hinder it. In the discussion below, the major findings are presented in a series of action steps regarding LDCs' Policy, Governance, and Global Collaboration for Data-Driven Sustainable Supply Chains (See Figure 4 and Table 2).

Step 1: Empowering Digital infrastructure and technological preparedness

LDCs experience an endemic lack of digital infrastructure, with internet penetration of only 36 years on average and way below developed economies. Poor connectivity to broadband, unreliable electricity, and a lack of technical capacity hinders the implementation of IoT, big data analytics, and blockchain technologies (Moktadir et al., 2019). The policymakers need to embrace the mobile-first and data-ready infrastructure approach. These include putting mobile broadband investment first, forming public-private alliances of digital infrastructure, and subsidizing rural data access. Governments ought to consider digital infrastructure as a national sustainable development plan and liaise with donors to invest in low-cost connectivity and data centres. These measures are beneficial as they not only increase the level of economic competitiveness but also social inclusion since local companies can engage in global digital supply chains.

Step 2: Development of Data Governance and Institutional Capability

The ineffectiveness of digital transformation is attributed to a weak governance structure, a lack of data standardization, and a lack of interoperable systems. Researchers underline that the lack of institutional governance leads to no sustainable results of digitalization (Sodhi & Tang, 2024). Governments ought to come up with measures in the form of national data governance frameworks that establish the standards of ownership, privacy, and interoperability in accordance with international norms. A consistent supervision of the ethical use and compliance with sustainability can be achieved by the creation of data councils or digital regulatory authorities. The capacity-building in the form of training civil servants, introducing e-government practices, and incorporating open data systems will help to enhance accountability and conduct more efficient monitoring of the sustainability indicators.

Step 3: Speeding up the Data analytics and AI adoption to make decisions

The use of big data analytics and AI applications is transformative, but there is a deficiency in their utilization because of gaps in capabilities, high prices, and technical expertise (Dubey et al., 2019). In LDCs, frequently, there is no absorptive capacity between firms and analytics to convert the analytics into sustainability results despite the presence of data (Prangan et al., 2025). The policymakers must encourage collaborative innovation centers between the universities and the privately established companies, and the government to work together. The local companies can use tax benefits and grants to adopt analytics and AI-based green innovations and incorporate predictive instruments to manage resources and risk. Analytics training programs could be funded by the national development banks to ensure that the sustainability data is part of the decision-making process.

Step 4: Connecting IoT and Blockchain Traceability and Transparency

IoT and blockchain innovations enhance traceability, yet connectivity gaps, high cost of implementation, and interoperability issues prevent their use. Pilot programs, conducted in Cambodia, Ghana, and Rwanda, prove that there is a high potential for improving transparency and fair-trade practices, but note that scalability is a challenge (Ndemo, 2025; Mohammed et a;, 2024). One of the recommendations that governments can make is to establish Digital Traceability Sandboxes that can be used to drive the integration of IoT and blockchain in priority sectors (agriculture, textiles, and health supply chains). To certify sustainable sourcing, International donors and lead firms can co-fund blockchain certification systems. Data silos will be minimized with the harmonization of blockchain standards in regions led by organizations like UNCTAD and ICT. This system of multi-level governance improves trust, reduces corruption, and makes it easy to comply with international standards of sustainable governance.

Step 5: Coherence and Adaptive Governance of Policies

Disjointed and old-fashioned policies have made the integration of technology slow. The governance structures of most LDCs are only reactive and not adaptive in how they combine digital innovation with sustainability goals (Govindan, et al., 2021). Implement dynamic policy modalities that keep up with advancements in technology. This entails frequent reviews of policy, consultation of stakeholders, and incorporation of sustainability impact assessment in every digital legislation. Governments ought to entail cross-sectoral administrative styles, in which ministries of ICT, environment, and commerce plan digital sustainability agendas. Adaptive governance creates agility in the institution and ensures that the new technology is innovative and ethical.

Step 6: Enhancing Global Cooperation and Multi-Actor Alliance

LDCs depend on transnational cooperation in terms of knowledge, financing, and the transfer of technology. Nevertheless, weak networks and power asymmetries, as well as low levels of trust, diminish the efficiency of partnerships (Siems et al., 2023). Establish institutionalized multi-stakeholder forums through which governments, donors, lead firms, and local SMEs are united. These are supposed to be run within open data-sharing criteria and common sustainability indicators. Peer learning between LDCs can be promoted by formalized systems of South-South cooperation. In addition, inclusive transfer of benefits and capacity by the donor firm models are supported by donor firm-firm partnership models that support funding and transfer to sustainability KPIs.

Step 7: Inclusion and Sustainability Socio-Economic Outcomes

The advantage of the digital supply chains should result in inclusive development results. Experience in Bangladesh, Rwanda, and Uganda indicates that in case digital transformation is in line with local empowerment and environmental objectives, long-term sustainability is attained (Lugada et al., 2022). There should be policies of inclusive digital participation where women, the young, and small-holder producers get access to data-driven supply chain opportunities. Governments could offer capacity-building grants for digital literacy and sustainability certification. Incorporation of social goals like fair trade, equitable financing, and rural inclusion as part of the digital strategies will make sure that data-driven systems are part of the UN Sustainable Development Goals.

Figure 4. Process Model for Implementing Data-Driven Sustainable Supply Chains in The LDCs

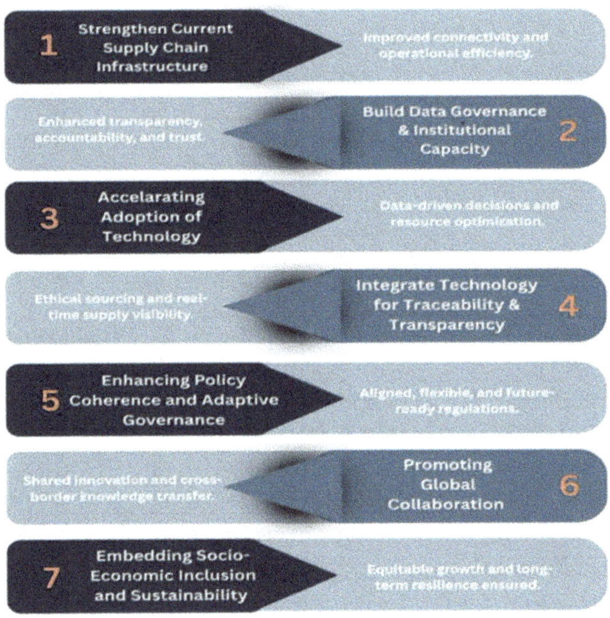

Source: Created by Authors

It has been concluded that an integrated policy process model, which comprises infrastructure development, data governance, technology adoption, and global cooperation, is needed to ensure transparency, resilience, and the sustainability of the supply chains of Least Developed Countries (LDCs). This holistic governance mechanism is to make sure that all phases of digital transformation lead to inclusive growth and long-term value creation as depicted in Figure 4 and table 3. The best business approaches to improving and leveraging supply chain infrastructure are to increase end-to-end visibility through live tracking and analytics, diversifying suppliers to reduce the impacts of disruption, and applying modern digital technologies, including AI, blockchain, and IoT, to ensure real-time data and automation. Cooperation with the suppliers as well as the stakeholders can be very important to harmonize the production strategies and increase agility and regular analysis of risks and performance measurement will offer continuity in the fluctuating conditions. The efficiency of operations, the cost saving, and the enhanced customer service can be even enhanced with the assistance of the ROTA-based logistics optimization of the routes, the incorporation of the warehouse management systems, and the manufacturing discipline. There should also be sustainability, knowledge sharing and inclusion approaches that should be adopted in order to attain long term sustainability and equitable development.

Table 3. Outcome of The Process Step

Process Steps	Key Focus	Policy Logic	Outcomes
Step 1	Infrastructure Readiness	1. Digital Platforms 2. Public–Private investment	3. Connectivity and accessibility
Step 2	Data Governance	4. Interoperable 5. Ethical data frameworks	6. Transparency and accountability
Step 3	Data Capability	7. Incentivized analytics and AI hubs	8. Predictive decision-making
Step 4	Traceability Systems	9. IoT–Blockchain pilots and harmonization	10. Ethical sourcing and compliance
Step 5	Adaptive Governance	11. Trans-sectoral regulation 12. Flexible regulation.	13. Policy coherence
Step 6	Global Collaboration	14. Multi-stakeholder information alliances	15. Knowledge exchange and sustainability
Step 7	Inclusive Development	16. Online accessibility and equality	17. Social equity and sustainability

Source: Created by Authors

CONCLUSION, IMPLICATIONS, LIMITATIONS, AND FUTURE DIRECTIONS

Conclusion

The analysis indicates that strategic policy interventions and international collaboration are essential for supply chain sustainability, despite significant challenges such as deficient institutional frameworks, insufficient digital infrastructures, and inadequate technical readiness. Effective governance, evidence-based practices, secure technical platforms, and collaborative approaches propel reform in LDC supply chains. The globalization of best practices, technology transfer initiatives, and the harmonization of national regulatory norms are aiding LDCs in achieving international sustainability standards. The research determines that sustainability in LDC supply chains has challenges related to technology, governance, and collaboration. Supply chains can provide enduring competitive advantages in socio-economic growth and environmental sustainability through contextually relevant legislation, enhancement of institutional capacity, and international collaboration.

Implications of the Research

Theoretical Implications: The research influences sustainable supply chain management, digitalization in resource-constrained environments, and international development partnerships, both conceptually and practically. It analyzes the impact of governance quality, regulatory frameworks, and technology innovation on sustainable supply chains in LDCs, contributing to academic research. This paper defines the notion of supply chain sustainability within the institutional and infrastructural contexts of LDCs and offers a comprehensive theoretical framework for research in operations management sustainability and development economics. This study will contribute to the literature on sustainable supply chain management and digital transformation in emerging nations, addressing a research gap that remains infrequently explored in least developed countries (LDCs). This study's theoretical approach can help scholars examine supply chain digitalization in resource-limited economies. It also underscores the need to empirically validate it across various LDC economies, which in turn requires a comparative developmental analysis.

Policy Implications: The results provide some feasible recommendations for policymakers. Supply chain professionals, international development organizations, and private sector entities operating in least developed countries (LDCs). The findings would prompt the establishment of robust legislative frameworks, investment in digital infrastructure, development of data governance standards, and creation of conducive conditions for collaboration among individuals and organizations. The article has shown that effective governance may diminish uncertainty, improve transparency, and facilitate the implementation of sustainable practices across supply chains.

Practical Implications: The research will assist practitioners and multinational corporations in overcoming institutional hurdles, developing local capabilities, using data-driven technologies, and aligning operations with worldwide sustainability standards while respecting local contexts. The paper underscores the significance of technology transfer, capacity building, financial support, and knowledge repositories in bridging the sustainability gap between developed and poor nations for international development agencies and donor organizations. The study paper advocates for coordinated international collaboration that respects sovereignty while establishing standards, enabling LDCs to engage in international supply chains without detrimental effects on the environment or society. The research identified the cognitive and operational dimensions of the issue, positioning policy, governance, and international cooperation as the foundational elements for sustainable supply chain transformation in least developed countries (LDCs). The results establish a foundation for future empirical research and provide stakeholders with a pragmatic approach to navigate the framework in emerging markets.

Limitations of the Research

Although this study provides valuable insights regarding policy, governance, and partnerships to enhance sustainable supply chains in LDCs, it possesses significant deficiencies. The theoretical article heavily utilized international reports, literature, and policy documents. The absence of primary empirical validation restricts the applicability of the findings to other LDCs with varying institutional maturity, economic structures, and cultural traits. This reliance on comprehensive global databases such as UNCTAD, the World Bank, and OECD may not accurately reflect country-specific factors, particularly regarding regulatory frameworks, cultural influences on governance efficacy, local supply chain obstacles, and industry sustainability. Each LDC possesses distinct infrastructural, political, and economic characteristics necessitating a customized response. A further disadvantage is that the framework emphasizes policy and governance at the expense of operational execution. The study reveals essential success factors; nonetheless, the ways in which LDCs might implement data-driven initiatives, overcome reluctance, and enhance institutional capacity and momentum are insufficiently explored. International collaboration is crucial; yet, the study fails to include power dynamics, knowledge asymmetry, and potential conflicts of interest between affluent and developing nations in sustainable partnerships. The study emphasizes structural and institutional constraints rather than behavioral aspects such as organizational culture, stakeholder motivation, change management, and human capital development methods that promote sustainability.

These limits indicate that next research ought to encompass empirical studies in various LDCs, comparative analyses of governance frameworks, sector-specific applications, and the human and organizational factors involved in sustainable supply chain reform.

Future Research Directions

Future LDC supply chain research should concentrate on field studies, surveys, and case studies to overcome constraints. LDC comparisons would disclose regional trends and scalable methods, while agricultural, manufacturing, textile, and service industry studies would identify challenges and regulation needs. Change management, capacity building, institutional resistance, and cultural issues in resource-limited situations should be addressed in implementation plan studies. Further research should examine LDCs' adoption of blockchain, IoT, AI, and cloud technologies, cost-benefit analyses, and digital preparedness. Public-private partnerships' governance frameworks and risk-sharing mechanisms must be evaluated, and longitudinal studies can assess their benefits and resilience to disruption. Finally, a behavioral and cultural study is needed to understand how organizational culture, leadership styles, and stakeholder incentives affect LDC sustainable supply chain transformation.

REFERENCES

Abtahi, A. T., Farhana, N., & Hasan, M. M. (2023). A study on the impact of E-commerce adoption for enhancing supply chain efficiency in Bangladesh SMES. *Business and Economics in Developing Countries*, *1*(1), 29–33. DOI: 10.26480/bedc.01.2023.29.33

Adjei-Bamfo, P., Maloreh-Nyamekye, T., & Ahenkan, A. (2021). The role of e-government in sustainable public procurement in developing countries: A systematic literature review. *Resources, Conservation and Recycling*, *142*, 189–203. DOI: 10.1016/j.resconrec.2018.12.001

Akbari, M., & Hopkins, J. L. (2022). Digital technologies as enablers of supply chain sustainability in an emerging economy. *Operations Management Research*, *15*(3), 689–710. DOI: 10.1016/j.ijpe.2020.107844

Bag, S., Kilbourn, P., & Pisa, N. (2023). Guest editorial: Data-driven quality management systems for improving supply chain management performance. *The TQM Journal*, *35*(1), 1–4. DOI: 10.1108/TQM-11-2021-315

Bagherpasandi, M., Salehi, M., Hajiha, Z., & Hejazi, R. (2025). Presenting a model for enhancing the performance of sustainable supply chain management using a data-driven approach. *Benchmarking*, *32*(6), 2164–2208. DOI: 10.1108/BIJ-12-2023-0846

Bahangulu, J. K., & Owusu-Berko, L. (2025). Algorithmic bias, data ethics, and governance: Ensuring fairness, transparency and compliance in AI-powered business analytics applications. *World Journal of Advanced Research and Reviews*, *25*(2), 1746–1763. DOI: 10.30574/wjarr.2025.25.2.0571

Bai, C., Quayson, M., & Sarkis, J. (2021). COVID-19 pandemic digitization lessons for sustainable development of micro-and small-enterprises. *Sustainable Production and Consumption*, *27*, 1989–2001. DOI: 10.1016/j.spc.2021.04.035 PMID: 34722843

Chalmeta, R., & Santos-deLeón, N. J. (2020). Sustainable supply chain in the era of industry 4.0 and big data: A systematic analysis of literature and research. *Sustainability*, *12*(10), 4108. DOI: 10.3390/su12104108

Chauhan, C., Kaur, P., Arrawatia, R., Ractham, P., & Dhir, A. (2022). Supply chain collaboration and sustainable development goals (SDGs). Teamwork makes achieving SDGs dream work. *Journal of Business Research*, *147*, 290–307. DOI: 10.1016/j.jbusres.2022.03.044

Chauhan, C., Singh, A., & Luthra, S. (2023). Barriers to industry 4.0 adoption and its performance implications: An empirical investigation of emerging economy. *Journal of Cleaner Production, 385*, 135649. DOI: 10.1016/j.jclepro.2020.124809

Chen, S., & Hasan, M. R. (2020). Impact of global competitiveness on logistics performance: Evidence from Asian countries. *The Journal of Asian Finance, Economics and Business, 7*(12), 693–703. DOI: 10.5281/ZENODO.3930252

Chen, Y. C., & Hasan, M. K. (2023). Impacts of liner shipping connectivity and global competitiveness on logistics performance: The mediating role of the quality of port and infrastructure. *Transport, 38*(2), 87–104. DOI: 10.3846/transport.2023.19372

Dubey, R., Gunasekaran, A., Childe, S. J., Bryde, D. J., Giannakis, M., Foropon, C., & Hazen, B. T. (2019). Big data analytics and artificial intelligence pathway to operational performance under the effects of entrepreneurial orientation and environmental dynamism. *International Journal of Production Economics, 226*, 107599. DOI: 10.1016/j.ijpe.2019.107599

Dutil, P., & Williams, J. (2017). Regulation governance in the digital era: A new research agenda. *Canadian Public Administration, 60*(4), 562–580. DOI: 10.1111/capa.12226

Dza, M., & Atsu, W. (2024). Supply Chain Intelligence and Operational Performance of Small and Medium Enterprises in Ghana: The Mediating Role of Collaboration. *International Journal of Business and Management, 7*(1), 12–31. DOI: 10.5281/zenodo.10684094

Emon, M. M. H., & Khan, T. (2025). The transformative role of Industry 4.0 in supply chains: Exploring digital integration and innovation in the manufacturing enterprises. *Journal of Open Innovation, 11*(2), 100516. DOI: 10.1016/j.joitmc.2025.100516

Govindan, K., Shaw, M., & Majumdar, A. (2021). Social sustainability tensions in multi-tier supply chain: A systematic literature review towards conceptual framework development. *Journal of Cleaner Production, 279*, 123075. DOI: 10.1016/j.jclepro.2020.123075

Hasan, M. K., Chun, C., Shengyong, Y., & Kemi, A. (2022). Forecasting the Quality of Port Infrastructure of Asian Port Countries: An Application of the Model GM (1, 1) and Clustering Them Using HCA Algorithm. *Operations and Supply Chain Management: An International Journal, 15*, 105–121. DOI: 10.31387/oscm0480334

Hasan, M. K., Latif, Z., Hlali, A., Xunping, L., & Aka, S. A. B. (2026). Hyperautomation: The Next Frontier in Supply Chain (SC) and Manufacturing. *Emerging Trends in Smart Logistics Technologies* (pp. 1-44). IGI Global Scientific Publishing.

Hasan, M. K., Lei, X., Hlali, A., & Bian, Z. (2024). Modelling capability factors of logistics industry based on ISM-MICMAC. *Heliyon, 10*, e40539. DOI: 10.1016/j.heliyon.2024.e40539 PMID: 39641072

Hasan, M. K., Lei, X. T. W., Nishi, N. N., & Latif, Z. (2025). Exploring logistics performance index (LPI) from global perspective: A study based on network analysis (NA). *Operations Management Research, 18*, 1088–1112. DOI: 10.1007/s12063-025-00550-3

Hendricks, S., & Mwapwele, S. D. (2024). A systematic literature review on the factors influencing e-commerce adoption in developing countries. *Data and Information Management, 8*(1), 100045. DOI: 10.1016/j.dim.2023.100045

Hosain, R. (2025). Digital transformation in Bangladesh's RMG supply chains: A case study on DBS Group. *International Journal of Research and Innovation in Social Science (IJRISS), 9*(6), 1696–1703. DOIl https://dx.doi.org/DOI: 10.47772/IJRISS.2025.906000133

International Trade Centre (ITC). (2023). *SME Competitiveness Outlook 2023,* Retrieved December 21, 2025from https://www.intracen.org/resources/publications/sme-competitiveness-outlook

Kamble, S. S., Gunasekaran, A., & Gawankar, S. A. (2020). Achieving sustainable performance in a data-driven agriculture supply chain: A review for research and applications. *International Journal of Production Economics, 219*, 179–194. DOI: 10.1016/j.ijpe.2019.05.022

Khan, M. R., & Arif, M. Z. U. (2025). Operational efficiency through disruptive innovation in dairy business: Evidence from an emerging economy. *International Journal of Productivity and Quality Management, 45*(1), 66–93. DOI: 10.1504/IJPQM.2025.146575

Khan, M. R., Arif, M. Z. U., & Rammal, H. G. (2025). Disruptive production process innovation for sustainable business: Evidence from an emerging economy. *Business Process Management Journal, 31*(4), 1349–1370. DOI: 10.1108/BPMJ-11-2023-0872

Khan, M. R., & Pervin, M. T. (2024). Technology disruption and its application in organizational management theories: A case study on Toyota Motor Corporation. *International Journal of Services and Operations Management, 49*(2), 198–220. DOI: 10.1504/IJSOM.2024.141998

Khan, M. R., & Sarkar, U. (2024). Business leadership in the digital age: IKEA's story in the retail and consumer sector. *Green Technologies and Sustainability, 2*(2), 100081. DOI: 10.1016/j.grets.2024.100081

Kshetri, N. (2021). Blockchain and sustainable supply chain management in developing countries. *International Journal of Information Management, 60*, 102376. DOI: 10.1016/j.ijinfomgt.2021.102376

Lugada, E., Komakech, H., Ochola, I., Mwebaze, S., Olowo Oteba, M., & Okidi Ladwar, D. (2022). Health supply chain system in Uganda: Current issues, structure, performance, and implications for systems strengthening. *Journal of Pharmaceutical Policy and Practice, 15*(1), 14. DOI: 10.1186/s40545-022-00412-4 PMID: 35232485

Mageto, J. (2021). Big data analytics in sustainable supply chain management: A focus on manufacturing supply chains. *Sustainability, 13*(13), 7101. DOI: 10.3390/su13137101

Mahajan, R., Lim, W. M., Sareen, M., Kumar, S., & Panwar, R. (2023). Stakeholder theory. *Journal of Business Research, 166*, 114104. DOI: 10.1016/j.jbusres.2023.114104

Mohammed, I., Nangpiire, C., Detoh, W. M., & Fataw, Y. (2024). The effect of blockchain technology in enhancing ethical sourcing and supply chain transparency: Evidence from the cocoa and agricultural sectors in Ghana. *African Journal of Empirical Research, 5*(2), 55–64. DOI: 10.51867/ajernet.5.2.6

Moktadir, M. A., Ali, S. M., Paul, S. K., & Shukla, N. (2019). Barriers to big data analytics in manufacturing supply chains: A case study from Bangladesh. *Computers & Industrial Engineering, 128*, 1063–1075. DOI: 10.1016/j.cie.2018.04.013

Mousavi, S. A., Pimenidis, E., & Jahankhani, H. (2008). Cultivating trust—an electronic-government development model for addressing the needs of developing countries. *International Journal of Electronic Security and Digital Forensics, 1*(3), 233–248. DOI: 10.1504/IJESDF.2008.020942

Munir, M. A., Hussain, A., Farooq, M., Habib, M. S., & Shahzad, M. F. (2023). Data-driven transformation: The role of ambidexterity and analytics capability in building dynamic and sustainable supply chains. *Sustainability, 15*(14), 10896. DOI: 10.3390/su151410896

Nakpodia, F., Ashiru, F., You, J. J., & Oni, O. (2024). Digital technologies, social entrepreneurship and resilience during crisis in developing countries: Evidence from Nigeria. *International Journal of Entrepreneurial Behaviour & Research, 30*(2/3), 342–368. DOI: 10.1108/IJEBR-01-2023-0012

Ndemo, B. (2025). The Role of Blockchain and Governance in Africa's Economic Development. In *Sustainable Digital Finance* (pp. 19–36). Springer Nature Switzerland.

Ngo, V. M., Nguyen, H. H., Pham, H. C., Nguyen, H. M., & Truong, P. V. D. (2023). Digital supply chain transformation: Effect of firm's knowledge creation capabilities under COVID-19 supply chain disruption risk. *Operations Management Research, 16*(2), 1003–1018. DOI: 10.1007/s12063-022-00326-z

Nguyen, D. T., Adulyasak, Y., Cordeau, J. F., & Ponce, S. I. (2022). Data-driven operations and supply chain management: Established research clusters from 2000 to early 2020. *International Journal of Production Research, 60*(17), 5407–5431. DOI: 10.1080/00207543.2021.1956695

Nkezabera, P., & Dinesh, R. (2025). Integrating IoT to Improve Real-Time Visibility and Efficiency in Rwanda's Healthcare Supply Chain. *IRASS Journal of Economics and Business Management, 2*(10), 74–80.

OECD. (2024). OECD Digital. *Economic Outlook, 2024*, •••. Retrieved December 21, 2025, from https://www.oecd.org/en/publications/oecd-digital-economy-outlook_f0b5c251-en.html

Poudel, N., & Shaw, R. (2024). Challenges in urban-rural food supply chains for disaster resilience in Nepal. *Regional Science Policy & Practice, 16*(8), 100073. DOI: 10.1016/j.rspp.2024.100073

Prangan, T. H., Ahmed, M. R., Islam, A. A., Islam, M. A., & Mim, J. S. (2025). Evaluating the Impact of Sustainable Supply Chain Management (SSCM) Practices on Business Performance Among Agro-Based SMEs in Bangladesh: Mediating Role of FinTech Usability. *Supply Chain Insider, 17*(1), 207–268. DOI: 10.5281/zenodo.17285206

Rajbhandari, S., Shrestha, R., & Alhassan, I. (2022). Industry 4.0 readiness of manufacturing industries in a developing economy: A case of Nepal. [External Link]. *Heliyon, 8*(8), e08919. DOI: 10.1016/j.heliyon.2022.e08919 PMID: 35243054

Shamout, M. D. (2019). Does supply chain analytics enhance supply chain innovation and robustness capability? *Organizacija, 52*(2), 95–106. DOI: 10.2478/orga-2019-0007

Shrivastava, B., Verma, M., & Dave, S. (2024). *Digital Entrepreneurship and E-Commerce: Opportunities and Challenges for Bhutan's International Trade. Convergence of Digitalization*. Innovation, and Sustainable Development in Business.

Siems, E., Seuring, S., & Schilling, L. (2023). Stakeholder roles in sustainable supply chain management: A literature review. *Journal of Business Economics, 93*(4), 747–775. DOI: 10.1007/s11573-022-01117-5

Sodhi, M. S., & Tang, C. S. (2024). Seeking and exploiting synergies among the UN sustainability development goals: Research opportunities for operations management. *Production and Operations Management*, *33*(4), 962–978. DOI: 10.1177/10591478241235004

Stroumpoulis, A., Kopanaki, E., & Chountalas, P. T. (2024). Enhancing sustainable supply chain management through digital transformation: A comparative case study analysis. *Sustainability*, *16*(16), 6778. DOI: 10.3390/su16166778

Suberi, H. K. (2022). Review analysis on challenges, opportunities, and implementation strategies for the success of green public procurement, the context of Bhutan. *Bhutan Journal of Research and Development*, *11*(1), 1–20. DOI: 10.17102/bjrd.rub.11.1.023

Tuyishime, K., & Adewusi, M. A. (2025). Data-driven prediction of cattle weight gain for evaluating key growth factors with machine learning approaches. *Discover Computing*, *28*(1), 275. DOI: 10.1007/s10791-025-09798-6

UNCTAD. (2023). *Digital Economy Report 2023: Enabling Data-Driven Development*. Retrieved October 13, 2025, from https://unctadstat.unctad.org/datacentre/

UNCTAD. (2024). *Technology and Innovation Report 2024: Opening Green Windows - Technological Opportunities for a Low-Carbon World*. Retrieved October 13, 2025, from https://unctadstat.unctad.org/datacentre/

Wasswa, J. H., Oundo, H., Oteba, M. O., Komakech, H., Ochola, I., Mwebaze, S., & Lugada, E. (2023). Leveraging electronic logistics management information systems to enhance and optimize supply chain response during public health emergencies: Lessons from COVID-19 response in Uganda. *Journal of Pharmaceutical Policy and Practice*, *16*(1), 6. DOI: 10.1186/s40545-023-00517-4 PMID: 36650571

World Bank. (2023). *World Development Report 2023: Migrants, Refugees, and Societies*. Retrieved December 01, 2025, from https://www.worldbank.org/en/publication/wdr2023

World Bank. (2024). *Digital Development: Data for Development*. Retrieved December 02, 2025, from https://www.worldbank.org/en/topic/digital

Zhao, N., Hong, J., & Lau, K. H. (2023). Impact of supply chain digitalization on supply chain resilience and performance: A multi-mediation model. *International Journal of Production Economics*, *259*, 108817. DOI: 10.1016/j.ijpe.2023.108817 PMID: 36852136

KEY TERMS AND DEFINITIONS

Big Data Analytics (BDA): The sophisticated procedure of analyzing extensive, heterogeneous information (both organized and unstructured) to uncover concealed associations, connections, and patterns.

Data-Driven Supply Chain: It employs real-time data and sophisticated analytics (artificial intelligence, machine learning) to influence choices, transitioning from reactive to proactive management to enhance efficiency, transparency, cost savings, and satisfaction with customers by consolidating information from Internet of Things, enterprise resource planning, and customer relationship management (CRM) platforms throughout the whole network.

Governance and Policy Frameworks: Organizations, ranging from governments to firms, are directed, regulated, and held responsible by systematic frameworks of regulations, processes, responsibilities, and norms that guarantee decisions align with strategic objectives, mitigate risks, and maintain moral standards through established legitimacy, accountability, and openness.

International Collaboration: collaborates with international organisations, including governments, corporations, and researchers, to address complex global issues, promote innovation, and accomplish feats that would be impossible for any one entity to do on its own.

Least Developed Countries (LDCs): LDCs are developing nations identified by the UN as those that have the most minimal socioeconomic growth indices.

Sustainable Supply Chain: It incorporates environmental, social, and economic accountability every step of the entire lifecycle of a good, from raw material procurement to disposal, with the objective of minimizing adverse effects (such as waste and emissions) and maximizing beneficial outcomes (including fair labour practices and community advantages) while maintaining profitability.

Compilation of References

Aarland, M. (2025). Cybersecurity in digital supply chains in the procurement process: Introducing the digital supply chain management framework. *Information and Computer Security*, *33*(1), 5–24. DOI: 10.1108/ICS-10-2023-0198

Aarthi, S., Aravinthan, K., Ravikumar, R. N., Sivakumar, N., & Wanglen, S. (2025). Cryptography securing data in motion within Blockchain, internet of everything, and Federated Learning. In *Convergence of Blockchain, Internet of Everything, and Federated Learning for Security* (pp. 39–78). IGI Global., DOI: 10.4018/979-8-3373-1424-2.ch002

Abdullah, F., Naeem, H. M., & Aslam, H. (2025). Big data, bigger ideas: The role of big data analytics management capability in supply chain sustainability. *Industrial Management & Data Systems*, •••, 1–23. DOI: 10.1108/IMDS-09-2024-0913

Abtahi, A. T., Farhana, N., & Hasan, M. M. (2023). A study on the impact of E-commerce adoption for enhancing supply chain efficiency in Bangladesh SMES. *Business and Economics in Developing Countries*, *1*(1), 29–33. DOI: 10.26480/bedc.01.2023.29.33

Abubakar, M., & Ahamad, S. (2023). Blockchain based platform for carbon credit. *NIET Journal of Engineering and Technology*, *12*(01W), 1–9. DOI: 10.62797/njet.vol.12.issue.01w.001

Adjei-Bamfo, P., Maloreh-Nyamekye, T., & Ahenkan, A. (2021). The role of e-government in sustainable public procurement in developing countries: A systematic literature review. *Resources, Conservation and Recycling*, *142*, 189–203. DOI: 10.1016/j.resconrec.2018.12.001

Agostinelli, S., Arman, A., Luzi, F. D., Monti, F., Manglaviti, M., & Mecella, M. (2024). Supporting business confidentiality in coopetitive scenarios: The B-CONFIDENT approach in blockchain-based supply chains. *Journal of Industrial Information Integration, 42*, 100730, ISSN 2452-414X, Elsevier BV, DOI: 10.1016/j.jii.2024.100730

Agrawal, N. (2022). Multi-criteria decision-making toward supplier selection: Exploration of PROMETHEE II method. *Benchmarking*, *29*(7), 2122–2146. DOI: 10.1108/BIJ-02-2021-0071

Ahsan, M., & Serrano, D. (2025). Lifecycle carbon mapping of well construction-blockchain carbon footprint profiling. *World Journal of Advanced Engineering Technology and Sciences*, *15*(3), 2268–2270. DOI: 10.30574/wjaets.2025.15.3.0800

Ajagekar, A., & You, F. (2024). Quantum-inspired optimization for sustainable supply chain management: A review. *Computers & Chemical Engineering*, *180*, 108125. Advance online publication. DOI: 10.1016/j.compchemeng.2023.108125

Ajalli, M. (2025). A hybrid approach of CFA-FAHP-SWARA-ARAS for evaluating the readiness criteria of zinc industry green suppliers in blockchain technology adopting. *Results in Engineering*, *27*, 106034. DOI: 10.1016/J.RINENG.2025.106034

Akbari, M. (2024). Revolutionizing supply chain and circular economy with edge computing: Systematic review, research themes and future directions. *Management Decision*, *62*(9), 2875–2899. DOI: 10.1108/MD-03-2023-0412

Akbari, M., & Do, T. N. A. (2021). A systematic review of machine learning in logistics and supply chain management: Current trends and future directions. *Benchmarking*, *28*(10), 2977–3005. DOI: 10.1108/BIJ-10-2020-0514

Akbari, M., & Hopkins, J. L. (2022). Digital technologies as enablers of supply chain sustainability in an emerging economy. *Operations Management Research*, *15*(3), 689–710. DOI: 10.1016/j.ijpe.2020.107844

Akram, M., Azam, S., & Kahraman, C. (2025). Group decision making method for site selection of car sharing stations in Istanbul using spherical fuzzy rough numbers. *Applied Soft Computing*, *169*, 112607. DOI: 10.1016/J.ASOC.2024.112607

Akter, S., & Wamba, S. F. (2016). Big data analytics in E-commerce: A systematic review and agenda for future research. *Electronic Markets*, *26*(2), 173–194. DOI: 10.1007/s12525-016-0219-0

Akter, S., Wamba, S. F., Gunasekaran, A., Dubey, R., & Childe, S. J. (2016). How to improve firm performance using big data analytics capability and business strategy alignment? *International Journal of Production Economics*, *182*, 113–131. DOI: 10.1016/J.IJPE.2016.08.018

Alam, T. (2020). *Blockchain-based Big Data Analytics Approach for Smart Cities.*, Wiley, DOI: 10.22541/au.160208029.93138178/v1

Al-Banna, A., Yaqot, M., & Menezes, B. C. (2024). Investment strategies in Industry 4.0 for enhanced supply chain resilience: An empirical analysis. *Cogent Business & Management*, *11*(1), 2298187. Advance online publication. DOI: 10.1080/23311975.2024.2298187

Aldrighetti, R., Zennaro, I., Finco, S., & Battini, D. (2021). Healthcare supply chain simulation with disruption considerations: A systematic literature review and bibliometric analysis. *Sustainability*, *13*(13), 7104. Advance online publication. DOI: 10.3390/su13137104

Al-Farsi, S., Rathore, M. M., & Bakiras, S. (2021). Security of Blockchain-Based Supply Chain Management Systems: Challenges and Opportunities. *Applied Sciences (Basel, Switzerland)*, *11*(12), 5585. DOI: 10.3390/app11125585

Alhathlaul, N., Lakhouit, A., Abdalla, G. M. T., Alghamdi, A., Shaban, M., Alshahir, A., Alshahr, S., Alali, I., & Mutlaq Alshammari, F. (2025). Assessing Waste Management Using Machine Learning Forecasting for Sustainable Development Goal Driven. *Sustainability*, *17*(19), 8654. DOI: 10.3390/su17198654

Alhodaib, A., Yahya, Z., Khan, O., Equbal, A., Equbal, M. S., Parvez, M., Kumar Yadav, A., & Idrisi, M. J. (2024). Sustainable coatings for green solar photovoltaic cells: Performance and environmental impact of recyclable biomass digestate polymers. *Scientific Reports*, *14*(1), 11221. DOI: 10.1038/s41598-024-62048-5 PMID: 38755253

Aljohani, A. (2023). Predictive Analytics and Machine Learning for Real-Time Supply Chain Risk Mitigation and Agility. *Sustainability*, *15*(20), 15088. DOI: 10.3390/su152015088

Almutairi, M. M., Sen, A. A. A., Bahbouh, N. M., Yamin, M., & Alsoqour, K. A. (2025). A Hybrid Framework for Flexible Waste Management During Crowded Events. *2025 12th International Conference on Computing for Sustainable Global Development (INDIACom)*, 1–7. DOI: 10.23919/INDIACom66777.2025.11115425

Alotaibi, E. M., Khallaf, A., Abdallah, A. A.-N., Zoubi, T., & Alnesafi, A. (2024). Blockchain-Driven Carbon Accountability in Supply Chains. *Sustainability, 16*(24), 10872. DOI: 10.3390/su162410872

Alwi, A., Sasongko, N., Adi, S., Suryana, Y., & Subagyo, H. (2024). Blockchain and big data integration design for traceability and carbon footprint management in the fishery supply chain. *Egyptian Informatics Journal, 26*, 100481, ISSN 1110-8665, Elsevier BV, DOI: 10.1016/j.eij.2024.100481

Alyahya, A., & Agag, G. (2025). Improving Corporate Environmental Performance Through Big Data Analytics Implementation: The Role of Industry Environment. *Sustainability 2025, Vol. 17, Page 2928, 17*(7), 2928. DOI: 10.3390/SU17072928

Andersen, T. (2022). A comparative study of national variations of the European WEEE directive: Manufacturer's view. *Environmental Science and Pollution Research International, 29*(14), 19920–19939. DOI: 10.1007/s11356-021-13206-z PMID: 33665699

Andronie, M., Lăzăroiu, G., tefănescu, R., U ă, C., & Dijmărescu, I. (2021). Sustainable, Smart, and Sensing Technologies for Cyber-Physical Manufacturing Systems: A Systematic Literature Review. *Sustainability, 13*(10), 5495. DOI: 10.3390/su13105495

Anjaria, K. (2025). *Analytics for Harnessing IoT and Industry 4.0: Data Flows in S-ERP* (pp. 197–219). https://doi.org/DOI: 10.1007/978-981-96-7734-4_7

Atagan Çetín, A. (2023). Using blockchain technology for carbon accounting in türkíye. *INTERNATIONAL REFEREED JOURNAL OF HUMANITIES AND ACADEMIC SCIENCES, 31*(0), 64–84. DOI: 10.17368/uhbab.2023.31.04

Atzori, L., Iera, A., & Morabito, G. (2010). The Internet of Things: A survey. *Computer Networks, 54*(15), 2787–2805. DOI: 10.1016/j.comnet.2010.05.010

Awan, U., Sroufe, R., & Shahbaz, M. (2021). Industry 4.0 and the circular economy: A literature review and recommendations for future research. *Business Strategy and the Environment, 30*(4), 2038–2060. DOI: 10.1002/bse.2731

Ayan, B., Güner, E., & Son-Turan, S. (2022). Blockchain Technology and Sustainability in Supply Chains and a Closer Look at Different Industries: A Mixed Method Approach. *Logistics, 6*(4), 85, ISSN 2305-6290, MDPI AG, DOI: 10.3390/logistics6040085

Aysan, A. F., Bergigui, F., & Disli, M. (2021). Blockchain-based solutions in achieving SDGs after COVID-19. *Journal of Open Innovation, 7*(2), 151. DOI: 10.3390/joitmc7020151

Baah, C., Afum, E., Agyabeng-Mensah, Y., & Agyeman, D. O. (2022). Stakeholder Influence on Adoption of Circular Economy Principles: Measuring Implications for Satisfaction and Green Legitimacy. *Circular Economy and Sustainability*, *2*(1), 91–111. DOI: 10.1007/s43615-021-00093-2

Bagherpasandi, M., Salehi, M., Hajiha, Z., & Hejazi, R. (2025). Presenting a model for enhancing the performance of sustainable supply chain management using a data-driven approach. *Benchmarking*, *32*(6), 2164–2208. DOI: 10.1108/BIJ-12-2023-0846

Bag, S., Gupta, S., & Kumar, S. (2021). Industry 4.0 adoption and supply chain sustainability: Empirical evidence from emerging economies. *International Journal of Production Economics*, *231*, 107831. DOI: 10.1016/j.ijpe.2020.107831

Bag, S., Gupta, S., Kumar, S., & Sivarajah, U. (2020). Role of big data and predictive analytics for supply chain sustainability. *International Journal of Production Research*, *58*(17), 5558–5582. DOI: 10.1080/00207543.2020.1735667

Bag, S., Kilbourn, P., & Pisa, N. (2023). Guest editorial: Data-driven quality management systems for improving supply chain management performance. *The TQM Journal*, *35*(1), 1–4. DOI: 10.1108/TQM-11-2021-315

Bag, S., Luthra, S., Mangla, S. K., & Kazancoglu, Y. (2021). Leveraging big data analytics capabilities in making reverse logistics decisions and improving remanufacturing performance. *International Journal of Logistics Management*, *32*(3), 742–765. DOI: 10.1108/IJLM-06-2020-0237

Bag, S., Rahman, M. S., Srivastava, G., Kilbourn, P., & Wood, L. C. (2024). System thinking skills and their effect upon supply chain resilience. *Systems Research and Behavioral Science*, *41*(6), 837–853. DOI: 10.1002/sres.3072

Bag, S., Wood, L. C., Mangla, S. K., & Luthra, S. (2020). Procurement 4.0 and its implications on business process performance in a circular economy. *Resources, Conservation and Recycling*, *152*, 104502. Advance online publication. DOI: 10.1016/j.resconrec.2019.104502

Bahangulu, J. K., & Owusu-Berko, L. (2025). Algorithmic bias, data ethics, and governance: Ensuring fairness, transparency and compliance in AI-powered business analytics applications. *World Journal of Advanced Research and Reviews*, *25*(2), 1746–1763. DOI: 10.30574/wjarr.2025.25.2.0571

Bahrami, M., & Shokouhyar, S. (2022). The role of big data analytics capabilities in bolstering supply chain resilience and firm performance: A dynamic capability view. *Information Technology & People*, *35*(5), 1621–1651. DOI: 10.1108/ITP-01-2021-0048

Bai, C., Quayson, M., & Sarkis, J. (2021). COVID-19 pandemic digitization lessons for sustainable development of micro-and small-enterprises. *Sustainable Production and Consumption, 27*, 1989–2001. DOI: 10.1016/j.spc.2021.04.035 PMID: 34722843

Baklaga, L. (2024). Synergizing AI and blockchain: Innovations in decentralized carbon markets for emission reduction through intelligent carbon credit trading. *Journal of Computer Science and Technology Studies, 6*(2), 111–120. DOI: 10.32996/jcsts.2024.6.2.13

Balawanth, R., Zomer, T., Gonçalves, P., & Savaget, P. (2025). Supply chain management in response to climate change: A system dynamics approach. *Sustainable Production and Consumption, 60*, 36–51. DOI: 10.1016/j.spc.2025.09.007

Banaeian, N., Mobli, H., Fahimnia, B., Nielsen, I. E., & Omid, M. (2019). Green supplier selection using fuzzy group decision making methods: A case study from the agri-food industry. *Computers & Operations Research, 89*, 337–347. DOI: 10.1016/j.cor.2016.02.015

Barney, J. (1991). Firm Resources and Sustained Competitive Advantage. *Journal of Management, 17*(1), 99–120. DOI: 10.1177/014920639101700108

Barykin, S. Y., Bochkarev, A. A., Kalinina, O. V., & Yadykin, V. K. (2020). Concept for a supply chain digital twin. International Journal of Mathematical. *Engineering and Management Sciences, 5*(6), 1498–1515. DOI: 10.33889/ijmems.2020.5.6.111

Basu, P., Deb, P., & Singh, A. (2024). Blockchain and the carbon credit ecosystem: Sustainable management of the supply chain. *The Journal of Business Strategy, 45*(1), 33–40. DOI: 10.1108/JBS-09-2022-0157

Batista, L., Bourlakis, M., Smart, P., & Maull, R. (2018). In search of a circular supply chain archetype – A content-analysis-based literature review. *Production Planning and Control, 29*(6), 438–451. DOI: 10.1080/09537287.2017.1343502

Bechtsis, D., Tsolakis, N., Iakovou, E., & Vlachos, D. (2022). Data-driven secure, resilient and sustainable supply chains: Gaps, opportunities, and a new generalised data sharing and data monetisation framework. *International Journal of Production Research, 60*(14), 4397–4417. DOI: 10.1080/00207543.2021.1957506

Beheshti, A., & Mansoor, W. (2025). Exploring the convergence of Internet of things and big data technologies in the age of generative artificial intelligence. In *Empowering IoT with Big Data Analytics* (pp. 333–354). Elsevier., DOI: 10.1016/B978-0-443-21640-4.00004-1

Belhadi, A., Mani, V., Kamble, S. S., Khan, S. A. R., & Verma, S. (2024). Artificial intelligence-driven innovation for enhancing supply chain resilience and performance under the effect of supply chain dynamism: An empirical investigation. *Annals of Operations Research, 333*(2–3), 627–652. DOI: 10.1007/s10479-021-03956-x PMID: 33551534

Berlato, M., Binni, L., Durmus, D., Gatto, C., Giusti, L., Massari, A., Toldo, B. M., Cascone, S., & Mirarchi, C. (2025). Digital Platforms for the Built Environment: A Systematic Review Across Sectors and Scales. *Buildings (Basel, Switzerland), 15*(14), 2432. DOI: 10.3390/buildings15142432

Beske-Janssen, P., Johnson, M., & Schaltegger, S. (2015). 20 years of performance measurement in sustainable supply chain management – What has been achieved? *Supply Chain Management, 20*(6), 664–680. DOI: 10.1108/SCM-06-2015-0216

Bocken, N. M. P., Boons, F., & Baldassarre, B. (2021). Sustainable business model experimentation by understanding ecologies of business models. *Journal of Cleaner Production, 295*, 126361. DOI: 10.1016/j.jclepro.2021.126361

Bouhtati, N., Alla, L., & Bentalha, B. (2023). Marketing Big Data Analytics and Customer Relationship Management. *Advances in Logistics, Operations, and Management Science*, 75-86, ISSN 2327-350X, IGI Global, DOI: 10.4018/979-8-3693-0225-5.ch004

Boyson, S., Corsi, T. M., & Paraskevas, J.-P. (2022). Defending digital supply chains: Evidence from a decade-long research program. *Technovation, 118*, 102380. DOI: 10.1016/j.technovation.2021.102380

Budak, A. (2020). Sustainable reverse logistics optimization with triple bottom line approach: An integration of disassembly line balancing. *Journal of Cleaner Production, 270*, 122475. DOI: 10.1016/j.jclepro.2020.122475

Bukhari, S. Danish (2024). Blockchain and Sustainability in Supply Chains. *Advances in Logistics, Operations, and Management Science*, 142-159, ISSN 2327-350X, IGI Global, DOI: 10.4018/979-8-3693-0482-2.ch009

Burgess, P., Sunmola, F., & Wertheim-Heck, S. (2024). Information needs for transparency in blockchain-enabled sustainable food supply chains. *International Journal of Information Management Data Insights, 4*(2), 100262, ISSN 2667-0968, Elsevier BV, DOI: 10.1016/j.jjimei.2024.100262

Burgos, D., & Ivanov, D. (2021). Food retail supply chain resilience and the COVID-19 pandemic: A digital twin-based impact analysis and improvement directions. *Transportation Research Part E, Logistics and Transportation Review, 152*, 102412. DOI: 10.1016/j.tre.2021.102412 PMID: 34934397

Burke, H., Zhang, A., & Wang, J. X. (2023). Integrating product design and supply chain management for a circular economy. *Production Planning and Control, 34*(11), 1097–1113. DOI: 10.1080/09537287.2021.1983063

Cai, Y., & Xiao, X. (2021). Application of Blockchain Technology in Management Accounting: Based on the Perspective of Frontier Literature Review. *Smart Innovation, Systems and Technologies*, 323-332, ISSN 2190-3018, Springer Singapore, DOI: 10.1007/978-981-33-6141-6_35

Calvão, F., & Archer, M. (2021). Digital extraction: Blockchain traceability in mineral supply chains. *Political Geography, 87*, 102381, ISSN 0962-6298, Elsevier BV, DOI: 10.1016/j.polgeo.2021.102381

Cao, S., Liao, W., & Huang, Y. (2021). Heterogeneous fleet recyclables collection routing optimization in a two-echelon collaborative reverse logistics network from circular economic and environmental perspective. *The Science of the Total Environment, 758*, 144062. DOI: 10.1016/j.scitotenv.2020.144062 PMID: 33333310

Carlan, V, Coppens, F, Sys, C, Vanelslander, T, & Gastel, G, V (2020). Blockchain technology as key contributor to the integration of maritime supply chain?. *Maritime Supply Chains*, 229-259, Elsevier, DOI: 10.1016/b978-0-12-818421-9.00012-4

Carter, C. R., Rogers, D. S., & Choi, T. Y. (2020). Toward the theory of the supply chain. *The Journal of Supply Chain Management, 56*(2), 18–28. DOI: 10.1111/jscm.12237

Cenci, M. P., Scarazzato, T., Munchen, D. D., Dartora, P. C., Veit, H. M., Bernardes, A. M., & Dias, P. R. (2022). Eco-Friendly Electronics—A Comprehensive Review. *Advanced Materials Technologies, 7*(2). Advance online publication. DOI: 10.1002/admt.202001263

Centobelli, P., Cerchione, R., Del Vecchio, P., Oropallo, E., & Secundo, G. (2022). Blockchain technology for bridging trust, traceability and transparency in circular supply chain. *Information & Management, 59*(7), 103508. DOI: 10.1016/j.im.2021.103508

Centobelli, P., Cerchione, R., & Esposito, E., & Shashi. (2020). Pursuing supply chain sustainability through Big Data Analytics: A systematic literature review. *Journal of Cleaner Production, 259*, 120705. DOI: 10.1016/j.jclepro.2020.120705

Centobelli, P., Cerchione, R., Esposito, E., & Oropallo, E. (2021). Surfing blockchain wave, or drowning? Shaping the future of distributed ledgers and the role of business models. *Technological Forecasting and Social Change*, *165*, 120463. Advance online publication. DOI: 10.1016/j.techfore.2020.120463

Chae, B. (2015). Insights from hashtag #supplychain and Twitter analytics: Considering Twitter and Twitter data for supply chain practice and research. *International Journal of Production Economics*, *165*, 247–259. DOI: 10.1016/j.ijpe.2014.12.037

Chang, Y., Iakovou, E., & Shi, W. (2020). Blockchain in global supply chains and cross border trade: A critical synthesis of the state-of-the-art, challenges and opportunities. *International Journal of Production Research*, *58*(7), 2082–2099. DOI: 10.1080/00207543.2019.1651946

Chauhan, C., Kaur, P., Arrawatia, R., Ractham, P., & Dhir, A. (2022). Supply chain collaboration and sustainable development goals (SDGs). Teamwork makes achieving SDGs dream work. *Journal of Business Research*, *147*, 290–307. DOI: 10.1016/j.jbusres.2022.03.044

Chauhan, C., Singh, A., & Luthra, S. (2023). Barriers to industry 4.0 adoption and its performance implications: An empirical investigation of emerging economy. *Journal of Cleaner Production*, *385*, 135649. DOI: 10.1016/j.jclepro.2020.124809

Chauhan, S., Singh, R., Gehlot, A., Akram, S. V., Twala, B., & Priyadarshi, N. (2022). Digitalization of Supply Chain Management with Industry 4.0 Enabling Technologies: A Sustainable Perspective. *Processes (Basel, Switzerland)*, *11*(1), 96. DOI: 10.3390/pr11010096

Chemingui, H., & Hrouga, M. (2025). Enhancing Reverse Supply Chain performance via artificial intelligence predictive solutions. *Supply Chain Forum: An International Journal*, 1–20. DOI: 10.1080/16258312.2025.2520737

Chen, C.-T. (2000). Extensions of the TOPSIS for group decision-making under fuzzy environment. *Fuzzy Sets and Systems*, *114*(1), 1–9. DOI: 10.1016/S0165-0114(97)00377-1

Chen, C.-T., Khan, A., & Chen, S.-C. (2024). Modeling the impact of BDA-AI on sustainable innovation ambidexterity and environmental performance. *Journal of Big Data*, *11*(1), 124. DOI: 10.1186/s40537-024-00995-6

Chen, H., Chiang, R. H. L., & Storey, V. C. (2012). Business intelligence and analytics: From big data to big impact. *Management Information Systems Quarterly*, *36*(4), 1165–1188. DOI: 10.2307/41703503

Chen, M., & Ogunseitan, O. A. (2021). Zero E-waste: Regulatory impediments and blockchain imperatives. *Frontiers of Environmental Science & Engineering, 15*(6), 114. DOI: 10.1007/s11783-021-1402-x

Chen, P., Gao, J., Ji, Z., Liang, H., & Peng, Y. (2022). Do artificial intelligence applications affect carbon emission performance?—Evidence from panel data analysis of Chinese cities. *Energies, 15*(15), 5730. DOI: 10.3390/en15155730

Chen, S., & Hasan, M. R. (2020). Impact of global competitiveness on logistics performance: Evidence from Asian countries. *The Journal of Asian Finance, Economics and Business, 7*(12), 693–703. DOI: 10.5281/ZENODO.3930252

Chen, Y.-C., & Hasan, M. K. (2023). IMPACTS OF LINER SHIPPING CONNECTIVITY AND GLOBAL COMPETITIVENESS ON LOGISTICS PERFORMANCE: THE MEDIATING ROLE OF THE QUALITY OF PORT AND INFRASTRUCTURE. *Transport, 38*(2), 87–104. DOI: 10.3846/transport.2023.19372

Chen, Y., & Jin, S. (2023a). Artificial intelligence and carbon emissions in manufacturing firms: The moderating role of green innovation. *Processes (Basel, Switzerland), 11*(9), 2705. DOI: 10.3390/pr11092705

Chen, Z., Hong, S., Ji, X., Shi, R., & Wu, J. (2022). Refurbished products and supply chain incentives. *Annals of Operations Research, 310*(1), 27–47. DOI: 10.1007/s10479-021-04016-0

Chen, Z.-S., Tan, Y., Ma, Z., Zhu, Z., & Skibniewski, M. J. (2025). Unlocking the potential of quantum computing in prefabricated construction supply chains: Current trends, challenges, and future directions. *Information Fusion, 120*, 103043. Advance online publication. DOI: 10.1016/j.inffus.2025.103043

Chibaro, M., Chikwere, D., Kanyepe, J., & Govere, E. (2024). End-of-Life Vehicle Management. *Advances in Civil and Industrial Engineering*, 309-344, ISSN 2326-6139, IGI Global, DOI: 10.4018/979-8-3693-3755-4.ch012

Chibaro, M., Mataba, A. T., & Mupfiga, C. (2024). Influence of Warehouse Management Practices on Service Delivery in Zimbabwean Local Authorities. *Logistic and Operation Management Research (LOMR), 3*(1), 1-16, ISSN 2830-2680, Research Synergy Foundation, DOI: 10.31098/lomr.v3i1.1882

Chibaro, M., Mupfiga, C., Mahwine, M. L., Chikwere, D., Mbudaya, J., & Kanyepe, J. (2025). Green supply chain management and agricultural performance: Towards ecological supply chain management from sustainable supply systems. In *Integrating Agriculture, Green Marketing Strategies, and Artificial Intelligence* (pp. 285–316). IGI Global Scientific Publishing.

Chikwere, D., Munuhwa, S., & Chibaro, M. (2025). Advancing sustainable green marketing agenda in Africa through green supply chain management. In *Sustainable Green Marketing Strategies for a Circular Economy: African Realities and Imperatives* (pp. 161–182). Springer Nature Switzerland.

Chikwere, D., Mbudaya, J., Chihwayi, H., & Chikwere, D. (2023). Food supply chain decarbonisation: Towards zero emissions in the beverages value chain – A case of Delta, Zimbabwe. *Journal of Tianjin University Science and Technology*, *10*, 1–15.

Choi, T. M., Wallace, S. W., & Wang, Y. (2018). Big data analytics in operations management. *Production and Operations Management*, *27*(10), 1868–1888. DOI: 10.1111/poms.12838

Choi, T. Y., Dooley, K. J., & Rungtusanatham, M. (2001). Supply networks and complex adaptive systems: Control versus emergence. *Journal of Operations Management*, *19*(3), 351–366. DOI: 10.1016/S0272-6963(00)00068-1

Choi, T.-M. (2018). Big data analytics in fashion supply chain. *IEEE Transactions on Engineering Management*, *65*(4), 819–831. DOI: 10.1109/TEM.2018.2797185

Contini, G., & Peruzzini, M. (2022). Sustainability and Industry 4.0: Definition of a Set of Key Performance Indicators for Manufacturing Companies. *Sustainability 2022, Vol. 14, Page 11004*, *14*(17), 11004. DOI: 10.3390/SU141711004

Dananjaya, H. R., Fabio, M., & Fakhrezzy, M. (2022). Coordination of Global Approach for Blockchain Supply Chains. *Blockchain Frontier Technology, 2*(1), 72-83, ISSN 2808-0009, Pandawan, DOI: 10.34306/bfront.v2i1.116

Dasaklis, T. K., Voutsinas, T. G., Tsoulfas, G. T., & Casino, F. (2022). A Systematic Literature Review of Blockchain-Enabled Supply Chain Traceability Implementations. *Sustainability*, *14*(4), 2439. DOI: 10.3390/su14042439

Das, C., & Jharkharia, S. (2018). Low carbon supply chain: A state-of-the-art literature review. *Journal of Manufacturing Technology Management*, *29*(2), 398–428. DOI: 10.1108/jmtm-09-2017-0188

David, I., Bork, D., & Kappel, G. (2024). Circular systems engineering. *Software & Systems Modeling*, *23*(2), 269–283. DOI: 10.1007/s10270-024-01154-4

de Jesus Pacheco, D. A., Koundal, D., Gunasekaran, A., Attaran, M., Sgarbossa, F., & Narayanan, A. (Chalam), & Zailani, S. (2025). Challenges and opportunities for empirical research on data analytics in supply chain management. *Supply Chain Forum: An International Journal, 26*(4), 431–436. https://doi.org/DOI: 10.1080/16258312.2025.2581507

De Marchi, V., & Alford, M. (2022). State policies and upgrading in global value chains: A systematic literature review. *Journal of International Business Policy*, *5*(1), 88–111. DOI: 10.1057/s42214-021-00107-8

Delmas, M. A., & Burbano, V. C. (2011). The Drivers of Greenwashing. *California Management Review*, *54*(1), 64–87. DOI: 10.1525/cmr.2011.54.1.64

Dempere, J., Alamash, E., & Mattos, P. (2024). Unveiling the truth: Greenwashing in sustainable finance. *Frontiers in Sustainability*, *5*. Advance online publication. DOI: 10.3389/frsus.2024.1362051

Dhaliwal, N., Aghera, S., Whig, P., & Remala, R. (2024). Advanced analytics and quantum computing for revolutionizing procurement strategies. In *Quantum computing and supply chain management: A new era of optimization* (pp. 304–330). IGI Global., DOI: 10.4018/979-8-3693-4107-0.ch016

Di Vaio, A., Latif, B., Gunarathne, N., Gupta, M., & D'Adamo, I. (2024). Digitalization and artificial knowledge for accountability in SCM: A systematic literature review. *Journal of Enterprise Information Management*, *37*(2), 606–672. DOI: 10.1108/JEIM-08-2022-0275

Diakoulaki, D., Mavrotas, G., & Papayannakis, L. (1995). Determining objective weights in multiple criteria problems: The critic method. *Computers & Operations Research*, *22*(7), 763–770. DOI: 10.1016/0305-0548(94)00059-H

DiMaggio, P. J., & Powell, W. W. (1983). The Iron Cage Revisited: Institutional Isomorphism and Collective Rationality in Organizational Fields. *American Sociological Review*, *48*(2), 147. DOI: 10.2307/2095101

Dörrenbächer, C., Geppert, M., & Hoffmann, A. (2021). Contemporary restructuring trends in European multinational corporations: Rationale and impact on labour and workers' participation. *Critical Perspectives on International Business*, *17*(4), 637–654. DOI: 10.1108/cpoib-03-2020-0017

Drissi Elbouzidi, A., Ait El Cadi, A., Pellerin, R., Lamouri, S., Tobon Valencia, E., & Bélanger, M.-J. (2023). The role of AI in warehouse digital twins: Literature review. *Applied Sciences (Basel, Switzerland)*, *13*(11), 6746. DOI: 10.3390/app13116746

Dubey, R., Gunasekaran, A., Bryde, D. J., Dwivedi, Y. K., & Papadopoulos, T. (2022). Blockchain technology for enhancing swift-trust, collaboration and resilience within a humanitarian supply chain setting. *International Journal of Production Research*, *60*(11), 3381–3398. DOI: 10.1080/00207543.2020.1722860

Dubey, R., Gunasekaran, A., & Childe, S. J. (2019). Big data analytics capability in supply chain agility. *Management Decision, 57*(8), 2096–2119. DOI: 10.1108/MD-01-2018-0119

Dubey, R., Gunasekaran, A., Childe, S. J., Bryde, D. J., Giannakis, M., Foropon, C., Roubaud, D., & Hazen, B. T. (2020). Big data analytics and artificial intelligence pathway to operational performance under the effects of entrepreneurial orientation and environmental dynamism: A study of manufacturing organisations. *International Journal of Production Economics, 226*. Advance online publication. DOI: 10.1016/j.ijpe.2019.107599

Dubey, R., Gunasekaran, A., Childe, S. J., Fosso Wamba, S., Roubaud, D., & Foropon, C. (2021). Empirical investigation of data analytics capability and organizational flexibility as complements to supply chain resilience. *International Journal of Production Research, 59*(1), 110–128. DOI: 10.1080/00207543.2019.1582820

Dubey, R., Gunasekaran, A., Childe, S. J., & Papadopoulos, T. (2020). Big data analytics and artificial intelligence for sustainable global supply chains. *Journal of Cleaner Production, 262*, 121313. Advance online publication. DOI: 10.1016/j.jclepro.2020.121313

Dubey, R., Gunasekaran, A., Childe, S. J., Papadopoulos, T., Luo, Z., Wamba, S. F., & Roubaud, D. (2019). Can big data and predictive analytics improve social and environmental sustainability? *Technological Forecasting and Social Change, 144*, 534–545. DOI: 10.1016/j.techfore.2017.06.020

Dumée, L. F. (2022). Circular Materials and Circular Design—Review on Challenges Towards Sustainable Manufacturing and Recycling. *Circular Economy and Sustainability, 2*(1), 9–23. DOI: 10.1007/s43615-021-00085-2 PMID: 34888565

Dutil, P., & Williams, J. (2017). Regulation governance in the digital era: A new research agenda. *Canadian Public Administration, 60*(4), 562–580. DOI: 10.1111/capa.12226

Dza, M., & Atsu, W. (2024). Supply Chain Intelligence and Operational Performance of Small and Medium Enterprises in Ghana: The Mediating Role of Collaboration. *International Journal of Business and Management, 7*(1), 12–31. DOI: 10.5281/zenodo.10684094

Elkington, J. (1998). Cannibals With Forks: The Triple Bottom Line of Sustainability. *New Society Publishers*, 37–51. https://books.google.com/books/about/Cannibals_with_Forks.html?hl=id&id=dIJAbIM7XNcC

Elkington, J. (1998). *Cannibals with forks: The triple bottom line of 21st-century business*. Capstone.

Elkington, J. (1999). *Cannibals with forks: The triple bottom line of 21st century business*. Capstone.

Ellen MacArthur Foundation. (2019). *Completing the picture: How the circular economy tackles climate change*. Ellen MacArthur Foundation.

Emon, M. M. H. (2025a). Circularity Meets AI: Revolutionizing Consumer Engagement Through Green Marketing. In *Transforming Business Practices With AI-Powered Green Marketing* (pp. 169–208). IGI Global Scientific Publishing. https://doi.org/DOI: 10.4018/979-8-3373-3017-4.ch007

Emon, M. M. H. (2025a). Cybersecurity in the Smart City Era: Overcoming Challenges With Modern Cryptographic Solutions. In *Securing Smart Cities Through Modern Cryptography Technologies* (pp. 43–74). IGI Global Scientific Publishing. DOI: 10.4018/979-8-3373-3326-7.ch002

Emon, M. M. H. (2025b). Ethical Intelligence in Motion: Leveraging AI for Responsible Sourcing in Supply Chain and Logistics. In *Navigating Responsible Business Practices Through Ethical AI* (pp. 207–240). https://doi.org/DOI: 10.4018/979-8-3373-3104-1.ch008

Emon, M. M. H. (2025b). Overcoming Hurdles: Navigating Challenges in the Adoption of Smart Logistics. In *Emerging Trends in Smart Logistics Technologies* (A. Hlali, pp. 197–228). IGI Global Scientific Publishing. DOI: 10.4018/979-8-3373-2434-0.ch007

Emon, M. M. H. (2025c). Purpose-Driven Intelligence in Green Marketing: Leveraging AI for CSR-Centric and Sustainable Brand Positioning. In *Transforming Business Practices With AI-Powered Green Marketing* (pp. 89–122). IGI Global Scientific Publishing. https://doi.org/DOI: 10.4018/979-8-3373-3017-4.ch004

Emon, M. M. H., & Chowdhury, M. S. A. (2025). AI and IoT-Powered Smart Logistics: Transforming Supply Chains for Efficiency and Sustainability. In *Emerging Trends in Smart Logistics Technologies* (A. Hlali, pp. 45–72). IGI Global Scientific Publishing. DOI: 10.4018/979-8-3373-2434-0.ch002

Emon, M. M. H., Mazid-Ul-Haque, M., Nath, A., Hamim, S. A., Fuad, M. N., & Islam, M. M. (2025). Determinants of AI-Powered Marketing Tool Adoption in E-Commerce: An Empirical Analysis within Intelligent Computing Systems. *2025 IEEE 7th International Conference on Sustainable Technologies For Industry 5.0 (STI)*, 1–6. DOI: 10.1109/STI69347.2025.11367588

Emon, M. M. H., Nath, A., Rahman, K. M., Kutub, J., Rifat, H. H., & Mahsin-Ul-Islam, M. (2025). Evaluating Artificial Intelligence Integration for Improving Supply Chain Efficiency in the Context of Bangladesh's E-Commerce Sector. *2025 IEEE 7th International Conference on Sustainable Technologies For Industry 5.0 (STI)*, 1–6. DOI: 10.1109/STI69347.2025.11367608

Emon, M. M. H., Rahman, K. M., Islam, M. S., Nath, A., Kutub, J., & Santa, N. A. (2025). Determinants of Explainable AI Adoption in Customer Service Chatbots: Insights from the Telecom Sector of Bangladesh. *2025 IEEE 7th International Conference on Sustainable Technologies For Industry 5.0 (STI)*, 1–6. https://doi .org/DOI: 10.1109/STI69347.2025.11367590

Emon, M. M. H., Rahman, K. M., Nath, A., Mahsin-Ul-Islam, M., Rifat, H. H., & Kutub, J. (2025). Exploring Drivers of Sustainable E-Commerce Adoption among SMEs in Bangladesh: A TOE Framework Approach for Industry 5.0 Transformation. *2025 IEEE 7th International Conference on Sustainable Technologies For Industry 5.0 (STI)*, 1–6. https://doi.org/DOI: 10.1109/STI69347.2025.11367600

Emon, M. M. H. (2025c). Digital transformation in emerging markets: Adoption dynamics of AI image generation in marketing practices. *Telematics and Informatics Reports*, *20*, 100267. DOI: 10.1016/j.teler.2025.100267

Emon, M. M. H., & Khan, T. (2025). The transformative role of Industry 4.0 in supply chains: Exploring digital integration and innovation in the manufacturing enterprises. *Journal of Open Innovation*, *11*(2), 100516. DOI: 10.1016/j.joitmc.2025.100516

Emon, M. M. H., & Khan, T. (2025a). Corporate Social Responsibility for Sustainable Development: A Systematic Review of Business Contributions to Address Global Challenges. *Review of Business and Economics Studies*, *13*(2), 6–39. DOI: 10.26794/2308-944X-2025-13-2-6-39

Emon, M. M. H., & Khan, T. (2025a). The Role of Traditional Media in Crisis Amplification: How Mainstream Media Magnifies Fake News and Ethical Dilemmas in Supply Chain Crises. In *Mass Media and Impact of Fake News on Supply Chains* (pp. 59–90). IGI Global., DOI: 10.4018/979-8-3373-2175-2.ch003

Emon, M. M. H., & Khan, T. (2025b). Exploring the mediating role of green logistics in enhancing green supply chain performance: Evidence from Bangladesh. *Journal of Engineering Research*. Advance online publication. DOI: 10.1016/j.jer.2025.10.003

Emon, M. M. H., & Khan, T. (2025b). Strengthening Bonds: The Strategic Role of Customer Relationship Management in Loyalty and Retention. In Ananthan, S., Kohli, A., Manickam, T., & Dhanabalan, T. (Eds.), *Strategic Innovation and Sustainable Customer-Centric Growth* (pp. 27–56). IGI Global Scientific Publishing., DOI: 10.4018/979-8-3373-6955-6.ch002

Emon, M. M. H., Nath, A., & Nipa, M. N. (2025). *AI for a Greener Tomorrow: Harnessing Artificial Intelligence for Environmental Sustainability*. IGI Global Scientific Publishing., DOI: 10.4018/979-8-3373-2387-9.ch010

Epede, M. B., & Wang, D. (2022). Global value chain linkages: An integrative review of the opportunities and challenges for SMEs in developing countries. *International Business Review*, *31*(5), 101993. DOI: 10.1016/j.ibusrev.2022.101993

Epstein, M. J., & Roy, M. J. (2001). Sustainability in Action: Identifying and Measuring the Key Performance Drivers. *Long Range Planning*, *34*(5), 585–604. DOI: 10.1016/S0024-6301(01)00084-X

Ethirajan, M., & Kandasamy, J. (2025). Quantum computing as an enabler for sustainable circular economy: Emerging trends and future directions. *Sustainable Operations and Computers*, *6*, 136–148. DOI: 10.1016/j.susoc.2024.12.001

European Commission. (2023). Regulation (EU) 2023/956 of the European Parliament and of the Council of 10 May 2023 establishing a carbon border adjustment mechanism. *Official Journal of the European Union, L, 130*(52).

Fan, M. (2023). Future of Blockchain: Data storage, carbon calculation, accounting, and emissions trading. *Journal of Student Research*, *12*(4). Advance online publication. DOI: 10.47611/jsrhs.v12i4.5665

Faraji, F., Hajipour, V., & Rahimnia, F. (2024). Quantum computing for climate resilience and sustainability challenges. *arXiv*. https://arxiv.org/abs/2409.10029

Farhana, K., Kadirgama, K., Mahamude, A. S. F., & Mica, M. T. (2022). Energy consumption, environmental impact, and implementation of renewable energy resources in global textile industries: An overview towards circularity and sustainability. *Materials Circular Economy*, *4*(1), 15. DOI: 10.1007/s42824-022-00059-1

Farshadfar, Z., Khajavi, S. H., Mucha, T., & Tanskanen, K. (2025). Machine learning-based automated waste sorting in the construction industry: A comparative competitiveness case study. *Waste Management (New York, N.Y.)*, *194*, 77–87. DOI: 10.1016/j.wasman.2025.01.008 PMID: 39787669

Feng, W., Chen, T., Li, L., Zhang, L., Deng, B., Liu, W., Li, J., & Cai, D. (2024). Application of neural networks on carbon emission prediction: A systematic review and comparison. *Energies, 17*(7), 1628. DOI: 10.3390/en17071628

Feng, X., Qiu, J., & Wei, C. (2025). Assessing Big Data Capabilities in Manufacturing Supply Chains: A Pythagorean Fuzzy MAGDM Framework. *International Journal of Fuzzy Systems, 27*(4), 1279–1302. DOI: 10.1007/S40815-024-01833-W/FIGURES/4

Fernando, Y., Shaharudin, M. S., & Abideen, A. Z. (2023). Circular economy-based reverse logistics: Dynamic interplay between sustainable resource commitment and financial performance. *European Journal of Management and Business Economics, 32*(1), 91–112. DOI: 10.1108/EJMBE-08-2020-0254

Fernando, Y., Sroufe, R., Tseng, M.-L., & Shaharudin, M. S., Wahyuni-TD, I. S., & Jawo, M. (2025). The circular supply chains in smart cities: A catalyst for sustainable development. *Journal of Industrial and Production Engineering, 42*(7), 730–754. DOI: 10.1080/21681015.2025.2497867

Folke, C. (2016). Resilience (republished). *Ecology and Society, 21*(4), 44. Advance online publication. DOI: 10.5751/ES-09088-210444

Freeman, R. E. (2010). *Strategic management: A stakeholder approach.* Cambridge University Press.

Fu, X., Alevizou, P. J., Cheng, R., & Ma, K. (2025). Explore the meanings beyond motives behind second-hand clothing consumption practice: From the theory of practice perspective. *Journal of Fashion Marketing and Management, 29*(7), 1320–1342. DOI: 10.1108/JFMM-05-2024-0196

García, Á., Bregon, A., & Martínez-Prieto, M. A. (2022). A non-intrusive Industry 4.0 retrofitting approach for collaborative maintenance in traditional manufacturing. *Computers & Industrial Engineering, 164*, 107896. DOI: 10.1016/j.cie.2021.107896 PMID: 36569781

Gaur, A., Gurjar, S. K., & Chaudhary, S. (2022). Circular system of resource recovery and reverse logistics approach: key to zero waste and zero landfill. In *Advanced Organic Waste Management* (pp. 365–381). Elsevier., DOI: 10.1016/B978-0-323-85792-5.00008-3

Gebhardt, M., Kopyto, M., Birkel, H., & Hartmann, E. (2022). Industry 4.0 technologies as enablers of collaboration in circular supply chains: A systematic literature review. *International Journal of Production Research, 60*(23), 6967–6995. DOI: 10.1080/00207543.2021.1999521

Geissdoerfer, M., Savaget, P., Bocken, N. M. P., & Hultink, E. J. (2017). The circular economy – A new sustainability paradigm? *Journal of Cleaner Production, 143*, 757–768. DOI: 10.1016/j.jclepro.2016.12.048

Genovese, A., Acquaye, A. A., Figueroa, A., & Koh, S. C. L. (2017). Sustainable supply chain management and the transition towards a circular economy: Evidence and some applications. *Omega*, *66*, 344–357. DOI: 10.1016/j.omega.2015.05.015

Gholami, H., Delorme, X., & Dolgui, A. (2025). An intelligent data-driven model for sustainable-resilient supplier scrutiny and selection in sustainable reconfigurable manufacturing systems. *International Journal of Production Research.* Advance online publication. DOI: 10.1080/00207543.2025.2581249;JOURNAL:JOURNAL:TPRS20;WGROUP:STRING:PUBLICATION

Ghorabaee, M. K., Amiri, M., Zavadskas, E. K., & Turskis, Z. (2017). Multi-criteria group decision-making using an extended EDAS method with interval type-2 fuzzy sets. *E+M. Ekonomie a Management*, *20*(1), 48–68. DOI: 10.15240/TUL/001/2017-1-004

Ghorbani, M., Yazdani, M., Govindan, K., & Basagni, S. (2023). Circular supply chains as complex adaptive systems: A simulation-based study. *IFAC-PapersOnLine*, *56*(2), 318–323. DOI: 10.1016/j.ifacol.2023.10.1596

Ghosh, P., Jha, A., & Sharma, R. R. K. (2020). Managing carbon footprint for a sustainable supply chain: A systematic literature review. *Modern Supply Chain Research and Applications*, *2*(3), 123–141. DOI: 10.1108/mscra-06-2020-0016

Giannakis, M., Papadopoulos, T., Dubey, R., Yan, Z., & Spanaki, K. (2025). Are we truly ready for what is coming? A reflection on supply chain resilience challenges in the face of megatrends. *International Journal of Production Economics*, *272*, 109238. Advance online publication. DOI: 10.1016/j.ijpe.2025.109238

Gokarn, S., & Kuthambalayan, T. S. (2017). Analysis of challenges inhibiting the reduction of waste in food supply chain. *Journal of Cleaner Production*, *168*, 595–604. DOI: 10.1016/j.jclepro.2017.09.028

González-Sánchez, R., Alonso-Muñoz, S., & Kocollari, U. (2025). Exploring the supply chain's transformation to achieve the sustainable development goals in the post-pandemic scenario: A review and a research agenda. *International Journal of Logistics Management*, *36*(7), 137–177. DOI: 10.1108/IJLM-05-2023-0221

Govindan, K., Khodaverdi, R., & Jafarian, A. (2013a). A fuzzy multi criteria approach for measuring sustainability performance of a supplier based on triple bottom line approach. *Journal of Cleaner Production, 47*, 345–354. DOI: 10.1016/j.jclepro.2012.04.014

Govindan, K., Shaw, M., & Majumdar, A. (2021). Social sustainability tensions in multi-tier supply chain: A systematic literature review towards conceptual framework development. *Journal of Cleaner Production, 279*, 123075. DOI: 10.1016/j.jclepro.2020.123075

Gualandris, J. (2021). Sustainable evaluation and verification. *The Journal of Supply Chain Management*. Advance online publication. DOI: 10.1016/j.pursup.2014.03.001

Gul, I., Raziq, A., & Khan, M. R. (2024). Towards Sustainable Supply Chains With Blockchain. *Advances in Logistics, Operations, and Management Science*, 18-37, ISSN 2327-350X, IGI Global, DOI: 10.4018/979-8-3693-0482-2.ch002

Gunasekaran, A., Papadopoulos, T., Dubey, R., Wamba, S. F., Childe, S. J., Hazen, B., & Akter, S. (2017). Big data and predictive analytics for supply chain and organizational performance. *Journal of Business Research, 70*, 308–317. DOI: 10.1016/j.jbusres.2016.08.004

Gupta, H., Kusi-Sarpong, S., & Rezaei, J. (2019). Barriers and overcoming strategies to supply chain sustainability innovation. *Resources, Conservation and Recycling, 146*, 307–316. DOI: 10.1016/j.resconrec.2019.03.015

Gupta, S., Chen, H., Hazen, B. T., Kaur, S., & Santibañez Gonzalez, E. D. R. (2019). Circular economy and big data analytics: A stakeholder perspective. *Technological Forecasting and Social Change, 144*, 466–474. DOI: 10.1016/j.techfore.2018.06.030

Gurtu, A., & Johny, J. (2019). Potential of blockchain technology in supply chain management: A literature review. *International Journal of Physical Distribution & Logistics Management, 49*(9), 881–900. DOI: 10.1108/ijpdlm-11-2018-0371

Gu, X. (2024). Exploration of carbon emission statistics and management in the supply chain of automobile industry based on Blockchain technology. *Academic Journal of Management and Social Sciences, 6*(1), 97–100. DOI: 10.54097/qfx8kh10

Haddud, A., DeSouza, A., Khare, A., & Lee, H. (2017). Examining potential benefits and challenges associated with the Internet of Things integration in supply chains. *Journal of Manufacturing Technology Management, 28*(8), 1055–1085. DOI: 10.1108/JMTM-05-2017-0094

Hader, M., Tchoffa, D., El Mhamedi, A., Ghodous, P., Dolgui, A., & Abouabdellah, A. (2022). Applying integrated Blockchain and Big Data technologies to improve supply chain traceability and information sharing in the textile sector. *Journal of Industrial Information Integration, 28*, 100345, ISSN 2452-414X, Elsevier BV, DOI: 10.1016/j.jii.2022.100345

Handoyo, S., & Anas, S. (2024). The effect of environmental, social, and governance (ESG) on firm performance: The moderating role of country regulatory quality and government effectiveness in ASEAN. *Cogent Business & Management, 11*(1). Advance online publication. DOI: 10.1080/23311975.2024.2371071

Hao, X., & Demir, E. (2024). Artificial intelligence in supply chain decision-making: An environmental, social, and governance triggering and technological inhibiting protocol. *Journal of Modelling in Management, 19*(2), 605–629. DOI: 10.1108/JM2-01-2023-0009

Hasan, M. K., Latif, Z., Hlali, A., Xunping, L., & Aka, S. A. B. (2025). Hyperautomation: The Next Frontier in Supply Chain (SC) and Manufacturing. In *Emerging Trends in Smart Logistics Technologies* (pp. 1–44). IGI Global Scientific Publishing. DOI: 10.4018/979-8-3373-2434-0.ch001

Hasan, M. K., Latif, Z., Hlali, A., Xunping, L., & Aka, S. A. B. (2026). Hyperautomation: The Next Frontier in Supply Chain (SC) and Manufacturing. *Emerging Trends in Smart Logistics Technologies* (pp. 1-44). IGI Global Scientific Publishing.

Hasan, M., Chun, C. Y., Yao, S., & Kemi, A. P. (2022). Forecasting the Quality of Port Infrastructure of Asian Port Countries: An Application of the Model GM (1, 1) and Clustering Them Using HCA Algorithm. *Operations and Supply Chain Management: An International Journal*, 105–121. DOI: 10.31387/oscm0480334

Hasan, M. K., Lei, X., Hlali, A., & Bian, Z. (2024). Modelling capability factors of logistics industry based on ISM-MICMAC. *Heliyon, 10*(22), e40539. DOI: 10.1016/j.heliyon.2024.e40539 PMID: 39641072

Hasan, M. K., Lei, X., Tang, W., Nishi, N. N., & Latif, Z. (2025). Exploring logistics performance index (LPI) from global perspective: A study based on network analysis (NA). *Operations Management Research, 18*(3), 1088–1112. DOI: 10.1007/s12063-025-00550-3

Hasan, R., Kamal, M. M., Daowd, A., Eldabi, T., Koliousis, I., & Papadopoulos, T. (2024). Critical analysis of the impact of big data analytics on supply chain operations. *Production Planning and Control, 35*(1), 46–70. DOI: 10.1080/09537287.2022.2047237;WEBSITE:WEBSITE:TFOPB;PAGE-GROUP:STRING:PUBLICATION

Ha, T., & Kim, S. (2024). Improving Trust in AI with Mitigating Confirmation Bias: Effects of Explanation Type and Debiasing Strategy for Decision-Making with Explainable AI. *International Journal of Human-Computer Interaction, 40*(24), 8562–8573. DOI: 10.1080/10447318.2023.2285640

Hazen, B. T., Boone, C. A., Ezell, J. D., & Jones-Farmer, L. A. (2016). Data quality for data science, predictive analytics, and big data in supply chain management: An introduction to the problem and suggestions for research and applications. *International Journal of Production Economics, 154*, 72–80. DOI: 10.1016/j.ijpe.2014.04.018

Hazen, B. T., Skipper, J. B., Ezell, J. D., & Boone, C. A. (2016). Big data and predictive analytics for supply chain sustainability: A theory-driven research agenda. *Computers & Industrial Engineering, 101*, 592–598. DOI: 10.1016/j.cie.2016.06.030

Hendricks, S., & Mwapwele, S. D. (2024). A systematic literature review on the factors influencing e-commerce adoption in developing countries. *Data and Information Management, 8*(1), 100045. DOI: 10.1016/j.dim.2023.100045

Hoberg, K. (2020). *Supply Chain and Big Data. Encyclopedia of Big Data*. Springer International Publishing., DOI: 10.1007/978-3-319-32001-4_242-1

Hoffmann, R., & Reich, C. (2023). A Systematic Literature Review on Artificial Intelligence and Explainable Artificial Intelligence for Visual Quality Assurance in Manufacturing. *Electronics (Basel), 12*(22), 4572. DOI: 10.3390/electronics12224572

Hofmann, E., Sternberg, H., Chen, H., Pflaum, A., & Prockl, G. (2019). Supply chain management and Industry 4.0: Conducting research in the digital age. *International Journal of Physical Distribution & Logistics Management, 49*(10), 945–955. DOI: 10.1108/IJPDLM-11-2019-399

Holland, J. H. (2014). *Complexity: A very short introduction*. Oxford University Press.

Holling, C. S. (1973). Resilience and stability of ecological systems. *Annual Review of Ecology and Systematics, 4*, 1–23. DOI: 10.1146/annurev.es.04.110173.000245

Hong, L., & Hales, D. N. (2021). Blockchain performance in supply chain management: application in blockchain integration companies. *Industrial Management & Data Systems, 121*(9), 1969-1996, ISSN 0263-5577, Emerald, DOI: 10.1108/imds-10-2020-0598

Hosain, R. (2025). Digital transformation in Bangladesh's RMG supply chains: A case study on DBS Group. *International Journal of Research and Innovation in Social Science (IJRISS), 9*(6), 1696–1703. DOII https://dx.doi.org/DOI: 10.47772/IJRISS.2025.906000133

Hunt, K., & Zhuang, J. (2022). Blockchain for Disaster Management. *Studies in Big Data*, 253-269, ISSN 2197-6503, Springer International Publishing, DOI: 10.1007/978-3-030-87304-2_10

Hussain, Z. (2022). Environmental and Economic-oriented Transport Efficiency: The Role of Climate Change Mitigation Technology. *Environmental Science and Pollution Research International*, *29*(19), 29165–29182. DOI: 10.1007/s11356-021-18392-4 PMID: 34993827

Huynh, P. L. T., Le, P. L., & Nguyen, T. T. (2025). Sustainability of FDI and domestic firms through big data analytics expertise: The moderating role of supply chain risk management. *Benchmarking*. Advance online publication. DOI: 10.1108/BIJ-09-2024-0735

Hu, Z., Du, Y., Rao, C., & Goh, M. (2020). Delegated proof of reputation consensus mechanism for blockchain-enabled distributed carbon emission trading system. *IEEE Access : Practical Innovations, Open Solutions*, *8*, 214932–214944. DOI: 10.1109/access.2020.3041689

Hwang, B. N., Jitanugoon, S., & Puntha, P. (2025). AI integration in service delivery: Enhancing business and sustainability performance amid challenges. *Journal of Services Marketing*. Advance online publication. DOI: 10.1108/JSM-10-2024-0511

Iftikhar, A., Ali, I., Arslan, A., & Tarba, S. (2024). Digital Innovation, Data Analytics, and Supply Chain Resiliency: A Bibliometric-based Systematic Literature Review. *Annals of Operations Research*, *333*(2–3), 825–848. DOI: 10.1007/s10479-022-04765-6 PMID: 35611176

International Trade Centre (ITC). (2023). *SME Competitiveness Outlook 2023,* Retrieved December 21, 2025from https://www.intracen.org/resources/publications/sme-competitiveness-outlook

Ivanov, D. (2020). Predicting the impacts of epidemic outbreaks on global supply chains: A simulation-based analysis on the coronavirus outbreak (COVID-19/SARS-CoV-2) case. *Transportation Research Part E, Logistics and Transportation Review*, *136*, 101922. DOI: 10.1016/j.tre.2020.101922 PMID: 32288597

Ivanov, D. (2021). Exiting the COVID-19 pandemic: Aftershock risks and avoidance of disruption tails in supply chains. *Annals of Operations Research*, *319*(1), 149–172. DOI: 10.1007/s10479-021-04092-6 PMID: 33840871

Ivanov, D. (2024). Viable supply chain model: Integrating agility, resilience, and sustainability perspectives—Lessons from and thinking beyond the COVID-19 pandemic. *Annals of Operations Research, 319*(1), 839–857. DOI: 10.1007/s10479-020-03640-6 PMID: 32836614

Ivanov, D., & Dolgui, A. (2021). A digital supply chain twin for managing the disruption risks and resilience in the era of Industry 4.0. *Production Planning and Control, 32*(9), 775–788. DOI: 10.1080/09537287.2020.1768450

Ivanov, D., Dolgui, A., & Sokolov, B. (2019). The impact of digital technology and Industry 4.0 on the ripple effect and supply chain risk analytics. *International Journal of Production Research, 57*(3), 829–846. DOI: 10.1080/00207543.2018.1488086

Jahin, M. A., Shovon, M. S. H., Islam, M. S., Shin, J., Mridha, M. F., & Tanweer, M. R. (2023). QAmplifyNet: Pushing the boundaries of supply chain backorder prediction using interpretable hybrid quantum-classical neural network. *Scientific Reports, 13*(1), 18225. Advance online publication. DOI: 10.1038/s41598-023-45406-7 PMID: 37880386

Jamshidi, A., Jamshidi, F., Ait-Kadi, D., & Ramudhin, A. (2019). A review of priority criteria and decision-making methods applied in selection of sustainable city logistics initiatives and collaboration partners. *International Journal of Production Research, 57*(15–16), 5175–5193. DOI: 10.1080/00207543.2018.1540892;WGROUP:STRING:PUBLICATION

Janssen, M., Hartog, M., Matheus, R., Yi Ding, A., & Kuk, G. (2022). Will Algorithms Blind People? The Effect of Explainable AI and Decision-Makers' Experience on AI-supported Decision-Making in Government. *Social Science Computer Review, 40*(2), 478–493. DOI: 10.1177/0894439320980118

Jeble, S., Dubey, R., Childe, S. J., Papadopoulos, T., Roubaud, D., & Prakash, A. (2018). Impact of big data and predictive analytics capability on supply chain sustainability. *International Journal of Logistics Management, 29*(2), 513–538. DOI: 10.1108/IJLM-05-2017-0134

Jeble, S., Kumari, S., Venkatesh, V. G., & Singh, M. (2023). Challenges of big data analytics for sustainable supply chains in healthcare – A resource-based view. *Benchmarking, 30*(9), 3461–3483. DOI: 10.1108/BIJ-07-2022-0433

Jensen, H. H. (2025). Internal IT: The Backbone System of Circular Business Models. In *Circular Economy Opportunities and Pathways for Manufacturers* (pp. 291–321). https://doi.org/DOI: 10.1007/978-3-031-75279-7_11

Ju, C., Shen, Z., Bao, F., Weng, P., Xu, Y., & Xu, C. (2022). A novel credible carbon footprint traceability system for low carbon economy using blockchain technology. *International Journal of Environmental Research and Public Health, 19*(16), 10316. DOI: 10.3390/ijerph191610316 PMID: 36011951

Kache, F., & Seuring, S. (2017). Challenges and opportunities of digital information at the intersection of Big Data Analytics and supply chain management. *International Journal of Operations & Production Management, 37*(1), 10–36. DOI: 10.1108/IJOPM-02-2015-0078

Kamble, S. S., Mor, R. S., & Belhadi, A. (2023). Big Data Analytics for Supply Chain Transformation: A Systematic Literature Review Using SCOR Framework. In *Digital Transformation and Industry 4.0 for Sustainable Supply Chain Performance* (pp. 1–50). https://doi.org/DOI: 10.1007/978-3-031-19711-6_1

Kamble, S. S., Gunasekaran, A., & Gawankar, S. A. (2020). Achieving sustainable performance in a data-driven agriculture supply chain: A review for research and applications. *International Journal of Production Economics, 219*, 179–194. DOI: 10.1016/j.ijpe.2019.05.022

Kandpal, V., Jaswal, A., Santibanez Gonzalez, E. D. R., & Agarwal, N. (2024). *Circular Economy Principles: Shifting Towards Sustainable Prosperity* (pp. 125–165). https://doi.org/DOI: 10.1007/978-3-031-52943-6_4

Kaneberg, E., Herold, D. M., Piotrowicz, W., & Gabellini, G. (2025). Supply chain resilience and critical dynamic capabilities: A balanced scorecard approach. *Logistics Research, 13*(1), 2523957. Advance online publication. DOI: 10.1080/21693277.2025.2523957

Kaniappan Chinnathai, M., & Alkan, B. (2023). A digital life-cycle management framework for sustainable smart manufacturing in energy intensive industries. *Journal of Cleaner Production, 419*, 138259. DOI: 10.1016/j.jclepro.2023.138259

Kanyepe, J. (2024). Data-Driven Logistics Optimisation. *Advances in Logistics, Operations, and Management Science*, 63-96, ISSN 2327-350X, IGI Global, DOI: 10.4018/979-8-3693-6205-1.ch003

Kanyepe, J., Chibaro, M., Morima, M., & Moeti-Lysson, J. (2024). AI-Powered Agricultural Supply Chains. *Advances in Marketing, Customer Relationship Management, and E-Services*, 33-64, ISSN 2327-5502, IGI Global, DOI: 10.4018/979-8-3693-6468-0.ch002

Karadgi, S., Kulkarni, V., & Doddamani, S. (2021). Traceable and Intelligent Supply Chain based on Blockchain and Artificial Intelligence. *Journal of Physics: Conference Series, 2070*(1), 12158, ISSN 1742-6588, IOP Publishing, DOI: 10.1088/1742-6596/2070/1/012158

Kayikci, S., & Khoshgoftaar, T. M. (2024). Blockchain meets machine learning: a survey. *Journal of Big Data, 11*(1), ISSN 2196-1115, Springer Science and Business Media LLC, DOI: 10.1186/s40537-023-00852-y

Kellogg, K. C., Valentine, M. A., & Christin, A. (2020). Algorithms at Work: The New Contested Terrain of Control. *The Academy of Management Annals, 14*(1), 366–410. DOI: 10.5465/annals.2018.0174

Kennedy, S., & Linnenluecke, M. K. (2022). Circular economy and resilience: A research agenda. *Business Strategy and the Environment, 31*(6), 2754–2765. DOI: 10.1002/bse.3004

Ketchen, D. J.Jr, Crook, T. R., Craighead, C. W., & Cheng, L. (2022). Toward a theory of supply chain entrepreneurial embeddedness in disrupted and normal states. *The Journal of Supply Chain Management, 58*(1), 5–26. DOI: 10.1111/jscm.12283

Ketokivi, M., & Choi, T. (2022). Building and testing necessity theories in supply chain management. *The Journal of Supply Chain Management, 58*(2), 3–22. DOI: 10.1111/jscm.12287

Khahro, S. H., Kumar, D., Siddiqui, F. H., Ali, T. H., Raza, M. S., & Khoso, A. R. (2021). Optimizing Energy Use, Cost and Carbon Emission through Building Information Modelling and a Sustainability Approach: A Case-Study of a Hospital Building. *Sustainability, 13*(7), 3675. DOI: 10.3390/su13073675

Khan, A., Hossain, E., Shahaab, A., & Khan, I. (2022). ShrimpChain: A blockchain-based transparent and traceable framework to enhance the export potentiality of Bangladeshi shrimp. *Smart Agricultural Technology, 2*, 100041, ISSN 2772-3755, Elsevier BV, DOI: 10.1016/j.atech.2022.100041

Khan, T., & Emon, M. M. H. (2025a). Preparing for the Next Disruption: Lessons Learned From Past Crises and Building a Playbook for Future Supply Chain Shocks. In *Supply Chain Disruptions and Impact on Global Inflation* (pp. 253–286). IGI Global Scientific Publishing. DOI: 10.4018/979-8-3373-1982-7.ch010

Khan, T., & Emon, M. M. H. (2025b). Resilient Supply Chains: Lessons From Past Crisis Strategies Companies Can Adopt to Create More Resilient Supply Chains. In *Mass Media and Impact of Fake News on Supply Chains* (pp. 285–318). IGI Global. DOI: 10.4018/979-8-3373-2175-2.ch011

Khan, T., & Hasan Emon, M. M. (2024). Determinants of AI Image Generator Adoption Among Marketing Agencies: The Mediating Effects of Perceived Usefulness. *2024 IEEE 3rd International Conference on Robotics, Automation, Artificial-Intelligence and Internet-of-Things (RAAICON)*, 177–182. https://doi.org/DOI: 10.1109/RAAICON64172.2024.10928548

Khan, T., Emon, M. M. H., & Nath, A. (2024). Quantifying the Effects of AI-Driven Inventory Management on Operational Efficiency in Online Retail. *2024 27th International Conference on Computer and Information Technology (ICCIT)*, 2092–2097. DOI: 10.1109/ICCIT64611.2024.11021996

Khan, T., Emon, M. M. H., & Rahman, S. (2024). Marketing Strategy Innovation via AI Adoption: A Study on Bangladeshi SMEs in the Context of Industry 5.0. *2024 6th International Conference on Sustainable Technologies for Industry 5.0 (STI)*, 1–6. https://doi.org/DOI: 10.1109/STI64222.2024.10951050

Khan, T., Emon, M. M. H., Rahman, M. A., Abdul Hamid, A. B., & Ya'akub, N. I. B. (2024). *Bridging the Gap: Realizing GreenTech Potential*. 91–121. DOI: 10.4018/979-8-3693-9879-1.ch004

Khanfar, A. A. A., Iranmanesh, M., Ghobakhloo, M., Senali, M. G., & Fathi, M. (2021). Applications of Blockchain Technology in Sustainable Manufacturing and Supply Chain Management: A Systematic Review. *Sustainability*, *13*(14), 7870. DOI: 10.3390/su13147870

Khan, M. R., & Arif, M. Z. U. (2025). Operational efficiency through disruptive innovation in dairy business: Evidence from an emerging economy. *International Journal of Productivity and Quality Management*, *45*(1), 66–93. DOI: 10.1504/IJPQM.2025.146575

Khan, M. R., Arif, M. Z. U., & Rammal, H. G. (2025). Disruptive production process innovation for sustainable business: Evidence from an emerging economy. *Business Process Management Journal*, *31*(4), 1349–1370. DOI: 10.1108/BPMJ-11-2023-0872

Khan, M. R., & Pervin, M. T. (2024). Technology disruption and its application in organizational management theories: A case study on Toyota Motor Corporation. *International Journal of Services and Operations Management*, *49*(2), 198–220. DOI: 10.1504/IJSOM.2024.141998

Khan, M. R., & Sarkar, U. (2024). Business leadership in the digital age: IKEA's story in the retail and consumer sector. *Green Technologies and Sustainability*, *2*(2), 100081. DOI: 10.1016/j.grets.2024.100081

Khan, M., Amin, F., Din, M. U., Abid, M. A., & de la Torre, I. (2025). Enhancing e-commerce logistics efficiency and sustainability via quantum computing and artificial intelligence-based quantum hybrid models. *The Journal of Supercomputing*, *81*(1), 1–32. DOI: 10.1007/s11227-025-07959-4

Khanna, R., Sharma, R. K., Sharma, A., & Mahajan, R. (2025). Circular supply chain management: Bridging business innovation and sustainability through best practices. *Journal of Circular Economy*, *3*(1), 1–15. DOI: 10.1007/s44251-024-00048-1

Khan, T., & Emon, M. M. H. (2025c). The role of digital supply chain practices in enhancing firm performance: Insights from the manufacturing sector of Bangladesh. *Brazilian Journal of Operations & Production Management*, *22*(2), 2493. DOI: 10.14488/BJOPM.2493.2025

Khan, T., Emon, M. M. H., Rahman, K. M., Nipa, M. N., & Fuad, M. N. (2025). The Role of AI in Driving Customer Engagement Through Technological, Organizational and Environmental Enablers in E-Commerce. *2025 International Conference on Quantum Photonics, Artificial Intelligence, and Networking (QPAIN)*, 1–6. https://doi.org/DOI: 10.1109/QPAIN66474.2025.11171949

Khan, T., & Hasan Emon, M. M. (2025). Harnessing Disciplinary Networks: A Global Educational Leadership Perspective on Positive Behavioural Management. In *International Dimensions of Educational Leadership and Management for Economic Growth*. IGI Global Scientific Publishing., DOI: 10.4018/979-8-3373-3616-9.ch012

Kim, S.-K., & Huh, J.-H. (2020). Blockchain of carbon trading for UN sustainable development goals. *Sustainability*, *12*(10), 4021. DOI: 10.3390/su12104021

Korhonen, J., Honkasalo, A., & Seppälä, J. (2018). Circular economy: The concept and its limitations. *Ecological Economics*, *143*, 37–46. DOI: 10.1016/j.ecolecon.2017.06.041

Kouhizadeh, M, Zhu, Q, Alkhuzaim, L, & Sarkis, J (2022). Blockchain Technology and the Circular Economy: An Exploration. *Circular Economy Supply Chains: From Chains to Systems*, 189-213, Emerald Publishing Limited, DOI: 10.1108/978-1-83982-544-620221010

Krasteva, I, Glushkova, T, Stoyanova-Doycheva, A, Moralivska, N, Doukovska, L, & Radeva, I (2021). Blockchain-based approach to supply chain modelling in a smart farming system. *2021 Big Data, Knowledge and Control Systems Engineering (BdKCSE)*, 1-6, IEEE, DOI: 10.1109/bdkcse53180.2021.9627309

Krishnan, R. (2024). Challenges and benefits for small and medium enterprises in the transformation to smart manufacturing: A systematic literature review and framework. *Journal of Manufacturing Technology Management, 35*(4), 918–938. DOI: 10.1108/JMTM-07-2022-0255

Kshetri, N (2021). Amplifying the value of blockchain in supply chains. *Blockchain and Supply Chain Management*, 67-88, Elsevier, DOI: 10.1016/b978-0-323-89934-5.00003-9

Kshetri, N. (2018). Blockchain's roles in meeting key supply chain management objectives. *International Journal of Information Management, 39*, 80–89. DOI: 10.1016/j.ijinfomgt.2017.12.005

Kshetri, N. (2021). Blockchain and sustainable supply chain management in developing countries. *International Journal of Information Management, 60*, 102376. DOI: 10.1016/j.ijinfomgt.2021.102376

Kumar, D., Singh, R. K., Mishra, R., & Vlachos, I. (2024). Big data analytics in supply chain decarbonisation: A systematic literature review and future research directions. *International Journal of Production Research, 62*(4), 1489–1509. DOI: 10.1080/00207543.2023.2179346

Kumar, G., Basri, S., Imam, A. A., Khowaja, S. A., Capretz, L. F., & Balogun, A. O. (2021). Data Harmonization for Heterogeneous Datasets: A Systematic Literature Review. *Applied Sciences (Basel, Switzerland), 11*(17), 8275. DOI: 10.3390/app11178275

Kumar, S., Mangla, S. K., Luthra, S., & Rana, N. P. (2021). Big data analytics and sustainability of supply chains: A bibliometric and framework-based review. *Technological Forecasting and Social Change, 163*, 120464. DOI: 10.1016/j.techfore.2020.120464

Kumar, S., Verma, A. K., & Mirza, A. (2024). *Opportunities and Challenges for Data-Driven and Circular Economy.*, DOI: 10.1007/978-981-97-5656-8_7

Lakhouit, A. (2025). Revolutionizing urban solid waste management with AI and IoT: A review of smart solutions for waste collection, sorting, and recycling. *Results in Engineering, 25*, 104018. DOI: 10.1016/j.rineng.2025.104018

Laney, D. (2001). 3D data management: Controlling data volume, velocity, and variety. *META Group Research Note, 6,* 1–4.

Lanzalonga, F., Marseglia, R., Irace, A., & Biancone, P. Pietro. (2024). The application of artificial intelligence in waste management: Understanding the potential of data-driven approaches for the circular economy paradigm. *Management Decision*. Advance online publication. DOI: 10.1108/MD-10-2023-1733

Lee, I., & Mangalaraj, G. (2022). Big Data Analytics in Supply Chain Management: A Systematic Literature Review and Research Directions. *Big Data and Cognitive Computing, 6*(1), 17, ISSN 2504-2289, MDPI AG, DOI: 10.3390/bdcc6010017

Le, T. T. (2023). Linking big data, sustainable supply chain management and corporate performance: The moderating role of circular economy thinking. *International Journal of Logistics Management, 34*(3), 744–771. DOI: 10.1108/IJLM-01-2022-0011

Lewandowski, M. (2016). Designing the business models for circular economy—Towards the conceptual framework. *Sustainability, 8*(1), 43. DOI: 10.3390/su8010043

Li, Y., Wang, X., Zhang, L., & Chen, J. (2025). Supply chain resilience: A literature review based on bibliometric analysis. *International Journal of Logistics Research and Applications*. Advance online publication. https://doi.org/DOI: 10.1080/13675567.2025.2554801

Li, Y., Xia, X., Qiao, N., Zhang, P., & Zhang, J. (2023). Research on carbon emission management of electric power enterprises based on blockchain technology. SHS Web of Conferences, 154, 01024. https://doi.org/DOI: 10.1051/shsconf/202315401024

Liao, H.-T., Pan, C.-L., & Zhang, Y. (2023). Smart digital platforms for carbon neutral management and services: Business models based on ITU standards for green digital transformation. *Frontiers in Ecology and Evolution, 11*. Advance online publication. DOI: 10.3389/fevo.2023.1134381

Lin, H., Lin, J., & Wang, F. (2022). An innovative machine learning model for supply chain management. *Journal of Innovation & Knowledge, 7*(4), 100276. DOI: 10.1016/j.jik.2022.100276

Lin, H., & Wang, J. (2024). Enabling AI into business operations: Investigating the impact of IoTs, big data, and IT-enabled technologies on supply chain performance. *International Journal of Electronic Business, 19*(2), 123–138. DOI: 10.1504/IJEB.2024.137703

Lin, K.-Y. (2024). Circular supply chain for smart production in Industry 4.0. *Computers & Industrial Engineering, 198*, 110682. DOI: 10.1016/j.cie.2024.110682

Liu, S., Liu, J., Li, Y., Zhou, C., & Wang, C. (2024). Research on the application of blockchain technology in the carbon trading market of substations. *Applied Mathematics and Nonlinear Sciences*, *9*(1). Advance online publication. DOI: 10.2478/amns-2024-0947

Loock, M. (2020). Unlocking the value of digitalization for the European energy transition: A typology of innovative business models. *Energy Research & Social Science*, *69*, 101740. DOI: 10.1016/j.erss.2020.101740

Lugada, E., Komakech, H., Ochola, I., Mwebaze, S., Olowo Oteba, M., & Okidi Ladwar, D. (2022). Health supply chain system in Uganda: Current issues, structure, performance, and implications for systems strengthening. *Journal of Pharmaceutical Policy and Practice*, *15*(1), 14. DOI: 10.1186/s40545-022-00412-4 PMID: 35232485

Lv, B. (2025). Supply chain resilience modeling based on dynamic hypergraph and quantum reinforcement learning for low-altitude-ground networks. *Transportation Research Part E, Logistics and Transportation Review*, *183*, 103467. Advance online publication. DOI: 10.1016/j.tre.2024.103467

Ma, L., & Chang, R. (2024). How big data analytics and artificial intelligence facilitate digital supply chain transformation: the role of integration and agility. *Management Decision*, ISSN 0025-1747, Emerald, DOI: 10.1108/md-10-2023-1822

Mageto, J. (2021). Big Data Analytics in Sustainable Supply Chain Management: A Focus on Manufacturing Supply Chains. *Sustainability, 13*(13), 7101, ISSN 2071-1050, MDPI AG, DOI: 10.3390/su13137101

Mahajan, R., Lim, W. M., Sareen, M., Kumar, S., & Panwar, R. (2023). Stakeholder theory. *Journal of Business Research, 166*, 114104. DOI: 10.1016/j.jbusres.2023.114104

Maheshwari, S., Gautam, P., & Jaggi, C. K. (2021). Role of Big Data Analytics in supply chain management: Current trends and future perspectives. *International Journal of Production Research*, *59*(6), 1875–1900. DOI: 10.1080/00207543.2020.1793011

Malik, S. (2024). Data-Driven Decision-Making: Leveraging the IoT for Real-Time Sustainability in Organizational Behavior. *Sustainability*, *16*(15), 6302. DOI: 10.3390/su16156302

Mallick, P. K., Salling, K. B., Pigosso, D. C. A., & McAloone, T. C. (2024). Towards a circular economy: Development of a support tool for designing reverse logistics systems. *Journal of Environmental Management*, *351*, 119819. DOI: 10.1016/j.jenvman.2023.119819 PMID: 38104465

Manavalan, E., & Jayakrishna, K. (2019). A review of Internet of Things (IoT) embedded sustainable supply chain for industry 4.0 requirements. *Computers & Industrial Engineering*, *127*, 925–953. DOI: 10.1016/j.cie.2018.11.030

Mansouri, N., Nasri, S., Mnassri, A., Lashab, A., Vasquez, J. C., Cherif, A., & Rezk, H. (2025). Electric Vehicle Charging Infrastructure: Impacts and Future Challenges of Photovoltaic Integration with Examples from a Tunisian Case. *World Electric Vehicle Journal*, *16*(7), 349. DOI: 10.3390/wevj16070349

Marabelli, M., Newell, S., & Handunge, V. (2021). The lifecycle of algorithmic decision-making systems: Organizational choices and ethical challenges. *The Journal of Strategic Information Systems*, *30*(3), 101683. DOI: 10.1016/j.jsis.2021.101683

Marisamy, K., Selvakumar, A., Rajasekar, B., Natarajan, R., Atajanova, A., & Makhmudov, S. (2025). Smart logistics integrating AI, IoT, blockchain, and Robotics for a sustainable Future. In *Emerging Trends in Smart Logistics Technologies* (pp. 73–104). IGI Global Scientific Publishing., DOI: 10.4018/979-8-3373-2434-0.ch003

Marques, L., & Cunha, J. (2020). Big data and supply chain management: A review and bibliometric analysis. *Production*, *30*, e20200020. DOI: 10.1590/0103-6513.20200020

Martin, K. (2015). Ethical issues in the big data industry. *MIS Quarterly Executive*, *14*(2), 67–85.

Masip-Bruin, X., Marín-Tordera, E., Ruiz, J., Jukan, A., Trakadas, P., Cernivec, A., Lioy, A., López, D., Santos, H., Gonos, A., Silva, A., Soriano, J., & Kalogiannis, G. (2021). Cybersecurity in ICT Supply Chains: Key Challenges and a Relevant Architecture. *Sensors (Basel)*, *21*(18), 6057. DOI: 10.3390/s21186057 PMID: 34577264

McCarthy, R. V., McCarthy, M. M., & Ceccucci, W. (2022). Introduction to Predictive Analytics. In *Applying Predictive Analytics* (pp. 1–26). Springer International Publishing., DOI: 10.1007/978-3-030-83070-0_1

Meredith, J. (1993). Theory building through conceptual methods. *International Journal of Operations & Production Management*, *13*(5), 3–11. DOI: 10.1108/01443579310028120

Michalski, D. (2024). Operationalization of ESG-Integrated Strategy Through the Balanced Scorecard in FMCG Companies. *Sustainability*, *16*(21), 9174. DOI: 10.3390/su16219174

Mihai, F.-C., & Ulman, S.-R. (2023). Circular economy in Green Deal strategies. In *Sustainable and Circular Management of Resources and Waste Towards a Green Deal* (pp. 49–63). Elsevier., DOI: 10.1016/B978-0-323-95278-1.00029-2

Mikalef, P., Boura, M., Lekakos, G., & Krogstie, J. (2020). Big data analytics capabilities and innovation: The mediating role of dynamic capabilities and moderating effect of the environment. *British Journal of Management*, *31*(2), 402–428. DOI: 10.1111/1467-8551.12324

Mikalef, P., Pappas, I. O., Krogstie, J., & Giannakos, M. (2019). Big data analytics capabilities: A systematic literature review and research agenda. *Information Systems and e-Business Management*, *17*, 547–578. DOI: 10.1007/s10257-018-0377-y

Mishra, A., Dutta, P., Jayasankar, S., Jain, P., & Mathiyazhagan, K. (2023). A review of reverse logistics and closed-loop supply chains in the perspective of circular economy. *Benchmarking*, *30*(3), 975–1020. DOI: 10.1108/BIJ-11-2021-0669

Mishra, D., Gunasekaran, A., Papadopoulos, T., & Childe, S. J. (2018). Big Data and supply chain management: A review and bibliometric analysis. *Annals of Operations Research*, *270*(1–2), 313–336. DOI: 10.1007/s10479-016-2236-y

Mishra, V., Ishdorj, A., Tabares Villarreal, E., & Norton, R. (2025). Collaboration in agricultural value chains: A scoping review of the evidence from developing countries. *Journal of Agribusiness in Developing and Emerging Economies*, *15*(6), 1168–1192. DOI: 10.1108/JADEE-12-2023-0311

Mohammed, I., Nangpiire, C., Detoh, W. M., & Fataw, Y. (2024). The effect of blockchain technology in enhancing ethical sourcing and supply chain transparency: Evidence from the cocoa and agricultural sectors in Ghana. *African Journal of Empirical Research*, *5*(2), 55–64. DOI: 10.51867/ajernet.5.2.6

Mohanraj, E., N, E., S, S., & S, S. (2024). Digital Twins for Automotive Predictive Maintenance. *2024 International Conference on Inventive Computation Technologies (ICICT)*, 1579–1584. https://doi.org/DOI: 10.1109/ICICT60155.2024.10544392

Mohanraj, R., & Balaji, S. N. (2025). Digital Twin Technology: A Comprehensive Review of Modeling, Applications, Challenges and Future Directions in Complex System Integration. *Archives of Computational Methods in Engineering*. Advance online publication. DOI: 10.1007/s11831-025-10397-3

Moktadir, M. A., Ali, S. M., Paul, S. K., & Shukla, N. (2019). Barriers to big data analytics in manufacturing supply chains: A case study from Bangladesh. *Computers & Industrial Engineering*, *128*, 1063–1075. DOI: 10.1016/j.cie.2018.04.013

Momena, A. F., Gazi, K. H., Rahaman, M., Sobczak, A., Salahshour, S., Mondal, S. P., & Ghosh, A. (2024). Ranking and Challenges of Supply Chain Companies Using MCDM Methodology. *Logistics 2024, Vol. 8, Page 87*, *8*(3), 87. DOI: 10.3390/LOGISTICS8030087

Mondragon, A. E. C., Mastrocinque, E., Tsai, J.-F., Flynn, B. B., & Hogg, P. J. (2025). Examining Industry 5.0 and supply chain performance. *Logistics Research, 18*(1), 2501181. Advance online publication. DOI: 10.1080/21693277.2025.2501181

Morana, J. (2013). Sustainable. *Supply Chain Management.* Advance online publication. DOI: 10.1002/9781118604069

Moshood, T., Nawanir, G., Sorooshian, S., & Okfalisa, O. (2021). Digital Twins driven supply chain visibility within logistics: A new paradigm for future logistics. *Applied System Innovation, 4*(2), 29. DOI: 10.3390/asi4020029

Möslinger, M., Ulpiani, G., & Vetters, N. (2023). Circular economy and waste management to empower a climate-neutral urban future. *Journal of Cleaner Production, 421*, 138454. DOI: 10.1016/j.jclepro.2023.138454

Mostaghel, R., & Chirumalla, K. (2021). Role of customers in circular business models. *Journal of Business Research, 127*, 35–44. DOI: 10.1016/j.jbusres.2020.12.053

Mousavi, S. A., Pimenidis, E., & Jahankhani, H. (2008). Cultivating trust—an electronic-government development model for addressing the needs of developing countries. *International Journal of Electronic Security and Digital Forensics, 1*(3), 233–248. DOI: 10.1504/IJESDF.2008.020942

Mukherjee, S., Nagariya, R., Mathiyazhagan, K., Baral, M. M., Pavithra, M. R., & Appolloni, A. (2024). Artificial intelligence-based reverse logistics for improving circular economy performance: A developing country perspective. *International Journal of Logistics Management, 35*(6), 1779–1806. DOI: 10.1108/IJLM-03-2023-0102

Munim, Z. H., Vladi, O., & Hossain, N. U. I. (2024). Data analytics applications in supply chain resilience and sustainability management: The state of the art and a way forward. In *IvySCI* (pp. 1–24). Springer., DOI: 10.1007/978-3-031-29823-3_1

Munir, M. A., Hussain, A., Farooq, M., Habib, M. S., & Shahzad, M. F. (2023). Data-driven transformation: The role of ambidexterity and analytics capability in building dynamic and sustainable supply chains. *Sustainability, 15*(14), 10896. DOI: 10.3390/su151410896

Munuhwa, S., & Chibaro, M. (2024). E-Commerce Logistics Unleashed. *Advances in Logistics, Operations, and Management Science*, 145-163, ISSN 2327-350X, IGI Global, DOI: 10.4018/979-8-3693-1578-1.ch008

Munuhwa, S., Mawonde, D., Mandere, T. S., & Nyemba, P. M. (2025). The role of robotics in enhancing green procurement practices: a systematic literature review. *Green Supply Chain Management in the Constrained Economy: Artificial Intelligence and Machine Learning*, 75-102.

Muralidharan, C., & Sirajudeen, Y. Mohamed, & Rajkumar, Y. (2022). Empowerment of Internet of Things Through the Integration of Blockchain Technology. *Studies in Big Data*, 147-157, ISSN 2197-6503, Springer International Publishing, DOI: 10.1007/978-3-030-95419-2_7

Nair, S., & Kumar, J. (2024). Blockchain Integration for Enhanced Traceability in Fijian Sugarcane Supply Chains. *2024 International Conference on Sustainable Technology and Engineering (i-COSTE)*, 1-7, IEEE, DOI: 10.1109/i-coste63786.2024.11024895

Nakpodia, F., Ashiru, F., You, J. J., & Oni, O. (2024). Digital technologies, social entrepreneurship and resilience during crisis in developing countries: Evidence from Nigeria. *International Journal of Entrepreneurial Behaviour & Research, 30*(2/3), 342–368. DOI: 10.1108/IJEBR-01-2023-0012

Nandi, S., Sarkis, J., Hervani, A. A., & Helms, M. M. (2021). Redesigning Supply Chains using Blockchain-Enabled Circular Economy and COVID-19 Experiences. *Sustainable Production and Consumption*, *27*, 10–22. DOI: 10.1016/j.spc.2020.10.019 PMID: 33102671

Narwane, V. S., & Raut, R. D., Mangla, S K, Dora, M, & Narkhede, Balkrishna E. (2021). Risks to Big Data Analytics and Blockchain Technology Adoption in Supply Chains. *Annals of Operations Research, 327*(1), 339-374, ISSN 0254-5330, Springer Science and Business Media LLC, DOI: 10.1007/s10479-021-04396-3

Natanelov, V., Cao, S., Foth, M., & Dulleck, U. (2022). Blockchain smart contracts for supply chain finance: Mapping the innovation potential in Australia-China beef supply chains. *Journal of Industrial Information Integration, 30*, 100389, ISSN 2452-414X, Elsevier BV, DOI: 10.1016/j.jii.2022.100389

Ndemo, B. (2025). The Role of Blockchain and Governance in Africa's Economic Development. In *Sustainable Digital Finance* (pp. 19–36). Springer Nature Switzerland.

Ngo, V. M., Nguyen, H. H., Pham, H. C., Nguyen, H. M., & Truong, P. V. D. (2023). Digital supply chain transformation: Effect of firm's knowledge creation capabilities under COVID-19 supply chain disruption risk. *Operations Management Research, 16*(2), 1003–1018. DOI: 10.1007/s12063-022-00326-z

Nguyen, D. T., Adulyasak, Y., Cordeau, J. F., & Ponce, S. I. (2022). Data-driven operations and supply chain management: Established research clusters from 2000 to early 2020. *International Journal of Production Research, 60*(17), 5407–5431. DOI: 10.1080/00207543.2021.1956695

Nibbering, D., & Paap, R. (2024). Forecasting carbon emissions using asymmetric grouping. *Journal of Forecasting, 43*(6), 2228–2256. DOI: 10.1002/for.3124

Niinimäki, K., Peters, G., Dahlbo, H., Perry, P., Rissanen, T., & Gwilt, A. (2020). The environmental price of fast fashion. *Nature Reviews. Earth & Environment, 1*(5), 278–278. DOI: 10.1038/s43017-020-0054-x

Nilashi, M., Baabdullah, A. M., Abumalloh, R. A., Ooi, K.-B., Tan, G. W.-H., Giannakis, M., & Dwivedi, Y. K. (2025). How can big data and predictive analytics impact the performance and competitive advantage of the food waste and recycling industry? *Annals of Operations Research, 348*(3), 1649–1690. DOI: 10.1007/s10479-023-05272-y

Niu, N., Zhang, H., Wang, M., Lu, Y., Ma, J., & Zhang, B. (2025). Circular economy efficiency improvements contribute to achieving Net-Zero: Empirical evidence from China. *Computers & Industrial Engineering, 201*, 110700. DOI: 10.1016/j.cie.2024.110700

Ni, Z., Chan, H. K., & Tan, Z. (2023). Systematic literature review of reverse logistics for e-waste: Overview, analysis, and future research agenda. *International Journal of Logistics Research and Applications, 26*(7), 843–871. DOI: 10.1080/13675567.2021.1993159

Nkezabera, P., & Dinesh, R. (2025). Integrating IoT to Improve Real-Time Visibility and Efficiency in Rwanda's Healthcare Supply Chain. *IRASS Journal of Economics and Business Management, 2*(10), 74–80.

Núñez-Merino, M., Maqueira-Marín, J. M., Moyano-Fuentes, J., & Castaño-Moraga, C. A. (2024). Quantum-inspired computing technology in operations and logistics management. *International Journal of Physical Distribution & Logistics Management, 54*(1), 1–28. DOI: 10.1108/IJPDLM-02-2023-0065

Núñez-Merino, M., Maqueira-Marín, J. M., Moyano-Fuentes, J., & Martínez-Jurado, P. J. (2020). Information and digital technologies of Industry 4.0 and Lean supply chain management: A systematic literature review. *International Journal of Production Research, 58*(16), 5034–5061. DOI: 10.1080/00207543.2020.1743896

O'Neil, C. (2017). *Weapons of math destruction: How big data increases inequality and threatens democracy* (First paperback edition). Broadway Books.

Odukoya, O. (2024). The Transformative Impact of Cloud Computing on Small and Medium-sized Enterprises (SMEs): A Comprehensive Analysis. *2024 International Conference on Smart Applications, Communications and Networking (SmartNets)*, 1–5. DOI: 10.1109/SmartNets61466.2024.10577703

OECD. (2024). OECD Digital. *Economic Outlook, 2024*, •••. Retrieved December 21, 2025, from https://www.oecd.org/en/publications/oecd-digital-economy-outlook_f0b5c251-en.html

Ogbuke, N. J., Yusuf, Y. Y., Dharma, K., & Mercangoz, B. A. (2022). Big data supply chain analytics: Ethical, privacy and security challenges posed to business, industries and society. *Production Planning and Control*, *33*(2–3), 123–137. DOI: 10.1080/09537287.2020.1810764

Ogwu, M. C., & Kosoe, E. A. (2025). Innovative Approaches to Recycling, Upcycling, and Downcycling for Sustainable Waste Management. *CleanMat*, *2*(3), 242–261. DOI: 10.1002/clem.70013

Olivares-Aguila, J., & ElMaraghy, W. (2021). System dynamics modelling for supply chain disruptions. *International Journal of Production Research*, *59*(6), 1757–1775. DOI: 10.1080/00207543.2020.1725171

Opricovic, S., & Tzeng, G.-H. (2004). Compromise solution by MCDM methods: A comparative analysis of VIKOR and TOPSIS. *European Journal of Operational Research*, *156*(2), 445–455. DOI: 10.1016/S0377-2217(03)00020-1

Papadopoulos, T., Gunasekaran, A., Dubey, R., Altay, N., Childe, S. J., & Fosso-Wamba, S. (2017). The role of big data in explaining disaster resilience in supply chains for sustainability. *Journal of Cleaner Production*, *142*, 1108–1118. DOI: 10.1016/j.jclepro.2016.03.059

Park, K. O. (2020). A Study on Sustainable Usage Intention of Blockchain in the Big Data Era: Logistics and Supply Chain Management Companies. *Sustainability*, *12*(24), 10670, ISSN 2071-1050, MDPI AG, DOI: 10.3390/su122410670

Park, S., Jung, D., Nguyen, H., & Choi, Y. (2021). Diagnosis of Problems in Truck Ore Transport Operations in Underground Mines Using Various Machine Learning Models and Data Collected by Internet of Things Systems. *Minerals (Basel)*, *11*(10), 1128. DOI: 10.3390/min11101128

Parmentola, A., Petrillo, A., Tutore, I., & De Felice, F. (2022). Is blockchain able to enhance environmental sustainability? A systematic review and research agenda from the perspective of Sustainable Development Goals (SDGs). *Business Strategy and the Environment*, *31*(1), 194–217. DOI: 10.1002/bse.2882

Pasupuleti, V., Thuraka, B., Kodete, C. S., & Malisetty, S. (2024). Enhancing Supply Chain Agility and Sustainability through Machine Learning: Optimization Techniques for Logistics and Inventory Management. *Logistics (Basel)*, *8*(3), 73. DOI: 10.3390/logistics8030073

Pathak, S., Krishnaswamy, V., & Sharma, M. (2025). A dynamic capability perspective on the impact of big data analytics and enterprise architecture on innovation: An empirical study. *Journal of Enterprise Information Management*, *38*(2), 532–563. DOI: 10.1108/JEIM-01-2024-0059

Patil, S. (2024). Blockchain Integration in Automotive Supply Chains: Overcoming Challenges and Revolutionising Industry Practices. Proceedings of the International Conference on Industrial Engineering and Operations Management, IEOM Society International, DOI: 10.46254/gc02.20240155

Pedersen, E. R. G., Gwozdz, W., & Hvass, K. K. (2019). Exploring the relationship between business model innovation, corporate sustainability, and organisational values within the fashion industry. *Journal of Business Ethics*, *155*, 623–641. DOI: 10.1007/s10551-017-3562-0

Phillipson, F. (2024). Quantum computing in logistics and supply chain management: An overview. *arXiv*. https://arxiv.org/abs/2402.17520

Pires, A., Oliveira, F. R., Azevedo, S. G., & Neto, J. (2025). Measuring the complexity of supply chains using Shannon entropy. *Applied System Innovation*, *8*(4), 105. Advance online publication. DOI: 10.3390/asi8040105

Polater, A. (2025). Building resilient supply chains: Unveiling the interplay of reflexivity, supply chain innovation and improvisation capability. *Benchmarking*, *32*(9), 3524–3555. DOI: 10.1108/BIJ-10-2024-0930

Ponomarov, S. Y., & Holcomb, M. C. (2009). Understanding the concept of supply chain resilience. *International Journal of Logistics Management*, *20*(1), 124–143. DOI: 10.1108/09574090910954873

Porkodi, S., & Kesavaraja, D. (2024). Blockchain and IoT Integration-Based Transparency of Supply Chain Social Sustainability. *Blockchain, IoT, and AI Technologies for Supply Chain Management*, 221-235, Apress, DOI: 10.1007/979-8-8688-0315-4_8

Poudel, N., & Shaw, R. (2024). Challenges in urban-rural food supply chains for disaster resilience in Nepal. *Regional Science Policy & Practice*, *16*(8), 100073. DOI: 10.1016/j.rspp.2024.100073

Powell, W, Cao, S, Foth, M, He, S, Turner-Morris, C, & Li, M (2022). Revisiting Trust in Supply Chains: How Does Blockchain Redefine Trust?. Blockchain Driven Supply Chains and Enterprise Information Systems, 21-42, Springer International Publishing, DOI: 10.1007/978-3-030-96154-1_2

Prajapati, M., Kant, R., Tripathi, S. M., & Shankar, R. (2025). Exploring sustainable pathways: A systematic literature review of triple bottom line in supply chain management. *Sustainable Operations and Computers*, *6*, 223–241. DOI: 10.1016/j.susoc.2025.03.002

Prangan, T. H., Ahmed, M. R., Islam, A. A., Islam, M. A., & Mim, J. S. (2025). Evaluating the Impact of Sustainable Supply Chain Management (SSCM) Practices on Business Performance Among Agro-Based SMEs in Bangladesh: Mediating Role of FinTech Usability. *Supply Chain Insider*, *17*(1), 207–268. DOI: 10.5281/zenodo.17285206

Psarommatis, F., May, G., & Azamfirei, V. (2025). Product reuse and repurpose in circular manufacturing: A critical review of key challenges, shortcomings and future directions. *Journal of Remanufacturing*, *15*(2–3), 273–310. DOI: 10.1007/s13243-025-00153-y

Putro, D. P., Suryani, P. E., & Amri, S. (2025). Comparative Analysis of AHP, SAW, TOPSIS, VIKOR, and MABAC in Pharmaceutical Supplier Selection. *Jurnal Transformatika*, *23*(1), 1–11. DOI: 10.26623/TRANSFORMATIKA.V23I1.12220

Rajbhandari, S., Shrestha, R., & Alhassan, I. (2022). Industry 4.0 readiness of manufacturing industries in a developing economy: A case of Nepal. [External Link]. *Heliyon*, *8*(8), e08919. DOI: 10.1016/j.heliyon.2022.e08919 PMID: 35243054

Rajesh, R. (2020). Exploring the sustainability performances of firms using big data analytics and circular economy strategy. *Journal of Cleaner Production*, *277*, 123632. DOI: 10.1016/j.jclepro.2020.123632

Rajput, S., & Singh, S. P. (2022). Industry 4.0 model for integrated circular economy-reverse logistics network. *International Journal of Logistics Research and Applications*, *25*(4–5), 837–877. DOI: 10.1080/13675567.2021.1926950

Ramanathan, U., He, Q., Subramanian, N., Gunasekaran, A., & Sarpong, D. (2023). Collaborative closed-loop supply chain framework for sustainable manufacturing: Evidence from the Indian packaging industry. *Technological Forecasting and Social Change*, *191*, 122489. DOI: 10.1016/j.techfore.2023.122489

Rane, S. B., Thakker, S. V., & Kant, R. (2021). Stakeholders' involvement in green supply chain: A perspective of blockchain IoT-integrated architecture. *Management of Environmental Quality*, *32*(6), 1166–1191. DOI: 10.1108/MEQ-11-2019-0248

Rashid, A., Baloch, N., Rasheed, R., & Ngah, A. H. (2025). Big data analytics-artificial intelligence and sustainable performance through green supply chain practices in manufacturing firms of a developing country. *Journal of Science and Technology Policy Management*, *16*(1), 42–67. DOI: 10.1108/JSTPM-04-2023-0050

Rauniyar, K., Wu, X., Gupta, S., Modgil, S., & Lopes de Sousa Jabbour, A. B. (2023). Risk management of supply chains in the digital transformation era: Contribution and challenges of blockchain technology. *Industrial Management & Data Systems*, *123*(1), 253–277. DOI: 10.1108/IMDS-04-2021-0235

Rivera, L., Gauthier-Umaña, V., & Chauhan, C. (2024). Blockchain: An opportunity to improve supply chains in the wake of digitalisation. *International Journal of Information Management Data Insights*, *4*(2), 100290, ISSN 2667-0968, Elsevier BV, DOI: 10.1016/j.jjimei.2024.100290

Rodrigues, S. P., Gomes, L. de C., Peres, F. A. P., Correa, R. G. de F., & Baierle, I. C. (2025). A Framework for Leveraging Digital Technologies in Reverse Logistics Actions: A Systematic Literature Review. *Logistics (Basel)*, *9*(2), 54. DOI: 10.3390/logistics9020054

Rossini, M., Powell, D. J., & Kundu, K. (2023). Lean supply chain management and Industry 4.0: A systematic literature review. *International Journal of Lean Six Sigma*, *14*(2), 253–276. DOI: 10.1108/IJLSS-05-2021-0092

Runtuk, J. K., & Sidjabat, F., Jsslynn, & Jordan, F. (2022). Big data in supply chain management: A systematic literature review. *Green Intelligent Systems and Applications*, *2*(2), 108–117. DOI: 10.53623/gisa.v2i2.115

Saberi, S., Kouhizadeh, M., Sarkis, J., & Shen, L. (2019). Blockchain technology and its relationships to sustainable supply chain management. *International Journal of Production Research*, *57*(7), 2117–2135. DOI: 10.1080/00207543.2018.1533261

Sachan, S., Barve, A., Muduli, K., Kumar, A., Samadhiya, A., & Luthra, S. (2025). Can smart manufacturing benchmark the complex landscape of global success? *Benchmarking*. Advance online publication. DOI: 10.1108/BIJ-10-2024-0879

Saeed, N., Malik, H., Naeem, A., & Bashir, U. (2023). Incorporating big data and IoT in intelligent ecosystems: State-of-the-arts, challenges and opportunities, and future directions. *Multimedia Tools and Applications*, *83*(7), 20699–20741. DOI: 10.1007/s11042-023-16328-3

Sahoo, S., Upadhyay, A., & Kumar, A. (2023). Circular economy practices and environmental performance: Analysing the role of big data analytics capability and responsible research and innovation. *Business Strategy and the Environment*, *32*(8), 6029–6046. DOI: 10.1002/bse.3471

Saidu, Y., Shuhidan, S. M., Aliyu, D. A., Abdul Aziz, I., & Adamu, S. (2025). Convergence of Blockchain, IoT, and AI for Enhanced Traceability Systems: A Comprehensive Review. *IEEE Access : Practical Innovations, Open Solutions*, *13*, 16838–16865. DOI: 10.1109/ACCESS.2025.3528035

Salwa, N. (2024). Real-time analytics and supply chain transformation in the digital era. *Sinergi International Journal of Logistics*, *1*(3). Advance online publication. DOI: 10.61194/sijl.v1i3.613

Samal, C. G., Biswal, D. R., Udgata, G., & Pradhan, S. K. (2025). Estimation, Classification, and Prediction of Construction and Demolition Waste Using Machine Learning for Sustainable Waste Management: A Critical Review. *Construction Materials*, *5*(1), 10. DOI: 10.3390/constrmater5010010

Santiago, F., Haraguchi, N., & Lavopa, A. (2024). Global Trends and World Order: Implications for New Industrial Policies in Developing Countries. *Journal of Industry, Competition and Trade*, *24*(1), 5. DOI: 10.1007/s10842-024-00419-4

Santos-de León, N. J. (2020). Sustainable supply chain in the era of Industry 4.0 and big data: A systematic analysis of literature and research. *Sustainability*, *12*(10), 4108. Advance online publication. DOI: 10.3390/su12104108

Saran, N., & Kesswani, N. (2025). An analytics-driven framework for securing industrial IoT-Enabled Supply Chain Management Systems. *Supply Chain Analytics*, *11*, 100128. DOI: 10.1016/j.sca.2025.100128

Šarić, J., & Abramović, B. (2025). Using SWARA for the Evaluation Criteria of Connecting Airports with Railway Networks. *Systems*, *13*(6). Advance online publication. DOI: 10.3390/SYSTEMS13060428/S1

Sarkis, J., Kouhizadeh, M., & Zhu, Q. S. (2020). Digitalization and the greening of supply chains. *Industrial Management & Data Systems*, *121*(1), 65–85. DOI: 10.1108/imds-08-2020-0450

Scarpi, D., & Pantano, E. (2024). "With great power comes great responsibility": Exploring the role of Corporate Digital Responsibility (CDR) for Artificial Intelligence Responsibility in Retail Service Automation (AIRRSA). *Organizational Dynamics*, *53*(2), 101030. DOI: 10.1016/j.orgdyn.2024.101030

Seidelson, C (2024). Data-Driven Approach to Agile Supply Chains. *Building Agile Supply Chains*, SAGE Publications, Inc., DOI: 10.4135/9781071941942

Seles, B. M. R. P., de Sousa Jabbour, A. B. L., Jabbour, C. J. C., & Dangelico, R. M. (2016). The green bullwhip effect, the diffusion of green supply chain practices, and institutional pressures: Evidence from the automotive sector. *International Journal of Production Economics, 182*, 342–355. DOI: 10.1016/j.ijpe.2016.08.033

Semenzin, S. (2023). 'Blockchain for good': Exploring the notion of social good inside the blockchain scene. *Big Data & Society, 10*(2), ISSN 2053-9517, SAGE Publications, DOI: 10.1177/20539517231205479

Setyadi, A., Pawirosumarto, S., & Damaris, A. (2025). Toward a resilient and sustainable supply chain: Operational responses to global disruptions in the post-COVID-19 era. *Sustainability, 17*(13), 6167. Advance online publication. DOI: 10.3390/su17136167

Seuring, S., & Müller, M. (2008). From a literature review to a conceptual framework for sustainable supply chain management. *Journal of Cleaner Production, 16*(15), 1699–1710. DOI: 10.1016/j.jclepro.2008.04.020

Shah, H. H., Amin, M., & Pepe, F. (2023). Maximizing resource efficiency: Opportunities for energy recovery from municipal solid waste in Europe. *Journal of Material Cycles and Waste Management, 25*(5), 2766–2782. DOI: 10.1007/s10163-023-01733-5

Shahidzadeh, M. H., & Shokouhyar, S. (2024). Unveiling just-in-time decision support system using social media analytics: A case study on reverse logistics resource recycling. *Industrial Management & Data Systems, 124*(6), 2251–2283. DOI: 10.1108/IMDS-12-2023-0921

Shamout, M. D. (2019). Does supply chain analytics enhance supply chain innovation and robustness capability? *Organizacija, 52*(2), 95–106. DOI: 10.2478/orga-2019-0007

Shamsuddoha, M., Kashem, M. A., Nasir, T., Hossain, A. I., & Ahmed, M. F. (2025). Quantum computing applications in supply chain information and optimization: Future scenarios and opportunities. *Information (Basel), 16*(8), 693. Advance online publication. DOI: 10.3390/info16080693

Shamsuddoha, M., Khan, E. A., Chowdhury, M. M. H., & Nasir, T. (2025). Revolutionizing Supply Chains: Unleashing the Power of AI-Driven Intelligent Automation and Real-Time Information Flow. *Information (Basel), 16*(1), 26. DOI: 10.3390/info16010026

Shang, M., & Luo, J. (2021). The Tapio decoupling principle and key strategies for changing factors of Chinese urban carbon footprint based on cloud computing. *International Journal of Environmental Research and Public Health, 18*(4), 2101. DOI: 10.3390/ijerph18042101 PMID: 33670040

Sharma, R., & Shishodia, A. (2022). Blockchain Technology Enablers in Physical Distribution and Logistics Management. *Studies in Big Data*, 329-344, ISSN 2197-6503, Springer International Publishing, DOI: 10.1007/978-3-030-87304-2_14

Shekarian, M., & Mellat Parast, M. (2021). An Integrative approach to supply chain disruption risk and resilience management: A literature review. *International Journal of Logistics Research and Applications, 24*(5), 427–455. DOI: 10.1080/13675567.2020.1763935

Shojaei, A., Ketabi, R., Razkenari, M., Hakim, H., & Wang, J. (2021). Enabling a circular economy in the built environment sector through blockchain technology. *Journal of Cleaner Production, 294*, 126352. DOI: 10.1016/j.jclepro.2021.126352

Shrivastava, B., Verma, M., & Dave, S. (2024). *Digital Entrepreneurship and E-Commerce: Opportunities and Challenges for Bhutan's International Trade. Convergence of Digitalization*. Innovation, and Sustainable Development in Business.

Siagian, A., & Gwynne, R. (2023). An Integrated Model for Selecting and Evaluating Logistics Outsourcing Decisions using AHP and PROMETHEE II. *Journal of Industrial Engineering and Education, 1*(1), 30–45. https://jiee.bksti.org/index.php/iee/article/view/11

Sibanda, V., Mhlanga, J., & Munuhwa, S. (2025). Circular Economy Practices in Supply Chain Management. In *Eco-Logistics and Sustainable Supply Chain Innovations* (pp. 13–38). IGI Global Scientific Publishing.

Siems, E., Seuring, S., & Schilling, L. (2023). Stakeholder roles in sustainable supply chain management: A literature review. *Journal of Business Economics, 93*(4), 747–775. DOI: 10.1007/s11573-022-01117-5

Sigmund, J. (2021). Advanced Analytics and Big Data in Supply Chain Planning. *Future of Business and Finance*, 121-135, ISSN 2662-2467, Springer International Publishing, DOI: 10.1007/978-3-030-61093-7_10

Sijariya, R., Garg, V., & Tiwari, P. (2025). SDGs for Organizational Sustainability: Integrating Digital Technologies for a Digital Circular Economy. In *Sustainable Innovations and Digital Circular Economy* (pp. 307–327). Springer Nature Singapore., DOI: 10.1007/978-981-96-1064-8_16

Simaei, E., & Rahimifard, S. (2024). AI-based decision support system for enhancing end-of-life value recovery from e-wastes. *International Journal of Sustainable Engineering*, *17*(1), 80–96. DOI: 10.1080/19397038.2024.2306293

Simionescu, M., & Strielkowski, W. (2025). The Role of the Internet of Things in Enhancing Sustainable Urban Energy Systems: A Review of Lessons Learned from the COVID-19 Pandemic. *Journal of Urban Technology*, *32*(1), 103–132. DOI: 10.1080/10630732.2024.2411932

Singh, R., Kukreja, D., & Sharma, D. K. (2023). Blockchain-enabled access control to prevent cyber attacks in IoT: Systematic literature review. *Frontiers in Big Data*, *5*, ISSN 2624-909X, Frontiers Media SA, DOI: 10.3389/fdata.2022.1081770

Singh, A., Goel, A., Chauhan, A., & Singh, S. K. (2025). Sustainability of electronic product manufacturing through e-waste management and reverse logistics. *Sustainable Futures : An Applied Journal of Technology, Environment and Society*, *9*, 100490. DOI: 10.1016/j.sftr.2025.100490

Singhvi, D., Singhvi, S., & Zhang, X. (2023). A Data-driven Approach to Improve Artisans' Productivity in Distributed Supply Chains. *SSRN Electronic Journal*, ISSN 1556-5068, Elsevier BV, DOI: 10.2139/ssrn.4531090

Sivarajah, U., Kamal, M. M., Irani, Z., & Weerakkody, V. (2017). Critical analysis of big data challenges and analytical methods. *Journal of Business Research*, *70*, 263–286. DOI: 10.1016/j.jbusres.2016.08.001

Smyth, C., Dennehy, D., Fosso Wamba, S., Scott, M., & Harfouche, A. (2024). Artificial intelligence and prescriptive analytics for supply chain resilience: A systematic literature review and research agenda. *International Journal of Production Research*, *62*(23), 8537–8561. DOI: 10.1080/00207543.2024.2341415

Snyder, H. (2019). Literature review as a research methodology: An overview and guidelines. *Journal of Business Research*, *104*, 333–339. DOI: 10.1016/j.jbusres.2019.07.039

Sodhi, M. S., & Tang, C. S. (2024). Seeking and exploiting synergies among the UN sustainability development goals: Research opportunities for operations management. *Production and Operations Management*, *33*(4), 962–978. DOI: 10.1177/10591478241235004

Souames, M. A., Mohammedi, L. A., Zouaghi, I., Gunasekaran, A., Beldjoudi, S., & Laghouag, A. (2025). Estimating Import Lead Times Using Business Intelligence and Machine Learning Within the CRISP-DM Framework: A Case Study in Oil and Gas Services Industry. *IEEE Access : Practical Innovations, Open Solutions, 13*, 119215–119234. DOI: 10.1109/ACCESS.2025.3584886

Spaltini, M., Poletti, A., Acerbi, F., & Taisch, M. (2021). A quantitative framework for Industry 4.0 enabled Circular Economy. *Procedia CIRP*, *98*, 115–120. DOI: 10.1016/j.procir.2021.01.015

Stefan Schaltegger, P. R. B. D., Beske, P., & Seuring, S. (2014). Putting sustainability into supply chain management. *Supply Chain Management*, *19*(3), 322–331. DOI: 10.1108/SCM-12-2013-0432

Stroumpoulis, A., & Kopanaki, E. (2022). Theoretical Perspectives on Sustainable Supply Chain Management and Digital Transformation: A Literature Review and a Conceptual Framework. *Sustainability*, *14*(8), 4862. DOI: 10.3390/su14084862

Stroumpoulis, A., Kopanaki, E., & Chountalas, P. T. (2024). Enhancing sustainable supply chain management through digital transformation: A comparative case study analysis. *Sustainability*, *16*(16), 6778. DOI: 10.3390/su16166778

Suberi, H. K. (2022). Review analysis on challenges, opportunities, and implementation strategies for the success of green public procurement, the context of Bhutan. *Bhutan Journal of Research and Development*, *11*(1), 1–20. DOI: 10.17102/bjrd.rub.11.1.023

Sun, L., Dong, H., Dai, Y., Dong, J., Fujii, M., Geng, Y., Lou, Z., & Liu, X. (2024). Environmental benefit of recycling plastics from waste electrical & electronic equipment. *Resources, Conservation and Recycling*, *211*, 107855. DOI: 10.1016/j.resconrec.2024.107855

Surati, S., Shrimali, B., Trivedi, H., & Chaudhari, P. (2023). Blockchain in Supply Chain Management. *Studies in Big Data*, 61-98, ISSN 2197-6503, Springer Nature Singapore, DOI: 10.1007/978-981-19-8730-4_3

Surucu-Balci, E., & Balci, G. (2022). Steering supply chains from a complex systems perspective. *European Journal of Management Studies*, *27*(1), 5–35. DOI: 10.1108/EJMS-04-2021-0030

Tajally, A. R., Babakhani, B., Jeyzanibrahimzade, E., Parvin, M., & Irani, S. (2025). Sustainable supplier selection and order allocation problem considering the agility and resilience dimensions: A novel multi-stage data-driven decision-making approach. *International Journal of Systems Science: Operations & Logistics, 12*(1), 2458756. DOI: 10.1080/23302674.2025.2458756

Talwar, S., Kaur, P., Fosso Wamba, S., & Dhir, A. (2021). Big Data in operations and supply chain management: A systematic literature review and future research agenda. *International Journal of Production Research, 59*(11), 3509–3534. DOI: 10.1080/00207543.2020.1868599

Tang, Q., & Tang, L. M. (2019). Toward a distributed carbon ledger for carbon emissions trading and accounting for corporate carbon management. *Journal of Emerging Technologies in Accounting, 16*(1), 37–46. DOI: 10.2308/jeta-52409

Tennakoon, G. A., Rameezdeen, R., & Chileshe, N. (2022). Diverting demolition waste toward secondary markets through integrated reverse logistics supply chains: A systematic literature review. *Waste Management & Research: The Journal for a Sustainable Circular Economy, 40*(3), 274–293. DOI: 10.1177/0734242X211021478 PMID: 34034580

Thanasi-Boçe, M., & Hoxha, J. (2025). Blockchain for Sustainable Development: A Systematic Review. *Sustainability, 17*(11), 4848. DOI: 10.3390/su17114848

Thinakaran, J., Paul, S., Latha, C., Beulah, C., & Jacob, G. (2023). Blockchain in Big Data for Agriculture Supply Chain. *Studies in Big Data*, 257-291, ISSN 2197-6503, Springer Nature Singapore, DOI: 10.1007/978-981-19-8730-4_9

Tian, H., Yan, M., Zhou, J., Wu, Q., Tiong, Y. W., Lam, H. T., Zhang, J., & Tong, Y. W. (2023). A closed loop case study of decentralized food waste management: System performance and life cycle carbon emission assessment. *The Science of the Total Environment, 899*, 165783. DOI: 10.1016/j.scitotenv.2023.165783 PMID: 37495140

Tombido, L. (2025). Resilient and sustainable closed-loop supply chains (CLSCs): A research agenda. *Journal of Responsible Production and Consumption, 2*(1), 256–289. DOI: 10.1108/JRPC-03-2024-0012

Torraco, R. J. (2016). Writing integrative literature reviews: Using the past and present to explore the future. *Human Resource Development Review, 15*(4), 404–428. DOI: 10.1177/1534484316671606

Tran-Dang, H., Kim, J.-W., Lee, J.-M., & Kim, D.-S. (2025). Shaping the Future of Logistics: Data-driven Technology Approaches and Strategic Management. *IETE Technical Review*, *42*(1), 44–79. DOI: 10.1080/02564602.2024.2445513

Tundys, B. (2023). Triple bottom line aspects and sustainable supply chain resilience. *Frontiers in Environmental Science*, *11*, 1161437. Advance online publication. DOI: 10.3389/fenvs.2023.1161437

Turskis, Z., & Šniokienė, V. (2024). IoT-Driven Transformation of Circular Economy Efficiency: An Overview. *Mathematical & Computational Applications*, *29*(4), 49. DOI: 10.3390/mca29040049

Tuyishime, K., & Adewusi, M. A. (2025). Data-driven prediction of cattle weight gain for evaluating key growth factors with machine learning approaches. *Discover Computing*, *28*(1), 275. DOI: 10.1007/s10791-025-09798-6

Ukoba, K., Olatunji, K. O., Adeoye, E., Jen, T.-C., & Madyira, D. M. (2024). Optimizing renewable energy systems through artificial intelligence: Review and future prospects. *Energy & Environment*, *35*(7), 3833–3879. DOI: 10.1177/0958305X241256293

UNCTAD. (2023). *Digital Economy Report 2023: Enabling Data-Driven Development.* Retrieved October 13, 2025, from https://unctadstat.unctad.org/datacentre/

UNCTAD. (2024). *Technology and Innovation Report 2024: Opening Green Windows - Technological Opportunities for a Low-Carbon World.* Retrieved October 13, 2025, from https://unctadstat.unctad.org/datacentre/

Vaghani, D. (2024). Big Data Analytics for Supply Chain Optimisation. *Advances in Logistics, Operations, and Management Science*, 101-150, ISSN 2327-350X, IGI Global, DOI: 10.4018/979-8-3693-4427-9.ch005

Van der Linde, L., Pretorius, L., & Oosthuizen, R. (2024). Sustainable Technology Management: A Causal Loop Analysis of Circular Economy Adoption and Stakeholder Dynamics. *2024 Portland International Conference on Management of Engineering and Technology (PICMET)*, 1–10. DOI: 10.23919/PICMET64035.2024.10653082

Vandyck, T., Temursho, U., Landis, F., Klenert, D., & Weitzel, M. (2022). Prices and Standards for Vertical and Horizontal Equity in Climate Policy. SSRN *Electronic Journal.* DOI: 10.2139/ssrn.4144282

Viriyasitavat, W., Bi, Z., & Hoonsopon, D. (2022). Blockchain technologies for interoperation of business processes in smart supply chains. *Journal of Industrial Information Integration, 26*, 100326, ISSN 2452-414X, Elsevier BV, DOI: 10.1016/j.jii.2022.100326

Vivaldini, M. (2020). Blockchain platforms in supply chains. *Journal of Enterprise Information Management, 34*(6), 1769-1797, ISSN 1741-0398, Emerald, DOI: 10.1108/jeim-12-2019-0416

Wacker, J. G. (1998). A definition of theory: Research guidelines for different theory-building research methods in operations management. *Journal of Operations Management, 16*(4), 361–385. DOI: 10.1016/S0272-6963(98)00019-9

Waller, M. A., & Fawcett, S. E. (2013). Data Science, Predictive Analytics, and Big Data: A Revolution That Will Transform Supply Chain Design and Management. *Journal of Business Logistics, 34*(2), 77–84. DOI: 10.1111/jbl.12010

Waltersmann, L., Kiemel, S., Stuhlsatz, J., Sauer, A., & Miehe, R. (2021). Artificial Intelligence Applications for Increasing Resource Efficiency in Manufacturing Companies—A Comprehensive Review. *Sustainability, 13*(12), 6689. DOI: 10.3390/su13126689

Wamba, S. F., Akter, S., Edwards, A., Chopin, G., & Gnanzou, D. (2015). How "big data" can make big impact. *International Journal of Production Economics, 165*, 234–246. DOI: 10.1016/j.ijpe.2014.12.007

Wamba, S. F., Akter, S., Edwards, A., Chopin, G., & Gnanzou, D. (2017). How "big data" can make big impact: Findings from a systematic review and a longitudinal case study. *International Journal of Production Economics, 165*, 234–246. DOI: 10.1016/j.ijpe.2014.12.035

Wamba, S. F., Gunasekaran, A., Dubey, R., & Childe, S. J. (2020). Big data analytics in operations and supply chain management: State of the art and research opportunities. *Annals of Operations Research, 270*, 313–336. DOI: 10.1007/s10479-016-2235-0

Wamba, S. F., Gunasekaran, A., Dubey, R., & Ngai, E. W. T. (2018). Big data analytics in operations and supply chain management: A systematic review and future research agenda. *International Journal of Production Economics, 194*, 828–844. DOI: 10.1016/j.ijpe.2017.11.020

Wamba, S. F., Queiroz, M., Trinchera, L., & Kamdjoug, J. R. K. (2020). Dynamics between big data analytics capabilities and firm's performance: Insights from a resource-based view and dynamic capabilities perspective. *Information & Management, 57*(2), 103207. DOI: 10.1016/j.im.2019.103207

Wang, L., Deng, T., Shen, Z.-J. M., Hu, H., & Qi, Y. (2022). Digital twin-driven smart supply chain. *Frontiers of Engineering Management, 9*(1), 56–70. DOI: 10.1007/s42524-021-0186-9

Wang, M., Wang, B., & Abareshi, A. (2020). Blockchain technology and its role in enhancing supply chain integration capability and reducing carbon emission: A conceptual framework. *Sustainability, 12*(24), 10550. DOI: 10.3390/su122410550

Wasswa, J. H., Oundo, H., Oteba, M. O., Komakech, H., Ochola, I., Mwebaze, S., & Lugada, E. (2023). Leveraging electronic logistics management information systems to enhance and optimize supply chain response during public health emergencies: Lessons from COVID-19 response in Uganda. *Journal of Pharmaceutical Policy and Practice, 16*(1), 6. DOI: 10.1186/s40545-023-00517-4 PMID: 36650571

Wijesinghe, S., Nanayakkara, I., Pathirana, R., Wickramarachchi, R., & Fernando, I. (2024). Impact of IoT Integration on Enterprise Resource Planning (ERP) Systems: A Comprehensive Literature Analysis. *Proceedings - International Research Conference on Smart Computing and Systems Engineering, SCSE 2024*. DOI: 10.1109/SCSE61872.2024.10550684

Wijewickrama, M. K. C. S., Chileshe, N., Rameezdeen, R., & Ochoa, J. J. (2021). Information sharing in reverse logistics supply chain of demolition waste: A systematic literature review. *Journal of Cleaner Production, 280*, 124359. DOI: 10.1016/j.jclepro.2020.124359

Wilson, M., Paschen, J., & Pitt, L. (2022). The circular economy meets artificial intelligence (AI): Understanding the opportunities of AI for reverse logistics. *Management of Environmental Quality, 33*(1), 9–25. DOI: 10.1108/MEQ-10-2020-0222

Wong, S., Yeung, J., Kun, W., Lau, Y., Kawasaki, T., & Kwong, R. (2024). *Sustainability of Blockchain Technology in Supply Chains: Implications from a Critical Literature Review.*, MDPI AG, DOI: 10.20944/preprints202404.1297.v1

World Bank. (2023). *World Development Report 2023: Migrants, Refugees, and Societies.* Retrieved December 01, 2025, from https://www.worldbank.org/en/publication/wdr2023

World Bank. (2024). *Digital Development: Data for Development.* Retrieved December 02, 2025, from https://www.worldbank.org/en/topic/digital

Wu, H., Liu, J., & Liang, B. (2024). AI-Driven Supply Chain Transformation in Industry 5.0: Enhancing Resilience and Sustainability. *Journal of the Knowledge Economy, 16*(1), 3826–3868. DOI: 10.1007/s13132-024-01999-6

Wylde, V., Rawindaran, N., Lawrence, J., Balasubramanian, R., Prakash, E., Jayal, A., Khan, I., Hewage, C., & Platts, J. (2022). Cybersecurity, Data Privacy and Blockchain: A Review. *SN Computer Science, 3*(2), 127. DOI: 10.1007/s42979-022-01020-4 PMID: 35036930

Xiao, B., Simsek, M., Kantarci, B., & Alkheir, A. A. (2022). Handling big tabular data of ICT supply chains: a multitask, machine-interpretable approach. *GLOBECOM 2022 - 2022 IEEE Global Communications Conference*, 504-509, IEEE, DOI: 10.1109/globecom48099.2022.10001253

Xu, D., Li, T., Li, Y., Su, X., Tarkoma, S., Jiang, T., Crowcroft, J., & Hui, P. (2021). Edge Intelligence: Empowering Intelligence to the Edge of Network. *Proceedings of the IEEE, 109*(11), 1778–1837. DOI: 10.1109/JPROC.2021.3119950

Xu, J., Pero, M., & Fabbri, M. (2023). Unfolding the link between big data analytics and supply chain planning. *Technological Forecasting and Social Change, 196*, 122805. Advance online publication. DOI: 10.1016/j.techfore.2023.122805

Yadav, S, & Rajput, S (2024). Modelling of blockchain interruptions for smooth integration with supply chain. *Blockchain Technology*, 49-65, CRC Press, DOI: 10.1201/9781003542766-5

Yarkoni, S., Plaat, A., & Aarts, E. H. L. (2022). Quantum-inspired algorithms for combinatorial optimization: A review. *ACM Computing Surveys, 54*(8), 1–36. DOI: 10.1145/3477141

Yildizbasi, A., & Arioz, Y. (2021). Green supplier selection in new era for sustainability: A novel method for integrating big data analytics and a hybrid fuzzy multi-criteria decision making. *Soft Computing 2021 26:1, 26*(1), 253–270. DOI: 10.1007/S00500-021-06477-8

Yu, S., Wang, X., Liu, J., & Wei, F. (2023). Role of mining waste trade on green development in China: Policy implications for circular economy. *Resources Policy, 86*, 104147. DOI: 10.1016/j.resourpol.2023.104147

Zareian Beinabadi, H., Baradaran, V., & Rashidi Komijan, A. (2024). Sustainable supply chain decision-making in the automotive industry: A data-driven approach. *Socio-Economic Planning Sciences, 95*, 101908. DOI: 10.1016/J.SEPS.2024.101908

Zarei, H., Rasti-Barzoki, M., Altmann, J., & Egger, B. (2023). Cooperation, coordination, or collaboration? A structured review of buyers' partnerships to support sustainable sourcing in supply chains. *Environmental Science and Pollution Research International, 30*(31), 76491–76514. DOI: 10.1007/s11356-023-27541-w PMID: 37280495

Zavadskas, E. K., Kaklauskas, A., & Šarka, V. (1994). *The new method of multi-criteria complex proportional assessment of projects*. https://etalpykla.vilniustech.lt/handle/123456789/111916

Zavadskas, E. K., & Turskis, Z. (2011). Multiple criteria decision making (MCDM) methods in economics: An overview. *Technological and Economic Development of Economy, 17*(2), 397–427. DOI: 10.3846/20294913.2011.593291;REQUEST-EDJOURNAL:JOURNAL:TTED21;JOURNAL:JOURNAL:TTED20;ISSUE:IS-SUE:DOI

Zavadskas, E. K., Turskis, Z., Antucheviciene, J., & Zakarevicius, A. (2012). Optimization of Weighted Aggregated Sum Product Assessment. *Elektronika ir Elektrotechnika, 122*(6), 3–6. DOI: 10.5755/J01.EEE.122.6.1810

Zekhnini, K., Cherrafi, A., Bouhaddou, I., Benghabrit, Y., & Garza-Reyes, J. A. (2021). Supply chain management 4.0: A literature review and research framework. *Benchmarking, 28*(2), 465–501.

Zhang, A., Venkatesh, V. G., Liu, Y., Wan, M., & Qu, T. (2021). A digital twin-enabled approach for improving circular supply chain performance. *Resources, Conservation and Recycling, 164*, 105119. DOI: 10.1016/j.resconrec.2020.105119

Zhang, X., Yu, Y., & Zhang, N. (2021). Sustainable supply chain management under big data: A bibliometric analysis. *Journal of Enterprise Information Management, 34*(1), 427–445. DOI: 10.1108/JEIM-12-2019-0381

Zhan, Y., Yeung, A. C. L., Tan, K. H., Xiong, Y., Xing, X., & Ye, F. (2025). Success and Failure of Blockchain Technology Providers: Founders' Power, Beyond-Blockchain Exploration and Centralised Decision-Making. *Journal of Operations Management, 71*(7), 893–916. DOI: 10.1002/joom.1364

Zhao, N., Hong, J., & Lau, K. H. (2023). Impact of supply chain digitalization on supply chain resilience and performance: A multi-mediation model. *International Journal of Production Economics, 259*, 108817. DOI: 10.1016/j.ijpe.2023.108817 PMID: 36852136

Zhong, R. Y., Newman, S. T., Huang, G. Q., & Lan, S. (2016). Big data for supply chain management in the service and manufacturing sectors: Challenges, opportunities, and future perspectives. *Computers & Industrial Engineering, 101*, 572–591. DOI: 10.1016/j.cie.2016.08.016

Zhou, W. (2024). Optimized application and potential impact of blockchain technology in carbon trading. *Finance & Economics, 1*(9). Advance online publication. DOI: 10.61173/7p5cjg77

Zhu, Q., Duan, Y., & Sarkis, J. (2024). Supply chain carbon transparency to consumers via blockchain: Does the truth hurt? *International Journal of Logistics Management, 35*(3), 833–864. DOI: 10.1108/IJLM-03-2023-0109

Zhu, Q., Duan, Y., & Sarkis, J. (2025). Blockchain Empowerment: Unveiling Managerial Choices in Carbon Finance Investment Across Supply Chains. *Journal of Business Logistics*, *46*(1). Advance online publication. DOI: 10.1111/jbl.12405

Zia, M., Mumtaz, S., & Raza, A. (2024). Green supply chain management practices and triple bottom line performance: Moderating role of total quality management and Industry 4.0 technologies. *Journal of Environmental Management*, *360*, 121082. Advance online publication. DOI: 10.1016/j.jenvman.2024.121082

Zreik, M. (2024). Assessing the Integration of Blockchain and Supply Chain Management. *Advances in Logistics, Operations, and Management Science*, 38-56, ISSN 2327-350X, IGI Global, DOI: 10.4018/979-8-3693-0482-2.ch003

Zuboff, S. (2020). *The age of surveillance capitalism: The fight for a human future at the new frontier of power* (First trade paperback edition). PublicAffairs.

About the Contributors

Mohammad Kamrul Hasan, obtained his Ph.D. in Management Science and Engineering from Shijiazhuang Tiedao University, Hebei, China, in 2024. Prior to this, he earned his second Master's degree in Business Administration in China. Currently, he serves at the School of Business Administration, Tongling University, Tongling, Anhui, China, where he is actively involved in teaching, research, and supervising undergraduate students. He teaches Qualitative and Quantitative Research Methodology, fostering both theoretical knowledge and practical skills among students. Dr. Hasan's research focuses on logistics management, green and sustainable logistics, explainable AI (XAI) in supply chain management, supply chain analytics, big data analytics, decision-making, and research methodologies. In addition to his research, Dr. Hasan actively contributes to the academic community as a reviewer for numerous journals.

Tahsina Khan is serving as Deputy Director (Research) at the Centre for Higher Studies and Research in Bangladesh University of Professionals (BUP). She is an Academician in Business Studies with more than 14 years of teaching, research & consulting experience in Higher Education Institutions. Over the years, she has successfully supervised multilateral academic programs in collaboration with the Government, NGOs, and Corporations from the Business sector. As a Visiting Lecturer, she has taught in the MBA program of the University of Gavle, Sweden. She has worked as Director of the research projects funded by the University Grants Commission (UGC) under the Ministry of Education. Her research papers were presented in National and International Conferences in Canada, France, Malaysia and Indonesia. As Session Chair, she presided over the conference organized by Higher Education and Innovation Group (HEAIG). She has also been invited as a resource speaker at the United Nations affiliated conference at the Yonsei University in Wonju, South Korea. She has published a number of peer-reviewed articles in reputed international journals and her policy brief paper on Rural Development has been included in the knowledge hub of the UN Task Force on SDG implementation. She is a member of International Sociological Association (ISA) which is associated with UNESCO, Economic & Social Council of the United Nations.

Arbia Hlali is a doctor of economics science from the Faculty of Economics and Management of Sfax, University of Sfax, Tunisia. She holds a master of transport and logistics sciences from the higher Institute of industrial management of Sfax, Tunisia. Currently, she is an Assistant Professor at Taibah University, Saudi Arabia. She has international experience in teaching, earlier worked at University of Puerto Rico at Rio Piedras, San Juan, Puerto Rico, and prior to that at different Universities in Tunisia. Her research interests include Logistics, Supply Chain, Transport Economics, Management, Maritime Transport, Transport Management, Transportation Science, Containers port, Port Management, Advanced Econometrics, Standard Statistical Analysis, Operation Management, strategic Management, Sustainability, among others. She is a prolific researcher and has several publications in renowned journals and books. She works also as editor and reviewer in several international journals.

Md Mehedi Hasan Emon is a research practitioner in Business and Management, with specialized in Supply Chain Management, Digital Transformation, Marketing, Information Systems, and Educational Technology (Edutech). His work bridges a diverse range of domains including Artificial Intelligence in Business, Human-Computer Interaction, Cognitive Behaviour, E-commerce, and Smart Logistics. His research extensively explores the integration of emerging technologies in business ecosystems focusing on AI-driven innovation, behavioral responses to technology adoption, and digital marketing strategies. He has also contributed significantly to sustainability-focused fields such as GreenTech, Green Finance, Renewable Energy, and Blockchain-enabled financial innovation. Additionally, his work in Smart Cities and IoT adoption emphasizes the importance of user trust, security, and operational efficiency. Emon has authored numerous peer-reviewed publications on topics including AI adoption intention, supply chain visibility, digital learning acceptance, and crisis-resilient supply chains. Many of his studies adopt behavioral and cognitive perspectives to understand how professionals and consumers interact with technology highlighting the psychological and user-centric aspects of digital transformation. He has participated in several research initiatives funded by the University Grants Commission of Bangladesh and the European Union. His work aligns closely with the United Nations Sustainable Development Goals (SDGs), particularly in areas such as poverty reduction, access to quality education, clean and affordable energy, inclusive economic growth, sustainable industrialization, responsible consumption, climate resilience, and ocean sustainability. His work also reflects a commitment to reducing inequalities and fostering international partnerships for sustainable development. In addition to his research contributions, he serves as a peer reviewer for several high-impact academic journals and is widely recognized for promoting academic rigor and ethical scholarship. As a prolific author, he continues to shape the discourse on sustainability, innovation, and digital advancement through his research, writing, and knowledge dissemination.

***

Mostofa Tanjil Ahmed is currently pursuing his Bachelor of Business Administration (BBA) at the Army Institute of Business Administration (Army IBA), Savar — an affiliated institute of the Bangladesh University of Professionals (BUP). With a strong academic record, he has maintained a CGPA of 3.99, reflecting his consistent dedication to academic excellence. Currently, he is majoring in finance. Tanjil's primary academic and research interests include strategic management, innovation, and behavioral aspects of consumer decision-making. His growing expertise lies in the intersection of business strategy, research analysis, and content communication. Tanjil has also participated in numerous academic competitions and research-based events such as IPESphere (SUST) and Research Mining 2.0, where he demonstrated his abilities in presentation design, idea generation, and research synthesis. Looking ahead, Tanjil aspires to pursue higher education and research in Finance and Strategic Management, aiming to contribute to Bangladesh's academic and financial development through innovative research and strategic insights.

Mowdud Ahmed is experienced in Supply Chain Management and Project Management, with a strong focus on integrating technology-driven strategies to enhance organizational performance. He holds a Master of Business Administration (MBA) with a major in Information Technology Project Management from Westcliff University, USA, and a Bachelor of Business Administration (BBA) in Operations and Supply Chain Management from the American International University-Bangladesh (AIUB). His expertise includes Supply Chain Information Technology, IT Governance, Project Integration, Technology Strategy, Management Information Systems, and Digital Transformation. His professional interests center on leveraging emerging technologies to improve efficiency, resilience, and sustainable growth in modern enterprises.

Amareen Omar Shabeeb is an economist and academic with extensive international experience in economic planning, strategic management, and higher education. He earned his Ph.D. in Economics (Economic Planning) from Moscow in 1988, following master's and bachelor's degrees in the same field, with his doctorate formally evaluated as equivalent to a U.S. doctoral degree. Over a career spanning more than three decades, Dr. Shabeeb has held senior executive and consulting roles in international business, marketing, and human resource development across Russia, Jordan, Saudi Arabia, Bahrain, and the United States. Dr. Shabeeb has served as a faculty member at several universities, including Delmon University (Bahrain), Petra Private University (Jordan), and currently Westcliff University, Irvine, USA. His teaching portfolio covers a wide range of undergraduate and postgraduate courses in economics, finance, management, quantitative methods, strategic management, and economic development. In addition to his academic work, he has contributed to national development initiatives, participated in Ministry of Planning studies, and designed and delivered specialized professional training programs for government and institutional stakeholders. His scholarly and professional contributions reflect a strong commitment to bridging economic theory, policy analysis, and practical management applications in diverse international contexts.

Mehedi Hassan Anik is an enthusiastic academic researcher in the field of Business and Management. His research interests focus on marketing, strategy, and emerging business practices. He is passionate about knowledge creation and actively contributes to scholarly research, aiming to generate practical and impactful insights for the business community.

Yeasin Arafat is an IT management professional with expertise in project management, financial analysis, and customer relationship strategies. He holds a Master of Business Administration (MBA) from Westcliff University, USA. His research interests focus on digital transformation, IT management, project integration, data-driven decision-making, and organizational performance optimization.

Reenu Bansal Actively involved in imparting quality education in the area of Finance & Accounting, Dr. Reenu Bansal has held the position of Assistant Professor in the Business & Management Department at Christ University. Before Delhi Metropolitan this she was working with Delhi Education (DME), Noida since 2021. Before joining DME, she worked as Assistant Professor in the Finance Department at IILM for 4 Years and worked as Program Director-UG with IMS Noida for 8 years. She has earned her BCCA & MBA degree from Maharshi Dayanand University, Rohtak (Haryana) in the year 2005 and 2007 respectively. She obtained her PhD from University of Rajasthan, Jaipur in the year 2016. She has rich corporate and academic experience of more than 16 years. She has guided successfully research scholars under her guidance and also invited as a resource person in various workshops and seminars. Participated in various National & International Conferences, she has presented more than 20 papers so far and 10 of her papers were published in International and National Journals & Conference proceedings. Also she has published book chapters. Her areas of teaching and research interests includes financial management, financial services, management of financial institutions, financial accounting, cost accounting, managerial accounting, and digital finance.

Beyzanur Cayir Ervural received PhD degree from Istanbul Technical University. She is currently an Associate Professor at Necmettin Erbakan University, Department of Aviation Management in Turkey. Her research interest covers decision-making, supply chain management, fuzzy applications and modelling, data analytics, optimization and forecasting studies. She has numerous publications in this field.

Munyaradzi Chibaro is a seasoned academic and industry expert with a strong background in logistics, supply chain management, and strategic leadership. His extensive experience spans over two decades, with notable roles in several institutions.

Jomon Jose M is an academic and researcher from Kerala, India, specializing in management studies, consumer behavior, and strategic marketing. His research interests span consumer psychology, behavioral finance, human resource management, tourism studies, and AI-driven customer experience, with a strong focus on contemporary business challenges.

James Kanyepe is a scholar and researcher specialising in supply chain management and operations management. He is currently a senior lecturer in the Department of Logistics and Supply Chain Management at the University of Botswana. His research focus covers topics like transport management, sustainable supply chains, artificial intelligence and logistics optimisation.

Md. Rahat Khan is working as a faculty member under the Army Institute of Business Administration (Army IBA), Savar (An Affiliated Institute of the Bangladesh University of Professionals) and as an editor for the South Asian Journal of Marketing (SAJoM by Emerald Publishing). Dr. Khan has a PhD in Strategic Management and an MBA in Marketing & Finance (Dual Major). He also has an MBS and a BBS (Hons) in management. He has three books, 44 journal articles, twelve conference papers, and one concept note. His primary research interests include strategic management and strategic marketing, such as disruptive innovation and technology, business sustainability, entrepreneurship development, and the behavioral and psychological aspects of business.

Wilbert Manyanga Have been a lecturer for several years. Currently a PDRF. Has vast experience in FMCG, Aviation, education and finance. His research interests are in customer experience, branding, online consumer behaviour and AI.

Jyothis Rachel Mathews is an Assistant Professor at Ahalia School of Management, Palakkad, Kerala, India. Her academic interests include sustainable marketing, digital transformation, and consumer psychology. She has participated in several national and international conferences and has contributed research papers and chapters in reputed publications. Passionate about bridging theory and practice, she focuses on promoting responsible business practices and ethical decision-making in management education.

Moeti-Lysson is a lecturer and researcher specializing in employee relations, industrial relations, labor relations, and human resource management.

Shakerod Munuhwa is a lecturer in Operations and Supply Chain Management at Glasgow Caledonian University. He specializes in teaching and research related to supply chain sustainability and digitalisation, catering to both undergraduate and postgraduate students. Dr. Munuhwa holds a PhD in Logistics and is a chartered member of the Chartered Institute of Logistics and Transport. Before joining academia, he gained six years of experience in distribution and courier logistics, which informs his practice-based teaching approach. Dr Munuhwa has so published more that 30 publications with reputable journals including Scopus.

Tinashe Musasa is a lecturer in marketing and international business at the University of Botswana. He has previously lectured at the Durban University of Technology. He is a Master's programme coordinator for the Faculty of Business, University of Botswana. His research interests are in disruptive and emerging marketing technologies, marketing sustainability, retail service quality, consumer behaviour, influencer marketing and supply chain resilience. He holds a D-Phil in Marketing, Master's in Marketing, and B-Tech in Retail Business Management from the Durban University of Technology.

Ravikumar R. Natarajan is an experienced academician with over 12+ years of teaching and research expertise across institutions in India, the UAE, and the Maldives. He currently serves as an Assistant Professor at Marwadi University, Rajkot, specializing in Machine Learning, Recommender Systems, and AI-driven applications in healthcare and security. He holds a Ph.D. in Machine Learning and Recommender Systems from Amity University, Jaipur, a Master of Engineering in CSE from VMRF University, Salem, and a Bachelor of Engineering in CSE from Anna University. He also has a MiniMBA from the Swiss eLearning Institute. Dr.

Ravikumar has authored more than 8+ multiple SCIE/Scopus-indexed journal articles, 25+ IEEE/Springer conference papers, and co-authored a book on Artificial Intelligence. He has also published 9 patents and contributed 10+ book chapters in emerging domains such as Federated Learning, Blockchain, and Digital Twins for IGI Global, Wiley and Springer publisher. He actively mentors students through initiatives like the Research Activities Club (RAC) and Student Research Internship Training (SRIT), promoting innovation and research culture.

Mohammad Al Refat Reyel is a research-focused professional with a strong interest in supply chain management and technology-driven business practices. His background includes extensive hands-on experience in sales, marketing, and retail operations, enabling a practical understanding of how digital technologies, data-driven strategies, and process optimization influence modern supply chains. He is actively engaged in academic research, with particular emphasis on technology-enabled supply chains, applied business analytics, and evidence-based managerial decision-making. He is academically affiliated with Ulster University and aims to bridge theoretical frameworks with real-world business applications through rigorous, practice-oriented research.

Aarthi S is a dedicated Assistant Professor in Computer Science with over six years of teaching experience. She is currently pursuing her Ph.D. at Marwadi University, Gujarat, and holds an M.Phil. and MCA from Bharathiar University, Tamil Nadu. Throughout her academic career, Aarthi has specialized in programming languages such as C++, Java, and C, and contributed to research in recommender systems and AI-related data privacy. She has published journal articles, contributed to book chapters, and actively participated in technical workshops. Known for her student mentorship and engagement in academic events, Aarthi remains committed to fostering innovation and excellence in computer science education.

Syed Waqar Ul Hassan Shah is currently affiliated with Ulster University. He holds a BSc in Computer Science and specializes in big data analytics, data-driven decision-making, and performance metrics analysis. He has expertise in research methodologies, data interpretation, and visualization, and is skilled in applying AI tools and advanced analytical techniques to extract insights from complex datasets.

Mukut Sikder is a postdoctoral researcher in Applied Economics and Environmental Resources at the Institute of Blue and Green Development, Shandong University, China. He holds a PhD in Logistics Engineering and Management from Chang'an University, China. His research focuses on green development planning within the broad areas of logistics and regional economy. He has published articles in journals including Science of the Total Environment and Journal of Cleaner Production.

Manjot Singh is a third-year Bachelor of Business Administration (BBA) student specialising in Finance and Marketing Analytics at Christ University, Bangalore. His academic interests lie in data analytics, business intelligence, and sustainable finance. He has undertaken multiple research and practical projects in analytics and finance, focusing on data-driven insights for decision-making and inclusive growth.

Nafisa Tasnuva is currently pursuing her Bachelor of Business Administration (BBA) with a major in finance at the Army Institute of Business Administration (Army IBA), Savar — an affiliated institute of the Bangladesh University of Professionals (BUP). She has maintained a strong academic record, demonstrating consistency and a deep interest in financial analysis, investment planning, and market dynamics. Her academic and research interests focus on corporate finance, investment behavior, and strategic management, with a growing curiosity about how financial decision-making influences organizational growth and sustainability. Through her coursework and analytical projects, she has developed strong competencies in problem-solving, data interpretation, and strategic communication. Nafisa aims to pursue advanced research in Finance and Business Strategy. Her long-term goal is to contribute to Bangladesh's financial sector by promoting data-driven decision-making and sustainable business practices that bridge theory with real-world impact.

Lei Xunping, PhD, is currently the vice president of the School of Business Administration, the vice president of the Anhui Economic Society, and the vice president of the Tongling Economic Society. He was selected as a young top-notch young teacher of the Anhui Province High-end Education Action Project, a top-notch talent in Anhui Province, and the first batch of young talents in Anhui Province. He serves as a part-time master's tutor of Anhui University of Technology, Anhui Normal University, and an expert in the appraisal of the achievements of the National Social Science Foundation. He has presided over and undertaken 21 scientific research projects, including 8 provincial and ministerial projects such as the National Social Science Foundation Youth Project, the Ministry of Education's Humanities and Social Sciences Youth Fund Project, and the Anhui Natural Science Foundation Project. He has published more than 80 academic papers, including CSSCI, SCI. He has published 2 monographs (including co-authors), and 2 provincial planning textbooks such as "Modern Logistics Management" as editor-in-chief and deputy editor-in-chief. He has presided over 9 quality engineering projects such as major education reform projects in Anhui Province and won the second prize of Anhui Province Teaching Achievement Award.

Index

A

B

C

D

E

G

I

L

M

T

W

www.ingramcontent.com/pod-product-compliance
Lightning Source LLC
LaVergne TN
LVHW062324300926
849161LV00007B/1559
9798337368962